A2 Essential
Business Studies for AQA

Jonathan Sutherland   Diane Canwell

United Kingdom: Folens Publishers, Waterslade House,
Thame Road, Haddenham, Buckinghamshire, HP17 8NT
Email: folens@folens.com

Ireland: Folens Publishers, Greenhills Road, Tallaght, Dublin 24
Email: info@folens.ie

Editor: Louise Wilson
Project development: Rick Jackman, Jackman Publishing Solutions Ltd
Design and layout: Patricia Briggs
Cover design: Jump to! www.jumpto.co.uk

First published 2009 by Folens Limited

British Library Cataloguing in Publication Data. A catalogue record for this
publication is available from the British Library.

ISBN 978-1-85008-362-7
Folens code: FD3627

CONTENTS

UNIT 3 STRATEGIES FOR SUCCESS   page iv

TOPIC 1 FUNCTIONAL OBJECTIVES AND STRATEGIES ▶ page 2

TOPIC 2 FINANCIAL STRATEGIES AND ACCOUNTS ▶ page 10

TOPIC 3 MARKETING STRATEGIES ▶ page 54

TOPIC 4 OPERATIONAL STRATEGIES ▶ page 92

TOPIC 5 HUMAN RESOURCE STRATEGIES ▶ page 130

CHECKLIST AND REVISION ▶ page 168

UNIT 4 THE BUSINESS ENVIRONMENT AND MANAGING CHANGE   page 170

TOPIC 1 CORPORATE AIMS AND OBJECTIVES ▶ page 172

TOPIC 2 ASSESSING CHANGES IN THE BUSINESS ENVIRONMENT ▶ page 184

TOPIC 3 MANAGING CHANGE ▶ page 248

CHECKLIST AND REVISION ▶ page 306

Picture credits ▶ page 309

Index ▶ page 310

UNIT 3
STRATEGIES FOR SUCCESS

Introduction

The core themes of Unit 3, the first of the two Business Studies A2 units, look at setting objectives, measuring performance and devising strategy. They are all issues that tend to be the focus of larger organisations than those you may have read about in AS Business Studies.

Much of the material covered in AS Business Studies will be very useful in helping you respond to the A2 questions for this unit. The examination itself is one hour and forty-five minutes long. It accounts for 25% of the total A-level mark, and 80 marks are available for the paper. You will be required to answer a number of extended questions, based on an unseen case study. You should be prepared to answer questions that relate to any or all of the five main parts of this unit.

The first topic, *Functional objectives and strategies*, examines how appropriate these objectives and strategies are in the context of corporate objectives. In other words, how the tactics a business might employ can be seen to contribute towards achieving corporate objectives.

The second topic, *Financial strategies and accounts*, builds on the finance work from AS Business Studies. It looks at the ways in which financial performance can be measured and the strategies that can be used by businesses.

The third topic, *Marketing strategies*, looks at how businesses develop their marketing strategies arising out of their broader objectives. It investigates how markets can be analysed in a business's search for patterns in sales and trends. It also investigates how businesses develop marketing plans in order to achieve specific objectives.

The fourth topic, *Operational strategies*, also builds on the material that you covered in Operations Management for AS Business Studies. It looks at the various objectives and strategies that businesses can use in order to achieve success in the market or markets in which they operate.

The final topic of this unit – *Human resource strategies* – builds on the AS Business Studies coverage of human resources. It looks at the strategies that are available to businesses in how they manage their human resources.

This unit follows the exact specification of the AQA Business Studies A2 Unit 3. Each of the core themes is broken down into topics and examined in detail. The topics consist of a number of double-page spreads, each of which looks at a particular aspect of that topic. On each spread there are either short answer questions to test your understanding, or mini case studies with extended questions. At the end of each topic there is an opportunity for you to try out a series of questions that are similar to the type you will encounter in the examination.

At the end of the unit there is another spread that provides you with a summary of the unit's key concepts and a full mock examination for you to try.

TOPIC 1: FUNCTIONAL OBJECTIVES AND STRATEGIES
▶ page 2

TOPIC 2: FINANCIAL STRATEGIES AND ACCOUNTS
▶ page 10

TOPIC 3: MARKETING STRATEGIES
▶ page 54

TOPIC 4: OPERATIONAL STRATEGIES
▶ page 92

TOPIC 5: HUMAN RESOURCE STRATEGIES
▶ page 130

CHECKLIST AND REVISION
▶ page 168

TOPIC 1 FUNCTIONAL OBJECTIVES AND STRATEGIES

Introduction

This is the first of the five core themes for *Strategies for success*. You will be expected to have an understanding of a range of functional objectives that a business could pursue and of how these can contribute to the achievement of the company's objectives.

It is important to remember that concepts such as corporate objectives tend to relate to far larger businesses than those studied during AS Business Studies. However, many of the actual functional objectives themselves can relate to any type of business, no matter what its size. These include areas such as minimising costs or gaining market share.

A business can use its broad and often vague corporate objectives to frame the type of functional objectives it chooses to employ in order to achieve the corporate objectives. It is important to remember that the driving force behind many businesses will begin with a corporate objective, or a series of corporate objectives. It is the role of the board of directors, led by the managing director, the owners, or key management to create, implement and monitor functional objectives and activities, which collectively aim to meet the corporate objectives of the business or organisation.

This is a relatively short topic, but some of the concepts you will encounter underpin other specific strategies covered later on in the unit.

FOCUS ON USING OBJECTIVES AND STRATEGIES

- Functional and corporate objectives ▶ page 4
- Functional objectives and strategies ▶ page 6
- Case studies, questions and exam practice ▶ page 8

Functional and corporate objectives

Corporate objectives

There is always potential confusion when using terms such as 'corporate objectives', 'strategies', 'mission statements', 'aims' and 'plans'. Perhaps the easiest way of understanding how all these terms interrelate is to consider the fact that businesses may have a number of different objectives. But as far as a corporate objective is concerned, this means their target or aim.

All the different terms fit into a framework or a hierarchy. They are all dependent upon one another and build both from the top down and the bottom up.

A typical hierarchy, which would show where all of these terms fit in, is outlined below:

Corporate aim or objective – such as to innovate, to grow or diversify.

▼

Corporate mission or mission statement – this is a short and catchy sentence or short paragraph, which aims to encapsulate the corporate aims and objectives of the business.

▼

Divisional objectives – how each part of the organisation is expected to contribute towards meeting the corporate aim or objectives.

▼

Departmental objectives – how each department within each division is expected to make a contribution towards the corporate aim or objectives.

▼

Specific individual targets – these are given to particular managers or supervisors, as their contribution towards achieving the overall corporate aims and objectives.

FOR EXAMPLE

An example in practice is Kingfisher – an international business with nearly 800 stores in nine markets. One of the business's key objectives is to produce  *above-average returns for its shareholders on a consistent, long-term basis. It has been able to achieve this consistently for the past 20 years. Considering the hierarchy that we have just looked at, this stated aim can be considered as a corporate objective and part of the mission. Kingfisher has a number of key brands, including B&Q and Screwfix. These are divisions within the overall group and they will be allocated specific targets as their contribution to achieving this corporate objective. Each store in turn will then be given a series of targets to help contribute towards the divisional objectives. Within each store, particular parts, such as electrical, paint, gardening and trade sales will be allocated targets to contribute towards the departmental sets of objectives. In this way, all parts of the organisation work in a coordinated manner towards achieving the overall corporate objective.*

Common corporate objectives are necessarily broad. This allows the business to employ a broad range of functional objectives in order to achieve the corporate objectives. In order for a business to be able to provide a good return for its investors, a number of different functional objectives will need to be employed, such as cost reduction, increasing sales or trying to gain market share. All of these will directly contribute towards maximising returns for investors.

Most corporate objectives will, in fact, need to incorporate a number of different functional objectives. Collectively they will contribute towards achieving the objective. Problems arise when corporate objectives are too vague or generalised. They need to say something about the business's future plans and to be part of a definite quantifiable target, even if that is not a financial target.

Functional objectives

Functional objectives can be seen as being specific but still quite general ways in which corporate objectives can be achieved. It is not until we consider functional strategies themselves that we can actually see specific steps that a business can take to, for example, minimise its costs. At this level, however, functional objectives can still be pretty broad, as can be seen below:

- *Growth* – there are many different ways in which growth itself can be measured. It can be measured in terms of sales achieved, number of employees, and number of stores, outlets or different markets in which the organisation operates. It could also be measured in terms of changes in the amount of profit that a business makes. The objective of growth itself is therefore fairly broad and will often be quantified by statements such as 'increasing the number of retail outlets from 110 to 140'. These can be specifically measured, and realisable targets can be set.

- *Maximising profits* – maximising profits as a functional objective can be seen as rather different from the broader objective of growth. Profits are used to either refinance further growth or to reward investors. The potential of making a profit is vital to balance the risks taken by business owners. However, maximising profits can be achieved by using a number of different functional strategies, such as cost-cutting, rises in prices, reduction of workforce or a reduction in distribution costs. One of the major problems in stating that profit maximisation is a principal objective is that short-term profits can undermine the long-term survival of the business, as it might encourage competitors to enter the market.

- *Increasing market share* – this is a more quantifiable objective. A business will have a fairly good idea of the overall size of the market or markets in which it operates, and the value of that market. It will also know its sales in that market, so it will be relatively easy to calculate its share of the market. It will also be able to monitor how particular initiatives affect sales, but it may not be immediately obvious whether the market has grown or whether sales have been taken from competitors.

- *Social, ethical and environmental objectives* – growth and expansion are often perceived in a negative way by the general public. By throwing profits into greater growth and increasing profits, businesses are often accused of being greedy and having little regard for social, ethical or environmental concerns. Low wages, for example, are not acceptable, nor is the use of underpaid overseas employees. These bring the business into conflict with the law and adverse publicity. Businesses need to trade off growth and profit with consideration of these issues in order to show a degree of public responsibility, regardless of whether they are based on genuine beliefs or not.

CASE STUDY KINGFISHER'S B&Q STRATEGY

In the period 2006–2008 B&Q redesigned 115 of its largest stores. New customer service initiatives were brought in and there was a 25% improvement in sales productivity. B&Q stated that it had four operational drivers: price competitiveness, customer service, new products and store environment. By the end of 2008 all of its large stores will have been converted to the new format.

Questions

1   What do you think is meant by an operational driver? Explain what you think is meant by the four examples given by B&Q. (*12 marks*)
2   If the four elements are operational drivers, the 25% improvement in sales can be considered as what type of objective and why? (*6 marks*)

Functional objectives and strategies

Functional objectives and strategies

Setting corporate objectives is just the first step. Achieving the corporate objective requires a considerable amount of planning. A business will go through a number of stages when planning the functional objectives and strategies that will help it achieve its corporate objectives. The first step will be to identify its missions and goals. This is still fairly broad and not very easy to translate directly into functional strategies. A broad mission or goal might be to increase market share over a period of time. Functional strategies will then be put in place that specify goals, such as achieving an increase in market share year on year.

The business will usually begin by analysing its current situation, looking at aspects from both inside and outside the organisation. You will already be familiar with the concept of SWOT analysis. By carrying out this type of analysis, the business can identify external factors that could be opportunities, or threats, such as increased competition. A business's internal strengths might give it a **competitive advantage**, but its weaknesses could undermine other initiatives.

A business will begin to develop a series of strategies and plans that could be used, perhaps to improve efficiency in certain areas, to increase brand loyalty, to introduce total quality management or to try to differentiate its products and services from those of the competition. Corporate objectives could also be achieved by merging or acquiring other businesses, or perhaps by setting up production facilities closer to the market.

Once a business has developed its strategies, it then needs to implement them. Both organisational and management systems will be required to carry out the strategies. New systems may have to be designed or existing ones adapted. At all times the business needs to be in a position to monitor, evaluate and redirect strategies if they are not proving to be as effective as hoped.

Leaving evaluation until a strategy has run its course is not the best option to adopt. It can be useful to evaluate strategies at the end of a given period, but by that stage it may be too late to make the necessary adjustments. By continually

evaluating strategies, subtle changes can be made in order to make them more effective, to remain on budget and to cater for internal and external changes as they occur.

Not all functional strategies are necessarily planned ahead of time: some simply emerge as a solution to a particular problem at a particular time. However, by simply responding to problems and creating strategies to deal with them, a business is often seen as being **reactive** rather than **proactive**.

In order for strategies to achieve their goal, a business needs to have a broader and longer-term vision. Each strategy is an integral part of the overall vision. Particular projects and initiatives, while having individual goals or targets, are part of a far broader approach. Businesses also need to consider the overall effect that strategies can have on their customers or clients. Approaching each corporate objective with a blinkered view that it should just be for the benefit of the business itself is likely to cause enormous problems with customers. Increased profitability is not simply a question of pushing up prices for customers. By doing so, customers can be alienated and would seek similar products and services from competitors.

All functional strategies need to be given a specific timescale. Often these are referred to as 'planning horizons'. This simply means the amount of time that a particular objective or initiative is given to set its plans and then to achieve them.

Contribution towards achieving corporate objectives

Each functional strategy needs to be suitable both for the business and for the goals that have been set. Therefore, businesses will use a wide variety of different strategies for different situations. Sometimes there will be clear functional plans, which could relate directly to human resources or marketing, for example. In other cases a business may have set up a **contingency plan**, which seeks to anticipate future problems and sets out a series of measures that the business will take if the worst-case scenario occurs.

All the functional strategies need to be flexible and dynamic. Corporate objectives and strategies are not cast in stone; they have to reflect and react to the economic environment in which the business is operating. A business needs to make sure that it is not necessarily deflected from its corporate objectives, but that it seeks to achieve them in a way that will not compromise its longer-term objectives and success. Short-term fixes in order to achieve corporate objectives can cause longer-term damage to a business.

Most functional strategies are designed to help a business get from where it currently stands to where it would like to be. For example, a business may forecast its sales for the next year based on historical data. These sales forecasts, however, may not be sufficient in order for it to achieve its corporate objectives. Functional strategies need to be implemented in order to amend and improve the sales forecasts to help bridge the gap. A series of new targets will be set, and initiatives put into place which could relate to training (human resources), increased customer awareness (marketing), customer incentives (sales), more stock available (production and purchasing), and greater commitment to customer support (customer services). Each element or functional strategy is designed to contribute to the overall objective; in this case, bridging the deficiency in sales, which would mean that a key corporate objective may or may not be achieved.

CASE STUDY KINGFISHER'S WAY OF MANAGING RISKS

The Kingfisher Group tries to manage its business and development risks in order to minimise their likelihood or impact. The risks that they identify are common to many business organisations and include:

- economic and market conditions
- entering new markets
- competitive product ranges, prices and customer service
- innovation in big, developed businesses
- attracting and retaining the best people
- financial resources
- crises affecting trading and Kingfisher's reputation
- in-store safety

Question

Kingfisher has identified eight principal risks in managing the business and its development. In each case, suggest at least one functional strategy that could be used to minimise the likelihood or impact of each risk. (*24 marks*)

Case studies, questions and exam practice

CASE STUDY KINGFISHER'S INTERNATIONAL EXPANSION

International expansion has been at the heart of Kingfisher's strategy for many years. Castorama opened its first overseas business in Italy in 1988, and B&Q entered Taiwan in 1996. This strategy has continued in a measured way over the years, leading to a strong and fast-growing portfolio of international business, which today provides strong growth and attractive economic returns for Kingfisher.

	Population (million)	Market size (£ billion)	Market share (%)
UK	61	26	15
France	61	31	9
Rest of Europe			
Poland	38	4	10
Italy	58	13	2
Turkey	74	4	3
Ireland	4	0.8	8
Spain	44	5	1
Russia	142	10	n/a
Asia			
China	1,300	27	2

Source: EIU

Kingfisher's international expansion has been based on several key principles:

- identify those markets that offer real scale, with opportunities for growth and returns
- research the market in depth
- build a strong local team from local nationals and allow local management autonomy, subject to close central monitoring of key performance indicators
- share ideas, resources and suppliers from around Kingfisher to create local advantage but adapt the business model to the local environment
- expand if the business case is proven, or exit if it is not.

To support continued expansion, £182 million, 40% of Kingfisher's total capital investment for the year, was invested in these businesses. Fifty-six new stores were opened in the year, taking the total in this category to nearly 270, with a similar number planned to open in 2007/08.

In France, Brico Dépôt added ten new stores, taking its total to 81. A major new system upgrade was implemented to enhance competitiveness and productivity. In the UK, Screwfix opened 31 new trade counter stores, taking the total to 38.

Castorama Poland continued to grow strongly and the first trial Brico Dépôt store was opened in Warsaw to target trade professionals. Castorama Italy and B&Q Ireland achieved strong growth.

In China, B&Q completed the integration of the OBI stores acquired in 2005 and returned to profitability. With 58 stores, B&Q China has consolidated its position as market leader.

B&Q is the market leader in the UK and is almost twice the size of its nearest rival. With the Warehouse store format and the smaller Mini-Warehouse format, B&Q offers customers the widest range of products in its stores – around 32,000 products in a Warehouse store.

B&Q's aim is to offer customers everything they need to improve their homes under one roof. Traditional DIY products can be found alongside 'room sets' displaying complete kitchens, bathrooms and bedrooms. Customers can also buy a large range of items online. A larger range of products can be purchased either over the telephone or via the 'special order' desk in-store.

B&Q UK is an official partner to the British Olympic Association and supported Team GB to the Beijing 2008 Olympic Games.

B&Q Ireland

B&Q Ireland offers a wide range of home improvement products, using both the larger, Warehouse stores and smaller, Mini-Warehouse stores.

B&Q China

B&Q China consolidated its position as market leader in 2005 with the purchase of OBI's stores in China, which have all been converted to the B&Q format. B&Q now has 60 stores in China and is twice the size of the nearest competitor. It is also one of the largest Western retailers in China. B&Q China has developed a full design and decoration service for Chinese apartments, which transforms an empty concrete shell into a stylish home. Customers select the designs, furnishings and colours

in-store and a B&Q service team undertakes all the work, from the installation of the kitchen and bathroom, to the painting of the walls. Over 30,000 apartments were designed and fitted out in the last year.

Source: adapted from www.kingfisher.com

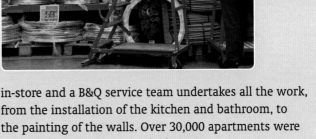

Questions

1 Comment on the key principles behind Kingfisher's international expansion. How have these contributed to ensuring continued success? (*15 marks*)

2 B&Q is the market leader in Britain and is almost twice as large as its nearest rival. To what extent do you think this gives B&Q a competitive advantage and why might this be the case? (*12 marks*)

TOPIC 2 FINANCIAL STRATEGIES AND ACCOUNTS

Introduction

Many of the concepts in this topic – the second part of *Strategies for success* – you will already have studied during AS Business Studies. This section examines the financial objectives of larger businesses. It looks at the ways in which financial performance can be measured and the strategies that can be used by these businesses.

The first focus area explores financial objectives, which are an integral part of a business's corporate objectives. They could include cash-flow targets, cost minimisation, return on capital employed and returns for shareholders.

In order to have any chance of succeeding in meeting its financial objectives, a business will need to measure and assess its performance over a period of time. The second focus area looks at working capital, depreciation, profit utilisation and profit quality.

In order for potential investors, current shareholders and financial analysts, both within and outside the business, to understand the financial performance of a business, published accounts need to be examined. The third focus area looks at how ratios can be used in order to measure a business's financial performance. It also looks at the value and the limitations of ratio analysis and how it often may not give the full picture.

The fourth focus examines the selection of financial strategies, such as raising finance, bringing in profit centres, minimising costs or allocating capital expenditure. It looks at how these strategies interrelate with other functions and how their value can be assessed in particular circumstances.

The final focus area for this topic looks at making investment decisions, primarily why businesses choose to invest and the ways in which particular types of investment can help a business fulfil its functional objectives. There are many different ways in which investment decisions can be selected and assessed, including payback, average rate of return and net present value.

FOCUS ON UNDERSTANDING FINANCIAL OBJECTIVES

- Financial objectives ▶ page 12
- Internal and external influences on financial objectives ▶ page 14
- Case studies, questions and exam practice ▶ page 16

FOCUS ON USING FINANCIAL DATA TO MEASURE AND ASSESS PERFORMANCE

- Analysing balance sheets ▶ page 18
- Analysing income statements ▶ page 20
- Working capital, depreciation, profit utilisation and profit quality ▶ page 22
- Using financial data for comparisons, trend analysis and decision-making ▶ page 24
- Strengths and weaknesses of financial data in judging performance ▶ page 26
- Case studies, questions and exam practice ▶ page 28

FOCUS ON INTERPRETING PUBLISHED ACCOUNTS

- Conducting ratio analysis (1) ▶ page 30
- Conducting ratio analysis (2) ▶ page 32
- The value and limitations of ratio analysis ▶ page 34
- Case studies, questions and exam practice ▶ page 36

FOCUS ON SELECTING FINANCIAL STRATEGIES

- Raising finance and implementing profit centres ▶ page 38
- Cost minimisation and allocating capital expenditure ▶ page 40
- Case studies, questions and exam practice ▶ page 42

FOCUS ON MAKING INVESTMENT DECISIONS

- Conducting investment appraisal ▶ page 44
- Investment criteria ▶ page 46
- Risks and uncertainties of investment decisions ▶ page 48
- Quantitative and qualitative influences ▶ page 50
- Case studies, questions and exam practice ▶ page 52

Financial objectives

Cash-flow targets

In the vast majority of cases, expanding a business will bring long-term benefits, but in the short term it can lead to some cash-flow problems. When a business expands, it will need to buy additional stock, and perhaps new fixed assets, and it may need to invest in new product development. These can all be considerable cash outflows. Ultimately, of course, these cash outflows should lead to greater cash inflows, but that will be at some point in the future.

Setting cash-flow targets is a two-fold task:

• The business needs to maximise its cash inflows. This can be achieved by either increasing sales or by finding some bridging funds, such as a loan, to see it over any cash-flow problems. The business could also chase its debtors to encourage them to pay on time.
• The business needs to minimise, or at least justify, any cash outflows or expenditure. Certain tactics are possible, such as delaying payment to suppliers or making staged payments for expensive fixed assets.

If a business does not set its cash-flow targets, then it could suffer from what is known as 'over-trading'. The business will have too much money invested in stock or will have spent too much money on fixed assets and, as a result, will have liquidity problems.

Cost minimisation

Cost minimisation has a close relationship to budgetary control. Budgeting aims to assist the business in planning and monitoring what is spent. Businesses will identify their major cost centres, such as sales and marketing, production or purchasing. They will then identify the major types of costs within each cost centre. Typically, these would include staff costs, raw materials, supplies and capital expenditure. In order to minimise costs, businesses will then focus on costs that offer the easiest savings. Alternatively, they will look at large costs which can be changed in the short term.

A business needs to initiate systematic cost control. It should establish standard costs for achieving its objectives and also create budgeted costs, based on actual experience. Against the budgeted costs the business would record its actual costs and compare them. This will alert the business to the fact that if costs are higher than budgeted costs, there may be opportunities to reduce them in the short term.

Lower costs could indicate good management (but this might also mean that quality issues could be a potential future problem). Each cost centre is usually the responsibility of a manager. It is obviously easier if one manager is given responsibility for a particular cost throughout the whole of the organisation.

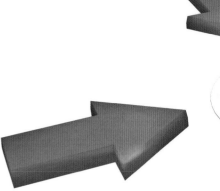

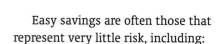

Easy savings are often those that represent very little risk, including:

• checking supplier invoices (over-charging or double-billing may have occurred)
• eliminating unnecessary costs
• reducing over-capacity, waste and useless processes
• eliminating excessive costs, looking for alternatives to first-class post, cheaper suppliers and wasteful luxuries
• inefficiencies – replace manual systems with computer-based systems, avoiding frequent small orders from suppliers and switching to monthly invoicing to cut out processing costs.

Return on capital employed (ROCE) targets

Return on capital employed (ROCE) is a primary efficiency ratio. It allows an assessment of the financial performance of the business as a whole. In effect it allows an organisation to identify whether the investments it has made are actually giving a better rate of return than just simply leaving the money in a deposit account in the bank.

Typically, a target ROCE would be in the range of 20% to 30%. However, most deposit accounts would only offer something around the Bank of England interest rate as a return.

The problem with setting ROCE targets is that they may not take into account short-term issues that could affect the actual return, and may not be a fair indication of the efficiency of the organisation. As ROCE is only ever shown as a percentage for comparison purposes, an underlying figure that appears to be poor either compared to the interest rate or to the previous year or indeed to a competitor may be somewhat unfair and would need further explanation.

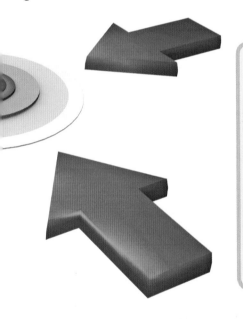

> ### KEY TERMS
>
> **Liquidity** – this is a measurement of a business's ability to meet its short-term debts (or liabilities).
>
> **Preference shares** – entitle the owner to a fixed payment from the business's profits.
>
> **Ordinary shares** – do not entitle the owner to a fixed payment from profits, but do give voting rights. The dividend will depend upon the amount of profit made by the business that is allocated to the payment of dividends.

Shareholders' returns

For public limited companies in particular, in order to retain existing investors and attract new ones, one of the primary financial objectives would be to maximise the returns for their shareholders. There are two ways in which this can be measured or quantified:

- Shareholders will be looking for a gradual increase in the actual value of their shares. They can then see that their original investment has increased in value and can make a decision about whether or not to sell these shares in anticipation of a fall.
- In the longer term, shareholders will look to receive a reasonable dividend each year on the shares that they hold. It is important to remember that there is a difference between preference shares and ordinary shares. Preference shares will always give a fixed return, whereas dividends paid on ordinary shares will fluctuate according to the profitability of the business.

Broadly, a business's financial objectives in terms of shareholder returns will be to provide a better investment than the majority of other alternative investment opportunities.

CASE STUDY PRELIMINARY RESULTS

A business operating in a global market saw sales increase from £8.676 billion to £9.364 billion – an increase of 7.9%. Its retail profits fell from £504 million to £498 million. Pre-tax profits also fell from £397 million to £386 million, and after-tax profits from £277 million to £265 million. The earnings per share fell 5% from 11.9p to 11.3p. The full-year dividend was also down from 10.65p to 7.25p. However, to offset any particular problems, the business also reported that it had a property portfolio valued at £3.6 billion.

Questions

1 Why might the profit have fallen even though sales were up? (*4 marks*)
2 Calculate the percentage change in both the pre-tax and after-tax profits. (*4 marks*)
3 As an existing investor in the business, what would be your decision about retaining or selling the shares and why? (*8 marks*)

Internal and external influences on financial objectives

LEARNING
OBJECTIVES

▶ Internal influences on financial objectives

▶ External influences on financial objectives

Internal influences on financial objectives

Internal influences on financial objectives range from the requirements, views and priorities of the board of directors, through various layers of management, including budget holders, to specific departmental managers. They are also expected to meet specific targets and remain within particular budgets.

Internal budgeting is a key consideration and this aspect incorporates both profit and cost centres. Profit centres contribute to the income received by the business. In this respect, as far as cash-flow targets are concerned, they will be responsible for maximising the amount of inflows of funds to the business. Profit centres also have running costs, which include staff, administration and contribution to overheads. As far as cash flow itself is concerned, profit centres are therefore likely to feature on both the income and expenditure of a cash-flow statement.

Cost centres, however, are not expected to generate any inward funds for the business organisation. They are therefore on the expenditure side of a cash-flow statement. This is not to say, however, that they do not have their own budgets, which set a maximum spend across the range of activities and expenses that they may incur as a result of their activities.

All areas of the organisation, whether it is a profit or cost centre, will be expected to minimise costs. In fact, costs are one of the three most vital areas that a business will monitor in terms of finance, the other two being sales and working capital. By splitting up a business into cost centres, and then matching those costs against revenue, a business will be able to monitor the profitability of each operation. Obviously, cash generation is a main priority for most businesses and cash is controlled by controlling the working capital – in other words the debtors, creditors, stock and work in progress.

Major investments in equipment or fixed assets will have to be justified and ROCE targets will usually be set. In order to argue the case successfully for the release of funds for an investment, the relevant part of the organisation, or the manager, will have to show that there are positive financial benefits by making the investment. Even the largest business does not have an inexhaustible supply of funds for investment. Divisions, departments and individual managers will have to compete for available investment funds, proving with accurate projections that an investment in their area will provide the business with a greater return compared to competing areas of the business.

External influences on financial objectives

The principal external influence on a business's financial objectives is the requirements of shareholders. Shareholders appreciate that they are entering into a financial risk when they buy shares in any business. The value of their initial investment in terms of the price they pay per share is dependent upon the fortunes of the organisation. Shares are openly traded on an hourly, daily and weekly basis by shareholders, who seek quick returns by buying shares at relatively low prices and then selling them as they rise in value.

Longer-term shareholders look for a combination of an increase in the value of their shares and a reasonable annual return, in the form of a dividend. The payment of dividends is also closely linked to the profitability and fortunes of the organisation.

A business that announces a rise in profits would see the demand for their shares increase, therefore driving up the price and hence the value of the investment of existing shareholders. At the same time, assuming that a reasonable portion of the profit is allocated for distribution to shareholders, those shareholders will be rewarded for keeping the shares by receiving a dividend.

Obviously there are other key drivers on the financial objectives of a business. Many businesses have short-, medium- or long-term loans, which need to be serviced by generating profit. There are also other external influences, which could include opportunities to increase export sales, or a requirement from a supplier or customer to undertake a certain level of business over a given period of time, in order to either fulfil a contract or to qualify for a discount or bonus payment.

FOR EXAMPLE

The budget airline Flybe had entered into an agreement with Norwich International Airport that it would carry 15,000 passengers from Norwich to Dublin during the 2007/08 financial year. On the penultimate day, March 30, they were 172 passengers short and would therefore have to pay a £280,000

commercial penalty to Norwich Airport. The airline laid on extra flights and paid actors to fill up the aircraft. In order to avoid the penalty charges, they paid the actors £80 per day and gave them 200 free return tickets to fill the seats.

CASE STUDY THANET DISTRICT COUNCIL FINANCIAL SERVICES

Strategic financial objectives

The Council's Financial Strategy aims to balance the Council's commitment to a regime of financial rigour, prudence and discipline with the need to facilitate innovation and strong financial management.

Aims of the General Fund revenue account

- To maintain a balanced General Fund Budget with expenditure matching income from Council Tax, fees and charges, and government and other grants, and to maintain that position.
- To maximise the Council's income by promptly raising all monies due and minimising the levels of arrears and debt write-offs.
- To maintain contingency reserves at no less than £1.5 million with a preferred target of not more than £2 million.
- To only incur additional spending when matched by increased income or identified budget savings.

- To increase future Council Tax levels by no more than 4.5%, subject to satisfactory grant awards.
- To ensure resources are aligned with the Council's strategic vision and corporate priorities.
- To actively engage local residents in the financial choices facing the Council.

Source: www.thanet.gov.uk

Questions

1 What is meant by 'to maintain a balanced General Fund Budget'? Explain how the Council intends to achieve this. (*6 marks*)
2 Why might the Council require a contingency reserve? (*4 marks*)
3 How does the Council intend to balance additional spending and why are the options uncertain? (*4 marks*)

Case studies, questions and exam practice

CASE STUDY CHELSEA'S FINANCIAL OBJECTIVES

Chelsea Football Club has been bankrolled by Roman Abramovich to the tune of £500 million since he took over in 2003, but the club aims to break even by 2010. Over the past two seasons, 300,000 more people have attended games, and Stamford Bridge is increasingly being used to the full extent of its 42,500 capacity. Match-day revenues are close to £1.5 million, which is approaching the amount taken by Manchester United. Eventually, the stadium may have to be expanded. Overall revenues were up by 40% last year, but controlling costs is an important part of the break-even strategy. Players' wages represent about 76% of turnover and the goal is to bring this down to a more sustainable level of 55%.

Chelsea losses over the past four years are a vast £384 million after the club announced an annual loss of £74.8 million in February 2008, but it still claims to be bigger than Arsenal, with a turnover that exceeds that of its London rival. The warning from Stamford Bridge was that Roman Abramovich's appetite for trophies has not diminished, despite sinking £578 million of his own money into the club.

The annual financial results for the richest football club in the world revealed that Chelsea's turnover has risen by 25% to £190.5 million, in excess of the £177 million turnover posted by Arsenal in September 2007. Chelsea's chief executive,

Peter Kenyon, said that the year's losses, down from £80.2 million last year, were the result of more expensive player contracts on the payroll.

Crucially for Chelsea, however, the man making it all happen has shown no sign of bailing out. The club put Abramovich's investment at £578 million, and for the past financial year it was the contracts for Andrei Shevchenko, Michael Ballack and a new deal for Didier Drogba that were the major factors in driving up losses. Kenyon claimed that Chelsea was still on course for its aim of breaking even in 2010.

The chairman, Bruce Buck, said that Abramovich was in Chelsea for the long term. 'We see him a lot and his enthusiasm for football and for Chelsea for the last four and three-quarter years has not waned, it has only increased,' Buck said. 'When a fellow puts more than £500 million into a football club of his own money he doesn't just walk away.'

Kenyon admitted that Chelsea would have to reduce the percentage of turnover spent on wages. Chelsea's proportion is 71%, giving it a payroll year of around £135 million.

There was a dramatic reduction in the net spending on transfers, which stood at £11.7 million, down from £85.4 million (2005/06) and £126.7 million (2004/05). In its accounts Chelsea spread the cost of a player across the length

of his contract. The sale of Eidur Gudjohnsen, Robert Huth, Damien Duff and Asier Del Horno has balanced those investments, leaving Chelsea with a respectable deficit. The next set of results will take into account the signings of Florent Malouda, Nicolas Anelka and Branislav Ivanovic, as well as the big pay-offs awarded to Jose Mourinho and his backroom staff, when they were sacked in September 2007.

Questions

1. Explain how Chelsea FC intends to break even and why this may not be as easy as they suggest. (*12 marks*)
2. Explain what is meant by 'spread the cost of a player across the length of his contract'. Why might this not be appropriate for many other types of business? (*6 marks*)
3. What are the internal and external influences on Chelsea's financial objectives? (*8 marks*)

Analysing balance sheets

LEARNING OBJECTIVES

▶ What is a balance sheet?
▶ Importance of balance sheets
▶ Reading and interpreting a balance sheet

What is a balance sheet?

A balance sheet records the assets or possessions owned by a business, as well as its liabilities (debts). It is important to remember that the balance sheet provides a snapshot of these assets and liabilities on a particular day, at the end of an accounting period. Balance sheets therefore always have a date to record when the valuations took place.

The balance sheet shows how the business has raised the capital and the uses the business has put the money to. It is an important and primary financial statement.

The key relationships on a balance sheet are:

- Assets are equal to liabilities – this is why it is called a balance sheet.
- The total assets of the business are equal to the fixed and current assets – these detail the range of assets that the business owns.
- The liabilities are equal to the share capital, borrowings, other creditors and reserves – these detail precisely in which area and to whom the business owes money.

Importance of balance sheets

For many financial analysts the balance sheet is the most important financial document for the following reasons:

- It provides the ultimate measure of the value or worth of the business. By looking at a business's balance sheets over a number of years, a clear indication of progress can be made.
- The balance sheet shows how the business's sources of finance are actually used. It can show whether the business is borrowing a large amount of money, which could indicate that it might be vulnerable if interest rates rise.
- It shows whether the business is using short-term or long-term sources of finance to fund the purchase of assets. Short-term finance, such as overdrafts, is relatively expensive. A business that has thought ahead will use longer-term sources of finance, like mortgages or loans, to purchase assets.

- The balance sheet also shows the liquidity of the business, in other words, the business's cash position. It can show whether the business will be able to meet its liability demands in the short term.

Balance sheets do not always give a full picture. Other information needs to be used alongside the balance sheet:

- A profit-and-loss account details the business's income, expenditure and profit or loss over the same trading period.
- Since the balance sheet is only a snapshot of the business's position on a specific day, it does not cover the current situation, which may have changed radically since the balance sheet was created.
- The balance sheet is only a record of financial dealings. There is no indication of how well the business is actually being managed, nor of the impact of external factors, such as a sudden change in customer demand or a rapid rise in interest rates.

Reading and interpreting a balance sheet

An enormous amount of information can be gleaned from a balance sheet. Broadly, it is possible to make an assessment of the short-term and long-term financial position and strategy of the business.

As far as the short-term position is concerned, the balance sheet shows the short-term debts (those that will have to be paid within the next 12 months). It also shows the state of the current assets that will be used to pay these debts. It is therefore possible to make an assessment of the available working capital. If a business has more current assets than it has current liabilities, then it has a positive working capital figure.

If the reverse is true, then the business may, in the short term, suffer cash problems or liquidity problems.

For the longer-term position, it is possible to note the following:

- *Fixed assets* – an increase in fixed assets could show that the business is growing at a fairly rapid pace, which could indicate that the financial performance will also increase.
- *Capital* – by looking at how a business has raised its capital, an assessment can be made as to whether or not it is vulnerable. If it has borrowed a great deal of money to fund the purchase

of assets, then an interest rate rise could cause difficulties. If the business is funding the purchase of assets through share capital or reserves, then it is less vulnerable.

- *Reserves* – if a business shows an increase in its reserves, this is an indication that it is profitable. Reserves give an indication of the profit being made by the business. If it is able to set aside cash to put into a reserve and make dividend payments to shareholders, as well as covering its liabilities and purchasing assets, then the business can be seen to be very profitable.

CASE STUDY FYFFES PLC

Fyffes Plc is primarily involved in the production, purchase, shipping, ripening and distribution and marketing of bananas, pineapples and melons. It is the largest tropical produce importer and distributor in Europe and one of the oldest fruit brands in the world. It is most closely associated with bananas.

This is the company's balance sheet, covering 2006/07. (Note that it is in Euros rather than £ sterling.)

Questions

1 What has happened to the total asset value in the two years? Which components of the current and non-current assets are responsible for the changes? (*8 marks*)
2 The business's total liabilities have fallen. Which parts of its liabilities have changed, and how does this affect the financial position of the business? (*10 marks*)

COMPANY BALANCE SHEET

	2007 (€000s)	2006 (€000s)
Assets		
Non-current		
Property, plant and equipment	462	604
Equity investments	265,436	269,736
Total non-current assets	265,898	270,736
Current		
Trade and other receivables	169,926	203,467
Cash and cash equivalents	17,106	41,681
Corporation tax recoverable	2	7
Total current assets	187,034	245,155
Total assets	452,932	515,495
Equity		
Called up share capital	21,844	21,600
Share premium	98,846	98,822
Other reserves	62,750	64,304
Retained earnings	169,319	190,123
Total equity	352,759	374,849
Liabilities		
Non-current		
Interest-bearing loans and borrowings	–	1,737
Total non-current liabilities		1,737
Current		
Interest-bearing loans and borrowings	479	1620
Trade and other payables	99,694	129,599
Provisions	–	7,500
Corporation tax payable	–	190
Total current liabilities	100,173	138,909
Total liabilities	100,173	140,646
Total equity and liabilities	452,932	515,495

Analysing income statements

LEARNING OBJECTIVES

▶ What is an income statement?
▶ Importance of an income statement
▶ Reading and interpreting an income statement

What is an income statement?

An income statement can simply show a summary of the business's revenue, although more commonly it is referred to as a 'trading profit-and-loss account'. In its more complete form this is a financial statement that sets out the business's revenues and expenses. It can, therefore, show whether or not the business has made a profit or a loss over a particular period of time. There are some important aspects of a profit-and-loss account:

- A business's income from sales minus its direct costs (such as raw materials and cost of sales) is equal to its gross profit.
- From the gross profit any other costs are deducted. These are known as 'indirect costs' (such as rent and wages). This provides the business's operating or trading profit and shows the underlying performance of the business.
- In order to work out the net profit before tax, the sales of fixed assets, or other profits from one-off activities, are added.
- The business pays tax on its net profits, including the one-off activities. In order to show its net profit after tax, corporation tax or income tax is deducted.
- From this remaining figure the business now has to decide what to do with the remaining profit. Usually some of it will be given to shareholders in the form of dividends. The remainder is known as a 'retained profit' and this is available for reinvestment.

Importance of an income statement

The profit-and-loss account gives useful information on the business's turnover and shows whether or not it has grown since the last financial year. It shows exactly where costs have been incurred and how the management has been able to control these. Of particular interest is the amount of net profit and precisely what the business has chosen to do with this. If it has retained a large proportion of it for re-investment then the hope will be that the business will grow faster in the near future and create even greater profits.

Interpreting profit-and-loss accounts is not always a straightforward exercise. Inflation can have a drastic effect and indicate that turnover has increased when in reality it has not. Businesses will try to bring forward sales from the next trading period in order to increase their turnover and show a higher profit. The document can also be massaged by including one-off activities as ordinary activities and by altering the way in which depreciation is calculated.

On its own, the profit-and-loss account is not good enough to really tell us how a business is performing. More than one year's figures are usually required, perhaps as many as five. By comparing five sets of accounts it is possible to find trends, as seen on p. 24.

Reading and interpreting an income statement

Just like a balance sheet, a profit-and-loss account can reveal some very useful information, that is of value to different groups or stakeholders. Shareholders will be looking at turnover and net profit. They will also be looking at how profits have been used. They may either be wishing to receive the highest possible dividend, or looking at reinvestment as a longer-term indicator of future profits.

The management of a business will use the profit-and-loss account to monitor performance. They can look at sales performance and monitor the cost of sales against sales revenue. Employees will be interested in the document, particularly if they are entitled to performance-related pay. It is an increasing trend for employees to actually be shareholders, so they will also be interested in dividend payments. More broadly, a profitable business may be able to afford pay increases to its employees and, at the very least, should be able to offer significant job security.

HM Revenue & Customs is also obviously interested in the profit-and-loss account, as it shows the tax liability of the business. For this reason, profit-and-loss accounts have to conform to particular standards, and the business needs to explain how the figures have been calculated.

FOR EXAMPLE

Fyffes Plc produces a summary income statement for its shareholders, which details precisely where the revenue has been generated. It shows the profit before and after tax and the amount of money that will be distributed to shareholders.

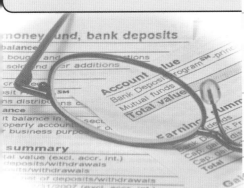

SUMMARY INCOME STATEMENT

	2007 (€m)	2006 (€m)
Group revenue	553.4	407.7
Adjusted earnings before tax and interest		
parent and subsidiaries	15.5	17.2
share of joint ventures	1.9	1.2
Total adjusted earnings before tax and interest	17.4	18.4
Net interest including share of joint ventures	1.0	3.5
Adjusted profit before tax	18.4	21.9
Share of profits of Blackrock	4.5	5.8
Exceptional items	(8.2)	(7.5)
Amortisation charge	(1.4)	(1.5)
Tax charge of joint ventures	(0.1)	0.4
Profit before tax per income statement	13.2	19.1
tax (charge)/credit (excl. share of joint ventures)	(3.1)	3.9
Minority interest charge	(0.8)	(0.7)
Profit attributable to equity shareholders	9.3	22.3
Adjusted fully diluted earnings per share (in cents)	4.42	5.70

CASE STUDY GLISTEN PLC

The business is a fast-growing confectioner, snack foods and specialist ingredient company. It owns Halo Foods, Lyme Regis Fine Foods and Nimbus Foods. The business was created in 2002 and employs around 650 people.

PROFIT-AND-LOSS ACCOUNT

	Year ended 30 June 2007 (£000s)	Year ended 30 June 2006 (£000s)
Turnover		
From continuing operations	58,611	55,630
Cost of sales	(45,254)	(44,000)
Gross profit	13,357	11,630
Administrative costs		
other	(8,752)	(7,333)
exceptional	(294)	(219)
Operating proft		
From continuing operations	4,491	4,078
Interest	(1,046)	(865)
Profit on ordinary activities before taxation	3,445	3,213
Taxation	(1,268)	(988)
PROFIT FOR THE FINANCIAL YEAR	2,177	2,225
Basic earnings per share	15.8p	16.6p
Diluted earnings per share	15.4p	15.8p

Questions

1 Briefly comment on the factors that contributed to the business's operating profits over the two years. (*6 marks*)

2 Why was there a drop in profit in 2007 and why was there a reduction in the basic earnings per share? (*6 marks*)

Working capital, depreciation, profit utilisation and profit quality

Working capital

Working capital is the essential amount of money a business has available to pay its day-to-day expenses. A business's working capital is what is left of its liquid assets once it has paid all its immediate debts. You will find that on a balance sheet, working capital is often referred to as 'net current assets'.

There can be a number of reasons why working capital problems emerge:

- A sudden change in interest rates will increase a business's interest payments and use up cash. Also, a drop in sales, and thus the business's receipts from those sales could fall while expenditure remains the same.
- Poor credit control is another problem. If there is not an effective system in place, bad debts can increase and the business will lose revenue.
- Internal mistakes can be another reason. If production costs increase while sales revenue declines, then working capital is used up. Also, if a business misjudges the level of sales and gears up to produce more, then costs have been incurred and continuing costs are incurred because the goods have to be stored.
- Mismanagement can also cause working capital problems. Costs can be underestimated or the amount of products that need to be produced can be overestimated. If considerable loans are taken out, then the business may have overstretched and find it impossible to service the debts.

Depreciation

Depreciation has an effect on both the balance sheet and the profit-and-loss account. Businesses depreciate their assets for the following reasons:

- It allows them to spread the cost of an asset over its useful life. This recognises that an asset often loses value due to its use, as it gets worn out. It also recognises that more modern assets are more efficient and have effectively devalued the older asset.
- Depreciation also allows a business to work out the true cost of production during a financial year. It takes into account the fact that by using an asset the business is devaluing that asset and this is a cost that needs to be worked into the cost of production.

Depreciation is important because it gives a real value to a business's asset throughout its life. This is a far more accurate figure than simply stating the original purchase price of the asset. Obviously, the depreciation affects both the profit and the value of the business:

- On the balance sheet, if an asset is depreciated too quickly, then the asset is valued at less than it is actually worth, understating the overall value of the business. If the asset is not depreciated enough then the asset is overvalued and the company appears to be worth more than it actually is.

'Since we downsized the board of directors' profits are up 300 percent.'
www.cartoonstock.com

- As far as the profit-and-loss account is concerned, if an asset is depreciated too quickly, then depreciation expenses are too high, which reduces the levels of profit. If it is too low, then the business's profits appear to be higher than they actually are.

You will not be required to actually calculate depreciation, but the concept recognises that assets lose value over a period of time.

Profit utilisation

Broadly speaking, the profits generated by a business can be put to two uses:

- They can be paid to shareholders in the form of dividends – this is known as 'distributed profit'. The profit is paid to shareholders so that they are given a sufficient dividend in order to attract additional share capital to the business. Some shareholders are only interested in short-term returns in the form of dividends and will not be interested in the prospect of longer-term profits if the business simply chooses to reinvest all its profits, rather than distributing them.
- Retained profit – as an alternative to distributing the profit, the business can choose to hold onto a significant proportion of it. This is known as 'undistributed profit'. It remains within the business, so that it can be used for reinvestment. A business may be planning research and development or the purchase of a major asset. Some businesses will also hold onto profit in case the forecasts for the next financial year are poor and they need it to pay shareholder dividends.

Profit quality

Although profit itself is a measure of the success of a business, it is fundamentally far more important in other ways. Not only does it provide funds for investment in the future, but it also acts as a way in which new shareholders can be attracted. It is also the major source of finance for businesses, which will ultimately allow them to grow. However, there are different types of profit and it is the profit quality that is an underlying factor in the actual success of the business.

Profit quality is high when the source of the profit is likely to continue into the future. A business showing profit may be able to do so because it has disposed of a major fixed asset. Once this asset has been sold and there are no more assets to sell, then the likelihood of being able to replicate this level of profit is extremely low. In this case, profit that incorporates the one-off sale of a fixed asset is said to be low in quality.

A business is said to have high-quality profit when the source of those profits can be seen to be sustainable. If a business has high-quality profit, it is more likely to be able to attract potential investors, as they will see that the business has the ability to produce sustainable profits into the future, rather than create profits by selling off assets that it cannot replace.

Questions

1. It should be easy for a business to be able to value its assets accurately. Discuss. (*12 marks*)
2. Businesses pay for their assets when they are acquired, so it does not really matter how depreciation is worked out. Discuss. (*12 marks*)

Using financial data for comparisons, trend analysis and decision-making

Comparisons

The first and most obvious use of financial data is that it allows fair comparisons between similar business organisations. This is particularly true of businesses that operate in the same sector, or are of roughly equivalent size. By using balance sheets and profit-and-loss accounts, it is possible to compare income and expenditure, use of profit, the source of that profit and how the profit is being utilised by the business.

In general, these comparisons are of particular value to potential investors. The precise relevance of different sets of figures will be dependent upon their own priorities in terms of making an investment decision. Some may be looking for businesses that can provide them with the prospect of short-term gains. This can be measured either in terms of a good dividend payment and/or an increase in share value. Potential investors will not be particularly concerned with investing in a business that decides to retain a high proportion of its profit for later reinvestment.

Longer-term orientated investors may be looking for businesses that are producing a healthy profit, but are also ploughing a good deal of that profit back into the business to fund expansion.

Obviously these are external comparisons, even though shareholders can be classified as being stakeholders in the business.

Trend analysis

Internally, a business will be concerned with assessing financial data to help it with its performance management. For many businesses it would appear that there is a fixation with the yearly planning horizon, as everything will be working up to the reporting of the financial results at the close of the financial year. However, businesses do tend to look further into the future, perhaps the medium-term of around three to five years. They will be looking for efficiency, performance outcomes and value for money. They do this by linking budgets to performance and integrating the two so that they can forecast potential results and then compare performance as accurate figures become available.

This form of trend analysis allows forecasts to be created on a rolling basis. They can be formally reviewed and updated on a quarterly basis. They are particularly useful for looking up to 18 months ahead, and the coming six months can be predicted with a fair degree of certainty. Each quarter's forecasts are compared with actual figures and then presented as a trend analysis. This combines financial trends with performance output and gives an overall picture.

Trend analysis for expenditure and income can be linked with trends in key performance indicators, so that a business can see the key drivers of costs and any variables in its area. By quarterly revision, resources can be redirected and the forecast can act as a tool for relating necessary funding to actual needs within the business.

The rolling approach to trend analysis is a continual process. It will not only pose challenges for the business but also indicate opportunities.

Decision-making

As we will see in the next spread, there are a number of strengths and weaknesses in terms of the scope of financial data. However, good quality financial data is absolutely essential for a business to be able to make informed decisions.

Effectively, financial data can provide the following to support decision-making:

- *Accuracy* – accurate data will provide a fair picture of performance and should enable informed decision-making.
- *Validity* – as financial data is recorded and used in compliance with generally accepted standards, there should be consistency and an ability to compare it with similar organisations. In effect it should measure what was intended to be measured.
- *Reliability* – financial data should be stable and consistent and there should be a confidence that all necessary data has been collected and included.
- *Timeliness* – the data is collected on a rolling basis, not just

presented as financial data at the end of a trading period. Financial data should be available quickly and frequently to support decision-making.

- *Relevance* – any related financial data should be captured so that it can be periodically reviewed to aid decision-making.

There are, of course, many different types of decision-making processes that can be used in order to assist the business in assessing risks. Effectively, a business will look at financial data and work out whether risks are acceptable. The data will also inform the decision-makers as to whether or not they can afford to make a decision. In this respect accurate financial data is at the foundation of most business decisions, as it will affect the business's profitability and shareholder value.

As we discover in the section covering investment decisions (on pages 44–52), there are a number of different ways in which financial data can be directly used in order to inform decision-makers of the most appropriate course of action. A business may use financial data to decide on entry into a new market, the adoption of new production techniques, the research and development of new products or services or whether changes need to be made to the organisational structure, management style and training.

Financial data can provide decision-makers with a very **quantitative** view of whether a decision is correct or not. As we will see, what accounts cannot do is address **qualitative** issues, which could perhaps improve the work situation for employees or managers, or perhaps simply make operations far easier to handle.

In dealing with financial data, only financial issues, primarily related to profit or loss, are the key considerations.

KEY TERMS

Quantitative – facts and figures based on numerical values, such as financial data.

Qualitative – views and opinions, rather than fixed quantitative figures.

CASE STUDY NEW HARDWARE

A sales director is deciding whether to implement a new computer-based contact management and sales processing system. The business will need ten PCs with supporting software at £2,450 each, a server at £3,500, three printers at £1,200 each, cabling and installation at £4,600, and sales support software at £15,000. An introductory computer course at £400 per person will be needed for eight employees and a keyboard skill course for the same number at the same price. Twelve more employees will need training on the sales support system at £700 per person. It has also been calculated that 40 man days will be lost at a cost of £200 per day. The disruption to the department would lead to lost sales of £20,000 and lost sales due to inefficiency during the first few months of another £20,000.

On the plus side, the department can triple its mailshot capacity, bringing in £40,000 extra each year.

Telesales campaigns will be improved, bringing in another £20,000 per year. Improved efficiency and reliability will net another £50,000. Improved customer service and retention will be worth a further £30,000. Improved customer information accuracy is worth £10,000 and other general improvements another £30,000.

Questions

1 What is the total cost of the proposed investment? (*4 marks*)
2 What is the total value of the benefits? (*2 marks*)
3 What is the payback time for the overall project? (*4 marks*)
4 This is an example of a cost benefit analysis. What are its key advantages and disadvantages? (*6 marks*)

Strengths and weaknesses of financial data in judging performance

LEARNING OBJECTIVES

▶ Nature of accounts
▶ Who uses accounts?
▶ What accounts do not cover
▶ Problems with accounts

Nature of accounts

A balance sheet is simply a statement of assets and liabilities at a point in time. Assets tend to be valued at their historic costs, which can be misleading. A balance sheet is also drawn up on a particular day, which allows the business to manipulate the figures in terms of their assets and liabilities.

A profit-and-loss account, or income statement, looks at the business's revenues and expenditure over the same period. In calculating profit there is a series of assumptions. This means that profit is an accounting opinion, whereas cash is always a matter of fact.

Financial accounts, which incorporate the balance sheet and profit-and-loss account (as well as a cash-flow statement) are required by Companies House and HM Revenue & Customs by law. A business also draws up management accounts. These are used to help managers make decisions. The accounts can be drawn up to cover the entire business, a division, a department, a product or a profit and cost centre. By using profit and cost centres managers will have detailed information that can help them with their decision-making.

Who uses accounts?

The actual value of financial data, as far as judging performance is concerned, very much depends on the user. Some of these users are internal to the business, such as employees, managers and shareholders. Others, however, are external, which could include competitors, customers, and providers of finance, suppliers and other stakeholders. The main priorities are outlined in the table below:

User	Type	Why used
Managers	Internal	They will be more interested in management accounts, as this shows the current situation. But the published financial accounts will need to show the business in a positive light.
Employees	Internal	Employees will be looking for stability, liquidity to pay wages, profitability for pay rises and generally a healthy state.
Shareholders	Internal	They want to see increased sales and profits and good cost control. They want to see rising dividends, which provide them with a better than average investment opportunity.
Customers	External	High profits could indicate that the business's products are priced too highly. They do want to see financial stability, particularly if they have a long-term relationship with the business.
Competitors	External	They want to be able to compare themselves with the business. They will look at profit margins, investment in new assets and sales trends.
Providers of finance	External	They want to know that the business has sufficient fixed assets to act as collateral for any loans. The cash flow needs to be good, so that the business will be able to make the interest payments and eventually repay the loan. They will also be interested in seeing how many other loans the business has taken out with other lenders.
Suppliers	External	These will be interested in seeing whether the business has sufficient funds to pay its invoices and whether they should give the business credit.
Other stakeholders	External	These are all other groups that may have a direct or indirect interest in the business. Trade unions will be concerned, as performance might affect their members. Local authorities will be concerned, as it may affect employment. Organisations such as Companies House and HM Revenue & Customs will be concerned that the accounts have been constructed in a legal manner.

KEY TERM

Collateral – a fixed asset that can be used as security against a loan.

What accounts do not cover

Accounts reveal very little beyond strict facts and figures. Accounts are historical documents: they do not take account of changes in the environment and neither do they really indicate the long-term prospects of the business.

Accounts say nothing about management or the workforce. There is no clue to the qualifications or experience of either. Nothing is mentioned about the technologies used by the business or the techniques it employs to create and market its products and services. There is also no indication as to whether the business's market share is growing or contracting, or whether the business needs to introduce new products to replace existing ones.

Problems with accounts

There is often a degree of confusion about the terms 'cash' and 'funds'. Normally the term 'cash' is used when the money has actually been received by the business or paid out by the business. This means that sales revenue is not the same as money that has been received from sales. Sales revenue includes sales that have been made on credit. The customer that has bought the products or services has not yet paid for them. They are a debtor and what is important is when that invoice will be paid.

Businesses that tend to deal with consumers rather than business customers do not usually tend to have this discrepancy between sales revenue and cash received from sales, as payment is normally immediate. Businesses that deal with other businesses, however, may see several months go by before an invoice is actually paid. This means that the profit-and-loss account may show that the business is doing well as it is generating sales, but it is in fact running out of cash because the invoices are not yet due.

We have already seen that profit quality is also important. Businesses that include the one-off disposal of an asset as part of their profit are said to have low-quality profit. Whereas those that generate profit from their normal trading activities have high-quality profit. The accounts will usually distinguish between the profit from trading and the profit from a one-off disposal.

Asset valuation is also a key concern, as can be seen in the following table:

Type of asset valuation	Potential problems
Debtors	The debtors figure does not show who actually owes money or whether there is a high likelihood of the debt being paid. It may be a bad debt that is never paid.
Depreciation	Depreciation reduces reported profit and therefore taxable profit, but reduced depreciation can boost reported profit.
Land and buildings	These assets are often shown at their historic cost, so are often valued at less than their current market value. This actually undervalues the whole business.
Intangible assets	Putting a value on brand names, licences, goodwill, copyright and patents is fairly subjective. If they are undervalued, it will make the business appear to be lower in value than it actually is.
Stock valuation	Stock needs to be valued at historic cost or its actual realisable value. There is no clear indication that a stock check was done correctly and that the quantities and values are right.

> ## Questions
>
> 1 Find out what is meant by the term 'window dressing'. How does this apply to accounts? (*8 marks*)
> 2 How can a business make a fair stock valuation? (*8 marks*)

Case studies, questions and exam practice

CASE STUDY SCHOOL UNIFORMS

Sandeep Sud is a qualified solicitor who also runs a school uniform business based in Hounslow, in partnership with his parents. The company, which has four full-time employees, uses its balance sheet to gauge how the business is progressing. It's also been a key factor in securing a bank loan for the improvement and expansion of the company premises.

Sandeep says: 'As a partnership we produce a balance sheet as part of our annual accounts and as an internal management exercise. A balance sheet gives a snapshot of how the business is doing at a particular time. This is useful, but you have to remember that it could change overnight. For example, if you were in debt on April 30 when you did your year-end accounts, but paid this off on May 1, you would get a completely different picture of the strength of the business. The balance sheet is useful when looked at alongside the profit-and-loss figures because then you get the whole picture. For example, if you borrowed lots in one particular year, but had made

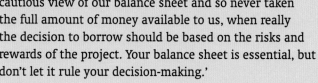

a profit, the profit would show on your profit-and-loss accounts, but what you owed would only be apparent on the balance sheet. It's important to be aware of both sets of numbers. Having a strong balance sheet helped when it came to borrowing. When we first applied for a refurbishment loan we couldn't provide up-to-date accounts to the bank manager. This could have been a problem, but we quickly got our accounts in order and the loan was approved straight away. Because our balance sheet was strong, the bank thought we were a good risk. Although we decided not to draw down on the loan – because we used cash flow instead – it did open our eyes to the importance of a strong balance sheet. I would have taken the bank loan to drive expansion. In the past we've taken a cautious view of our balance sheet and so never taken the full amount of money available to us, when really the decision to borrow should be based on the risks and rewards of the project. Your balance sheet is essential, but don't let it rule your decision-making.'

Source: adapted from Business Link

Sandeep's top tips

- 'Pay your creditors – especially suppliers – as soon as possible. Not only does it help your balance sheet but it improves your bargaining position.'
- 'Consider off-balance sheet financing if appropriate, e.g. for leased vehicles – this will improve the asset side of your balance sheet.'
- 'Never have too much cash in hand. If you are cash rich, this will show on your balance sheet and you should move this money to a high-interest bank account.'

Questions

1 What does Sandeep mean by 'we produce a balance sheet as part of our annual accounts and as an internal management exercise'? What is the purpose of doing this? (*10 marks*)
2 What does Sandeep mean by saying that he used cash flow rather than a loan to fund the refurbishment? (*6 marks*)
3 Consider Sandeep's top tips and comment on their value to a business. (*12 marks*)

Conducting ratio analysis (1)

LEARNING
OBJECTIVES
► Liquidity ratios
► Profitability ratios
► Gearing ratio

Liquidity ratios

Liquidity ratios are also known as 'solvency ratios'. They allow someone to monitor a business's precise cash position. They measure the actual liquid assets that are held by a business, such as cash and other assets that can easily be turned into cash. The purpose of the ratio is then to compare these assets with short-term debts or liabilities.

There are two relevant liquidity ratios, the first being the current ratio:

$$\text{current ratio} = \frac{\text{current assets}}{\text{current liabilities}}$$

The current ratio is always shown as a ratio, such as 3:1. In this instance the business has £3 worth of current assets (cash, debtors and stock) for every £1 of current liability (creditors, tax, proposed dividends).

Usually a current ratio of 1.6:1 is considered to be perfectly acceptable. But many businesses operate with far lower ratios and manufacturing businesses, for example, will have far higher ratios. The higher ratio could show that a business is actually hanging onto too much cash and not investing that money into fixed assets. In the short term, businesses can improve their current ratio by selling off fixed assets or negotiating longer-term loans.

The second liquidity ratio is known as the acid test, or quick ratio:

$$\text{acid test ratio} = \frac{\text{liquid assets}}{\text{current liabilities}}$$

The key difference between this and the current ratio is that it counts liquid assets as being current assets minus stock. It is seen as a more accurate indicator of liquidity because stock is actually quite difficult to turn into ready cash.

Many businesses can operate successfully with an acid test figure of 0.7:1, rather than what would normally be expected to be 1:1. Businesses that tend to deal primarily in cash will have far lower ratios, perhaps 0.4:1. Manufacturing businesses will tend to be closer to 1:1.

Again a business should not have a high ratio, as it will be hanging onto cash rather than investing it. A business can improve its ratio by selling off fixed assets and changing over to long-term loans.

Profitability ratios

There are three key ratios related to profitability. The first is the gross profit margin:

$$\frac{\text{gross profit}}{\text{margin}} = \frac{\text{gross profit} \times 100}{\text{turnover}}$$

This is expressed as a percentage.

FOR EXAMPLE

A business that has a gross profit of £150,000 against a turnover of £2,875,000 would have a gross profit margin of 5.21%.

Businesses that turn their stock over rapidly, such as retailers, will have low gross profit margins. Businesses that have significant fixed assets and turn their stock over more slowly will have a higher ratio. Businesses can improve this by increasing prices or reducing their direct costs.

The second profitability ratio is the net profit margin:

$$\frac{\text{net profit}}{\text{margin}} = \frac{\text{net profit} \times 100}{\text{turnover}}$$

FOR EXAMPLE

Again, using the same example as above, the business shows a net profit of £125,000 on a turnover of £2,875,000. Its net profit margin is therefore 4.34%.

The higher the net profit margin, the better it is for the business. By comparing the gross and net profit margins, much can be discovered. If a business has a relatively stable gross profit margin but a falling net profit margin, then indirect costs may be out of control. It is usually indirect costs that are the key to improving net profit margin, but again improvements can be made by increasing prices.

The final profitability ratio is known as return on capital employed (ROCE). This is often referred to as 'primary efficiency ratio', as it allows someone to assess the overall financial performance of the business:

$$\text{ROCE} = \frac{\text{operating profit} \times 100}{\text{capital employed}}$$

A business may show an operating profit of £24 million and this is on £389 million of capital employed. The ROCE is therefore 6.16%.

In our example, the ROCE is relatively poor, as it is usually initially compared to the rate of interest that a business would receive if it had simply placed its money in the bank. Usually ROCE is expected to be between 20% and 30%, which is considerably higher than just leaving the money in a deposit account. However, it is also important to compare ROCE figures with competitors in order to see just how the business is performing compared to similar businesses.

ROCE can be improved by increasing operating profit, repaying long-term debt or actually reducing the amount of capital that is being employed.

Gearing ratio

Gearing looks at the long-term liquidity situation of a business and for many is classed as a liquidity ratio. The ratio itself looks at how the business has raised its long-term capital:

$$\text{gearing} = \frac{\text{long term loans}}{\text{total capital employed}}$$

A highly geared business is said to have more than half of its capital employed in the form of loans. A low-geared business has a gearing figure of less than 50%.

A business has equity capital of £200 million and fixed interest capital of £82 million. Therefore its gearing ratio is 0.4 or 41%. In this example the business can be considered to have low gearing.

Businesses can improve their gearing by repaying their long-term loans or by issuing more shares or redeeming debentures.

KEY TERM

Debenture – a long-term loan to the business that carries a fixed rate of interest and is repayable on a specific date.

CASE STUDY THREE SIMILAR BUSINESSES?

Three businesses are operating in the same market. They are not, however, precisely the same, as they have different amounts of current assets, stock, liabilities and sources of finance and capital employed:

- Buchan's has current assets of £150,000; stock valued at £60,000, current liabilities of £100,000, equity capital and reserves of £180,000 and fixed interest capital of £120,000.
- Carlisle has current assets of £200,000, stock worth £50,000, current liabilities of £400,000, equity capital and reserves of £100,000 and fixed interest capital of £70,000.
- Finally, Stimpsons has current assets of £280,000, stock worth £80,000, current liabilities of £220,000, equity capital and reserves of £90,000 and fixed interest capital of £20,000.

Questions

1 Calculate the current ratio, acid test ratio and gearing of Buchan's. (*6 marks*)
2 Calculate the current ratio, acid test ratio and gearing of Carlisle. (*6 marks*)
3 Calculate the current ratio, acid test ratio and gearing of Stimpsons. (*6 marks*)

Conducting ratio analysis (2)

Financial efficiency ratios

Financial efficiency ratios look at how well the management is controlling the operations of the business. They show how assets are being used to generate profit, how well stock is being managed and how the business is paying for its purchases and carrying out credit control.

The first key efficiency ratio is the asset turnover ratio. This looks at business sales and how assets are being used to generate the sales:

$$\text{asset turnover} = \frac{\text{sales (turnover)}}{\text{net assets}}$$

In this ratio, net assets are total assets minus total liabilities. If this ratio increases over a period of time it shows that the business is becoming more efficient. A fall usually shows that there has been a decline in sales or an increase in the value of the assets being employed.

Many retail outlets will have high asset turnover ratio because they have high sales and relatively few assets and they actually earn very little profit on each sale. A business that sells high-value products is likely to have a low asset turnover ratio because they have high-value assets but relatively few sales. They do, however, earn a great deal of profit on each sale that they make. A business would be able to improve the asset turnover ratio by either selling off any surplus or under-utilised assets or by improving its sales performance.

The second efficiency ratio looks at stock turnover. It compares the value of stock with sales achieved, valued at cost. The business should make a profit on each sale, sell its stock relatively fast and it will then earn larger profits. The ratio is:

$$\text{stock turnover ratio} = \frac{\text{cost of sales}}{\text{stock}}$$

FOR EXAMPLE

A business holds stock valued at £27,000. However, over the year the business achieved sales of £323,000. Therefore by dividing the sales by the stock held, we can see that the business's stock turnover ratio was 11.96, or the stock turned over approximately 12 times (perhaps once a month) throughout the financial year.

Businesses such as supermarkets may have a stock turnover of around 100 times in a financial year. Other businesses, such as second-hand bookshops might only have a ratio of 2 or 3. A low stock turnover ratio may be as a result of the business holding stock that nobody wants to buy, whereas a high figure can show that the business is efficient, but that it could easily run out of stock. In order to improve the ratio, a business needs to hold low levels of stock or achieve higher sales without increasing their stock levels.

It is also valuable to see how quickly a business pays its debts to its creditors and how quickly it receives payments from its debtors. The creditor turnover is:

$$\text{creditor turnover} = \frac{\text{average creditors}}{(\text{cost of sales} \div 365)}$$

FOR EXAMPLE

A business has a cost of sales of £106,000 and owes £22,000 to creditors, with those amounts falling due within the year. The creditor turnover ratio is 75.75 days.

The debtors' collection period ratio, also known as 'debtor days', is designed to calculate how long it takes for the business to collect any money that it might be owed. A business that is suffering from liquidity problems may actually be granting customers longer periods of credit than it can actually afford. The ratio is:

$$\text{debtors} = \frac{\text{debtors} \times 365}{\text{turnover}}$$

It is commonplace for businesses to offer 30 to 90 days' credit. Using this ratio, the lower the ratio, the quicker the money is coming into the business. The ratio can be improved by reducing the credit period offered to customers and persuading the slowest payers to pay more promptly.

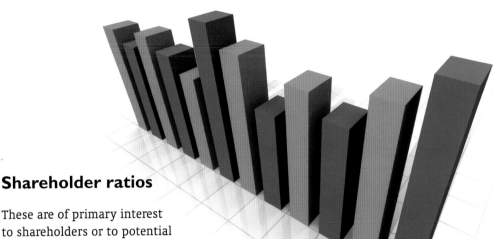

Shareholder ratios

These are of primary interest to shareholders or to potential investors. They are often referred to as 'investment ratios'. It is important to remember that shareholders receive a return on their investment in two different ways: they receive a dividend payment based on profits that the business has made during the financial year; the other major consideration is the potential rise in the price of the shares, which is known as a 'capital gain'.

The dividends themselves offer the shareholders a short-term return, whereas the share price is more long-term. Shareholders more interested in the share price type of return will not be that concerned that they are not receiving a high dividend, as they will expect that the business will grow and the value of their shares will increase.

The first ratio is the dividend per share, which is a simple calculation made by dividing the total dividend available to shareholders by the number of shares that have been issued:

$$\text{dividend per share} = \frac{\text{total dividends}}{\text{number of issued shares}}$$

> **FOR EXAMPLE**
>
> *A business decides that it will distribute £160.2 million to its shareholders as their share of the profits. They have issued 1,454.6 million shares. The dividend per share is therefore 11.01p.*

The shareholder will usually be paid an interim dividend part-way through the financial year, and then the balance at the end of the year. Shareholders looking at the shorter term will probably want a high figure, but those looking at the investment in the long term will hope that they will receive greater returns in the future and that the share price will continue to rise. Investors will compare the dividend per share with other businesses. One other key issue is the fact that the actual purchase price of each share may not be the same from company to company. Some shares will be significantly more expensive, but still produce the same dividend per share.

A business can increase its dividend per share by reducing the amount of profit it retains, but this may not be in the long-term interests of the business or the shareholders.

The second shareholder ratio is the dividend yield. This compares the dividend received on the share with the current market price of that share. This gives an investor an opportunity to compare the return with the amount that has been invested to purchase the share. The ratio is:

$$\frac{\text{dividend}}{\text{yield}} = \frac{\text{dividend per share} \times 100}{\text{market price per share}}$$

> **FOR EXAMPLE**
>
> *If the dividend per share was 11.01p and the share price was £3.62, then the dividend yield would be 3.04%.*

Investors looking for a quick return will be looking for a higher figure. Longer-term investors will be content that the business is reinvesting its profits. This ratio will change as the share price fluctuates, and the ratio can be improved by increasing the amount of profit given to the shareholders.

> (Question)
>
> Which ratio provides a better indication of company performance and why, when comparing dividend yield ratio and dividend per share ratio? (*8 marks*)

The value and limitations of ratio analysis

LEARNING OBJECTIVES
▶ Value of ratio analysis
▶ Limitations of ratio analysis

Value of ratio analysis

By using a broad range of ratios, it is possible for an existing shareholder, stakeholder or potential investor to make direct comparisons between different businesses. Liquidity ratios are primarily designed to look at the ability of a business to pay its immediate debts, principally of interest to the management of the business, their suppliers and their creditors. The efficiency ratios provide specific evidence as to how well the management is controlling the business. This is of particular interest to shareholders, the management itself, employees and competitors.

Profitability ratios measure the fundamental success of the business and are of interest to a broad range of different groups, including shareholders, creditors, the management, employees and competitors.

Gearing measures the extent to which the business is running on borrowed money. This is of particular concern to shareholders, creditors and the management. Finally the value of shareholder ratios provides vital information to investors on returns on their investment.

By using ratios it is possible to extract data that allows a direct comparison from business to business, regardless of the size of the businesses, their complexity, or the gross figures involved.

Limitations of ratio analysis

While ratios can provide us with a great deal of information about a business's performance and can be useful tools, they do have limitations. Limitations include:

- Ratios are only really averages.
- Ratios are taken over the whole business, which may actually conceal parts of the business that are performing quite badly.
- In isolation a ratio tells us nothing. It must be compared with another business, or with historical data or trends.
- Ratios can hide true cash gains and losses. For example, a reduction in the net profit margin may actually hide an increase in the actual profit.
- It is perfectly possible for businesses to distort the true picture and it is important to know which accounting policies have been adopted.
- Inflation needs to be taken into account. For example, an increase in sales may actually hide the fact that no real improvement has been made.
- The financial statements used to create the ratios are historical ones and may not necessarily indicate future prosperity.
- Extracting ratios from one set of accounts for one year will tell us nothing about where the business is going.
- Ratios actually pose more questions than answers. The ratios need to be looked at in context. Why are trends increasing or decreasing?

- The balance sheet itself is only a snapshot in time and may not be typical of the business.
- Balance sheet values may be out of date or unrealistic. Stock may actually be unsaleable; debtors may be bad debtors; and by the time the ratio is worked out, money sitting in a bank may have been spent.

It is important to look at some of these aspects in a little more detail, firstly by considering the fact that information gained from ratio analysis needs to be subject to comparison:

- It is advisable to compare ratios for the same business over previous years, as this allows trends to be identified.
- A comparison with businesses in the same industry can reveal how they are performing compared to their closest, similar competitors.
- It is also valuable to compare the business with other businesses from a wider range of industries, such as choosing two that are growing fast.

Performance should also be a key consideration when looking at ratios. There are other elements that need to be taken into account when considering the figures:

- It is important to understand the market in which the business is operating. Poor ratios, such as return on capital employed, may not necessarily indicate that the business is performing badly, but that it is operating in a very competitive market where there must be low profits per unit.

- The strength of the business in the marketplace itself is important. A business that has gained a degree of market leadership should be providing better performance results than one that has just entered the market. The smaller business may be investing heavily in assets and new products and ideas, as well

as trying to establish its brand. This will depress many of the ratios, but in the longer term the business may generate bigger profits.

- Little is known about the management or the quality of the employees. Neither of these factors is revealed in ratio analysis. If a business is spending considerable sums on training and development, this will not show up as a positive in ratio analysis.

- As already mentioned, the economic environment itself can have a drastic impact on the ratio analysis results. If the economy is strong, where there is low unemployment, low interest rates and a generally upbeat economy, then most businesses should be doing well. If the economy is precarious and there are difficulties, then it should be expected that the ratios will reflect this.

CASE STUDY IT FIGURES

A business has prepared a comprehensive set of ratio analysis results contained in the following table:

Year end	31 April 07	31 April 06	31 April 05	31 April 04
Consolidation	Yes	Yes	Yes	Yes
Exchange rate used	GBP	GBP	GBP	GBP
Number of employees	10	9	11	11
Gross profit margin (%)	65.52	63.54	57.50	52.38
Operating profit margin (%)	31.90	29.17	32.50	26.19
Pre-tax profit margin (%)	26.72	29.17	33.75	26.19
Return on capital employed (%)	44.03	53.64	58.70	46.03
Return on investment (%)	110.71	93.33	180.00	110.00
Current ratio	1.30	1.06	1.21	1.19
Quick ratio	1.14	0.94	1.06	1.07
Debt ratio	0.57	0.43	0.67	0.58
Times interest earned	12.33	14.00	26.00	5.50
Stock turnover	7.41	7.95	8.10	8.00
Credit given (days)	35	48	50	45
Credit taken (days)	45	40	35	30
Fixed asset turnover	1.93	1.96	2.35	2.21
Debtor turnover	10.55	7.62	7.27	8.07
Value added (£)	106,280	86,290	74,700	26,855
Sales per employee (£)	50,000	53,333	36,364	19,091
Average wage	13,500	13,889	10,909	10,909
Growth in sales (%)	20.83	20.00	90.48	
Change in employees (%)	11.11	−18.18	0.00	

Questions

1 Outline the key trends in profits over the period 2004–2007. (6 marks)
2 What other improvements have been made over the same period? Comment on their significance. (8 marks)

Case studies, questions and exam practice

CASE STUDY AVERAGES

A business has prepared a set of ratios based on the industry in which it operates. It has only been able to access financial data from the larger competitors which are public limited companies. It hopes to be able to compare its own results with the industry averages.

INDUSTRY AVERAGES

	2003	2004	2005	2006	2007
Gross profit margin (%)	45.55	48.11	43.23	48.66	49.00
Operating margin (%)	10.89	9.56	11.32	11.00	10.25
Pre-tax margin (%)	8.99	9.03	8.55	8.89	9.06
Return on capital employed (%)	14.73	22.17	25.28	19.89	23.00
Return on investment (%)	26.03	30.45	26.90	35.03	32.88
Current ratio	1.34	1.29	1.25	1.28	1.31
Debt ratio	0.69	0.65	0.66	0.66	0.64
Stock turnover (per year)	15.68	16.04	15.52	15.83	14.69
Average credit given (days)	70	60	63	63	65
Average credit taken (days)	37	54	55	52	55
Fixed asset turnover (per year)	5.95	5.37	4.95	4.85	5.23
Debtor turnover (per year)	6.31	6.60	6.38	6.33	6.99
Value added (% of turnover)	-0.78	1.68	2.45	1.79	0.3
Average sales per employee (£)	85,580	84,796	84,428	81,877	77,670
Average wage per employee (£)	18,488	16,995	17,390	18,127	18,637
Total sales (% of base year)	89.45	94.32	100	101.35	107.98
Operating profit (% of base year)	121.95	118.24	100	88.99	100.15

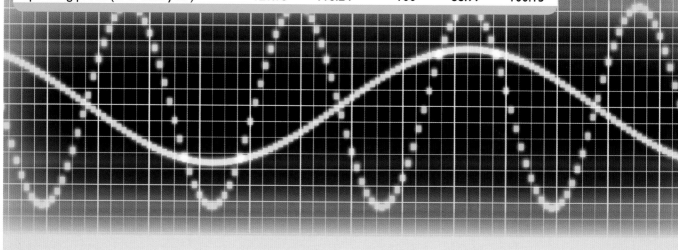

BUSINESS RESULTS

Year end	31 April 07	31 April 06	31 April 05	31 April 04
Gross profit margin (%)	65.52	63.54	57.50	52.38
Operating profit margin (%)	31.90	29.17	32.50	26.19
Pre-tax profit margin (%)	26.72	29.17	33.75	26.19
Return on capital employed (%)	44.03	53.64	58.70	46.03
Return on investment (%)	110.71	93.33	180.00	110.00
Current ratio	1.30	1.06	1.21	1.19
Quick ratio	1.14	0.94	1.06	1.07
Debt ratio	0.57	0.43	0.67	0.58
Times interest earned	12.33	14.00	26.00	5.50
Stock turnover (per year)	7.41	7.95	8.10	8.00
Credit given (days)	35	48	50	45
Credit taken (days)	45	40	35	30
Fixed asset turnover (per year)	1.93	1.96	2.35	2.21
Debtor turnover (per year)	10.55	7.62	7.27	8.07
Value added (£)	106,280	86,290	74,700	26,855
Sales per employee (£)	50,000	53,333	36,364	19,091
Average wage per employee (£)	13,500	13,889	10,909	10,909
Growth in sales (%)	20.83	20.00	90.48	
Change in employees (%)	11.11	-18.18	0.00	

The business intends to extend the analysis and is proposing the following:

- *The largest companies* – Identifying the companies with the largest turnover in the industry to give an idea of market concentration and market size. Market share data is difficult to compute since many companies are in several distinct sectors or because in some sectors there are many small companies that are either not limited or not filing full accounting records. The ranking of the largest companies gives a feel for this important marketing data.
- *The fastest-growing companies* – Evaluating the companies whose turnover has grown the fastest in the last four years. The faster growth companies might be attractive takeover targets or companies offering products to emulate, if it is this that is fuelling their growth.

- *The new entrants to the market* – Listing the newly formed companies that are operating in the market. This might be important in protecting market share or in identifying new trends of customer behaviour if combined with knowledge of the product lines being offered.

Questions

1 Comment on how valuable this exercise may be to the business. (*18 marks*)
2 Highlight the key relevant comparisons and comment on them. (*16 marks*)
3 How useful would the second part of the research be and why? (*8 marks*)

Raising finance and implementing profit centres

Raising finance

Finance, or money, is a scarce resource. For any business to obtain it from a third party, such as a bank, it will have to compete to get it. This means a company has to show that it is less of a risk than other businesses, and that the lender (or the investor) has a reasonable chance that they will see their money again and receive a reasonable rate of return (profit) from the investment.

When we look at loans, the implication is that the bank or building society is only lending the money for the short term. They will expect the business to pay interest on the loan and at the end of the loan period to pay back the capital sum (the amount that was originally loaned). Investment, on the other hand, infers a longer-term relationship between the investor and the business. A shareholder as a part owner of the business will expect the business to provide them with cash dividends on their shares and for the value of the shares to gradually increase.

Once a business is trading and more established, one of the major sources of finance is from the retained profit resulting from selling products and services to customers. However, if a business is just starting up, or it needs extra finance to expand, it will have to find money from a different source.

The key questions for a business to ask itself are:

- How long will we need the money for (duration of loan needed)?
- How much will it cost to borrow the money (rate of interest and perhaps payment protection insurance)?
- How much will we have to pay on a regular (monthly) basis (what is the repayment schedule)?

In effect, a business will obtain finance from either:

- internal sources – such as the owner's capital (in the case of new businesses) or retained profits (in the case of existing businesses), or
- external sources – overdrafts (both new and existing businesses), hire purchase, loans and mortgages.

The main problem with issuing shares in order to raise finance is the fact that the business owners are diluting their ownership of the business. As investors buy shares, they become part owners in the business and, to some extent, the original owners of the business

lose ownership and some control over the business. Investors may want different things, such as improved profits, more cautious expansion, and a lower reliance on borrowing. They may have fundamental problems with the way in which the originators of the business run the operation.

Providing the original owners retain at least 51% of the shares, they will always have the final say over decision-making, even at the annual general meeting, but if they sell more than a 50% stake in the business, then they run the risk of losing control over the business that they created.

Overdrafts in particular can be seen as an extremely expensive way of borrowing money. Overdrafts not only have to be agreed with the bank or building society (in terms of the amount that the business can be overdrawn), but the overdrawn amounts attract a relatively high level of interest.

Bank loans tend to be fixed term, with interest payments due on a monthly basis (they either include a contribution to the capital amount rather like an endowment mortgage, or the capital sum is due at the end of the loan period). The longer the period of the loan, the more interest will have been paid over the term of the loan.

In the case of loans, the business needs to make sure that it can afford to pay the monthly instalments and that these repayments do not eat into their working capital, affecting their ability to pay other current liabilities.

Rather like the sale of shares, the involvement of venture capitalists inevitably means some loss of ownership of the business. Unlike smaller shareholders who may only own relatively few shares, a venture capital business will tend to own a substantial block of shares or be a partner in the business. This means that they will want to exert an influence on the day-to-day running of the business and be involved in key decisions.

Usually a specified cash sum will be invested by a venture capital business in return for a specified share of the business; the business owner needs to weigh up the comparative loss of ownership and control as well as proportionate loss of the profits.

Implementing profit centres

Profit centres, or cost centres, involve the dividing up of large organisations into areas where individual managers are responsible for the profits generated or the costs incurred. As far as accounting procedures are concerned, cost and profit centres are ideal, as individual performance of particular areas of the business can be analysed.

The purpose of these is to allocate costs and attribute profit to various areas of the business. Cost centres, for example, will incur direct and indirect costs, as will profit centres, but they will also generate income for the business.

As we will see on the next spread, the allocation of costs, in particular, has significant implications and can affect different parts of the business in different ways, depending on how the profit and cost centres have been created.

By establishing cost and profit centres according to products, particular groups of machines in a factory, a department, the location or even an individual, a business is able to allocate its overheads or indirect costs. This will have an impact on the performance of each of the centres, but it is seen as a fairer way of allocating actual costs and assigning the source of income to the business.

Typically, a business will create a series of mini profit-and-loss accounts for each of the cost and profit centres. These can then be consolidated into a full profit-and-loss account, as part of the main financial summary of the business's activities. It is important to remember that these mini profit-and-loss accounts are for internal consumption only, as public awareness of them would reveal far too much about the internal workings of the business and would be of considerable value to competitors.

Questions

1 List at least five common direct costs and five common indirect costs. (*10 marks*)
2 What do you understand by the term 'full costing', and what are the implications for a profit or cost centre? (*6 marks*)

Cost minimisation and allocating capital expenditure

LEARNING OBJECTIVES

▶ Cost minimisation
▶ Allocating capital expenditure
▶ Implications and value of financial strategies

Cost minimisation

Cost minimisation is part of a broader cost management function. It requires strategic planning, and the foundations of ensuring that costs are maintained at a reasonable level involve cash-flow forecasting, the monitoring of working capital, credit control and managing relationships with suppliers.

Cash-flow forecasting should alert the business to planned capital expenditure, and decisions can be made as to whether they are appropriate and will bring reasonable benefits to the organisation.

Working capital can also be drastically affected by spiralling costs, particularly if purchasing is being funded by using an overdraft or unsustainable credit from suppliers.

Credit control, of course, handles the incoming of funds to the business, but it is the relationship with suppliers that perhaps holds the key to cost minimisation. This relates primarily to products and services that are purchased from outside the organisation. It means making use of the best credit terms, renegotiating credit limits and, of course, driving a hard bargain for each and every product and service purchased.

Cost minimisation also needs to extend into the business itself. This can be measured in a variety of different ways, but broadly costs can be more clearly identified if a business has broken up its organisation into profit and cost centres. Effectively they charge these centres for services carried out by other parts of the business. This alerts them to the sometimes hidden costs involved in support services and partner services within the business.

Cost minimisation is key to ensuring that the income received by the business is in excess of its expenditure.

Allocating capital expenditure

Capital expenditure involves the spending by a business to purchase fixed assets, such as a vehicle, machinery or a building. Businesses will routinely carry out what is known as a 'cost benefit analysis', in order to assess the value that will be brought to the business by the purchase of the fixed asset.

Again, by breaking down the business into cost and profit centres, each budget holder will be expected to effectively bid and argue the case for any capital expenditure that they wish to be allocated to their centre. The business will always have a limited amount of funds available to purchase these types of assets and it needs to be assured that any investment in these assets will provide the greatest possible benefits and financial returns to the business. Some capital expenditure costs are unavoidable, perhaps when a fleet of vehicles needs to be replaced, or an adjacent property needs to be purchased.

Each capital expenditure item is analysed within the context of the overall activities of the organisation, and assessed to see if it is central to the smooth running of the operation. Not only will the costs and benefits be measured, but also the potential consequences if the capital expenditure is not approved. What might be the consequences of not replacing worn out machinery, or upgrading the computer network to cope with industry standard software?

Of course this scientific approach to allocating capital expenditure is designed to dissuade the business from making unnecessary and ill-considered fixed asset purchases. The process, however, needs to be managed in such a way that it does not inhibit growth or delay necessary purchases.

Implications and value of financial strategies

It is vital for a business to seek the most appropriate sources of finance not only to provide sufficient funds, but also to make sure that its financial position is not adversely affected. Over-borrowing can seriously affect gearing ratios. A business saddled with large loans that attract considerable interest may find it difficult to get itself out of that position. Businesses would far rather raise finance through retained profits, or through the timely sale of a fixed asset no longer central to their operations.

However, in diverting profits away from shareholders, a business runs the risk of not being as attractive a prospect for potential investors. This, in turn, means that its prospects of being able to raise capital through the sale of shares are diminished.

Although not a solution to the problems of raising finance, cost control can go a long way towards reducing the need for additional injections of finance. The more efficient a business is in returning a profit on its sales or activities, the more attractive the business is to investors, and in most cases the less it will have to borrow.

Many businesses begin this process of cost awareness by creating profit and cost centres. Individual budget holders will be expected to work within strict limits and to justify every additional pound spent, as well as to account for any lost forecast income. By creating these centres, each part of the organisation can be encouraged to consider cost minimisation. This is a key driver to improving efficiency and, of course, returning a higher level of profit.

Cost minimisation does not just apply to the day-to-day running of the business, so it extends further than the purchase of products and services from suppliers, the using up of consumables

and whether someone has left a computer running overnight. It extends to every part of the business's operations and how the business decides to make sizeable investments in fixed assets.

Collectively, these financial strategies are designed to improve the financial results of the business. But they need to be viewed with caution, as it is sometimes not possible or appropriate to apply all these measures in every case. Growing businesses may be more concerned with making rapid investment, knowing that they will make mistakes. Established businesses may look across the activities of their organisation and seek out expensive areas that can be trimmed. The precise effectiveness of these financial strategies, therefore, depends on the priorities of the business.

Question

Why might it be unfair to allocate the full costs of overheads to particular cost and profit centres, purely based on the amount of space that they occupy or the number of employees in that centre? (*12 marks*)

41

Case studies, questions and exam practice

CASE STUDY CENTAUR MEDIA PLC'S STRATEGY

Centaur's strategy is to establish and market high-quality weekly publications focused on distinct business communities, attracting a committed base of readers and advertisers. Centaur builds on this established reader and advertiser base by adding monthly magazines and directories and organising exhibitions, awards and conferences. Online products complete Centaur's integrated offering.

Typically Centaur seeks out new markets, or niches within markets, with growth potential, high value and limited competition. In creating products that meet the needs of its markets, it has sought first to define the audience that advertisers wish to meet. Then it identifies the information needs of that audience. Finally it ensures the maintenance of the highest standards of editorial integrity. This strategy reflects the fact that, while Centaur only creates products that advertisers want, having done so, it positions itself primarily as being in the readership business and thereby is successful in establishing market-leading brands.

As the information needs of these communities drive the content development of the weeklies, they also reveal further opportunities to supply information and services in other ways. The second element of Centaur's strategy is therefore to extend its trusted community brands into other product offerings. The most important of these extensions are conferences, exhibitions and Internet services.

This strategy of building on existing brand strength is best illustrated by the example of *Marketing Week*. The 'subsidiary' products built up around the market-leading weekly title include specialist titles such as *Precision Marketing* and *In-Store*, conferences, newsletters, directories, awards ceremonies and the online portal, mad.co.uk. This strategy is being successfully deployed across all of Centaur's main communities.

Management's experience has demonstrated that it is only market-leading brands that consistently attract the high-quality audiences that are able to command premium advertising rates and avoid heavy discounting.

Description of business and culture

Centaur is a federation of small businesses. Its focus on selected business communities is reflected in its community-based organisation. Apart from the Exhibitions and Conferences divisions, all other products constitute discrete profit centres grouped by business community under the leadership of a Group Publisher. The Exhibitions and Conferences divisions' primary objective is to develop profitable extensions of the magazine brands. Centaur's culture is entrepreneurial, innovative and customer-focused.

The business comprises essentially 18 main profit centres, the largest of which employs no more than 45 staff. The publishers and other profit centre heads all demonstrate an advanced level of skill in selling, buying, promotion and research. They and their teams have a marked sense of identity with, and ownership of, their respective businesses. The profit centre organisation recognises that there are certain activities and resource requirements common to all the business units, which benefit from economies of scale.

Accordingly, Centaur operates an efficient central service infrastructure comprising accounting, IT support, circulation fulfilment and marketing, HR, art and various legal, administrative, risk management and property services.

The central service teams deliver to the profit centres the most cost-effective and appropriate infrastructure and services, so that profit margins and revenue growth potential are optimised. They also ensure that the company can absorb growth with minimal additional cost, so that future internal profitability can be enhanced and additional value can be created from acquisitions and organic growth.

Launches and acquisitions

Centaur's strategy is principally one of organic growth. The company looks for opportunities or angles that others have not identified, in which the information and communications needs of the communities it serves can be met by new products and services developed from existing titles. This awareness creates organic growth at low risk within known markets.

Source: adapted from www.centaur.co.uk

Questions

1 Explain why the business has decided to set up profit centres. (*8 marks*)
2 Briefly explain why profit centres might be appropriate to this particular type of business. (*6 marks*)
3 What is the purpose of the central service teams? (*4 marks*)

Conducting investment appraisal

LEARNING
OBJECTIVES

▶ What is investment?
▶ What is investment appraisal?
▶ What information is needed?
▶ Does it work?

What is investment?

All businesses have to make investment decisions, and investments can mean the purchasing of assets, such as equipment, buildings or vehicles, or indeed improving existing fixed assets.

Some investment decisions are in fact even more complex, as they may require the business to consider relocation or the scrapping of all their machinery and its replacement with more high-tech items.

Making sure the investment works requires a good deal of planning, regardless of the nature of the investment, whether it means replacing worn-out computer screens, buying a new van or acquiring new premises to cope with an expanding level of activity.

What is investment appraisal?

Investment appraisal focuses on the viability of an investment project. In other words, how profitable the investment is likely to be or whether it is actually desirable. This can, of course, apply to the business itself wishing to reinvest in its own activities, or an external provider of finance and investment looking to sink cash into a promising-looking business.

Many of the investment appraisal techniques are quantitative in the sense that they are figure-based, but there are also many qualitative factors to take into account. Not all businesses carry out a formal investment appraisal, particularly in the case of new businesses or businesses that are largely controlled by a dominant entrepreneur. They will tend to use their intuition rather than try to explain or justify a particular investment. However, in the majority of cases more formal techniques are used before a project is given the go ahead or it is revealed that the project is not viable and it is scrapped.

Inevitably any investment means the spending of cash, which represents a cash outflow to the business or to the investor. Regardless of the source of the funds, whoever is making the investment will be expecting a return in the form of cash inflows and these cash inflows will be considered over the viable life of the asset being purchased.

Using strictly quantitative methods, a relatively simple comparison can be made between the cost of the project (cash outflow) and the income that the asset will generate (cash inflow). We will consider the different types of quantitative and qualitative methods used later on in this focus area.

What information is needed?

Focusing on the quantitative techniques in the first instance, a great deal of information needs to be assembled before any kind of appraisal can take place. Typically the following will be needed:

- The actual initial total costs of the investment – to incorporate the costs of any machinery, equipment, installation and running costs.
- The life expectancy of the asset being purchased – for how many years will the business be able to use the asset effectively and for what period of time will the asset be able to produce returns or cash inflows for the business?
- What will the asset be worth after its useful life? Will there be any residual value in the asset, and what can it be sold for, as any funds received will also be a cash inflow?
- What are the forecasted net returns or the cash inflows? The business needs to figure out the expected returns of the investments over its life expectancy and make sure that it has worked out accurate running costs, that then need to be deducted from these returns.

As we will see, working out these quantitative figures in the first instance can be very difficult, as there is a high level of uncertainty. This is because apart from knowing the initial costs of the investment, everything else is a forecast or an estimate. This is why investment appraisals are notoriously inaccurate and although clear figures may be available, they can be very subjective and may diverge wildly from the actual figures achieved.

See also Evaluating qualitative and quantitative influences on investment decisions on pp. 50–1.

Does it work?

By relying on quantitative figures, it is easy for the business to be misled. Forecasts and estimates are never certain or definite. A business cannot possibly predict how operating costs may change in the future, factor in changes in the interest rate or know with any certainty that certain cash flows are accurate.

The best that an investment appraisal can do is to give an indication or a set of guidelines on which decision-makers can base their final appraisal of the investment. As we will also see, many of the investment appraisal calculations give contradictory results. Some projects will pay back the investment faster than others, while some will provide a higher annual rate of return to the business. The organisation needs to balance the risks of making or not making the investment and judge how this may or may not affect future profits.

Businesses will make investment decisions in line with the overall objectives of the organisation. If short-term profits have to be sacrificed in order to fund a major project, then the business is looking for a higher level of profit in the future and will have to argue its case as far as shareholders are concerned, who may be looking for shorter-term gains.

Investment appraisals are necessary, but they cannot provide the business with a certain forecast of the future. Neither can the business necessarily guarantee that any of the assumptions it has made about the impact of the investment will be correct. There are simply too many other variables to make any investment appraisal a certainty.

CASE STUDY PROPOSAL

To convert unused outbuildings at the business's premises and develop an indoor cricket school (outline planning permission applied for).

Purpose

To provide both indoor facilities throughout the year for local clubs on a hire basis and to provide a coaching facility for schools and colleges and other interested parties.

Promotion of existing company products

To make the cricket community more aware of the company's range of products.

Capital expenditure

Property conversion: £44,000
Nets and artificial wickets: £16,500
Other equipment: £7,500

Total = £68,000

Projected annual cash flow

Coaching fees and hire: £50,000

Operating costs (excluding depreciation)
Coach's fees: £16,500
Heating and lighting: £3,100
Insurances: £1,500
Consumables: £1,250
Repairs and maintenance: £750
Administration: £1,100
Coach's professional fees: £250

Total = £24,450

Net cash flow
(£50,000–£24,450) = £25,550

Questions

1 How would you go about considering this investment appraisal? (*10 marks*)
2 Without carrying out quantitative investment appraisal techniques, would you approve or reject the proposal? Explain your reasons. (*10 marks*)

Investment criteria

Types of investment criteria

In effect, investment appraisal really focuses on the business's objectives, its opportunities and any constraints that it may work within. It is important to remember that the capital investment will require a cash outflow and that ultimately it should have an impact on the profitability of the business.

Setting aside the quantitative considerations, a business that is interested in profit maximisation will take a very different view on an investment than one that simply wants to improve its position in the marketplace. A profit-maximising business will always use the criteria of opting for the project that offers the largest return. A business concerned with its market position will be more concerned with providing a better quality product, so that it can firmly establish itself in the marketplace, even though smaller returns will be expected.

External costs and benefits are also part of the investment criteria. If a business is considering making an investment that would adversely affect its reputation, this impact could be seen as being more important than the strict financial rewards it would receive as a result of making the investment. The business may also consider the economic situation and whether it should make an investment now or delay it until the economic situation has improved.

Another set of criteria may be related to the business's past experience. If they are confident that an additional or replacement asset has in the past provided them with a good rate of return and that the supplier of that asset has always given them good service, then this may be a key consideration.

Ethical investment criteria can be a consideration, particularly as far as individual shareholders or ethical fund managers and advisers are concerned. Although the criteria tend to apply to inward investment into a business, organisations such as the Cooperative Society and Fair Trade would also avoid investment in businesses related to the right-hand side of the following table:

Encourage	Avoid
Animal welfare	Acid rain
Birth control	Alcohol
Communications	Animal farming
Community relations	Animal testing
Companies with good employee records	Companies with bad employee records
Disaster relief	Armaments
Education and training	Deforestation
Energy conservation and efficiency	Gambling
Environmental technology	Genetic research
Equal opportunities	Human rights abuse
Firms with environmental aims	Land abuse
Food retailers with good policies (e.g. organic)	Food retailers with bad policies (e.g. fast food, high salt, high sugar)
Forestry	Military
Healthcare sector	Motor industries
Healthy eating	Nuclear power
Land use	Oil companies
Plant welfare	Oppressive regimes
Pollution control	Ozone depletion
Positive products and services	Pesticides
Public transport	Political donors
Recycling	Polluters
Renewable energy projects	Pornography
Research (selected types)	Research (re human tissue)
Safety concerns	Road building
Sustainable Third World aid	Third World exploitation
Waste management	Tobacco
Water management	Water pollution

Internal and external investment criteria

So far as investment criteria are concerned, we have primarily focused on businesses making their own reinvestments. Another key consideration to add to this is the confidence of management to be able to make major decisions that bring with them a series of risks, albeit with the promise of future profits. Whether they are prepared to take the risk, given their own position in the business, could be a prime consideration. It is important to remember that unless the senior managers of a business are also the owners of the business, they will be making decisions on behalf of the owners or shareholders. Not only would a poor decision adversely affect the owners and shareholders, but it would also undermine the manager's own position and call into doubt their decision-making abilities and position.

When businesses seek external funds in order to finance capital expenditure, they will have to show that they are a well-managed organisation, and that the proposed investment will provide the new investor with potential earnings in the future. You will already be aware of organisations known as 'venture capitalists', or 'business angels'. They are prepared to take risks on businesses that wish to make investment, in return, of course, for a share of the business itself. In many respects their investment criteria are all the more stringent and they approach the question of investment decisions in a far more objective manner than the potentially subjective approach of individuals closer to the needs of the business itself.

CASE STUDY THE SOUTH WEST VENTURES FUND

The South West Ventures Fund seeks to provide venture capital funding to companies which:

- are small or medium sized and located in the south-west of England
- have a talented and ambitious management team fully committed to the success of their venture
- show potential for significant growth in their market
- deal with products or services with a strong competitive advantage
- have a detailed plan to achieve strong, sustainable growth in profits
- can show effective financial systems and controls
- are committed to achieving an exit for shareholders either through a stock-market flotation or trade sale within a three- to seven-year timeframe.

Investment criteria include:

- the Fund being able to invest up to £330,000 initially, and a further £330,000 after six months
- in certain circumstances, alongside other new investors, the Fund being able to follow on its investments to provide a total of £2.1 million to any one company
- an interest in companies at all stages of development from early stage to those seeking to expand organically or by acquisition as well as management buy-outs (MBOs) and management buy-ins (MBIs). Start-up companies will also be considered

- most sectors, although there are some restrictions, principally relating to property, financial services, agriculture and some state-aided sectors.

Post-investment requirements:

- typically a non-executive director (NED) is appointed to the Board. His or her principal role will be to provide support and advice to the executive directors. The NED will normally have relevant industry experience and often help to strengthen a particular skill set in the team. The NED provides a brief monthly report on progress. Each investee company is also expected to provide regular financial reports, including cash-flow projections, management accounts and audited financial statements.

Questions

1 Comment on the implications of South West Ventures Fund's investment criteria as far as a business looking for funding is concerned. (8 marks)
2 What do you think is meant by 'post-investment requirements' and what might be their implications? (6 marks)

Risks and uncertainties of investment decisions

LEARNING OBJECTIVES

▶ Identifying options
▶ Non-financial benefits
▶ Costs and incomes
▶ Risks and uncertainties

Identifying options

It is important for a business to look at all feasible options, including doing nothing or doing the minimum. Businesses will include these as a base case, even if they are unacceptable in operational terms. Projects that need high levels of investment will need a long list of all other options. Some of the options will be quickly eliminated as unfeasible, but a shortlist of options will be left – perhaps between three and six – which can be analysed in some detail.

The time spent considering the various options is usually reflected by the level of investment. For major projects, with a significant expenditure, a team will be set up to identify options. For example, a building project might have options such as refurbishing, demolishing and rebuilding, purchasing an alternative site, leasing accommodation, or erecting a new build on a different site.

A business will also look at the various ranges of financing the project, although some projects will have only a limited range of options. When replacing computer equipment, a company really has only three options: to do nothing, to lease or to buy.

Non-financial benefits

The financial viability of any investment is of major importance, but it is also important to appreciate that some benefits cannot be measured in purely financial terms. An assessment needs to be made of the various non-financial benefits. The comparison of these benefits is usually quite subjective, but can assist the decision-making process.

One of the standard approaches used in investment appraisal is a weighting and scoring method. This means identifying a list of relevant criteria (usually five to eight) against which each option is scored. The criteria are then weighted to reflect their importance, with weightings totalling 100. The shortlisted options are then scored out of ten. For each criterion a weighted score is calculated by multiplying the criteria score by its weighting. This should demonstrate the merits of each option.

Costs and incomes

There are various considerations to be addressed that could add to the risks and certainties in making a decision about a potential investment, including the following:

- Capital costs – such as land, demolition, construction, refurbishment, equipment purchase and replacement.
- Residual values of the asset at the end of the appraisal period – this is a benefit that could be stated at the current prices or base year and then based on the remaining useful life of the asset.

FOR EXAMPLE

If a new building is given an estimated useful life of 50 years then the building will have a residual value at the end of the 25-year appraisal period of 50% of its initial cost. Land and buildings will always have a residual value that is equal to their initial cost at least.

Risks and uncertainties

- Opportunity cost – if assets that are currently owned by the business are required for one or more options then the relevant options should include an opportunity cost for the assets, even if no expenditure takes place. Assets could be sold or used for alternative purposes if a particular option that is being considered does not occur. The opportunity cost of the asset will be its market value or its value in an alternative use, whichever is higher.

- Revenue costs – staff costs, premises costs including rates and maintenance, equipment maintenance and other recurrent costs. These need to be included in the investment appraisal and valued at the current cost levels.

- Income or financially quantifiable benefits – income over the investment appraisal period should include any increased income for anticipated improvements and any other financially quantifiable benefit that the option will bring.

As we have already seen, estimated expenditure and income that assist in the investment appraisal invariably involve assumptions about the future. Even a small change in assumptions, particularly those related to future income levels, would significantly affect the ranking of options.

A business will repeat the appraisal calculations with estimates set at the upper or lower end of likely outcomes. This is often referred to as sensitivity analysis and it takes into account the fact that both expenditure and income are variable.

There are other areas of risk associated with individual options and it is not always possible to express these in financial terms. A proposed new building's planning permission could be delayed or denied; utilities that need to be laid on to make a new building operational may also be delayed; or the business might decide to purchase a new site, but be unable to find the ideal one in the local area.

In order to minimise risk and uncertainty a business will begin with an initial investigation of the proposal. This simply aims to make sure that it is technically feasible and commercially viable. At this point it will assess the risks and decide whether the project is in-line with the business's long-term objectives.

The second stage sees a more detailed evaluation, where projected cash flows can be looked at and a sensitivity analysis performed. At this point the business will also consider how it intends to fund the project.

Authorisation is the next key stage, but this will be given only once everyone is satisfied that a detailed evaluation has been carried out and that the project will contribute to the profitability of the business and is consistent with business strategy. The project is now passed on to a project manager, who is responsible for implementation. They will be set specific targets.

Throughout, the project will be monitored by senior management. There may have to be a reassessment of costs and benefits if unforeseen events take place. Finally, at the end of the project, an audit will take place to see if any lessons can be learned in order to help future project planning.

Question

To what extent does a systematic project appraisal take the risk and uncertainty out of investment decisions? (*12 marks*)

Quantitative and qualitative influences

Quantitative influences

There are various ways in which a business can make quantitative investment appraisals, the first of which is known as the payback method. This measures the length of time it will take for net cash inflows to pay back the original investment. The calculation used is shown in the following example:

Year	Cash outflow (£)	Cash inflow (£)
1	250,000	50,000
2		100,000
3		100,000
4		50,000

The example above shows that by the end of the third year the investment will be paid back, and from that point onwards the investment will continue to provide cash inflows. However, the calculations are not always this straightforward, as can be seen in the next example:

Year	Cash outflow (£)	Cash inflow (£)
1	250,000	50,000
2		150,000
3		100,000
4		100,000

Here, the project pays back its full amount in year 3. But year 3 also provides an additional cash inflow to the business. Therefore by the end of year 2 the project has already paid back £200,000 and the remaining £50,000 is paid back in the first six months of year 3.

Payback has the advantage of being a very quick and easy way in which to work out how quickly a project will pay its own way. It is widely used and it helps to minimise risks by giving greater weight to earlier cash inflows. What it does not do, however, is take into account the value of money at the time the paybacks are being received. It also ignores cash flows received after the end of the payback period and does not take into account the overall profitability of the project.

The second quantitative method is known as average rate of return, or ARR. This is more complex but it provides a more meaningful investment appraisal. It also allows a business to compare a project with

other investment opportunities. The formula used for ARR is:

$$\frac{\text{Estimated average profits}}{\text{Estimated average investment}} \times 100\%$$

The last quantitative investment appraisal that you will need to consider is known as 'net present value'. This method forecasts the expected outflows and inflows. Each inflow or outflow is discounted back to its present value. In order to work out net present value the following information is needed:

• The cost of the original investment
• The rate of discount
• Any expected inflows or outflows of money
• The duration of the investment project
• The residual value of the project at the end of the investment

The outflows of cash are subtracted from the discounted inflows to provide a net figure, known as the net present value. This is an important

FOR EXAMPLE

A business has estimated that a new project will cost it £150,000. It has also calculated that over a four-year period the investment will bring in cash inflows of £560,000. Using the formula we first have to work out the annual return per year, which is 560,000 divided by 4. This gives us £140,000. We then apply these figures to the formula:

$$\frac{£140,000}{£150,000} \times 100 = 93\%$$

So 93% of the initial investment is paid back each year. This is an extreme example, as normally an average rate of return higher than the prevailing interest rate would represent a more than attractive investment proposition.

part of the calculation because if the net present value is negative then the project should not be pursued because the present value of the earnings is actually less than the cost of the investment. A business can use the present value figure to rank a range of investment projects, with the one showing the highest net present value figure being the most worthwhile.

Effectively this system incorporates what is known as discounted cash flows. It recognises that if a business were to have £100,000 today, this would be preferable to it being given £100,000 in a year's time. If it invested the £100,000 immediately and put it into a bank account paying 10% interest, in a year's time, the £100,000 would have swelled to £110,000. However, if the business received the £100,000 in a year's time, the money would actually be worth 10% less then than it is worth today.

A business will use a discount table to work out the value of money in future years. An example of such a discount table is shown below.

Qualitative influences

Not all investment appraisal techniques can necessarily be carried out by simply referring to the financial data. Qualitative issues can also have a bearing on the decision. We have already seen that some of the potential considerations, such as environmental issues that may arise out of the investment decision, could bring bad publicity to an organisation. A prime example would be the continuing disputes over the expansion of airports such as Heathrow and Stansted. The expansion plans make financial sense to the airport operators, but are detrimental to their reputation.

There is also the concern about whether planning permission would be allowed for such a major building project, or indeed whether the local infrastructure is capable of dealing with larger trucks or vehicles. Added to this there may be environmental concerns and resistance from the local community, who will be affected by the increased pollution.

The overall aims and objectives of the business also need to be part

FOR EXAMPLE

If the business was to receive £100,000 in five years' time and the average expected interest rate was 12% per year then the calculation would be:

$£100,000 \times 0.57 = £57,000$

If the interest was in fact 8% rather than 12% then the money would actually be worth £68,000.

of the deliberations. Some years ago many banks began closing branches to replace them with telephone banking and Internet services. They saw that the capital expenditure required for the projects was worth the risk, as it would bring them long-term savings. What they did not anticipate was that local branches were the cornerstone of their business. Banks that closed down branches have found that many customers have left.

The final qualitative consideration is that many managers are risk averse. They simply do not want to take the responsibility of spending the business's money when there is a risk involved in doing so.

Years ahead	6%	8%	10%	12%	15%
0	1.00	1.00	1.00	1.00	1.00
1	0.94	0.93	0.91	0.89	0.87
2	0.89	0.86	0.83	0.80	0.76
3	0.84	0.79	0.75	0.71	0.66
4	0.79	0.74	0.68	0.64	0.57
5	0.75	0.68	0.62	0.57	0.50

In this way the business is able to calculate with a degree of clarity the exact value of each cash inflow, taking into account that the rate of interest will affect its actual value.

Questions

1 What would be the value of a cash flow of £56,000 in four year's time if the interest rate was reckoned to be 8%? (*2 marks*)
2 If a business made an investment of £100,000 and expected £25,000 net inflow per year, what would be the payback period? (*2 marks*)

Case studies, questions and exam practice

CASE STUDY A TALE OF TWO CITIES

An insurance company is currently looking at two major options: one would see a considerable investment in London and the other in Norwich. Both would cost the business £550,000.

The two competing divisions of the business have prepared a series of figures, anticipating the cash inflows from years one to five. What neither of them has done is to take into consideration the fact that the business needs to apply a 10% discount factor to the values of those cash flows.

The first project, based in London, anticipates a cash inflow of £88,000 in year one, £92,000 in year two, £96,000 in year three, £94,000 in year four and £162,000 in year five.

The competing project, based in Norwich, has calculated the following figures. They anticipate that the project will bring in £95,000 in each of years one, two and three, then rise to £104,000 in year four, before falling back to £95,000 in year five.

Years ahead	6%	8%	10%	12%	15%
0	1.00	1.00	1.00	1.00	1.00
1	0.94	0.93	0.91	0.89	0.87
2	0.89	0.86	0.83	0.80	0.76
3	0.84	0.79	0.75	0.71	0.66
4	0.79	0.74	0.68	0.64	0.57
5	0.75	0.68	0.62	0.57	0.50

Questions

1 Calculate the net present value for each of the projects at the end of year five. Show your workings. (*12 marks*)
2 Which of the two projects would you recommend? Why? (*4 marks*)

Introduction

The second theme of *Strategies for success* is *Marketing strategies*. Again the primary focus is on larger businesses and how they develop marketing strategies by adopting a scientific approach to decision-making. Much of the material that you covered in AS Business Studies, in the Marketing section, will prove useful as a background from which to build a deeper knowledge of how marketing works, the nature of marketing plans and how businesses select marketing strategies.

In a highly competitive world market, businesses will use a variety of scientific processes in order to analyse the market, market trends and the activities of competitors. They do this to create workable solutions to deal with the competition and to ensure that the most efficient and cost-effective measures are used to bring their products and services to the attention of potential customers.

The first focus area looks at broader marketing objectives and how these are framed by the business. It is important to appreciate that both internal and external influences have an impact on a business's marketing objectives. Internal considerations could include finance, operational issues and, importantly, the business's corporate objectives. External influences include the actions of competitors, how the market is behaving, and changes in technology.

The second focus area looks at how markets can be analysed and how businesses increasingly use information technology to help them analyse markets. Businesses will seek to discover patterns in sales and trends and then try to exploit these trends to their advantage.

The third focus area looks at how businesses can select marketing strategies. Businesses do not use just price or short-term sales promotions to achieve a temporary advantage. Many marketing strategies are long term and an embedded part of the overall corporate objectives of the organisation. Businesses need to consider the risks and benefits of everything they do in terms of marketing and positioning their products and services in the marketplace. They will consider product development and market development, whether their products are sufficiently differentiated from the competition, and, if not, whether they should opt for low-cost competition. There are various ways in which marketing strategies can be framed and assessed and one of the key ways of doing this is to use what is known as the Ansoff Matrix.

The final focus area looks at developing and implementing market plans. You will already have seen how business plans are created and used in AS Business Studies. A marketing plan can be an integral part of a business plan, or can be a separate document focusing solely on the achievement of marketing objectives through a series of specified strategies.

Marketing plans will not only set out objectives, but will also detail budgets, sales forecasts and marketing strategies. We will also look at how a marketing plan can be influenced by issues of finance, operational factors and competitors' actions.

FOCUS ON UNDERSTANDING MARKETING STRATEGIES

- Marketing objectives ▶ page 56
- Internal and external influences on marketing objectives ▶ page 58
- Case studies, questions and exam practice ▶ page 60

FOCUS ON ANALYSING MARKETS AND MARKETING

- Reasons for and the value of market analysis ▶ page 62
- Methods of analysing trends ▶ page 64
- The use of technology in analysing markets ▶ page 66
- Difficulties in analysing marketing data ▶ page 68
- Case studies, questions and exam practice ▶ page 70

FOCUS ON SELECTING MARKETING STRATEGIES

- Low cost versus differentiation ▶ page 72
- Market penetration ▶ page 74
- Product development and market development strategies ▶ page 76
- Diversification ▶ page 78
- Assessing effectiveness of marketing strategies ▶ page 80
- Case studies, questions and exam practice ▶ page 82

FOCUS ON DEVELOPING AND IMPLEMENTING MARKETING PLANS

- Components of marketing plans ▶ page 84
- Assessing internal and external influences on marketing plans ▶ page 86
- Issues in implementing marketing plans ▶ page 88
- Case studies, questions and exam practice ▶ page 90

Marketing objectives

Deciding on the objectives

Marketing objectives are goals that a business wishes to achieve as part of its overall marketing programme, such as increasing sales, market share or profitability. All good objectives need to be measurable, attainable and, increasingly, socially significant.

Marketing objectives need to be based on the business's understanding of its strengths and weaknesses, and relevant to the business environment in which it operates. Above all, they need to be linked to the general corporate or business objectives.

Objectives should always conform to the SMART criteria:

Specific – the objective should be clear – for example, the business will aim to get 100 new customers.

Measurable – it is important for the business to be able to check whether it has achieved the objective and, if not, to review the plan.

Achievable – the business needs to have the necessary resources to achieve the objective – usually expertise and money.

Realistic – the business needs to identify objectives that can be reasonably achieved given the current status of the business and its priorities.

Time-bound – there should be a deadline for achieving the objective, such as getting 100 new customers within the next 12 months.

A marketing objective aims to ensure that a business knows what its strategies are: without objectives, strategy decisions are meaningless. However, setting objectives is more complex than it might at first appear. Usually the starting point is the mission statement, out of which broad company objectives are created.

The marketing objectives need to be: consistent, obtainable within budget limitations, and compatible with the strengths, weaknesses and external factors that could affect the business.

There are in fact just four main types of marketing objective:

- selling existing products into existing markets
- selling new products into existing markets
- selling existing products into new markets
- selling new products into new markets.

Everything else is a variation on these four, or simply a focus on an aspect of one of the four. We will look at these different options in more detail in the next section.

FOR EXAMPLE

If a business's objective is to increase sales by 10% in the next year, then the marketing objective would be to target a new market segment to help achieve this growth.

Types of objective

In your AS you will have studied product lifecycles. Marketing objectives can often be linked to the lifecycle of a product and the following are logical marketing objectives:

- For an established product in an established market the marketing objective may be to maintain the product's position.
- For a product that is relatively new to the market and seems to have high demand, the business may seek to improve its sales and position in the market.
- If the product is not selling very well, the business may have only one option: to try to get back as much money as it can before demand falls away altogether. It will try to make short-term profit, or harvest from the product.
- Although this may not seem like a marketing objective, a product that is reaching the end of its useful life can still provide valuable income to the business, but the business itself needs to exit gradually from the market and this too can be a marketing objective.
- The final and most dangerous type of marketing objective is to try to launch a product into a new business or market area. The product or service itself might also be new. The objective will be to enter the market and create a presence.

The four most common types of marketing objective are therefore:

- *Market penetration* – selling more of an existing product or service into an existing market, either by increasing consumer demand or by taking customers away from the competitors.
- *Market development* – selling more of an existing product or service to new customers, perhaps by offering them in a new country or radically changing the advertising or outlets in which the product or service can be purchased.
- *Product development* – selling a new or improved product to existing customers by encouraging them to upgrade.
- *Diversification* – moving into a new area of business with new products and services that are targeted at new customers.

Within these four different marketing objectives we can find a range of objectives, for example, improving market share, increasing profitability or sales, or becoming market leader.

What is of vital importance is that marketing objectives can either be short term or long term. This can be determined by the types of products or services involved, by the nature of the market in which the products and services are sold, or by the objectives of the business itself:

- *Determined by the product or service* – marketing objectives for products or services that rapidly change, such as innovative consumer electronics, need to be constantly changed and rethought in order to cope with the rapid change and development of products.

> **FOR EXAMPLE**
>
> *Successively, different types of mobile phone have entered the market, rendering older versions obsolete. By continuing to market outdated technology, a business will inevitably fall behind its competitors.*

- *The nature of the market* – markets or market segments have radically different characteristics. Some are consumers, while others are businesses. Added to this are factors such as lifestyle, income, age, gender and geographic location. The market rapidly changes in terms of its tastes and fashions, and if a business does not respond to these by adapting its objectives it will undoubtedly fail.

> **KEY TERM**
>
> **Market segment** – a recognisable part of the overall market that shares common characteristics.

For more about external influences see Internal and external influences on marketing objectives on pp. 58–9.

> **FOR EXAMPLE**
>
> *Only two or three years ago most people purchased music by buying CDs. Now the general trend is to buy music via downloads. The music industry was slow to adapt to this and saw CD sales fall while people illegally downloaded copies of music from the Internet.*

- *The objectives of the business* – there will inevitably be problems if the marketing objectives are different from the overall objectives of the organisation. Different parts of the organisation will be moving in different directions; there will be a lack of coordination and conflict between senior management; and it is likely that the business will not be able to satisfy its customers.

> **FOR EXAMPLE**
>
> *There has been much criticism of utility companies, which provide us with gas and electricity. As private companies, one of their key objectives is to provide shareholder value by generating maximum profits. However this has meant that they have driven up prices, alienating their customers. Their marketing efforts to suggest that they are competitively priced seem to be at variance with their desire to create profit for the owners.*

> **Question**
>
> What are the four main types of marketing objective and why do all marketing objectives fit within these four descriptions? (*8 marks*)

Internal and external influences on marketing objectives

Internal influences

There are many factors that can limit a business's ability either to choose appropriate and effective marketing objectives, or to achieve those objectives once they have been set. Returning to the concept of SWOT analysis, the internal strengths and weaknesses of the business itself are as relevant to marketing objectives as they are to the general fortunes of the business and its chances of success or failure.

Although marketing does not necessarily have to be prohibitively expensive, finance is the first key internal influence that could impact on marketing objectives. Developing, launching and maintaining a new product or service in the marketplace can be extremely expensive. Often innovative ideas created by smaller businesses that lack funds are doomed to failure. Equally, large businesses that fail to financially support new product development often fail to achieve their fundamental marketing objectives.

The second internal influence can be categorised as either human resource or organisational based. The business may lack the necessary skills and expertise to frame and implement a marketing objective. Not all businesses have their own marketing departments, while others split the effort between different divisions or product areas. There is always the option of buying in marketing expertise by using marketing or advertising agencies or marketing consultants. However this returns to the funding problem.

Operational issues can also be a key influence, as the business may simply not be geared up to cope with the demand that may be generated through an effective marketing campaign. Other operational problems may arise, such as a high defect rate in production, difficulties in distributing the product to the new market, unexpectedly high costs that drive down the profit margins, or pricing at a level that is unacceptable to consumers.

Of equal importance is the final internal influence, which we have already mentioned. That is, ensuring that the marketing objectives are consistent with the corporate objectives of the business.

External influences

Just as there are many internal influences that can impact on marketing objectives, there are also a wide range of external influences. The first are known as political factors, and include laws or regulations that prohibit the sale of particular products and services, or limit them to the extent that they are no longer as profitable as the business had hoped.

FOR EXAMPLE

The government is considering legislation banning the advertising of toys and unhealthy snack foods during children's television programmes. This would have a drastic impact on the sale of these products, as children could become aware of their existence.

The second set of external influences can be broadly described as economic. Interest rates, inflation, unemployment, economic uncertainty and a host of other factors could have a direct impact on the business's ability to meet its marketing objectives. Added to this is the complication of there inevitably being competitors in the marketplace. A business cannot accurately predict what a competitor may be planning or how it will react in certain circumstances.

The market itself, or social factors, can have an impact on marketing objectives. Changes in customer tastes, fashions and trends make particular products and services more or less popular over a period of time. These changes can be temporary, permanent, or may simply shift sales from the business to competing brands.

Technological factors can either make products obsolete or less attractive as alternatives are available. Businesses whose products are associated with out-of-date technology eventually lose market share and in many cases, regardless of the actions of the business, they find it impossible to regain their position.

FOR EXAMPLE

The VHS videotape recorder and player became the industry standard and pushed the competing technology, Betamax, out of the market. More recently this has happened with high-definition DVDs. Support for the losing technology has virtually stopped. No more DVDs are being produced, and manufacturers are switching over to the winning technology.

Increasingly, green and environmental influences are playing a major role in both business strategy and in the framing of marketing objectives. What may appear to be a perfectly acceptable and profitable course of action may face difficulties if the product is seen to be environmentally unfriendly, over-packaged, or less efficient than competing brands. Government legislation may actually restrict production, and certain products, because of the way in which they have been made, may be banned.

FOR EXAMPLE

Many clothing manufacturers have entered into voluntary agreements to ensure that their clothing products are not produced by underpaid children in underdeveloped countries. Nonetheless scandals still arise concerning some popular high-street brands.

CASE STUDY THE OLYMPIC MOVEMENT'S MARKETING OBJECTIVES

Turin 2006 was the most 'international' Olympic Winter Games in history, as a record 80 Olympic teams participated, and television viewers in more countries than ever before shared in the experience. Likewise, the sixth generation of The Olympic Partner (TOP) Programme is the most globally inclusive ever. The TOP VI sponsors have headquarters in seven countries across three continents – demonstrating global participation in the programme that mirrors the worldwide nature of the Olympic Movement.

The Turin 2006 domestic sponsorship programme stands as the most lucrative and successful sponsorship programme in Italian history, generating €269.8 million and include 57 companies and 63 brands across three tiers: main sponsors, official sponsors and official suppliers. The programme accounted for nearly 1% of the total advertising spend in the Italian market, 35 times greater than that of the Salt Lake 2002 Olympics, and reached 35 million people in Italy in terms of interest and awareness, surpassing the reach of sponsorships in football (€27 million) and motor racing (€24 million).

Turin 2006 accounted for 6.14% of the total sponsorship spending in the market, which was significantly higher than previous Olympic Winter Games sponsorship programmes.

The Turin Olympic Broadcast Organisation provided nearly 1,000 hours of live content – the most in Olympic Winter Games history. Our broadcast partners, in turn, provided viewers with a combined total of more than 16,000 hours of coverage – by far a record in Olympic Winter Games broadcasting. The Olympic broadcasters also maximised opportunities in new media technology, providing viewers with more access and greater choice through the Internet, mobile phones and multiple television channels.

Question

Olympic events are unique, but what do you think are the key marketing objectives of the Olympic Movement? How are these affected by external factors? (*10 marks*)

Case studies, questions and exam practice

CASE STUDY THE HOME OF THE OLYMPICS

In 2004, the Olympic Games returned to the city where it was created – Athens.

Olympic marketing seeks:

- To create continuing long-term marketing programmes and to build on and support the successful activities developed by each organising committee, thus ensuring the financial stability of the Olympic movement.
- To ensure appropriate distribution of revenue throughout the Olympic movement, including future organising committees, national Olympic committees, international federations and other recognised organisations.
- To ensure that the whole world can view and experience the Olympic Games via a variety of broadcast platforms.
- To preserve the special character of the Olympic Games, to protect and promote the Olympic image and ideals throughout the world, and to work with all marketing partners to enhance Olympism.

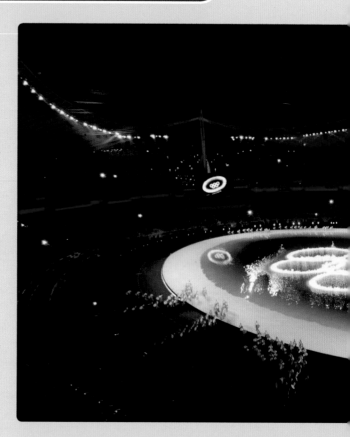

The Athens 2004 sponsorship programme was the second largest source of revenue for the staging of the Olympic Games, providing approximately 23% of the organising committee's balanced budget.

The Athens 2004 domestic sponsorship programme exceeded initial targets by 57%, generating more than US$300 million in domestic sponsorship of the Olympic Games and sponsorship of the Athens 2004 Olympic torch relay.

The Athens 2004 Olympic broadcast partners provided unprecedented levels of support for the Olympic Movement and the staging of the 2004 Olympic Games. The Athens 2004 Olympic Games broadcast generated over US$1,400 million in rights fees revenue.

More than 300 television channels provided 35,000 hours of dedicated Olympic Games coverage over 17 days, delivering images from Athens 2004 to an audience of 3.9 billion people in 220 countries and territories.

An audience of 3.9 billion television viewers in 220 countries and territories had access to the Athens 2004 Olympic Games broadcast, marking a significant increase over the previous Olympic broadcast record of 3.6 billion viewers with access to Sydney 2000. Each television viewer worldwide watched an average of 12 hours of Olympic Games coverage on television over the 17 days of the Olympic Games.

Several satellite and cable channels devoted their entire programming to 24-hour coverage of Athens 2004. A number of Olympic broadcast partners offered Olympic coverage on dedicated channels 24 hours per day for 17 days.

Several broadcasters enhanced viewer choice by providing extended coverage on digital and interactive channels. Broadcasters in certain countries used 3G technology to make streaming video and highlight clips of the Athens 2004 Olympic Games available through mobile phone handsets. Broadcasters in several markets offered streaming video via the Internet and dedicated Olympic web sites. For the first time in summer Olympic history, the host broadcaster provided the live feed of Olympic Games competitions and ceremonies in high definition.

Questions

1 How closely do the events in Athens match the Olympic marketing objectives? (*8 marks*)
2 Which new technologies have been embraced by the Olympic Movement to bring the games to a wider audience? (*4 marks*)

Reasons for and the value of market analysis

LEARNING OBJECTIVES

▶ Market analysis
▶ Value of market analysis
▶ Devising new strategies
▶ Identifying patterns in sales

Market analysis

Market analysis involves the business undertaking a detailed look at the characteristics of a particular market. Specifically it will look at the following:

- *Market position* – whether a product or service is a market leader, follower or challenger, or whether it is being sold into a market niche.
- *Market objectives* – the business may have to take into account its key marketing objectives, or at the very least the market analysis may reveal the priority of its market objectives. These could include growth; ethical issues; market share; focus on the consumer or the product; image; social responsibility; maximisation of revenue and profit; maximising shareholder value and dealing with competitors.

KEY TERMS

Leader – a business that has a dominant position in the marketplace, probably dictating price and ways in which the products or services are marketed.

Follower – a business that usually follows the market leader in terms of product development, pricing and marketing.

Challenger – a business that is trying to create new strategies to challenge the position of the market leader.

- *Market segments* – part of the analysis will look at the different market segments, categorising them in terms of age, gender, income, lifestyle, ethnic background, social class, geographical region, behaviours and family circumstances.
- *Categorisation of market segments* – the business will categorise each segment as being either a mass-market segment, which will have a large number of people with similar characteristics, or smaller, definable segments that need specific attention (also known as niche markets).
- *Market structure* – is the market highly competitive? Does supply outstrip demand? Or does demand outstrip supply? Is it dominated by one, two or three major businesses (all forms of imperfect competition)?

Value of market analysis

The main purpose of carrying out market analysis is to identify the existing state of the market. From this the business may be able to make some estimates of future trends in that market. The market analysis itself is an essential part of the marketing process because it allows the business to see where it is today and then frame its objectives to get where it wants to be tomorrow.

Essential to the analysis is a determination of the market size. It can be measured in terms of

volume (i.e. the actual number of units sold) or the expenditure of the market (i.e. the hard cash that is actually spent on products and services). Once this figure is known the business can then compare its own numbers of units sold or income received to work out its market share. A vital final part of the analysis is to make a judgement as to where the market will be moving in the short, medium and long term. By considering figures over a period of time the business will be able to assess whether the market is stagnant (neither growing nor contracting), growing (rapidly or slowly) or contracting (quickly or slowly). This information will have an enormous impact on the future marketing objectives of the business.

A shrinking market is not attractive because sales will be falling. A growing market may be attractive but not if it also attracts a higher level of competition from other businesses.

Devising new strategies

The market analysis should reveal to the business that either its current marketing objectives are relevant and effective, or that it needs to give serious consideration to reframing them. Subtle changes in the market may require only slight adjustment to the strategies used by the business in order to fulfil the marketing objectives.

More radical changes or forecasts of changes may require a drastic rethink of not only the strategies, but also the objectives behind them.

In a highly competitive market a business that is seeing the market itself grow, while its own market share remains the same, will have experienced some increases in sales and profits. However it may need to seriously consider changing the way in which it markets its products, and be more aggressive to gain more market share. Aggressive marketing is also relevant in order to ensure continued sales in a shrinking market.

Identifying patterns in sales

One of the key parts of market analysis is to analyse a business's own patterns in sales. Sales for products and services inevitably fluctuate over a period of time. Traditionally, many different types of products enjoy higher sales at different times of the year. An ice-cream manufacturer, for example, would not expect to be selling as much in the winter as it would in the summer months.

Market analysis tries to iron out these seasonal fluctuations and look for underlying patterns in sales. There are many different ways to analyse these trends, as we will see on the next spread.

FOR EXAMPLE

The graph below shows the comparative sales of the Nintendo Wii, the Sony PS3 and Microsoft's Xbox360 over a period of eight months. All three businesses would probably have to estimate the sales of their competitors' products, as much of this information would be confidential. We can see from the example that Microsoft's sales are relatively stable and low. Sony's sales gradually increase and then suddenly, due to seasonal fluctuations, increase dramatically from October to November. Nintendo's sales peak in the summer months and then fall away, which is a worrying trend, considering there is only a slight increase just before Christmas.

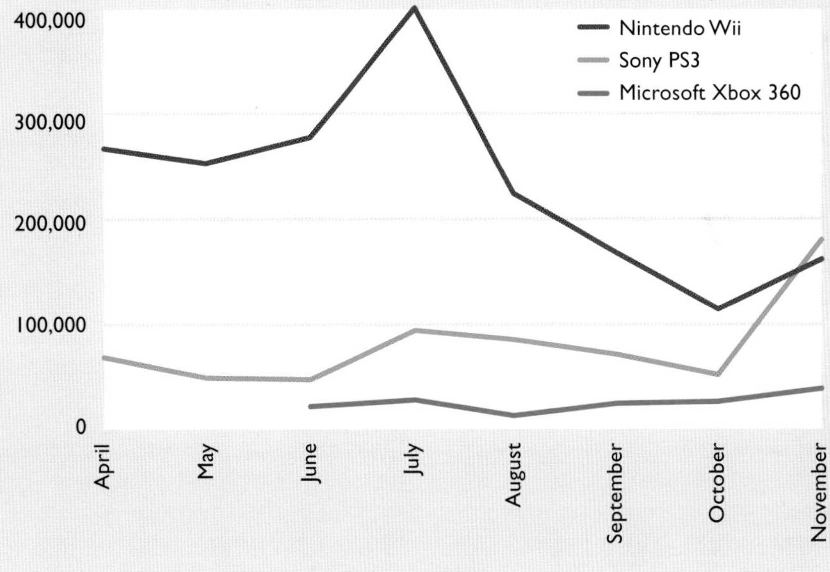

Question

For the past five years a business has steadily sold £50 million of products into the market each year. Next year it predicts that this will increase to £60 million as the market is growing. Five years ago the market was worth £550 million and has grown steadily at a rate of 10% each year, but is expected to grow by 20% next year.

What is the market share of the business over this period of time and into next year, and what is the underlying pattern of that market share? (*6 marks*)

Methods of analysing trends

Moving averages

The first way in which sales data can be analysed is known as moving averages. For our purposes a three-month moving average is sufficient to work out an underlying trend in sales. Obviously sales change from month to month and what the business is looking for is the overall trend underlying the sales figures. To find this, it reduces particularly high or particularly low figures and works out an average.

The following table outlines an example of sales figures over a year. Note that in order to use three sets of monthly figures no calculations can be made for January or December.

Month	Sales (£000s)
January	24
February	27
March	29
April	29
May	32
June	27
July	31
August	32
September	34
October	38
November	39
December	39

In order to work out the three-month moving averages we need to add together three consecutive months, as shown in the table below:

Month	Sales (£000s)	Calculation	Three month moving average (£000s)
January	24		
February	27	$(24 + 27 + 29) \div 3$	26.6
March	29	$(27 + 29 + 29) \div 3$	28.3
April	29	$(29 + 29 + 32) \div 3$	30
May	32	$(29 + 32 + 27) \div 3$	29.3
June	27	$(32 + 27 + 31) \div 3$	30
July	31	$(27 + 31 + 32) \div 3$	30
August	32	$(31 + 32 + 34) \div 3$	32.3
September	34	$(32 + 34 + 38) \div 3$	34.6
October	38	$(34 + 38 + 29) \div 3$	33.6
November	39	$(38 + 29 + 39) \div 3$	35.3
December	39		

Test markets

One of the ways in which a business can try to predict future sales for a product or service is to launch it into a limited test market area. For many years towns such as Nottingham were seen to be ideal examples of containable communities that had similar characteristics to those more broadly seen across the whole of the British Isles.

The product or service is launched using a smaller-scale version of what will be used for its national launch, including television advertising, radio advertising, promotions, and a maximum effort to try to ensure that as many different outlets as possible stock the product or provide the service. The launch period should not only give the business a clear

indication of the sales potential and the effectiveness of marketing methods used, but it should also highlight any potential problems in distribution, sales, marketing or servicing.

Once the business is satisfied that it has carried out this form of market analysis and figured out sales and marketing trends, it is then in a position to roll the product out on a national basis.

Extrapolation and correlation

Extrapolation is another way in which a business can try to predict the expected level of sales of a product or service. It looks for trends and for correlation between different variables and the level of sales. For example,

it might be expected that additional advertising would generate additional sales. This would be a positive correlation between the two variables, meaning that there is a direct link. There can also be a negative correlation, which means that the two variables are inversely related. A prime example of this is an increase in price, which is likely to lead to a fall in sales.

Businesses will plot the level of advertising spend per month against the level of sales in the same month and then see whether there is a correlation between the two. It should show both figures increasing simultaneously, while a drop in advertising spend might show a drop in sales.

In fact, extrapolation is not as exact a science as we are sometimes led to believe. It assumes that trends in the future will be identical to trends in the past. After all, the correlation between two variables is being worked out on the basis of data that has already been collected. What extrapolation cannot handle is a sudden change in the market, such as the introduction of a new and more desirable product or service. Neither can it predict the fact that there may be a sudden change in demand for other reasons, such as a health scare over a food item, a scandal related to the production of a particular product, or the fact that the business does not have sufficient units available for sale because of unexpectedly high demand in another market.

Businesses can learn from past trends, but they need to be cautious about jumping to conclusions when using extrapolation. In effect the business is looking for one of the three following types of correlation:

- A perfect negative correlation – where one of the variables has a negative impact on the other. This is often labelled as −1.
- A perfect positive correlation – where there is a direct link between the variables and an increase in one leads to an increase in the other. This is often labelled as +1.
- No correlation between the variables – where there appears to be no discernible pattern or relationship between the two variables. They simply do not affect one another.

Like many things, correlation is never perfectly positive or perfectly negative. It is measured in degrees of correlation. Therefore −0.6 correlation would show that it is close to perfect negative correlation, but not absolute, whereas +0.2 would show that there is a weak but positive correlation as there is some relationship between the two variables.

The key difference between extrapolation and correlation is the fact that businesses use extrapolation to try to extend a series of figures at the same rate of growth or decline into the future, by plotting them on a graph. On the other hand, correlation takes individual factors that are part of the trend and tries to link them together to anticipate trends.

Questions

There is a clear relationship between elasticity and correlation. Price elasticity of demand usually shows a negative correlation because sales fall when prices increase. Price elasticity of demand measures the relationship between price changes and changes in quantity demanded. Income elasticity measures the changes in income and quantity demanded.

1 What would normally happen to cheap, own-brand food sales if customers have more disposable income? What type of correlation is likely to be shown? (*4 marks*)
2 Correlation can help a business to target a specific part of the market. If there is a strong correlation between income levels and demand for its products, what should the business do and what would be the likely outcome? (*4 marks*)

The use of technology in analysing markets

Why use technology?

Market analysis, if comprehensively carried out, is a complex issue with many different areas of necessary research. The business needs to collate the broadest possible range of information and then to analyse any underlying trends in order to help decision-making. Typically, market analysis software can assist in the following areas:

- competitive research
- customer segmentation
- demographic analysis
- market penetration and potential
- market screening and share
- market trends
- possible site and distribution locations.

The complexity of market analysis depends on the business's access to relevant information. Increasingly, market analysis software contains many of the fundamental elements that can assist a business in putting together a comprehensive analysis. It would pull in information from a variety of different sources, including data from banks, research companies, the census and even mapping such as Google Earth.

Applications

The available range of applications covers customer analysis, building of databases, campaign management, the targeting of markets, the analysis of responses to marketing, competitor analysis and software that focuses on trying to extrapolate trends.

Although there are many specific proprietary brands of market analysis software, what many businesses actually use is known as a marketing information system. This is an integrated network of information designed to help marketing managers collate and analyse information that can be used for planning, decision-making and control.

Normally these systems are part of a broader management information system.

FOR EXAMPLE

The clothing retailer, Benetton, has linked all its stores using a management information system and when an item is sold its fabric and colour are noted. The data collected makes it possible for the company to determine the shade and amount of fabric that needs to be dyed each day, enabling the business to respond more quickly to colour trends.

Marketing information systems need to be carefully designed and developed, so that they provide timely and accurate information. Because information is not cost-free, it may not be feasible to input or obtain all the kinds of information needed. The benefit of information always needs to be compared with the cost of obtaining and maintaining it. The system design needs to take into account how the information will be transformed into data that can readily be used.

It is desirable for these systems to be both effective and efficient – they need to be user-orientated, systematic, expandable, flexible, integrated, reliable, timely and controllable.

An additional complication is when an international marketing information system is set up in order to support a business's international marketing strategy and market analysis. Additional criteria incorporate cultural and linguistic differences, legal differences and peculiarities about locations.

While many businesses will routinely collect data, they are reliant upon relevant secondary data in order to fill in the gaps between what they already know and what they need to know, in order to make an effective market analysis. They will collect data from general reference, trade journals, business associations, syndicated services and market research agencies. Government sources can also provide a useful pool of relevant data.

It is not always necessary for the business to gather primary data, as this is not only more expensive, but also far more time-consuming. Businesses will set up a marketing information system to handle the information as efficiently and effectively as possible. They will aim to integrate all the information inputs from various sources and this requires a high degree of integration and coordination from areas that generate usable data.

With the development of artificial intelligence it is becoming possible for computers to perform many of the necessary functions, specifically the laborious and time-consuming ones of collating the data and analysing it. Some of the software systems available today can actually make recommendations for marketing strategies.

Examples

For the past ten years or more the car manufacturer, BMW, has been using Claritas's marketing data and software to help with market analysis. One of the main steps was for Claritas to have access to BMW's Intranet, so that they could assist in providing the market information data and perform the analysis required. The system helped BMW focus on primary marketing areas, to understand the lifestyle characteristics of potential customers, to increase their market share, to ensure that their dealerships did not overlap and compete with one another and to help them develop a customer-focused marketing strategy.

The Peterborough-based business, Technologies4Targeting Ltd, boasts a range of customers as broad as BSkyB, British Airways, the National Trust, American Express, Microsoft and Thomas Cook. The company provides a range of software solutions that primarily focus on analysing existing and potential customers and their purchasing habits. This has allowed the various businesses to target their marketing communications and create more effective marketing campaigns.

The Warwickshire-based business, Apteco, provides an even broader range of software, including marketing data analysis software, known as FastStats. It allows businesses to measure their marketing results, consider customer behaviour, focus on investment returns, increase response rates and generally assist in decision-making. One of their clients was the People's Dispensary for Sick Animals (PDSA), as can be seen in the following case study and questions.

CASE STUDY PDSA AND TECHNOLOGY

PDSA has a small direct marketing team who manage the wide range of products and campaigns run to increase funding. Despite having an excellent IT support department, the direct marketing department was unable to get the information it needed to define and drive campaigns in the timescales required. The IT team started a major project to build a new marketing database system, but Direct Marketing needed a way to reach marketing information themselves.

FastStats and Cascade were chosen by PDSA Direct Marketing to deliver the analysis, counts and selections needed to plan and deliver effective direct mail campaigns. All four million supporter records, 15 million transaction records and 60 million items of mailing history have been loaded into FastStats to deliver 50 or more campaigns a year. These campaigns range from small tactical mailings of a few thousand people, to major monthly lottery mailings of up to one million people. FastStats is a strategic part of the new marketing database development which refreshes weekly data including full postal address details, allowing FastStats to drive the campaign production process.

PDSA makes extensive use of effectiveness testing by key-coding all segments of all mailing campaigns. Testing includes both the database selections and the creative element of each campaign and ensures an optimised return. Telemarketing is used to follow up mailings and improve the response rates to very high levels by most marketing campaign standards.

Questions

1 What is the principal reason why the PDSA is using this software? (*4 marks*)
2 What do you understand by the term 'direct marketing'? (*2 marks*)

Difficulties in analysing marketing data

LEARNING OBJECTIVES

▶ Analysis of analysis
▶ Different problems for different markets

Analysis of analysis

Market analysis tries to make sense of the constituent components of markets and the factors that influence them. Ultimately, a market's primary characteristics are determined by who is involved. This extends beyond just customers, consumers and the competitors. It should include suppliers, distribution channels and the threat from substitute products, services or technologies.

The results of any market analysis should provide valuable quantitative and qualitative snapshots of the size, structure, and distinguishing features of the markets. They should also identify the environmental factors that drive change and indicate future trends and scenarios.

All effective marketing needs to be linked to the strengths of the business and the market opportunities. In theory any type of market research should inform the business, help with decision-making and reduce risk of failure.

Techniques such as extrapolation enable a business to estimate future sales. Plans can then be developed to accommodate the projections. Correlation can help a business identify the key drivers of demand. The business can then try to influence these and thus to control demand. The use of moving averages highlights underlying trends in the market. Theoretically the business can then use these to help with their planning.

However the value of extrapolation depends on the extent of market changes. Some markets are radically transformed by the introduction of new technology or the arrival of a new competitor, suggesting that the value of extrapolation is fairly limited. Correlation relies on a stable relationship between variables. There may well have been a stable relationship in the past, but this does not mean to say that there will be one in the future. Manufacturers of traditional toys may have used correlation to estimate the demand for children's toys in forthcoming Christmas periods, but what they could not have worked into that equation was the dominance of games consoles and handheld games.

Different problems for different markets

Market analysis will inevitably be different if a business's own approach is different from the outset. A business that is asset-led – in other words that looks at what the market wants and then is prepared to deliver it – should find market analysis an extremely valuable tool. It will alert the company to market opportunities and maximising chances of success.

A market-led strategy can also be successful because the business aims to put customers first and make what the market wants. The problem is that businesses cannot always match customer requirements. If a business chases the market it may enter a market where it has little or no knowledge or experience. It may be facing competitors who know the market inside out and have already assumed market leadership. Equally, it could mean that the business is unable to deploy enough resources and this could be disastrous in terms of its relationship with customers.

What then of a product-led organisation and its use of market analysis? A product-led business is looking for somewhere to sell what it wants to sell to customers, not necessarily to supply them with what they want. However, market analysis can find a market for them. It will look to find a market that has little competition, and where the customers therefore have very little choice. If market analysis reveals this, then the business also needs to be fortunate enough to find customers who are still prepared to buy.

There is also a considerable difference between industrial and consumer markets as far as market analysis is concerned. It would be fair to say that many businesses do try to produce the right product, at the right price, at the right time and then of course to make sure that their potential customers hear about it. This is the basis of the marketing mix, but market analysis may be more or less difficult, depending on the type of customer that provides the bulk of buyers for a business.

In industrial markets the tendency is for businesses to interact directly with their customers. Only in some cases are intermediaries used and the entire market may consist of only a few hundred customers. Market analysis may be valuable to analyse trends, work out average prices and spending, or to examine the location of the majority of customers, so that for example a service or delivery centre could be located close to them. But each of the customers will inevitably be large. They will also have radically different requirements, so the business, no matter how much market analysis has been undertaken, will still need to be flexible and cater for the precise needs of each customer as if they were individuals.

We can compare this business-to-business approach with the business-to-consumer market. Here a business may produce tens or hundreds of thousands of products a day. They may rely on a host of intermediaries to get their products to the marketplace and to sell their products to the consumer on their behalf. Where should the focus of their market analysis be? Should they focus on the intermediaries, as after all these are their prime customers? But their customers are not their end-users and it is the consumer that drives the demand. It is the consumer that has specific preferences, characteristics and buying habits, not the intermediaries. This makes the process of market analysis all the more complex, as research needs to bypass the intermediaries and focus on the consumer.

Information gathered from the consumer may well inform the manufacturer, but will it have any influence on the intermediary? Increasingly, in order to streamline the supply chain, information from all parties involved in manufacture and distribution is usually shared. This adds to the pool of information available for market analysis and should lead to more accurate analysis and amendment of activities to match the consumers' requirements.

CASE STUDY DESTINATION FAILURE

The Royal Armouries in Leeds (*below*), the Earth Centre in Doncaster (*right*), and the National Centre for Popular Music in Sheffield (*far right*) all suffer from low attendance levels, mounting debts and public criticism. Would better market analysis have prevented these downturns, because visitor numbers were clearly overestimated?

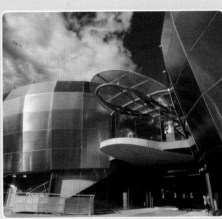

Questions

1 When carrying out a market analysis for a destination such as those in the case study, is competitor analysis really important? (*4 marks*)
2 Given the choice, would a visitor go to a new museum or an existing museum? Give reasons for your answer. (*4 marks*)
3 Suggest how a market analysis could be carried out for the sighting of an attraction. (*10 marks*)

Case studies, questions and exam practice

CASE STUDY PACKAGING MARKET ANALYSIS

Packaging is a massive industry and worldwide it is worth $424 billion, with Europe being the largest single regional market.

Europe market worth (*Europe packaging market worth is estimated as US$127 billion*)

REGIONAL BREAKDOWN OF EUROPEAN PACKAGING INDUSTRY

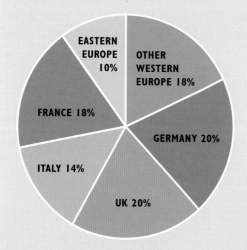

Region	Value (US$ billion)	Percentage (%) European market
Eastern Europe	13	10
Germany	26	20
UK	25	20
France	23	18
Italy	17	14
Other Western Europe	23	18
Total	127	100

EUROPE PACKAGING MATERIAL BREAKDOWN

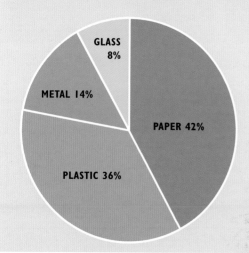

Product	Share (%)
Paper	42
Plastic	36
Metal	14
Glass	8
Total	100

EUROPEAN PACKAGING SECTORS BREAKDOWN

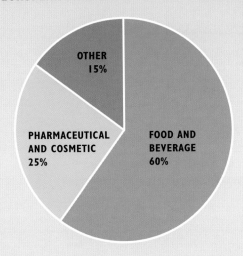

Sectors	Value (US$ billion)	Percentage (%) European market
Food and beverage	76	60
Pharmaceutical and cosmetic	32	25
Other	19	15
Total	127	100

European packaging market trends from 1998–2008

PROJECTED MARKET GROWTH (1.2%)

Year	Worth (US$ billion)
1998	124
2000	125
2002	126
2004	127
2006	128
2008	130

Questions

1 Looking at the regional breakdown, which markets appear to be the most attractive and why? (*4 marks*)

2 Having considered which regional markets are the most attractive, which packaging material and sector would provide a business with the most potential for success? (*2 marks*)

3 Using a three-year moving average, with 2006 as the centre point, what is the moving average for that year? (*2 marks*)

Low cost versus differentiation

LEARNING OBJECTIVES

▶ Porter's generic strategies
▶ Low-cost strategy
▶ Differentiation strategy

Porter's generic strategies

Writing back in the 1980s Michael Porter suggested that there were generic strategies that could be applied to all products and services in all industries, regardless of the type of organisation or its size.

Porter suggested that each of the strategies was a way of gaining a competitive advantage, or edge, over the competition:

- *Cost leadership strategy* – increasing profits through reducing costs, while still charging industry average prices. The alternative would be to increase market share by charging lower prices, while still making a reasonable profit because costs have been reduced.
- *Differentiation strategy* – this means making products and services different or more attractive than those of the competitors. It requires having good research, development and innovation, the ability to deliver high-quality products and services and, above all, effective sales and marketing so that the market understands the benefits.
- *Focus strategy* – either cost focus or differentiation focus. Cost focus means developing a unique low cost compared to that of the competitor, probably by virtue of the fact that the business is in a position to produce an enormous number of units at a low cost to itself due to economies of scale. The alternative is the differentiation focus, which means producing something that has strong brand loyalty, is unique and probably serves market niches.

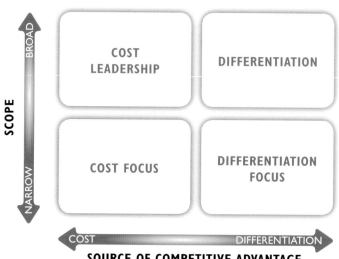

SOURCE OF COMPETITIVE ADVANTAGE

Choosing the right generic strategy underpins every strategic decision that the business will make, so it is important to get it right. Porter warned specifically about 'hedging your bets' by trying to follow more than one strategy. The business needs to focus on making the strategy work once it has chosen the most appropriate one.

One of the problems, however, was that Porter did not really take into account several key changes that inevitably occur in the competitive environment, broad corporate objectives and strategies and, above all, recognisable business changes that have taken place over the last fifty to sixty years. The key changes are outlined in the table opposite, which also shows exactly where Porter's generic strategies fall into the trends in using management tools.

Low-cost strategy

Low-cost strategy actually rests on many of the requirements that cost leadership needs:

- Access to funds that will allow an investment in technology to bring overall costs down.
- Efficient logistics in the case of tangible products or a comprehensive distribution system of some kind for services.
- A low base cost in terms of labour, materials and facilities.
- A strategy in place to ensure the sustainability of cutting costs below those of the competition.

KEY TERM

Logistics – essentially the whole management of the supply chain, from acquiring raw materials through the movement of part-finished goods, finished goods, packaging and distribution to stockist or end user.

Differentiation strategy

A differentiation strategy is possible when a business can successfully convince its customers that their product is unique. However even unique products are inevitably copied, like Coca-Cola, Pringles and Dyson. For a time, if they are unique, the business can charge a premium price, but this requires a strong brand, probably a new invention and almost certainly a unique selling point (USP). The product or service needs to appear to be exclusive and of better quality. In many cases the business seeks to keep very tight control over the distribution in order to maintain the image.

Any marketing focuses on making sure that customers understand that the product is superior and markedly different from any rival products.

	Period of stable growth	Period of competition	Period of hyper-competition
Period	1945 – mid-'70s	Mid-'70s – mid-'90s	Mid-'90s onwards
Characteristics of competitive environment	• Growth • Chances	• Competition • Cyclical growth	• Rapid, non-linear change
Corporate objectives	• Revenue growth • Spread of risks	• Survival • Profitability	• Management of unpredictable developments
Corporate strategies	• Expansion	• Refocusing to core businesses • Restructuring • Niche marketing • Mergers and acquisitions	• Re-definition of industry borders • Re-definition of business • Management of partnerships
Management tools and models	• Ansoff's matrix • Product lifecycle model • Boston matrix	• Porter's Generic Strategies • Core Competencies • Business Process Re-engineering	• Chaos theory • Game theory • Industry Breakpoints

CASE STUDY EUROPEAN ORGANIC FRUIT JUICES – THE OPTIONS

The European organic juices market is becoming increasingly competitive, with growth rates slowing and consumer demand stabilising in many countries. Competition is stepping up and companies need to re-examine their strategies if they are to achieve positive business growth.

Juice companies can acquire competitive advantage via a cost leadership strategy. This is usually gained by companies that are able to achieve economies of scale in production and marketing. Such companies buy raw materials in bulk and they produce organic juices on a large-scale. They are thus able to market organic juices at low prices and this is usually to the mainstream food retailers. France and the UK have organic juice companies that have gained market leadership via this strategy. Conventional juice companies undertake this strategy in the organic juices market because of their large production capacity and established contacts. This strategy is not viable for new entrants that have low financial resources and specialised products.

A differentiation strategy involves companies marketing a product that is clearly distinguishable from others in the marketplace. In the organic juices market, this means the product has attributes that are distinct from others, which can be in the form of flavour, juice type or other characteristics.

A cost focus strategy involves a company gaining competitive advantage by being the low-cost provider to the segment. An example would be a company that offers a wide range of specialised juices (e.g. organic mixed vegetable juices) at low prices.

A differentiation focus strategy involves companies marketing a distinct or unique product in the target segment. There are many examples of companies undertaking this strategy in the European organic juices market. The leading companies in Germany specialise in supplying organic juices to certain marketing channels. An example is the Demeter brand of organic juices.

The cost leadership strategy is the most fancied route of conventional juice companies and has achieved success in countries such as Italy and the UK.

A focus strategy is probably the most practical for smaller companies, but the potential of target segments has to be accurately measured.

Source: adapted from www.organicmonitor.com

Questions

1 Comment on the advice given to organic juice companies in relation to Porter's four generic strategies. (*8 marks*)
2 Why is there a suggestion that there should be a different strategy adopted for large and small producers? (*4 marks*)

Market penetration

Ansoff's matrix

Back in the 1950s Igor Ansoff designed a matrix that sought to identify the four key options as far as business strategy was concerned. He created a matrix, cross-referencing new and current products with new and current markets and then suggesting specific strategies to handle the situation that a business would find itself in if it chose each option.

Over the next three spreads we will look at the matrix and explain how each option is relevant to marketing. For now, however, we can see that the four generic growth strategies identified in the matrix below are:

- *Market penetration* – selling existing products to existing customers
- *Market development* – selling existing products to new customers
- *Product development* – selling new products to existing customers
- *Diversification* – selling new products to new customers

As we will see, the Ansoff matrix suggests certain degrees of risk. Market penetration has the lowest risk, while both market development and product development could be described as being moderately risky. Diversification, however, is the most risky, as the business is dealing with a new product and a new market.

Two prime examples show how the Ansoff matrix works in practice

– the activities of Tesco and The Royal Bank of Scotland are compared in the table below.

Before moving on to look at market penetration in more detail, there is a variation of Ansoff's matrix that extends it to a nine-box format. This is becoming a preferred way of looking at the matrix, as it takes into account the fact that businesses do not necessarily throw themselves wholeheartedly into one of the four basic strategies. They may partially involve themselves, perhaps by extending their product line – for example, a Mars bar can now be purchased as an ice cream or a drink – this is an example of product extension.

Strategy	Tesco	Royal Bank of Scotland
Market penetration	Increased market share by taking customers from Sainsbury's and Asda	Became dominant bank in Scotland
Market development	Expanded abroad and entered the convenience store market	Bought Halifax and Williams & Glyn (this runs Tesco's bank)
Product development	Expanded into petrol sales and financial services	Sold insurance and revolutionised motor insurance through Direct Line
Diversification	Moved into catalogue sales and home delivery services	Moved into selling insurance in England and in other territories

MARKET DEVELOPMENT	PARTIAL DIVERSIFICATION	DIVERSIFICATION
MARKET EXPANSION	LIMITED DIVERSIFICATION	PARTIAL DIVERSIFICATION
MARKET PENETRATION	PRODUCT EXTENSION	PRODUCT DEVELOPMENT

MARKETS: NEW — EXPANDED — EXISTING

PRODUCTS AND SERVICES: EXISTING — MODIFIED — NEW

Market penetration

Market penetration can be achieved if one or more of the following factors exists in the market:

- There is an opportunity for the business to be able to encourage additional usage of products or services by existing customers
- There is a chance that the business may be able to attract customers away from competitors
- There is scope to take market share away from at least one key competitor or from a number of smaller competitors
- The business can focus on trying to increase frequency of use of its products and services
- The business can come up with new applications or uses for its products and services
- It can encourage non-buyers to make a purchase

It may be necessary for the business to re-jig its marketing mix in order to ensure that market penetration works. Market penetration can be a valuable and effective strategy if the following sets of circumstances exist:

- The market is not already saturated with products and services offered by a broad range of strong competitors
- The market is actually showing signs of continued growth
- The business has already identified the fact that one or more competitor's market share is vulnerable
- Increasing the amount of products or services sold brings about economies of scale
- There is scope for the business to sell additional products and services to its existing customer base

It is widely believed that once market penetration has reached about half of what it could possibly achieve overall, the process actually slows down. The business still needs to support the efforts, perhaps through price cuts and additional advertising, to convince those that have so far been resistant to its products, to buy.

CASE STUDY CROCS

Crocs Shoes, rather like plastic clogs, have been described as the must-have middle-class shoe. The business is based in Colorado and has been making the shoes since 2002. Factories in China and the US are making up to 5 million pairs per month and their profits are up on average nearly 300% per year. But fakes are flooding into the market for £5 a pair. Crocs can be seen to have followed Ansoff's matrix. They focused on their

original markets, Canada and the US (market penetration). They then moved to Europe (market development). They then moved on to producing accessories, bags and t-shirts when the markets became saturated with original Crocs.

Questions

1 What is the development of bags and t-shirts an example of in relation to the Ansoff matrix? (*2 marks*)

2 Crocs has recently announced that it is about to launch a line of clothing featuring a form of the plastic resin that is used in its shoes. It has also bought Bite Footwear, the clothing company, Ocean Minded, and the sports company, Fury. Explain how these acquisitions also relate to Ansoff's matrix. (*12 marks*)

Product development and market development strategies

Product development

Product development means the development of new products for existing markets. These products can be genuinely new, innovative products, or one of the following:

- A new product that is designed to replace a current product
- A genuinely new, innovative product
- A product improvement
- An extension of the product line
- A new product that supplements or complements an existing product
- A product that is of a different quality (either lower or higher) than an existing product

Businesses that have well-respected brands may be able to sell the customer other things. The business can use the goodwill it already has in the market to successfully launch a new product.

Not every new product development based on a well-known brand works. Coca-Cola, for example, launched its premium bottled water, Dasani, into the UK consumer market. Customers quickly realised that the product was nothing more than bottled tap water. It nearly ruined Coca-Cola's reputation. The company had already tried to change the formula of the main Coca-Cola brand but customers were resistant to it and the business had to make a humiliating back step.

FOR EXAMPLE

The pen manufacturer, Mont Blanc, had a 100-year reputation for producing some of the finest quality pens in the market. A Mont Blanc pen was highly desirable, but the business realised that once loyal customers had bought a pen, a ballpoint and a pencil there was nothing else for them to buy. This was because the pens lasted for life and even the most loyal customers might never buy anything from them again. As a result, Mont Blanc went into producing cuff links, wallets and notebooks, transferring their well-established brand name onto new products.

Product development is often used by businesses in the following sets of circumstances:

- When the business has a strong research and development department
- When the market is growing
- When there is rapid change in technology
- When the business can actually build on an existing brand
- When the competitors are seen to have better products

New product development is often a way in which businesses can refresh their appeal to new customers. Bringing out new, fresh products keeps the customer interested and can give the business a competitive advantage.

Projects always start with an idea, but what is crucial is making sure that an effective new product or service is developed in the quickest possible time, as product development is expensive and time-consuming. While the product is being developed, costs are being incurred with no immediate prospect of profits. Businesses will try to reduce development time, terminate projects that are not achieving their goals and, above all, make sure that any product development is in line with the business's strategic objectives and long-term plans.

Market development

Market development means selling the same product to new customers. This can be achieved by entering new markets or segments with products and services that the business already offers. In many cases it may mean entering an overseas market.

One of the key issues of market development is that there will have to be a major change in marketing strategy. New distribution channels will have to be developed and new pricing policies adopted. New promotional strategies can be created, to attract different types of customer.

Market development involves a moderate risk, largely because the exact behaviour of the new potential customers is unknown, but at least the business has a strong knowledge of its own products and services. A business will usually opt for market development when:

- Market analysis has identified that there are untapped markets that could be interested in the products and services
- The business has, or could easily achieve, excess capacity
- There appear to be attractive ways in which to access the new markets

Selling the same product into a new market is a fairly difficult proposition, but a number of businesses have managed to do this, such as Guinness, Lucozade and Skoda. Perhaps one of the most successful was the repositioning of the Sony PlayStation. It had originally been developed as a product for children, but Sony decided to re-launch it to the adult market. Since then it has shown continued success.

Not all market development by repositioning has worked. A strange example was the repositioning of the sport of cricket, when clubs adopted strange names, like American baseball teams. Although this approach worked perfectly well in America and appealed to younger markets, it did not work in Britain.

CASE STUDY FIREANGEL

Sam Tate co-founded Sprue Aegis plc in 1998 when he and his business partner came up with an innovative smoke detector. The FireAngel fits between a light fitting and the bulb, taking its energy from the mains. FireAngel charges up its rechargeable battery when the light is on – and runs off the battery when the light is off. It's now stocked in around 6,000 outlets.

Sam explains: 'We spent months digging out market research reports, talking to the Fire Brigade and the Office of the Deputy Prime Minister – the government department responsible for fire safety (now the responsibility of Communities and Local Government). Once we confirmed the FireAngel was a valuable idea, I went out on to the street to see if there was a market for it. We basically just stopped people, showed them the prototype and asked a set list of questions. We also looked closely at our competitors' products and who their market was. We initially worked out a sales strategy involving the Internet, direct marketing and advertising. However, we soon knew on a cost-per-sale basis this wouldn't be feasible – we would have sold less and had to charge twice as much. We then realised an ideal way to reach consumers who wanted a quick solution was through supermarkets. Most smoke detectors retail at between £5 and £10. We knew we could charge a premium because fitting the alarm is as simple as changing a bulb. It doesn't need a battery and it lasts for up to ten years. We set the price at around £20 but the retailer obviously takes a margin. Remember – it's a lot harder to put the price up than drop it down, so don't go in too cheaply. It's really important to be able to get your message across in 30 seconds flat. It took three years to get our product to market. A lot of this time was spent on design and safety testing, but it took 18 months of talking to one well-known high-street retailer before they agreed to stock the alarm. Once you're in there with one retail chain, it gets much easier to approach others. But you definitely have to be persistent to succeed.'

Source: adapted from Business Link

Questions

1 Explain how the business carried out its research to determine whether there was a market for the new product. (*8 marks*)
2 Setting the price is a difficult task initially. How did the business go about setting a price? (*6 marks*)

Diversification

Diversification

As far as Ansoff's matrix is concerned, diversification involves either selling new products to new markets or new products to new customers. It is the most risky strategy that a business can adopt because selling new products into new markets offers the greatest prospect for growth, but it also offers the greatest risk of failure.

A business does not usually go into a new market with a new product without amassing a great deal of information first. It is very easy to get diversification wrong. Two examples of getting it right come from very different types of industry:

- Caterpillar – primarily makes bulldozers and diggers and sells them to construction companies. They now sell boots and clothing to consumers.
- Apple – used to sell computers to graphic designers. Now there are few children and adults without an iPod.

Diversification can often go horribly wrong. One of the first home entertainment systems was designed by an inventor and entrepreneur, Sir Clive Sinclair. It was called the ZX Spectrum and despite it being extremely primitive by today's standards, it sold in astonishing numbers. He diversified into a new form of personal transport, the Sinclair C5, an electric single-seat car, which looked like a plastic pram. It was a complete failure, but today its rarity is such that a car sells for several hundred pounds.

Related diversification

Related diversification involves the business moving out of the market in which it is best known, but still remaining within a particular industry, such as a CD shop selling DVDs and computer games.

The idea is that either the market or the product that the business is moving into has some features in common with the existing range of products that the business sells. The business is not taking such an enormous risk because it is building on its own expertise and areas of activity, which it may have developed over a number of years.

Sometimes related diversification is known as synergistic diversification. This means that the business is using its existing product and market knowledge in order to help it broaden either the range of product it sells or the markets in which it operates. The fact that the business already has some knowledge of either the product or the market means that the risk is significantly reduced. A prime example would be a bank moving into selling insurance.

Related diversification is not quite as simple as it would immediately appear. There are three main types of related diversification:

- Horizontal diversification – the business chooses to introduce new products into its existing markets.
- Vertical diversification – the business actually moves up or down the supply chain. A distributor, for example, may either buy or replicate what its retail customers do, or the same business may begin to manufacture products that are similar to those originally bought from its suppliers.
- Concentric diversification – the business brings new products, closely related to its existing products, into new markets.

PC World is owned by the same company that owns Dixons and Currys. As a group it has grown through market penetration, by establishing new stores, and through product development by offering a wider range. However, it has also grown

through related diversification, particularly in the case of PC World. To begin with, PC World sold only computer products. The first related diversification was into digital photography, then MP3 players, then flat-screen TVs. The company now sells a wide range of products that could all be broadly described as related to digital technology.

FOR EXAMPLE

An example of vertical diversification was the purchase of travel agencies by tour operators such as Thomson. An example of concentric diversification is easyJet, which has moved into offering not just flights, but also car hire and hotel booking services.

Unrelated diversification

Unrelated diversification can occur when businesses moves to sell products that are completely new into markets that are completely unknown to them. They are effectively developing products and markets that have little to do with what they already know and there is no commonality between their existing product range and what they intend to sell.

Sometimes this type of diversification is referred to as conglomerate diversification. A single parent business will own a wide range of completely unrelated companies that sell an enormously different range of products and services in a number of different markets. The energy provider, British Gas, provides home emergency services, and many film studios in Hollywood own hotels, casinos and cruise liners.

CASE STUDY MITCHELL CHARLESWORTH

Mitchell Charlesworth is a chartered accountancy practice with five offices in the North West and over 100 years' experience. Aware of the need to maintain a competitive edge in an increasingly tough market, the company launched a specialist small business development service two years ago. The new service has increased profitability per customer and boosted business volumes. Business development manager Greg Harris explains how it was done.

'Even a well-established business like ours has to evolve. Most chartered accountants offer the same basic package of services such as tax planning and payroll services. Although we were confident that ours were some of the best around, we wanted to offer something that would really add value for our clients. The first step in developing a new service was consulting our existing clients. Through listening to feedback, we identified a market for a trusted business development service that leveraged the chartered accountancy 'brand'. We also researched our competitors and found that there were only two other practices in our area offering a similar service. From talking to clients, we realised that many SMEs need specialist help in developing and growing their businesses, but often don't know who to trust. Small firms tend to be wary of anyone who styles

themselves as a general business consultant. They think that they'll end up spending a lot of money for promises that aren't ultimately delivered. In launching our own business development service we already had the advantage of the chartered accountancy brand behind us. It represents an assurance of quality that helps small business owners overcome their qualms. This meant we could logically offer new products and services to our existing customer base that were natural extensions of our accounting services, without our customers being surprised or concerned. We initially thought the new service would expand our business by attracting new clients. In practice, I'd say about 75 per cent of the increase in business volume we've experienced has come from existing clients, although having the service in our portfolio does help to attract new clients. The cost of marketing to existing customers is obviously lower than recruiting new ones as well.'

Source: adapted from Business Link

Question

Using this business as an example, explain how it is possible for even a relatively small business to successfully achieve diversification. (*12 marks*)

Assessing effectiveness of marketing strategies

LEARNING
OBJECTIVES

▶ Overseas marketing strategy
▶ Why change strategy in the first place?
▶ Evaluating strategy

Overseas marketing strategy

For many larger businesses, framing a marketing strategy can be complex because they are focusing on moving into overseas markets. This tends to be the case when the domestic market is already saturated, when there are many competitors, and when there is a desire to make inroads into overseas markets.

Overseas marketing brings its own particular problems because a business is far less likely to be familiar with the market. It will have to research consumer behaviour, the response of the competition and any relevant economic or legal factors. Many businesses actually enter overseas markets in collaboration with a local partner that understands the market. The business has to decide whether it needs to adapt its products and services to match the new market (for example there are dozens of different formulae of Nescafé coffee available around the world, but all with the same brand name).

Products and services will easily transfer into new markets with very little adaptation, such as soft drinks, jeans and cigarettes. The biggest advantage of being able to operate in multiple overseas markets is that businesses will gradually acquire economies of scale. This does not just mean in production terms, but by having to develop only one style of advertising, packaging and distribution.

Why change strategy in the first place?

Although some businesses will make the positive decision to review and then change their marketing strategy, others may have to change it for a variety of reasons:

- They may have changed their marketing objectives and perhaps want to focus on diversification rather than trying to get additional sales out of their existing products and markets
- The market conditions may have changed – perhaps the markets in which they operate are either stagnating or declining
- The competition may be too fierce so the business may decide to focus on areas in which they have a competitive advantage
- The business may have developed new strengths over a period of time and is now particularly good at developing new products, providing excellent customer service, or offering some other key advantage

FOR EXAMPLE

The retailing chain Boots was primarily a pharmacist, but with the diversification of supermarkets into chemists and health-related products it has, over time, moved into new market segments – including photography, dental care and optical services.

Evaluating strategy

Businesses need to look at different ways in which they can assess whether or not their strategies have been successful. Clearly, they will have to set SMART targets (Specific, Measurable, Achievable, Realistic and Time-based). In this way they can see whether they have reached set targets and indicators.

However, not all assessments are necessarily financial or figure-based. Clearly a big change in marketing strategy will have had cost implications for the business. It will have affected profits at least in the short to medium term. But there are different ways in which the ultimate success of a new marketing strategy can be judged, as outlined in the table opposite.

Evaluation measure	Explanation
Earnings	Could be measured in terms of increases of earnings per employee, earnings per customer, earnings per outlet, or earnings per square metre.
Profit	Could be measured in a very similar way to earnings, but focusing on profit only. This would be calculated over a period of time and compared perhaps month by month.
Return on capital	Could be a key measurement tool, either in terms of returns on capital employed or earnings per share in organisations where share capital has been issued to fund changes in marketing strategy.
Volume	Sales, production or even throughput per employee could be the focus when looking at changes in volume produced. Alternatively the volume of products or services sold per customer or per outlet, or in other cases, such as retail, the volume turnover per outlet could be considered.
Costs	Costs obviously have a strong connection with both earnings and profits, but they will be particularly relevant to businesses that have a desire to make cost improvements part of their overall objectives. They will look at costs, charges, overheads, purchasing and any additional costs that have been incurred as a result of implementing or running the marketing strategy. Typically target costs per employee, square metre, outlet or department might be used.
Comparisons	It is always a useful process for a business to compare itself with similar businesses, particularly those in the same industry. It could look at similar businesses both before and after the marketing strategy has been introduced. Specific comparisons can be made, such as pricing, customer satisfaction, awareness of the product or service and how the competition has responded to the new marketing initiative. Typically, output, volume, turnover, and profit margins will be compared.
Percentages and annual comparisons	Could be an internal comparison or a 'before and after' comparison. The business will already be aware of its performance and will have almost certainly assigned particular desired improvements such as increased sales, reduction in complaints or greater market penetration and market share.
Qualitative	Qualitative measures could include being recognised more publicly, and by the industry itself as having achieved a higher level of awareness or success. Media coverage would also be a strong measure in terms of a qualitative evaluation.

CASE STUDY THE REAL THING REALLY

In the 1970s and 1980s, Pepsi Cola was outselling Coca-Cola, despite the fact that Coca-Cola was outspending Pepsi on marketing and advertising. In blind taste tests Pepsi always came out on top. So, after 99 years, Coca-Cola decided to abandon its original formula and come up with a new formula that was sweeter. In blind-tests people thought it was Pepsi and it beat Pepsi in taste tests. Nearly 200,000 people were used in the test marketing across thirteen cities in the United States. According to Coca-Cola's own results, 55% of people preferred the new formula. Coca-Cola decided to replace the original formula and it proved to be an absolute disaster. Complaints were coming in at a rate of 5,000 a day. People accused Coca-Cola of being un-American and daring to change something that people felt should never be tampered with. New Coke lasted only 79 days before Coca-Cola was forced to switch back to the classic formula.

Question

It would seem from the response of customers that the market research was a waste of time. Comment on this view. (8 marks)

Case studies, questions and exam practice

CASE STUDY ANSOFF AND APPLE

For most of the 1990s, Apple was stuck in the personal computing world. Rather than adding customers and products, it shrank in market share and abandoned some markets (handhelds, printers). It was plainly stuck way down in the lower left quadrant, with little in the way of great growth prospects until the new iMacs, released in 1998, spurred interest among existing customers. The message of the market was clear. Making Macs better was not the problem. The market needed something more compelling than a computer that was slightly better than a Windows PC to convince new customers to give the company money.

Apple's core audience is multimedia-oriented, so a Mac music player was a step in the right direction. It also helps that Apple is well-known for charismatic product design; the public is a little more willing to give an Apple innovation a try. When early models of the iPod got rave reviews, even Windows users who were deep into downloading wanted one. Once the iTunes software was released on Windows the iPod zoomed. In Ansoff terms, a successful product development strategy that succeeded immediately had positioned Apple for a market development strategy. Suddenly Apple was not just developing new revenues, it was also growing a new customer base.

The iTunes online music service was a diversification strategy which took Apple out of its traditional business model – cool, elegant, user-friendly hardware – into a retail services entertainment business. Everything about the business, from frequency of customer contact to how profits are taken, is different.

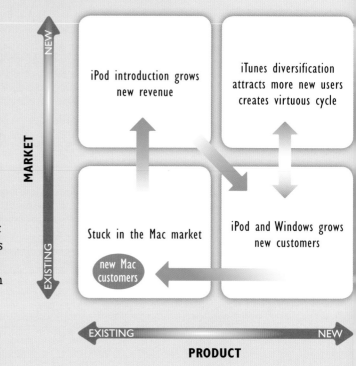

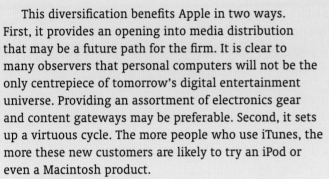

This diversification benefits Apple in two ways. First, it provides an opening into media distribution that may be a future path for the firm. It is clear to many observers that personal computers will not be the only centrepiece of tomorrow's digital entertainment universe. Providing an assortment of electronics gear and content gateways may be preferable. Second, it sets up a virtuous cycle. The more people who use iTunes, the more these new customers are likely to try an iPod or even a Macintosh product.

As Apple puts iPods into millions of new hands each quarter, it is creating iTunes users and developing potential customers for the Macintosh and new products yet to come, such as future video iPods and newer iPod phones. Think of Apple's groups of users as interpenetrating communities –Mac users, iPod users, iTunes users, and so forth. Each improvement to hardware, to the iTunes software and the music store, is leading to enhancements in the user experience for all those groups. Apple has unique strengths that have enabled it to succeed with this multi-level strategy which all started with a great product (the iPod) and an awareness of how it could quickly integrate with market development and diversification strategies.

Source: adapted from Transcend

Questions

1   Explain how Apple has been able to use all four of Ansoff's key sets of marketing strategies. (*12 marks*)
2   Outline how a retailer such as Marks and Spencer or Tesco might also have used all four strategies. (*16 marks*)

Components of marketing plans

LEARNING OBJECTIVES

▶ Marketing plans and corporate strategy
▶ The building blocks of a marketing plan
▶ Components of a marketing plan

Marketing plans and corporate strategy

It is important to remember how the marketing plan fits into overall corporate strategy. It is easy to confuse the fact that the environmental analysis in the marketing planning process means that the marketing plan is the same thing as the overall corporate strategic plan.

The marketing plan and the corporate strategic plan are not the same thing. The difference is largely one of scope: the corporate plan has to consider all aspects of the organisation's business, while a marketing plan is principally about marketing activities. The marketing plan is aligned with the corporate plan and aims to support it.

The building blocks of a marketing plan

There are four basic building blocks upon which all marketing plans are designed. These are:

- Situation analysis – the planning process should start with the collection and analysis of basic

data. This includes the wider environmental factors of the PESTEL model, SWOT analysis, marketing research data, current and planned products and services and other critical issues.

- Marketing strategy – this is a statement of all the marketing concepts, practices and activities that will be used by the business. It will probably also include how the marketing mix is to be used.

- Numerical forecasts – this will be quantitative data about the resources that will be used and the forecasts that have been estimated. The costs will be given in some detail and there will have to be realistic sales estimates. In particular, the costs of any marketing activities will be expected.

- Controls – this is the focus of the plan as it will not work without them. The controls may include sales and organisational milestones, routine performance measures and some indication of a contingency plan.

The components of a marketing plan

There are probably as many formats of marketing plans as there are marketing plans themselves. However, it is common practice to begin with an executive summary to provide a fast overview of the plan.

Ideally, the summary should include:

- Background information that helps explain why the particular proposals are being made and decisions taken

- A description of the proposed actions and the timescales involved

- A summary of the key aims and targets that it is hoped will be achieved

- A short assessment of the wider implications of the action

- Where the investments will be made and how much they will be

The marketing plan's summary is also likely to have some basic information on the marketing research that has been carried out, the proposed targets and segments identified and the proposed marketing techniques to be used (essentially the marketing mix) and finally a summary of the sales forecasts.

The next main part of the plan is the situational analysis. This is generally broken down into sections, but it looks at how the business interacts with its environment and really represents the first stage of the data collection. The plan needs to cover the external and the internal environment, as shown in the table opposite.

The next key section is the marketing strategy. This can be looked at under a number of broad headings:

- Marketing objectives – derived from the corporate plan and a clear statement of the overall purposes of the objectives. They aim to provide a focus for activities and are broken down into targets. They provide a framework for

KEY TERMS

PESTEL model – external factors that may have an impact on the business – political, economic, social, technological, environmental and legal.

Gap analysis – a comparison of the projected performance with the actual performance.

External environment	Internal environment
• The macro-environment may be analysed into six elements: political, technological, economic, environment or ecological or 'green', social and legal.	• The marketing plan should reflect the characteristics of the business concerned. It will inevitably refer to current and planned products and capabilities, and be designed to exploit the organisation's resources to the maximum.
• The micro-environment consists of the markets in which the business operates or plans to operate. It includes current and prospective customers and existing and potential competitors. The micro-environment also includes any distribution systems used by the business. This would therefore include: target markets, products and services, market needs, competition, market geography, costs, market demographics, suppliers, market trends and forecasts, market growth and other key issues.	• An important aspect of the internal analysis is the product and market background. This sets the scene for those that are less aware of the products and the markets involved.
	• The environmental analysis is usually summarised and entered on a SWOT analysis grid to highlight the overall situation of the business.
• Likely to be a very substantial part of the marketing plan.	

a profit is made. This is one of the key determinants of the marketing plan if profit is the major driver.

The control section of the plan aims to ensure that any of the planning targets are actually met. Typically this means that standards and targets need to be set, then they have to compare favourably in relation to actual performance, and finally corrective action needs to be taken if necessary. Usually this means one or more of the following:

• Performance measurement – collection of results so that comparisons can be made with the forecasts that have been created. This means either carrying out sales analysis (comparisons with budgeted turnover, etc.) or market-share analysis, often measured alongside turnover (because the growth or decline of the market can distort market-share figures)
• Marketing organisation – responsible for parts of the plan and the preparation of the performance reports
• Milestones – dates when the progress of the plan will be monitored

The final part of the plan will deal with contingency provision. It is highly unlikely that things will happen exactly as set out in the plan. Problems will arise and these will need to be handled. For example:

• Does the business have the capability to adapt to situations that could arise?
• What are the options or responses to a given contingency?
• How quickly will the business be able to respond to a given contingency?

coordination of activity and are fundamental to the control process as they define success or failure. When the objectives have been looked at in some detail, it is possible to refine them using gap analysis. The objectives will relate to both the dynamics of the market and the financial results. Typically, objectives could include revenue growth, market share, profitability, opening of outlets, customer retention, brand recognition, marketing spend and employee levels.

• Target markets – these will be defined and will tend to depend on the scale of the marketing operation.
• Product positioning – clearly defining how the target markets perceive the products or services (essentially whether the products and services aim to do exactly what the main competitors do – known as 'me too' positioning – or whether they are designed to meet an unmet demand in the market – known as gap filling).

• Marketing mix – the plan might not give full details of all the elements of this, but will tend to focus on the main parts that are aimed at ensuring success.
• Marketing research – how research has helped frame the plan and how it will continue to be a major part of the plan (in terms of monitoring and seeking feedback).

The next component is the numerical forecast (sometimes referred to as the budget). This will tend to cover forecasts including turnover, market share, spending on marketing, units sold, costs and break-even analysis. Usually, the numerical forecasts are broken down in two ways:

• by time period – the forecasts are broken down into either monthly or quarterly figures, or
• by marketing characteristic – analysed by product or market segment.

The break-even analysis is an important measure of the marketing plan as it shows the number of units that will need to be sold in order to ensure that

Questions

1 What is gap analysis? (2 marks)
2 Why are contingency plans important? (6 marks)

Assessing internal and external influences on marketing plans

Internal influences

Marketing does not operate in isolation within a business. It will work closely with other functional parts of the business, such as sales, product development, purchasing and human resources. The relationships and influences depend on a number of factors, including:

- *The corporate culture* – how the organisation actually works internally and whether cooperation and collaboration is positively supported and encouraged
- *The size of the business* – the larger the business, the more difficult it is at times to coordinate the work of different departments and for them all to appreciate their precise role
- *The nature of the industry* – how dependent the creation and manufacturing of products is on different parts of the organisation, or the role that different departments play in the provision of services
- *The lifecycle of the product or service* – products and services that have been sold for a number of years will be well-known to different parts of the organisation, whereas new products and services may be unknown quantities.

Not all businesses are well coordinated and many businesses allow their functions to operate in a fairly independent manner. Other businesses are far more integrated and their operations operate with a high level of coordination.

Marketing needs to work closely with other departments in order to ensure that the marketing concept extends across the whole of the organisation. Some of the other departments will have key roles to play, such as:

- *Finance department* – ensures that there is sufficient working capital to pay for marketing initiatives and organises relationships with customers
  – for example, setting credit terms
- *Human Resources* – responsible for the recruiting and training of staff, and specifically important in terms of training staff to understand that their actions have a bearing on the business's image and reputation
- *Purchasing* – responsible for ensuring that products and services used by the business are of a consistently high quality and are reliable

In some organisations cross-functional teams will have been set up. These are groups of individuals who are experts in their own particular specialism. Other businesses try to encourage inter-departmental relationships, to promote cooperation and integration. Customers themselves have very little interest in how a business organises itself or coordinates its activities, providing the products and services they receive from the business are of a satisfactory standard.

As we have seen when we considered the components of the marketing plan, it is important to appreciate that the plans will have very definite objectives. It would be incorrect to assume that only the finance department would have any basic interest or influence in a marketing plan that focuses on increasing profitability or sales income. It would also have implications for the sales department, and for purchasing, production and distribution. It would also have an implication for Human Resources, who may have to recruit more staff to cope with increased demand and train staff in order to ensure that they are fully up-to-date with the new objectives of the business.

Each different department of the business would therefore have either a direct or indirect influence, as there will inevitably be implications for them and they will be expected to play their part. In return they will expect to be able to have some input into the framing of the plan itself.

External influences

As far as external influences on a marketing plan are concerned, again there are both direct and indirect influences. As far as direct influences are concerned, we should consider organisations, groups and individuals that are close enough to the business to exert a major influence on the organisation. Typically this group would include shareholders, providers of finance, suppliers, and supply-chain partners such as distributors and, of course, customers. Ultimately it is the response of the customer that will have the greatest influence on the success or failure of a marketing plan. Their likely reactions will have been a major part of any market research prior to the framing of the plan and their continued opinions will be sought while the marketing objectives are being implemented and evaluated.

The business also needs to consider the fact that other external groups could have a marked impact on the plan, and their reactions are far less easy to predict. Typically this would focus on the competition and

how they respond once they have seen that the business has taken a different turn as far as marketing strategy is concerned.

Some established competitors may not necessarily feel that their position will be adversely affected by the actions of the business; others will feel more threatened and may well implement contingency plans of their own in order to offset the negative impact that the business's new marketing initiatives have caused.

A business may encounter unforeseen circumstances or reactions as a result of implementing new marketing initiatives. For example, a business that has made the decision to sell direct to consumers for the

first time and not simply to rely on distributors and retailers may experience a violent reaction from these distributors and retailers. Understandably they will feel that their position is being threatened, they may look to the competition to supply them with similar products and services and they may even sever relations with the organisation.

The actual marketing plan and its consequences also have to be within legal parameters. A business cannot adopt a marketing strategy that makes unsubstantiated claims or will cause them difficulties with trading standards, government departments, the Advertising Standards Authority or the Office of Fair Trading.

CASE STUDY SHOCKVERTISING

This statement was made by Luciano Benetton:

'The purpose of advertising is not to sell more. It is to do with institutional publicity, whose aim is to communicate the company's values. We need to convey a single strong image, which can be shared anywhere in the world.'

In the last few years Benetton has been one of the businesses that have caused great controversy by using photographs of cemeteries, priests and nuns kissing, AIDS sufferers and soldiers' clothes covered in blood to promote their brand name.

Question

Using the Internet, find out more about this style of advertising, whether it works and how people respond to it.

Issues in implementing marketing plans

Common implementation problems

It is not always just the implementation of a marketing plan that could present a major problem. Often it is the initial design. There are a number of identifiable problems in both design and implementation, including:

- Lack of support from the managing director, chief executive or senior management
- The fact that the business has not actually planned for the planning
- A lack of line management support, which could mean hostility, lack of skills and information, lack of resources and a poor overall organisational structure
- Confusion about terms used in the planning
- The fact that the plan may have focused more on forecasting figures than setting out written objectives and strategies
- The plan was too detailed and looked too far ahead
- The plan was seen as a yearly ritual, to be endured but not to be implemented
- The fact that the business may have separated operational planning from strategic planning
- The marketing plan was not integrated into the total corporate plan
- Responsibility for implementing parts of the plan was given to people lacking the skills to do the job

One of the major reasons why marketing planning fails is that businesses tend to put too great an emphasis on procedures and paperwork, rather than generating the information that can be used to inform real decision-making. Many businesses actually hand marketing planning over to a planner who has little real knowledge of the operational realities of the business. If a planner is involved, they should work in conjunction with those responsible for implementing the plan.

Many plans also fail because businesses try to do too much too quickly. They often attempt this without having trained their staff in the use of procedures, or they may not have provided them with sufficient resources.

Implementation, monitoring and budgets

Marketing plans are worthless if they do not encourage actions. The implementation is the steps and activities that are needed to bring the plans to life. Implementation should include detailed scheduling of planning activities, detailed timetables, staffing and budgeting. They all need to be designed in order to make sure that the plans are effectively implemented. So, for a plan to work all the necessary structures need to be in place, including people, budgets and processes.

Broad objectives and strategies need to be translated into actions. The detailed actions need to have someone assigned to them. They need to know when and what costs are involved. This raises the issue of marketing budgets, because obviously without the necessary supporting financial resources there is no chance that a marketing plan will be successfully implemented. A marketing budget, of course, represents the resources that have been allocated to supporting a series of marketing activities over a period of time. The resources include human resources, facilities and time, but financial resources are also required. However, marketing budgets are not soley financial.

Usually there are four ways in which the budgets are determined:

- The affordable method – which aims to ensure that the business does not overspend and this usually means that the marketing budget is fairly modest
- Percentage of profits – the marketing department will negotiate a certain percentage of the profits, so the higher the profit the bigger the potential budget. However this method does not actually match up the benefits of particular objectives with the spending.
- Percentage of sales – this is usually based on a sales forecast and it is a widely used method. There is some logic to it, as the business seeks to match actual levels of activity with marketing spend.
- Objectives and tasks – budgets are allocated according to the total costs required to support the marketing plan. These are seen to be more realistic, as they reflect actual costs, but require that each activity is cost effective.

While large businesses may be able to cope with the costs of a failed marketing plan, it can be disastrous for small or medium-sized businesses. Equally it is important to realise that a marketing plan can fail even if it succeeds, if it costs several times more than it ends up generating in sales.

The problem for many businesses is that at the point at which it begins to implement a marketing plan it will begin to spend money. If there is no response to the spending then the business can easily stop incurring costs by terminating the marketing initiative. If there is a minimal or below forecast response then the business will be tempted to continue spending in the hope that more sales will be generated. The problem is to know when to stop or when to continue to invest.

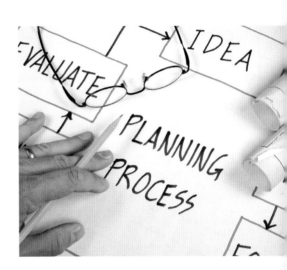

CASE STUDY FACEBOOK

The social networking site, Facebook, has recently been valued at an astonishing $15 billion. But is it really worth $15 billion, considering the fact that analysts believe that Facebook's own poor marketing plan is costing the business on average $1 billion of lost income in the last few years? There are at least sixty million online users and their marketing plan should produce between $5 and $10 in gross revenue per user. This should bring in between $300 million and $600 million per year, but in 2006, for example, their revenues were just $100 million. The poor marketing in Britain has seen the loss of 400,000 users in just the first three months of 2008. This is very bad news for Facebook. Similar drops have hit competitors such as Bebo and Myspace.

Questions

1 How would Facebook find out whether this is a problem of their making or an industry-wide problem? (*6 marks*)
2 Microsoft invested $240 million for a 1.6% share of Facebook. How might they view their investment now? (*6 marks*)

Case studies, questions and exam practice

CASE STUDY SPY AND CHIPS

In July 2003, the Tesco supermarket chain conducted some business research, in conjunction with Gillette, using a so-called 'smart shelf' system at its store in Cambridge. This entailed attaching a Radio Frequency Identification (RFID) microchip to packs of Gillette Mach 3 razor blades.

When a customer removed a pack of the blades from a shelf, the RFID chip would trigger a hidden camera to take a picture of the customer. When the razor pack was passed through the check-out counter, another photo was taken. The objective of capturing such a series of photos seems to be to identify people who

have picked up a razor pack but not paid for it through the check-out system. The RFID chips do not necessarily have to be linked to a camera or video recorder facility. However, the chips can be tracked outside the shop unless they are electronically neutralised at the checkout. A Tesco spokesperson has indicated that the research with the tags was very much of an exploratory nature. 'We are just looking at the benefits. It is blue-sky stuff. The camera use was a side project to look at the security benefit.' The police were reported to be impressed with the system but civil rights activists were less enthusiastic.

At one stage, Benetton was considering embedding RFID chips in some of its clothing but abandoned the idea in the face of customer unhappiness. A successful implementation of RFID technology has been at the Star City Casino in Sydney, Australia, where it has been embedded in employee uniforms to deter against theft. Currently there are strong sensitivities to the use of chips which trigger photos of customers purchasing feminine personal hygiene products.

In February 2005, the Brittan Elementary School in California, USA, attempted to implement RFID name tags so that it could monitor the whereabouts of its students during the day. However, the school was forced to withdraw the scheme because of parents objections based on the maintenance of civil liberties.

On the one hand, there is the argument that if you have done nothing wrong or are not planning to do anything wrong, there is nothing to hide. What is the problem if there are chips that can track your movements and whereabouts? On the other hand, there are equally valid arguments concerning the individual right to privacy.

The current situation seems to be that manufacturers and retailers have put aside their plans to attach RFID chips on products sold to consumers. Instead, the chip is being used for tracking bulk packages of stocks in warehouses. There is a vision that RFID chips might be incorporated into credit cards, mobile phones and other devices thereby providing people with the benefit of being able to buy a train ticket, pay for parking or get a drink from a vending machine without needing to have a handful of cash.

Whether RFID technology will be acceptable or not to consumers will depend on circumstances. If the risks

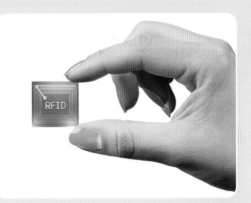

of crime and terrorism persist or increase, people may begin to accept the benefits of being able to keep track of people and things that might potentially be used as weapons.

Questions

1 How might a business justify the use of a new product development such as this and why might customers be reluctant to accept its introduction? (*8 marks*)

2 Radio frequency identification (RFID) technology provides a means of automatic identification. It is already widely used in animal tagging and electronic payment, such as Transport for London's Oyster cards. Many other potential applications such as improving supply chain efficiency and reducing crime are being investigated. Why might this be an ideal solution for businesses such as transport providers? (*4 marks*)

TOPIC 4 OPERATIONAL STRATEGIES

Introduction

Many of the key concepts that you will encounter in this topic will be familiar to you, as they build on factors that you looked at in AS Business Studies. This topic examines operational objectives and strategies, such as quality, production, economies and diseconomies of scale, innovation, location and lean production.

There are five main focus areas in this part of the unit, each of which examines a specific part of operations management and how it contributes to a business's ability to set and achieve its operational objectives.

The first focus area looks at understanding operational objectives. These could be quality, cost and volume targets, innovation, efficiency and, increasingly, environmental targets. The focus also considers the fact that operational objectives can be influenced by a number of different factors, including the type of product being produced, the demand, the resources available to the business and competitors' performance.

The second focus area looks at the first component of operational strategies: the scale and resource mix. This begins by examining how a business chooses an appropriate scale of production, which may give it economies of scale or make it face diseconomies of scale. It also looks at the benefits

and drawbacks of capital-intensive and labour-intensive strategies.

The second component of operational strategies – innovation – is dealt with in the third focus area. This examines how a business researches and develops products and services and the costs, benefits and risks of innovation. Innovating brings its own series of risks and implications, particularly for finance, marketing and human resources.

The next component of operational strategies is location and this is covered in the fourth focus area of this topic. Of particular importance is expansion and relocation and which methods might be used by a business in order to quantify the location options in financial terms, as well as qualitative considerations. This focus area will also look at international location, particularly in the light of global markets, avoiding trade barriers and cost reduction.

The final part of this topic looks at the last component of operational strategies – lean production. It will look at critical path networks, or critical path analysis. Of equal importance is the effective management of resources through lean production techniques, which include Just-In-Time production and Kaizen.

FOCUS ON UNDERSTANDING OPERATIONAL OBJECTIVES

- Operational objectives ▶ page 94
- Assessing internal and external influences on operational objectives ▶ page 96
- Case studies, questions and exam practice ▶ page 98

FOCUS ON SCALE AND RESOURCE MIX

- Choosing the right scale of production ▶ page 100
- Choosing the optimal mix of resources ▶ page 102
- Case studies, questions and exam practice ▶ page 104

FOCUS ON INNOVATION

- Innovation, research and development ▶ page 106
- Purpose, costs, benefits and risks of innovation ▶ page 108
- Case studies, questions and exam practice ▶ page 110

FOCUS ON LOCATION

- Methods of making location decisions ▶ page 112
- Benefits of optimal location ▶ page 114
- Advantages and disadvantages of multi-site locations ▶ page 116
- International locations ▶ page 118
- Case studies, questions and exam practice ▶ page 120

FOCUS ON LEAN PRODUCTION

- Time management ▶ page 122
- Critical path analysis ▶ page 124
- Time management of resources ▶ page 126
- Case studies, questions and exam practice ▶ page 128

Operational objectives

LEARNING
OBJECTIVES

▶ What is operations management?
▶ Operations management and stakeholders
▶ Quality
▶ Speed and dependability
▶ Flexibility and cost

What is operations management?

Formerly, operations management was known as production management and was applied almost exclusively to the manufacturing sector. In many organisations, the term 'production management' is still used, though in most of these the management function related to manufacturing has broadened to incorporate many other aspects related to the supply chain. The term 'operations management' is used to describe activities related to both manufacturing and, increasingly, the service sector. At its heart, operations management deals with the design of products and services, the buying of components or services from suppliers, the processing of those products and services, and the selling of the finished goods. Across all these disparate areas of business, operations management can be seen as an overarching discipline that seeks to quantify and organise the whole process. Nonetheless, there is still a considerable emphasis placed on issues directly related to manufacturing, stock control and, to a lesser extent, the management of the distribution systems. A large manufacturing organisation will include aspects of operations management under a wide variety of different, but closely related managerial disciplines. Primarily, Human Resources, Marketing, Administration and Finance and, of course, the Research and Development department of an organisation, are mutually dependent upon the Operations division.

Given the wide spread of different job roles and tasks within operations management, it is notoriously difficult to give a perfect definition of what operations managers actually do. Certainly they are responsible for a wide range of different functions, but the functions themselves will often be determined by the nature of the business – whether it is a service-based industry or an organisation primarily concerned with manufacturing.

Operations management can be broadly described as being the activities that produce and deliver products and services. All organisations have operations management because they all produce a mixture of products and services.

In larger organisations the term operations management will be generally used, whereas in smaller businesses the role is often performed by individuals who also do other jobs, such as accounting or marketing.

Operations management is important because it has an impact on the cost of producing products and services. In turn this has an impact on revenue and, therefore, on costs.

Operations management and stakeholders

There are various groups, both within the organisation and beyond, which have an interest in or are affected by operations management, these include:

- customers
- suppliers
- shareholders
- employees
- society

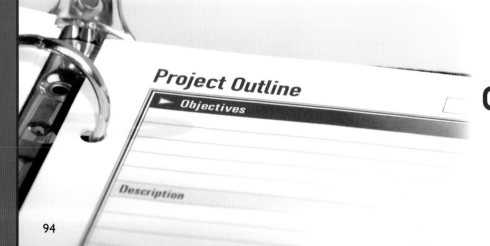

To see what influence these stakeholders have in a business's operational objectives see Assessing internal and external influences on operational objectives on pp. 96–7.

Quality

Quality is usually placed at the top of the list in terms of operations objectives and certainly much more has been written and said about quality than about any other aspect of operations management. Quality is much to do with the term 'conformance'. This simply means that a product or service conforms to the specifications or requirements that have been set down by the business, in terms of the quality of that product or service and what it can do.

Obviously the external effect of good quality is that consumers continue to purchase the products and services, and, if they conform to the specifications, then the customers will continue to consume them and bring in revenue to the business. Internally it is slightly more complicated, but as long as products and services conform to quality standards, fewer mistakes are made and the products and services are considered to be more dependable.

Speed and dependability

Essentially speed means speed of response, or the time taken between a customer asking for a product or service and them receiving it. As far as external influences are concerned it is important for the business to be able to respond quickly, as this is often viewed in a positive light by customers and they are more likely to return to the business to purchase on another occasion. Swift response also means that the business could probably charge slightly higher prices. Internally, speed also has a cost implication: fast throughput in manufacturing, for example, can mean reduced costs. Even in services, such as an airport, processing passengers through a terminal gate reduces the turnaround time of the aircraft.

Dependability essentially means providing products and services on time. But actually defining what 'on time' means is difficult. It may mean when delivery is expected or when it was promised, or even when it was promised the second time after the first delivery failed. Dependability is important to most customers; it is often the most important criteria when choosing a supplier. Again dependability has an internal impact on cost. Dependability saves time, money, and provides the business with a level of stability that allows it to become more efficient.

Flexibility and cost

Flexibility can also mean many different things. But essentially it is the notion of being able to change the operation in some way if required. This could mean product or service flexibility, volume flexibility or delivery flexibility. Externally, customers will expect the business to be relatively flexible, perhaps to incorporate new ideas that customers have suggested, or for the business to be able to cope with unexpected changes in demand and still deliver products and services on time. Internally, it means being able to speed up response to new demands. Flexibility also saves time and money and helps maintain dependability.

The cost structure of different organisations differs and there are many different categories of costs. If a business is managed properly and produces high quality at a high speed as well as being dependable and flexible, then costs are inevitably driven down. It is important to remember that these four performance objectives will always contribute to costs. Getting them wrong usually results in higher costs.

Cost-volume analysis focuses on the relationships between cost, revenue and volume of output. It is one of the common methods used in the evaluation of capacity planning. Variables used in the analysis are:

FC = Fixed cost
VC = Variable cost per unit
TC = Total cost
TR = Total revenue
R = Revenue per unit
Q = Quantity or volume of output
Q_{bep} = Break-even quantity
P = Profit

The assumptions of cost-volume analysis are:

- One product is involved.
- Everything produced is sold.
- The variable cost per unit is the same regardless of the volume.
- Fixed costs do not change with volume changes (or they are step changes).
- The revenue per unit is the same regardless of volume.

The cost-volume analysis is therefore the total cost (TC), which is the sum of the fixed cost (FC) and the variable cost per unit (VC), multiplied by the output volume (Q), or:

$$TC = FC + VC \times Q$$

Questions

1 What do you understand by the term 'operations management'? (*2 marks*)
2 In an organisation that does not have a distinct operations management team, where would the responsibilities lie in meeting operations objectives? (*8 marks*)

Assessing internal and external influences on operational objectives

Competitors' performance

Just as there can be many different types of operational objectives, there can also be many different ways in which competitors' performance can be measured. This has a great deal to do with trying to obtain a competitive advantage in at least one or two areas, as can be seen in the following table:

FOR EXAMPLE

In fashion retailing, customers want a broad range of styles, qualities and colours. Some are willing to pay more for premium or exclusive styles and quality, and retailers want reliable and speedy suppliers. In terms of the competition it is easy to enter the market, and there is a high concentration of similar retailers in the same areas. Some of the competitors have strong buying power and others use price or non-price competition. The key success factors are to combine a customised service for customers with a low-cost operation, to be able to respond quickly to changes in styles and fashions, to listen to customers and to have low overhead and labour costs.

Competitive advantage	Operational objective or policy	Operational requirements
Products and services that satisfy the widest possible range of customers	Flexibility	Versatile organisation and labour, rapid changeovers, broad range of products and flexible working systems
More sophisticated and advanced products and services	Technology	High use of research and development, good use of technology, excellent project management skills
High-quality products and services	Quality	Error-free processes and systems, good quality assurance and controls
Faster delivery time and shorter waiting times for customers	Speed	Fast throughput, good capacity, shorter queues, specialised work systems
Lowest price	Cost	High productivity and use of resources, limited standardised range, low stock levels
Highly serviceable products	Reliability	Good systems and resource maintenance, rapid response to problems with new products and services, high process quality
Fast response time to new customer requirements	Responsiveness	Rapid new product development
Consistent good service	Dependability	Ability to repeat processes and systems at a high level

Resources

As with almost any activity undertaken by a business, their success or failure very much depends upon the resources that are available to them. This is not strictly limited to financial resources, although this does play an important role in being able to fund the necessary machinery, processes and training. The more important consideration is the actual utilization of the resources that are available to the business.

Resource utilisation is an entire subject in itself, concerned with the maximum utilisation of machinery, labour and materials. Even if the resources available to the business are limited, maximum utilisation of what is available makes the business more efficient and ultimately more profitable. For example, it reduces the amount of time that machines lie idle, ensures that correctly trained employees are doing the right jobs to match their skills and, in terms of materials, ensures that wastage is reduced and that only materials required are ordered and stored.

Nature of the product

As we will see when we look at the capital-intensive and labour-intensive strategies, the exact nature of the product or service being produced will have a marked impact on the operational objectives. Some products and services are far more time- or labour-intensive to deliver to the customer. This means that they take longer to produce, longer to sell and have more implications in terms of ongoing customer support and service.

Other products and services are simpler. They are relatively quick to produce, and quick to sell and have very few after-sales implications. Businesses must therefore try to match their operational objectives with the nature of the product itself. This also means that some products have to be sold or processed in a specific period of time, otherwise their value is lost. This is while others can be made over a period of time and then stored until required.

For more about capital and labour-intensive strategies see Choosing the optimal mix of resources *on pp. 102–3.*

> **FOR EXAMPLE**
>
> *The operational challenges for a strawberry farm and a major airline are in fact very similar. The strawberry farmer has a narrow window in which the fruit becomes ripe, can be picked and then processed. The airline knows that at a specific time on a specific day an aircraft will leave. This is regardless of whether they have sold one seat or every seat on the aircraft. The nature of both the farmer's and the airline's products and services means that their operational objectives are determined by the nature of what they sell.*

Demand

In many respects demand is the ultimate determinant of any operational objective. On the one hand the business seeks to supply enough products or services to meet the forecasts of demand. On the other hand it should retain a degree of excess capacity in order to step up supply if demand unexpectedly increases.

By overestimating demand, however, the business may be overproducing and will therefore be left with products or services that it cannot sell. Fluctuations in demand are always inevitable as they are influenced by so many other different factors. As we have seen, competitors can have a marked impact on the demand for products and services. Equally, the resources available to a business may determine the level of supply that it can achieve.

There are many other external factors that influence demand, for example: the availability of other products, interest rates, inflation, levels of disposable income, seasonality and a host of other possibilities. One of the key issues in operations management is to be able to match potential demand as closely as possible with a capacity to produce at that level, with some flexibility. It also means that the business needs to be assured that it can maintain production at a variety of different levels while also maintaining its operational objectives, including profitability.

> **Questions**
>
> 1 How might the nature of a product have an impact on the business's operational objectives? (*4 marks*)
> 2 How might a business compare itself to a competitor's performance? (*4 marks*)

Case studies, questions and exam practice

CASE STUDY JAGUAR

Jaguar Cars was originally known as the Swallow Sidecar Company and was founded in 1922. In 1990 Jaguar was bought by Ford. At the time Jaguar was well known for its high-quality performance, however even the most enthusiastic supporters of the company had to admit that their cars were extremely poor in terms of reliability. For years the business had suffered from under-investment. It was technically led rather than customer led. The problem was that the company's old production facilities were struggling to meet increasing demands for quality. In a customer survey in America only one other manufacturer scored lower than Jaguar in terms of customer satisfaction. All this changed with the arrival of Ford's money. The company could begin to invest in training, especially in high-quality areas. Payment systems such as piece work were abandoned and so too was clocking in. From now on there would be a general productivity bonus and flexible working would be encouraged. New multi-skilled teams were created,

as well as continuous improvement teams and the business began benchmarking itself against the best in the industry. Changes encouraged Ford to make further investments and new models were developed. Customer satisfaction soared. Jaguar had once been at the bottom of the league and now it was at the very top.

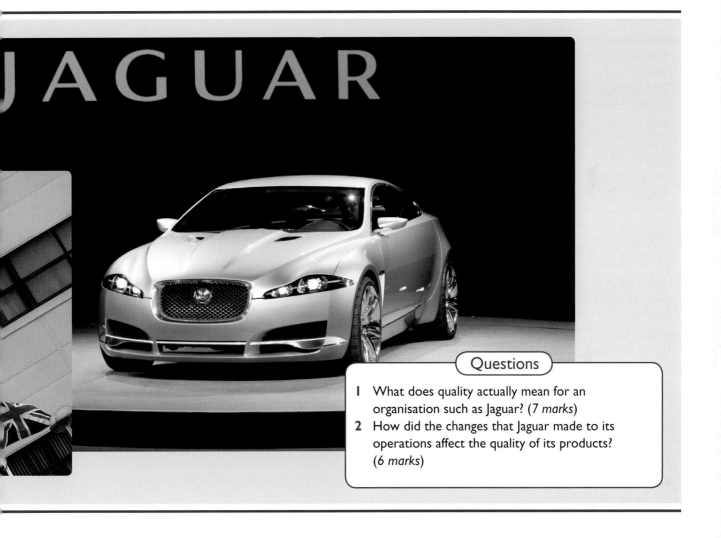

Questions

1. What does quality actually mean for an organisation such as Jaguar? (*7 marks*)
2. How did the changes that Jaguar made to its operations affect the quality of its products? (*6 marks*)

Choosing the right scale of production

LEARNING OBJECTIVES

▶ Economies of scale
▶ Diseconomies of scale

Economies of scale

Strictly speaking, the term economies of scale is an economics related issue. However, it has considerable implications in terms of operations management and production. The basic concept is that a business needs to build up a critical mass. In other words, it needs to be large enough to be able to enjoy the benefits associated with larger-scale production. Once a business has reached a point where it is a larger trading entity, it can enjoy many of the benefits associated with larger-scale production or distribution. In other words, as the size and scope of the business increases, the generally held view is that the unit costs are driven down. Having achieved economies of scale, a greater amount of funds are available to further improve the market position and efficiency of the business.

The table on the right outlines some of the key economies of scale that can be derived from the size of the business.

Economy	Explanation
Bulk buying	When businesses grow larger they increase their average order to suppliers. The large orders are very valuable to suppliers and there is a greater opportunity cost if they were to lose the order. This gives the buying business considerable leverage to demand discounts.
Technical	As a business grows it will have the ability to invest in new technology. By using more and more machinery the business is able to generate cost savings. The latest machinery is less wasteful. Ultimately, this will cut the business's variable costs.
Managerial	Larger businesses can afford to employ more specialised managers. Smaller businesses tend to have to use management that has a broader range of skills but not in any particular depth. Specialist managers should mean better quality decision-making.
Financial	Larger businesses are less of a risk to lenders, so it is easier for them to find potential lenders and pay lower rates of interest.
Marketing	Larger businesses can spread the costs of marketing across many thousands or millions of unit sales. This cuts the cost of marketing per unit.
Risk reduction	If a large business is able to diversify into producing different products and services and enter new markets, they will be less dependent on single products or services compared to smaller businesses. Large businesses can achieve diversification quickly by takeovers and mergers.
Capacity utilisation	Capacity utilisation is a measure of the current output as a percentage of the total theoretical or maximum output possible. By increasing capacity utilisation, fixed costs are spread out over more units, reducing the total cost per unit.

KEY TERMS

Bottleneck – a system, or a part of a system, that prevents the business from reaching levels of production that are demanded.

Lead-time – the length of time that a business takes to produce a product or component from the point that it was ordered by a customer.

Diseconomies of scale

Diseconomies of scale arise when a manufacturing process simply becomes too large and the normal rule of economies of scale ceases to apply. In certain cases, as capacity continues to increase, the manufacturing organisation may encounter the problem of average unit costs increasing, rather than falling. There are usually three reasons for this, these are:

- The different processes within the manufacturing process may have already reached their optimum *capacity* and they are unable to produce any more products, thus causing difficulties for other processes which are capable of a higher rate of production. This means that various parts of the production process are literally starved of parts and components by these bottlenecks.
- As the organisation grows, there are attendant difficulties related to the coordination of activities. To support the production process there is an attendant increase in administration and a proliferation of bureaucratic procedures which may inhibit the production process itself, while adding indirect costs to each unit of production.
- Under the assumption that the capacity levels of the organisation could, up to a point, be supplied by other organisations within a viable geographical area, as production increases the manufacturing organisation may

need to cast its net wider in order to secure sufficient supply. The company may also need to make compromises on the lead-times, quality and delivery costs of these supplies from the additional suppliers. All these issues will add cost overall, which in turn is applied to each unit of production.

Diseconomies of scale, therefore, occur as a mixture of internal and external diseconomies.

There are three main reasons why large businesses may face diseconomies of scale. The table below outlines these three sets of circumstances and suggests ways in which the business could deal with them.

Diseconomy	Explanation	Action needed
Employee motivation	If motivation is low then this is probably as a result of there being little contact between the employees and the management. Larger businesses may not view employees as individuals, but as merely parts of a larger business machine. Poorly motivated staff work less hard, absentee rates are higher, output falls and labour costs per unit rise.	Decision-making needs to be delegated, job enrichment programmes introduced and the business could be split up by creating profit and cost centres.
Communication	If communication up and down and across the organisation is poor, then the employees will feel that they are out of the communications loop. Larger organisations tend to use written communication rather than verbal communication. Written communication is more easy to ignore and usually generates less feedback.	The business needs to use similar techniques as for the improvement of employee motivation, and create new communication structures, such as work councils.
Coordination	In smaller businesses coordination is relatively straightforward. The larger the business, the more difficult it is to control. Managers tend to find that if they do not delegate then they become overwhelmed with work. It is difficult for everyone to focus on the same goals and follow through the same strategies. Large meetings are expensive and can be ineffective.	The business needs to decentralise, empower employees and encourage managers to cope with wider spans of control.

> ## Questions
>
> 1 Why might many businesses fall into the trap of creating diseconomies of scale even though they have been successful in growing? (*10 marks*)
> 2 At which point will a business be able to enjoy the lowest cost of production? (*2 marks*)

Choosing the optimal mix of resources

Labour-intensive

A labour-intensive process is one that requires a relatively high level of labour to carry it out. The processes that are used by a labour-intensive business tend to be focused on producing individual or personalised products on a relatively small scale. The amount of labour used will affect wages, benefits, recruitment and training.

The principal problem is capacity flexibility. In labour-intensive operations, overtime and the use of temporary staff has to be used to cope with increased demand. Suppressed or reduced demand means that the business may have to reduce the working hours of employees or permanently make them redundant.

For businesses that are reliant upon labour-intensive operations their long-term growth is often determined by their ability to recruit sufficiently experienced and skilled employees. Labour-intensive processes tend to be used for job production in many smaller-scale enterprises.

Labour-intensive businesses are obviously exposed to wage increases. It is difficult for businesses to forecast their wage bills as they are inevitably influenced by industry and economic factors. Businesses that find it difficult to manage their labour-intensive operations often try to reduce their dependency by either outsourcing some of the work or by gradually introducing machinery.

Capital-intensive

A capital-intensive business uses relatively heavy capital investment to buy assets, typically machinery. The capital refers to machinery, vehicles and equipment.

The business's levels of capital investment are high compared to their labour costs. In most cases the businesses are on a fairly large scale and use highly automated processes. As expensive equipment is being purchased, a capital-intensive business is more likely to be involved with flow production. It will try to ensure that it maximises efficiency by getting as close to full capacity utilisation as possible.

One of the problems with switching levels of production is that it is both costly and time-consuming. Setting up costs is high, both in terms of the expertise needed and the fact that the production line will be down and inoperative while the changes are being made.

A capital-intensive business has to make a long-term investment, so there are additional concerns about financing. Added to this, the equipment is likely to depreciate at a fairly rapid rate. Generally, equipment costs represent a substantial overhead. There will therefore be a substantial amount of fixed assets on the business's balance sheet.

As the cost of introducing equipment to the production process is high, there are relatively high barriers to entry. This means it is difficult for a business that has been labour-intensive to switch over to capital-intensive operations owing to the amount of investment needed.

Capital-intensive businesses can, however, reduce the amount of capital they need to finance the equipment that they must use. Usually this is achieved by leasing or renting assets rather than purchasing them outright.

Managing capacity and resources

A simple definition of capacity is that it is the maximum rate of output for a given process. It is usually measured in output per unit of time. Businesses will tend to use different units of time in order to calculate their capacity, such as per minute, per hour, per day or per shift. In truth, the maximum capacity is much better described as being the demonstrated capacity, as this is the true level of capacity achieved. Some organisations and analysts will attempt to calculate a theoretical capacity, which is largely based on the capacity of the machines involved and rarely takes into account any variables which may affect the capacity. Businesses will attempt to operate at their optimum capacity. This means that they will attempt to reduce costs or loss of capacity associated with waiting time.

An organisation's capacity cushion is equal to the amount of capacity it has in excess of expected demand. It is normally calculated using the following formula:

$$\frac{\text{capacity} - \text{expected demand}}{\text{expected demanded}}$$

The figure is expressed as a percentage. Normally the higher the level of uncertainty that the organisation has in terms of future demand, the larger the capacity cushion. Organisations that wish to be able to respond quickly to customer demand will build in a sizeable capacity cushion, enabling them to quickly increase the productivity of the production lines to soak up that new demand. Businesses with standard products and a high level of capital intensity tend to have smaller capacity cushions in order to offset the fixed costs of the equipment they use.

Capacity focus revolves around the notion that a manufacturing facility tends to believe that it works best when it focuses on a fairly limited set of production objectives. In other words, the organisation should not attempt or expect to excel in every aspect of manufacturing performance.

This means that the organisation should concentrate on a fairly limited range of goals (cost, quality, flexibility, new product development, reliability, shorter lead times or low investment) and not all of these issues. It should choose the goal that most closely matches its organisational objectives.

As manufacturing technology has become more advanced and the competition more fierce, there is an increasing trend for organisations to attempt to do everything well and have multiple objectives. It is, however, also true that in certain sectors a business does not have to be excellent on all issues in order to compete effectively.

The capacity focus concept can be achieved by having plants within plants (PWPs). Each of the PWPs will not only have separate sub-organisations, but will also use different equipment and process policies. They will also be able to institute different workforce management policies and production control methods. In this way, the desire to achieve efficiency and excellence in every area can be achieved in part by excellence in one of the PWPs.

Capacity management is the discipline that ensures that infrastructure is provided at the right time in the right volume at the right price. It also ensures that all the inputs are used in the most efficient way.

Capacity management also involves input from various areas of the business, including the infrastructure to support the services, contingencies and the associated costs. Typically, the inputs related to capacity management include:

- performance monitoring
- workload monitoring
- application sizing
- resource forecasting
- demand forecasting
- modelling

These processes create the results of capacity management, in other words, the plan itself, the forecasts, data and level of service guidelines.

Questions

1 How can capacity be calculated? (*4 marks*)
2 What do you understand by the term 'capacity cushion'? (*2 marks*)

Case studies, questions and exam practice

CASE STUDY BROWN SUGAR

There are two categories of brown sugar: those produced directly from the cane juice at the place of origin and those produced during the refining of the raw sugar. The first type includes a variety of molasses and syrups, Demerara, muscovado and turbinado sugars. The second type is coated brown or 'soft' sugars, manufactured Demerara, and a variety of refinery molasses and golden syrups.

Those produced directly from the cane juice at the place of origin can be made using relatively low-cost and low-technology processes suitable for small-scale production. However, this level of production still requires experience, skill and knowledge to be successful.

The refined brown sugars are produced in modern vacuum pan (VP) sugar factories which are capital-intensive, have high throughputs and are not suitable for small-scale production.

The brown sugar types can be further divided into those where the crystals are separated (centrifuged) and those that are not separated (non-centrifuged) from the molasses.

Scale	Cane processed/ day	Type of enterprise
Small	up to 50 tonnes	Cottage and small village industry using traditional technology
Medium	50 to 500 tonnes	Small- to medium-sized enterprise using modified traditional, OPS or small-scale VP technology
Large	500 tonnes upwards	Large industry using modern VP technology

Small-scale brown sugar production

The following sugars can be produced using relatively simple low-cost technologies and are currently in use in India, Pakistan, Bangladesh, East Africa and South America. In all cases these sugars can also be produced in medium and large factories.

Syrups

Syrup is a liquid sugar made using relatively simple production processes. The cane is crushed using roller-type crushers extracting the juice and discharging the waste residue. The juice is collected in containers and allowed to stand for a few hours before use, to allow particles to precipitate out. The juice is then poured into the boiling pan through a coarse cotton cloth to filter out remaining particles.

The juice is boiled until the required concentration is reached at around 105°C when most of the moisture has been boiled off and crystallisation begins. The viscous juice (massecuite) is then removed, a step known as the 'strike', and allowed to cool before bottling.

Non-centrifugal sugars

In Asia, Africa and South America non-centrifugal sugars are made for direct consumption and are known by a range of names: *gur* in India and Bangladesh, *desi* in Pakistan, *jaggery* in Africa, and *panela* in South America. These sugars are a concentrated product of the cane juice without separation of the molasses and crystals. They can vary from golden brown to dark brown in colour and contain up to 50% sucrose, up to 20% invert sugars, moisture content of up to 20%, and the remainder made up of other insoluble matter such as ash, proteins and bagasse fines.

Khandsari

Khandsari is a basic raw crystalline sugar, developed in India, that has been separated from most of the molasses. It varies in colour from golden-yellow to brown and contains between 94% and 98% sucrose.

Khandsari is produced by the small- to medium-scale sector and has a considerable market in India. At its most basic, it is manufactured using simple animal-drawn crushers, is subjected to simple clarification, boiled to the consistency of a thick syrup, and allowed to stand until sugar crystals are formed. The small crystals are then separated in manually operated centrifuges and sun-dried.

At the other end of the scale, the production plant can use diesel or electrically driven crushers, crystalliser to ensure even formation of crystals, power-driven centrifuges, and forced-air driers to dry the product. Factories processing between one and two hundred tonnes of cane per day are common, yielding between 6.5 and 13 tonnes per day respectively.

Medium-scale brown sugar production

Medium-scale sugar processing can use either relatively low-cost, labour-intensive open pan sulphitation (OPS) technology or modern vacuum pan (VP) technology. Although OPS is a low-cost technology compared to VP technology, it still requires substantial capital investment in plant and equipment.

The following brown sugars are normally produced using modern VP plants but could be produced using OPS technology.

Demerara sugar

Named after the area in Guyana where it was first produced, Demerara is a centrifuged sugar prepared from the first crystallisation of cane syrup and has large yellow crystals and a slightly sticky texture. Production of this sugar is not suitable for the small sector as the juice needs to be carefully clarified to ensure purity, and crystallisers are required to ensure uniform grain size.

Muscovado

Also known as Barbados sugar, muscovado is the product of the third crystallisation. It is dark brown in colour with small grains and a sticky texture.

A by-product of both the OPS and VP scale of production, it tends to be produced as an alternative to white sugar if the standard is not very high.

Large-scale brown sugar production

Large-scale sugar production is anything over 500 tonnes of cane processed per day and uses modern VP technology. However, due to the high capital cost of the technology it is usual for plants to be capable of processing at least 1000 tonnes of cane per day.

Refinery brown sugars

All of these sugars are produced during the refining of raw sugars and are known as 'soft' sugars because their small, free-flowing grains give the impression of a soft texture. These are produced by boiling crystals from a dark massecuite or by coating refined sugar with a thin film of molasses, known as painted or London brown sugars (where the system was first developed). In some cases, caramel and invert sugars are added in small amounts to enhance the colour and texture. These sugars tend to be produced by the large-scale white sugar manufactures and not by the small to medium-scale producers.

Source: adapted from Practical Action

Questions

1   Identify which of the sugar production process are capital-intensive or labour-intensive, and explain why. (*10 marks*)
2   Why might certain types of production not be appropriate or possible in under-developed countries? (*6 marks*)

Innovation, research and development

Innovation

The quest for growth through innovation is stronger than ever. Businesses scramble to find the next blockbuster development in order to achieve their ambitious growth goals. There is never any shortage of imaginative, creative, differentiated and profitable new products and services. The problem is the cost of developing them and the time it takes to go from idea to launch.

Innovation can be described as the successful exploitation of new ideas. Often it will involve new technologies or new applications. It should deliver better products and services, more efficient production and processes, and improved business models. It should also mean higher quality, better value products and services, and businesses that can enjoy sustained, improved growth.

Britain ranks fourth in the world (after the USA, France and Germany) for its expenditure on research and development, which, as we will see, lies behind the creation of innovative products and services.

Usually there are two ways in which the level of innovation can be measured. These are:

- the actual spending on research and development by businesses
- the number of patents successfully applied for

In terms of the second measure, Britain lies well behind Japan and America and is slightly behind the EU average.

Research and development (R&D)

New product development, and the bright ideas associated with such an endeavour, must be tempered with the practicalities of production. While many good ideas appear to be workable on paper, the realities of the situation may mean that the product cannot be produced in a cost-effective and efficient manner.

An organisation has to assess whether it is looking for a new product which its current production process is capable of producing. It would serve no purpose for an organisation to develop an idea for a new product only to discover that the actual production process has to be carried out elsewhere, possibly by subcontractors or business partners. After all, one of the key considerations in developing new products, regardless of their design, is that the organisation should make full use of its production facilities.

The design of new products is often changed gradually as design problems are identified and solved. This process, although not enjoyable for the designer, needs to be considered in terms of efficiency and overall benefit to the organisation. Whether the design process is undertaken by the organisation itself or by external organisations, the business must ensure that it carries out feasibility studies at the earliest possible stage to ensure that resources are not wasted in the development of a new product design when there is no likelihood of that product being produced in a cost-effective way. This screening process

needs to be rigorously enforced to make sure that the business does not invest in product design that is impractical and that will never come to fruition. The development of new products can be not only time-consuming but expensive. The desire to develop new products should be tempered by an awareness that many small businesses fail as a result of over-investing in new product development. And only a small percentage of new products is ever successful. However, the success of new products is central to the long-term success and growth of an organisation. It is imperative for an organisation to plan its new product development using the following steps:

- Allow an initial screening period in which an investigation is carried out to assess how the product fits in with current products and services.
- Investigate whether the new product could be produced using current production methods.
- Test the production process.
- Fully cost the production process.
- Carry out the necessary market research.
- Produce a test batch of new products and test-market them.

However, the long-term success of a new product or service depends upon it meeting customer requirements:

- Initial market research will have to identify the specific needs of the customer and the product, or design around these needs
- The business will have to be able to consistently provide the same quality level of product or service, regardless of output or demand

Research and development is therefore vital. But investment in research does not necessarily mean that the product or service will be successful.

Obviously research and development takes place before the product or service is launched. The business is spending money without actually earning anything for it, which causes cash-flow problems. This means that a business needs to think long and hard about its research and development spending. A truly innovative product or service can give a competitive advantage. Examples are the pyramid-shaped teabag, the ticketless airline, and razors with additional features and comfort.

Businesses need to think ahead, invest money and take risks, knowing both that they could be wasting funds, and that there are opportunity costs involved. How much a business spends on research and development will depend on its overall strategy. In fast-changing markets the demand for new products is high and the need for businesses to spend on research and development is also high. This is a combination of customer demand and the knowledge that if a business does not carry out research and development and bring out innovative products, its competitors will.

There can be no absolute guarantees with research and development. There is no direct link between spending on research and development and the creation of successful, innovative products and services. This leads some businesses to consider whether they can afford to take the risk of research and development. They may lack internally generated funds, so any research and development will have to be funded by external finance.

CASE STUDY DIRECT AIR DRIERS

The UK insurance industry spends £1.5 billion per year on flood restoration. The cost of flood damage across the country in recent years has reached as much as £2 billion. Direct Air Driers Ltd has produced a revolutionary new product that reduces drying time by half. It is lightweight and easy to install and manage.

Questions

1 The product is not only an innovative one, but it is also environmentally friendly. How might this be the case? (*4 marks*)
2 Up to 27,000 homes and 5,000 businesses are affected by flooding each year. How might this product be of benefit to the general economy? (*6 marks*)

Purpose, costs, benefits and risks of innovation

LEARNING
OBJECTIVES
▶ Purposes and benefits
▶ Costs and risks

Purposes and benefits

Not all businesses can necessarily afford to invest in research and development and produce innovative products. But there are considerable benefits to an organisation that chooses to do this, as can be seen in the table below.

Costs and risks

The research and design process can be time-consuming and extremely expensive. As we have seen, there is no absolute guarantee that the product or service will either work or will find a market at a price that is acceptable to both the manufacturer

and the consumer. There is also the danger that the business may find that its products or services are quickly copied by competitors. If the innovation is genuinely new then the business would be advised to purchase a patent in order to protect it. This effectively means that the owner of the patent has the sole right

Benefit	Explanation	Examples
New products	If a business can produce a genuinely new product or service then it will be able to enjoy a competitive advantage. If the business can also obtain a patent for this new product then it will be in a position to be able to sell it without it being imitated for a period of time. This can mean that the business can charge a premium price and make a higher profit.	Dyson's bagless vacuum cleaners
New materials	New man-made materials are able to be put to far more extreme uses than natural resources. They may be durable, cheaper, lighter or heat resistant. This is a general benefit, as it reduces the demand for natural resources and puts less environmental pressure on the planet.	DuPont's lightweight fabric has great strength and has dominated the ski-wear market
New production techniques	Rather than focus on products and services for end-users, some businesses focus on the production of new machinery to improve other manufacturers' outputs. The introduction of computer-controlled machinery, for example, helps cut costs and raise productivity. The machines are more efficient, safer and cleaner.	Machines that have been designed to improve the environment for employees and are more ergonomic
Improved image	Although research and development is risky, breakthroughs can provide the business with an enormous amount of positive publicity. Customers are often impressed by the fact that a business reinvests a considerable amount of its profits back into improving product design.	Drugs companies that spend millions developing cures and solutions to diseases and illnesses
Improved employee motivation	Research and development involves a great deal of creativity. If you recall, Abraham Maslow's theory of motivation, research and development can contribute towards esteem and self-actualisation.	If the research and development department is successful then a general sense of achievement will be felt across the whole of the organisation
Benefits to customers	Research and development means a wider range of products and services become available to the consumer. The introduction of new technology drives down costs and therefore prices. The use of technology also means better quality products using better quality materials.	New simple solutions to consumer problems can be developed and offered at a relatively low cost, such as corrective eye surgery, which in the past would have cost thousands of pounds but now costs hundreds

to the process or manufacture of the product for twenty years. This does not, however, mean that the product cannot be copied in some way.

As invention and innovation are long-term activities, businesses concerned with making short-term profits are unlikely to take the risk of spending money on innovation. Businesses, however, that do take a broader view and are perhaps not as influenced by the short-term requirements of their investors, are more likely to spend heavily on research. However, most are constrained by the demands of shareholders for high dividend payments, which means that they cannot retain much profit for investment in research and development. This is not necessarily a particularly bad thing, as not many businesses are actually in a position where they need to produce innovative products and services through expensive research and development.

However, innovative ideas do not necessarily need to be expensive ones and neither do they really need to be massive leaps in technology, process or design. The vast majority of new products are actually adaptations or refinements of existing products or services. Many businesses prefer to take this approach, gradually adapting and improving the range of products and services they offer over a period of time. This not only gives the business the opportunity to make incremental investments in research and development, but it also gives customers an opportunity to gradually move over to more sophisticated products without having to be re-educated in the use of a radically new and innovative product design.

Critics of this approach may suggest that the businesses prefer incremental changes as they can sell and re-sell the product or service each time a minor improvement is made. There is, however, an enormous risk to this strategy: while making incremental changes, competitors may opt for a more drastic and all-encompassing leap in product design. This would leave the incremental organisation in a much weaker position, and the innovative one would adopt a dominant position.

CASE STUDY APPLE

Two enormous businesses – Apple and AT&T – found themselves being sued for purportedly stealing a patent on visual voicemail in March 2008. Apple's iPhone allows users to identify individual voicemail messages in their voicemail box and selectively listen to them using the iPhone interface, without having to go through all the messages to find the ones they want.

A business called Klausner Technologies claims that both Apple and AT&T infringed their patent of a 'telephone answering device linking displayed data with recorded audio message'. This was the second time that the New York based toymaker had tried to sue Apple over the voicemail technology.

Question

Why would losing this court battle be disastrous for an organisation such as Apple? (*6 marks*)

Case studies, questions and exam practice

CASE STUDY FREEMINER BREWERY

This case illustrates multiple innovation processes: a new product for a new distribution channel, with innovative packaging and labelling. A key ingredient in this process has been a sustained entrepreneurial mission: to get high-quality beers onto the dining table and to a status level with wine. A new product concept was developed to interest the large supermarkets, and its success means that high-quality beer from the Forest of Dean is now being consumed nationally and in ever-increasing volumes.

The post-war history of Britain's beer and ale industry is that it has experienced more than its fair share of consolidation. The large-scale promotion of premium brands, and vigorous price competition in the drinks industry, has had major effects, most notably a reduction in consumer choice as regional and local breweries have been acquired and closed.

One of the counter-trends to this process of consolidation and globalisation has been the proliferation of small-scale micro-breweries, typically founded and managed by brewing enthusiasts and serving the local market. In order to compete with the big brands, these brewers have tended to concentrate on the craft nature of their ale, often using a promotional strategy of unusual names to make their products distinctive.

Don Burgess founded the Freeminer Brewery – the name being based on the local tradition of independent mining in the Forest of Dean – some 13 years ago, and

has continuously developed the sales and reputation of its products over that time. During these years there have been many changes and challenges, including the relocation of the brewery and the catastrophic effect of the 2001 Foot and Mouth epidemic on the local market, as tourist visitors to the Forest of Dean simply disappeared. However, throughout all this change Don has maintained his driving commitment to the production of high-quality real ales and to educating consumers to understand and appreciate the complex qualities and variety of beers – in a nutshell, to achieve for beer an equal status with wine.

In the pursuit of this vision, Don had been looking for new distribution channels to a wider national market, for some time but this search was intensified after foot and mouth disease struck. He had long been aware of the importance of packaging and presentation and developed a complete new product concept with which to approach the national and regional supermarkets. This was the origin of the highly successful Gold Miner bottled beer.

In line with Don's mission, the central concept was for a high-quality naturally conditioned beer in an elegant bottle that would be attractive on a supermarket shelf and not look out of place on the dining table. A great deal of effort went into the design of the bottle and of the labelling: 'It's all about raising expectations' says Don. The labelling includes a high-quality printed label on the front and a particularly innovative 'double label' on the rear.

The double label concept was a solution to the problem of incorporating a lot of information on the provenance of the ingredients and the beer, as well as the supermarket requirements of bar-code and statutory information, while maintaining an uncluttered and sophisticated appearance. The problem was solved by developing the double label for the rear of the bottle, in which the outer layer that carries the statutory information can be peeled back to reveal the inner label that carries the educational details of the provenance of the malt, hops and water and of the brewing process.

The rest of the story is now history – great commercial success. Freeminer succeeded in persuading the Co-op supermarket chain to take Gold Miner Ale on a trial basis and the results were astounding, with the first year's sales target being exceeded within three months. Gold Miner is now reaching a national market in ever-increasing volumes. However, Don's appetite for innovation and his mission to push beer up the league table of sophistication and to roll back the homogenisation of food, drink and life in general, are undiminished.

Source: adapted from the University of Gloucester

Questions

1 What were the problems facing the brewery and how were they overcome? (*10 marks*)
2 How would you describe Don's mission? (*6 marks*)

Methods of making location decisions

Factors affecting location

New businesses in particular are faced with a major and difficult decision as to where to locate. The location will have a massive impact on the business's costs, its access to customers and markets and, ultimately, its income and profitability.

As we will see, location decisions can be broadly split into quantitative and qualitative factors. The quantitative factors relate primarily to costs and revenue, whereas the qualitative factors focus on other issues that are not so easy to put a monetary value on, such as quality of life.

There are many factors that could affect a business's location decision. These are outlined in the table on the right.

Quantitative factors

Quantitative analysis, related to location, focuses on the impacts on costs and revenues. A business will generally try to find a location that offers a financially attractive package. One of the ways in which it can do this is to use break-even analysis to demonstrate how many units it needs to sell in order to break even. This variation can incorporate the particular costs of a variety of different locations and see how this impacts on the break-even level of output.

Locational cost-profit-volume analysis is a statistical technique which is used to evaluate location options. The graphical assumptions

Factor	Explanation
Costs of the location	Costs of land or buildings can vary from area to area. Equally, additional costs, such as business rates, can vary. If the business is considering an international location then lower-cost employees can often make overseas locations more attractive.
Grants and incentives	Governments and local authorities may offer lower taxes or lower rents to attract businesses to locate in a particular region. Grants help draw businesses into an area.
Infrastructure	This incorporates the transport, energy and communications in a particular area. Good infrastructure will help push down costs of production, speed up distribution and make the business's operations easier.
The nature of the business	Some businesses that deal directly with consumers need to be close to their markets. Industries may need to be close to their raw materials. Service-based industries may not need to be near either their customers or their suppliers.
Market location	Some businesses need to be near their markets, either because they offer direct services or because their products benefit from being close to their customer base by reducing distribution costs, etc.
Market access	A business needs to be assured that it can get its products and services into the market without incurring additional and unnecessary costs.
Exchange rates	Overseas businesses will usually quote prices in their own currency, but if they are selling into other countries the actual value of the sale can be affected by fluctuations in the exchange rates.
Political and economic stability	Political uncertainty and economic disruption can adversely affect businesses, particularly if they feel that it is unwise to invest at a particularly uncertain time.
Availability of resources	This primarily refers to the availability of human resources, particularly potential employees that have a recognised level of qualifications, expertise or skills.
Company image	Certain areas have a degree of prestige attached to them and the business may wish to use this as a part of its overall corporate image.
Quality of life	This is a qualitative factor and it may be an important decision for the business to locate in an area that offers a good standard of living and is attractive and desirable.
Ethical issues	Some businesses will continue to invest and expand in areas with which they have long-standing associations. Others will avoid areas where wages are traditionally low, so that they are not seen to be exploiting the local workforce.

Example

Many businesses locate their manufacturing in the Far East for these reasons.

There are development agencies all around Britain with a variety of incentives to attract businesses.

The proximity of a good road network or spending on infrastructure projects can make areas attractive to businesses.

A retail outlet must be inside a large enough catchment area to draw in sufficient customers.

A retail outlet needs to be either in a high-street location or a retail park, rather than in a remote location.

Businesses located outside the EU are required to pay a tax to import their products and services into the region. Many overseas businesses (particularly the Japanese and Koreans) have set up production facilities for this reason.

A strong currency makes it difficult for home producers to export, whereas it is cheaper for them to purchase products made abroad, which they then import.

Terrorist threats in certain countries have made businesses reluctant to locate or invest.

Businesses that focus on innovation often locate close to major universities to recruit the best graduates and use the best research facilities.

The supermarket chain Waitrose tends to locate in more affluent areas. Fashion designers may wish to be associated with London, Paris or Milan.

Although many businesses have relocated to more rural areas, inner cities are becoming more attractive, with inward investments, such as Cardiff, Newcastle and parts of London.

Businesses such as Café Direct have long-standing associations with particular suppliers.

are that fixed costs will remain constant over a range of probable output and that variable costs are linear. The required level of output can then be estimated (usually one product is considered). The total cost lines for each alternative location are plotted onto the same graph, using the familiar fixed costs (FC) plus variable cost (VC) multiplied by quantity of output (Q) to calculate the total cost.

Investment appraisal is another quantitative technique, where the business can look at issues such as the average rate of return, net present value and expected payback period of particular location options. Naturally, businesses will tend to choose a location that offers them the highest net present value, the highest average rate of return and the quickest payback. However, a single location is never likely to offer all three advantages, and it may ultimately rest on other decision factors before the location is finally chosen.

Question

How important would the location decision be in determining the success of a retail clothes chain? (*15 marks*)

Benefits of optimal location

Qualitative factors

Although businesses may primarily focus on the quantitative factors in their location decision analysis, there are other important factors that may well be taken into account before the decision is finally made. Foremost is the appeal of any area and the quality of life it may offer. Equally, many overseas businesses have chosen to locate in Britain because English is the dominant business language in the world.

Other businesses may choose to locate in a particular area because it is already associated with that type of business or industry. In the US, film companies gravitate towards Los Angeles, as Hollywood is the film capital of the world. In Britain the Thames Valley is associated with high-tech industries and has often been referred to as Britain's Silicon Valley.

As we have already seen, some particular locations appear to give the business a boost in terms of their image. Many businesses will have small offices in London for this reason, despite the fact that their main production facilities are elsewhere.

Push and pull factors

We have already examined the key quantitative and qualitative factors. Many of them can be classified as being push or pull factors. A push factor can be described as a feature of a particular area that either makes it less attractive to a business or forces a business to consider relocation. In other words, there are few advantages to the business in either locating there or remaining there. Typical push factors include:

- increased competition
- rising costs
- poor communications
- falling sales

As a counterbalance there may be pull factors, which attract businesses to a particular area, or convince them that they should remain there. Pull factors can include:

- government incentives and grants
- lower labour costs
- good communications and infrastructure
- developing markets

Location costs and benefits

Although location decisions are important to new businesses, they can also have a major impact on an established organisation. Usually at some point in a business's development it will have to consider relocation. It will need to move to an optimal location, which can offer it room to grow but also presents a balance of positive quantitative and qualitative factors.

Relocation does bring problems: some staff may not wish to move, which means provision has to be made for them, and could include redundancy and compensation. The business will also suffer disruption during the move, making it difficult to maintain a steady income. Added to this, the customers need to be told about the location change, as do the suppliers.

However, an optimal relocation can offer the business enormous benefits. New premises can mean that new systems, processes and management systems can be installed without many of the problems that would have been associated with trying to do this at the old location. The business can redefine itself, reassign roles and streamline production and operations.

An optimal relocation can offer even an established business an opportunity to reinvent itself. It can take advantage of all of the benefits of the new location while seeking to discard any problems it may have had in operating at its old premises. Of course, an ideal relocation would put the business at the centre of its market; allow smoother distribution; retain key personnel and set the business up in a situation where it can continue to enjoy these advantages for some years to come.

Low-cost location

Businesses will tend to assume that after the costs of the move have been taken into account they should be able to increase their efficiency and have a positive impact on their overall costs. This does not necessarily mean, however, that a business will always seek to find the lowest cost location, as there may be very good reasons why that location is so inexpensive compared to others. A low-cost location may not really offer a solid platform for future expansion and success. In fact the new location may have a drastic impact on the long-term profitability of the business.

A business will therefore have to weigh up the 'cost only' factors and compare them to qualitative factors and other long-term issues before it finally makes a decision. Shifting operations to an overseas location may appear financially attractive, but there could be basic problems, such as language difficulties. Moving to an area where there are insufficiently trained staff may bring with it problems of ensuring quality of production or quality of raw materials and components.

Many supermarkets and retail outlets had to make the very difficult decision some years ago that in order to expand they had to move out of the high streets. Not only was there insufficient space for them, but also the rents and rates were prohibitively expensive. Moving to out-of-town locations was a considerable risk, but ultimately it has usually proved to be more profitable.

Like many business decisions, relocation cannot solve all problems, certainly not in the short term. As it is such an expensive option, the business needs to think long and hard about whether it should relocate, considering all the relevant factors, and should make an assessment of the short-term and the long-term viability of the move.

CASE STUDY HOME OR AWAY?

A plastics manufacturer has outgrown its factory near Manchester and faces a major location decision. The management has worked out that their average employees cost them £18 per hour and that to move to a new factory of sufficient size they will need to pay £125 per square metre per year in rent. The finance director has just returned from a fact-finding trip abroad. He has discovered that the average cost of a Malaysian worker would be just £4 per hour and that a factory would cost them just £25 per square metre per year. He proposes that they shut down the factory and shift production abroad.

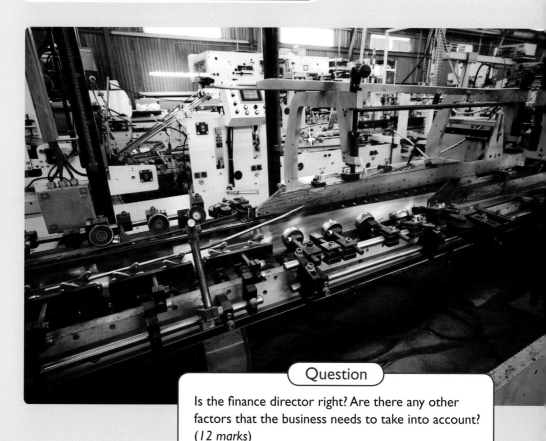

Question

Is the finance director right? Are there any other factors that the business needs to take into account? (*12 marks*)

Advantages and disadvantages of multi-site locations

LEARNING OBJECTIVES

► What are multi-site locations?
► Managing multi-site locations

What are multi-site locations?

As an alternative to wholesale relocation, businesses often find the need to establish additional locations as their primary strategy in achieving growth. This means that the senior management of a business has the challenge of managing not only multiple offices, factories and sales teams, but also a number of individuals who may work from home.

Managing parts of the operation in different geographical locations requires the organisation to adapt its reporting procedures and processes, in order to ensure that the business still continues to move in the same direction, with these separate divisions contributing in a timely manner. As we will see, this is a particular concern if the business becomes a multinational operation, with separate parts of the organisation located in different countries. While this means that there are particular complications, such as languages and different time zones, the challenges facing a business in operating across a whole country with numerous outlets or offices can be equally challenging.

Business opportunities may arise that mean that they may shift production or fulfilment to a new location. They may merge or acquire other businesses. The net result is that the business begins to operate from multiple work sites. The problem is maintaining a clear reporting relationship to the main headquarters and inevitably there are positive and negative factors to take into account.

KEY TERMS

Autonomy – a degree of freedom to make decisions and to problem-solve.

Empowerment – the authority to make decisions and take responsibility for particular actions.

Managing multi-site locations

Usually outside of the main office the atmosphere in subsidiary locations is often more informal or relaxed. The management and employees in these sites will have a degree of autonomy and empowerment. The subsidiary sites are often smaller, both in terms of numbers of employees and physical size. The sites have their own specific management and more often than not these sites have more motivated and productive employees, as they usually have slightly more freedom.

However, less formal structures have some negative impacts. It can be difficult for the main office to give them the support and direction that they need. Mistakes can easily be made and decisions may be at variance with the main objectives of the organisation. A common situation is the 'them versus us' feeling. Each of the sites feels that it is perfectly capable of making its own decisions without interference from head office. However, the same is true from the opposite point of view. The main office can feel frustrated by the subsidiary site's lack of adherence to common goals and objectives.

Communication can often be a significant problem, particularly if a communication structure is not put into place at the earliest possible opportunity. The use of ICT has certainly improved this situation, with the main office being able to access data generated by the subsidiary sites. In this way it can monitor progress and information such as sales figures or production totals.

There are many different challenges to managing a multi-site organisation. It is usually recognised that the following issues need to be addressed:

- A structure needs to be created – either formal or informal – with clear reporting relationships.
- Informal and formal power relationships and lines of authority need to be established.
- Standardised hours need to be established so that sites operating in other time zones can have direct communication during opening hours
- Productivity levels and outcomes need to be mutually agreed.
- Goals, milestones and deadlines need to be clearly identified.
- The main office needs to make both scheduled and impromptu visits to other sites.
- Daily contact may need to be established via videoconferencing or conference calls.
- Remote sites need to be encouraged to communicate on a regular basis with the main office to seek answers to specific problems.
- The whole business needs to be knitted together by methods such as joint meetings, newsletters and the general encouragement of cooperation and collaboration.

Businesses that open in new locations may impress potential investors by their drive and sales growth. However, operating in different areas can be as complicated as managing multiple brands of products or services.

CASE STUDY FLOWER POWER

KaBloom is America's fastest growing floral retail chain. John Halaris, owner of three KaBloom franchises in Rhode Island, actually prefers owning multiple locations to owning just one.

It was KaBloom's potential for growth and its novel mission – educating consumers that fresh flowers don't have to be limited to special occasions – that attracted the entrepreneur in Halaris.

'With three locations, I have a much larger budget for marketing and can do the kinds of promotions I want to do. If one store doesn't have a certain type of flower, you can usually find it at another store. Plus, we order our flowers directly from the growers – with several locations, your buying power is much better. With more designers and managers on board, you can increase your business without stressing out, if we have three weddings in a weekend, I don't worry about having enough people to do those jobs. With multiple locations, you can assign people to help you out in a pinch. Some industries have to fight turnover of people always in search of a better-paying job, better hours. Fortunately, the people interested in working with our product are unique, creative people who are more likely to stay. Floral designers love working with the product and find that it's a better job than going to work 10–20 hours a week at any other retail business.'

Source: adapted from Kabloom

Questions

1 Outline Halaris's reasoning behind the advantages he enjoys from multiple locations. (*8 marks*)
2 What disadvantages might there be? (*8 marks*)

International locations

LEARNING OBJECTIVES
▶ Multinationals
▶ Why become a multinational?
▶ Advantages of multinationals

Multinationals

A multinational organisation is one that has its headquarters in one country and carries out operations in a range of other, different countries. Household names such as Microsoft, Canon, Coca-Cola, McDonald's, Shell and Ford are all examples of successful multinationals.

FOR EXAMPLE

Ford has manufacturing operations on six continents. They include assembly plants, engine plants, casting and aluminium plants. In Europe they have over thirty sites in nine different countries.

Multinationals are large organisations with enormous power and influence and, as we will see, despite criticism of multinationals, they are much desired as potential investors in countries around the world.

Why become a multinational?

There are many reasons why a business may ultimately decide to become a multinational organisation. We have seen that some of the first steps towards overseas involvement can come from location decisions. Consequently, one of the first reasons why a business might become a multinational is to benefit from lower costs if it was operating overseas. It may also gain the advantage of not having to adhere to such strict rules and regulations – health and safety may be more lax. Additionally, the business will be able to tap into a new labour pool. This may be cheaper than in countries that it is already operating in, and may be prepared to be more flexible.

Another reason why a business may locate abroad would be to gain closer access to raw materials

and components. New market opportunities might also present themselves. This has particularly been a trend when businesses have discovered that the domestic market has become saturated and that they are experiencing only slow growth. Operating abroad offers a brand new market and an opportunity for rapid growth. This may ultimately give the business greater economies of scale.

Being closer to overseas markets also means that a business can understand that market. It can appreciate customer requirements and if it is based in that country it can respond to customer service issues with greater efficiency.

Some countries and regions take steps to try to protect their domestic industries. China, for example, can be described as being protectionist. It puts up trade barriers to prevent its markets from being flooded with overseas products, affecting domestic businesses. To get around this issue businesses have entered into joint ventures with Chinese businesses, so that they can enjoy the benefits of the protectionist barriers.

When we considered location decisions, we mentioned the fact that there could be problems with exchange rate fluctuations. If a business is able to produce products in the country in which it sells them, then fluctuating exchange rates are no longer an issue.

It is not necessarily the case that multinationals locate in underdeveloped countries in order to access a cheap workforce and cheap resources. Britain has been especially attractive for Japanese and Korean businesses in particular. They have invested heavily in production facilities, especially in the vehicle market. This has mainly been to avoid the trade barriers set up by the EU to discourage EU businesses and customers from purchasing products and services from outside the EU.

Advantages of multinationals

As we have already mentioned, countries are keen to attract multinational organisations because they bring investment into the country. When a multinational business locates in a particular country it will need land and labour and it will be spending money that will find its way into the local economy. Local people will be employed and existing resources can be exploited, with the possibility of attracting additional multinationals.

Many argue that multinational companies not only bring with them new techniques and ideas, but also improve the human capital in the host country. In other words they train the local labour force and give it new skills.

We have already seen that Japanese car manufacturers decided to locate in Britain to give them access to the EU and avoid trade barriers. As far as Britain is concerned, it has not only provided valuable employment opportunities, particularly in the North East, but has also generally improved working practices and driven down the cost of vehicles by bringing new competition into the market.

The multinational business will also pay tax to the host government. It very much depends on the accounting policies of the multinational, and whether profits are actually exported as payment to the parent company for the investment in setting up the operation. Multinationals often invest in infrastructure to improve communications and road and rail networks. This also provides a valuable set of investments for the host country.

Some countries, however, are suspicious of multinational companies and their motives. There are costs associated with

the establishment of multinational companies, including the following:

- The employment opportunities may not be as good as expected. If the business needs skilled workers they may be overseas nationals and not locals
- The relocation of the multinational to the host country may be temporary and they may only stay for the duration of a particular set of incentives, or until the tax advantages of moving elsewhere become too tempting
- Employment prospects may be good in the early stages, particularly for construction workers, but if the business is using capital-intensive production facilities then the longer-term employment prospects are actually quite poor
- Weak or corrupt governments are susceptible to bribes and exploitation by powerful multinationals. Multinationals may target countries that they believe they can manipulate in order to get the best deal
- Regulations may not be as rigorous in the host country, and the business may cause significant pollution and environmental damage that it would not be allowed to cause in its own country. It may also dump waste products and have a long-term negative impact on the country
- The multinational may actually set up in the country specifically to sell products that are falling in popularity or have been heavily regulated in its home country, such as tobacco products or certain types of drugs.

> **Question**
>
> What might be the advantages and disadvantages to an underdeveloped country in attracting a multinational corporation? (*12 marks*)

Case studies, questions and exam practice

CASE STUDY HOW I CHOOSE MY BUSINESS LOCATION

Who: Patcharee Shaweewan of Oaka

What: Peterborough-based pub and restaurant business

The issue: Choosing the right location for your business

The solution: 'My partner and I have four businesses based in Peterborough and Birmingham and we are about to open our fifth restaurant and pub, Oaka, in Kennington, London. It was important for us to find a freehold property because we wanted the flexibility to make changes to the premises, which is much harder to do if you buy leasehold. Looking for a freehold put us in a more difficult position – we wanted a freehold property with a licence to serve food and drink. They're really hard to come by, especially in London. We settled on a location in Kennington, on a busy road. It was important for us to find a place where there are lots of people passing by, because footfall is a major consideration for our type of business. Ultimately, we'd like to get customers travelling to Oaka as a destination place, but in the beginning we'll be relying on passing trade. We're right opposite a Tube station, which is a real advantage because most people in London don't drive. Being close to transport links will also help us recruit staff. But, because

we're also on a major A-road, we will be very visible to people driving past. There is free parking outside after 7pm and we hope people will stop and come in. Being on a major road is also helpful to our suppliers, who should have no problem finding us. London is such a big city, it has different 'rules' from other cities and people like to go to eat in certain places, such as the West End. Kennington has an up-and-coming restaurant trade, too, and we're hoping to take advantage not only of local custom, but people who come here especially for the restaurants. It also helps that we're located close to The Oval cricket ground, which we will be targeting with marketing leaflets. We'll be selling real ale, which is a big plus point for cricket fans.'

Lessons learned: One of our restaurants in Peterborough is located on a large barge, on the south bank of the River Nene. We don't have a car park, so we rely heavily on footfall. Its location on the outskirts of the city centre is quite unique and works to our advantage, even though it is quieter. It's much safer than the town centre, so much more desirable to our customers. Town centres don't always provide the best location; you should base your location on where customers want to go.'

Source: adapted from Highlands and Islands Enterprise

Questions

1 Explain why the restaurant site in Kennington was an optimal one? (*10 marks*)
2 Different criteria were used to choose the Peterborough site. Why could they still be considered to be optimal? (*6 marks*)

Time management

LEARNING
OBJECTIVES

▶ Time management
▶ Time management tools
▶ Time management grid
▶ Time studies

Time management

Time management skills are essential, both to the individual and to the organisation in general. Applying time management techniques should ensure that the business runs far more effectively and that managers and employees are able to function well, even under extreme pressure.

Time management is all about taking control of workloads and reducing stress due to work overload. Ultimately if time cannot be managed then nothing else can be managed.

Time management tools

There are literally dozens of different ways in which time management can be introduced and techniques that can be employed in order to manage time in an effective manner. The following table outlines some of the key techniques:

Technique	Explanation
Weekly planning	A weekly plan should give a manager an overview of the tasks they need to complete. A much-used technique is to use an ABC and 123 priority system. A priority is a high-value, urgent activity and then each task is also assigned a number, signifying its importance.
Planning software	Microsoft Project is often used by managers as a planning mechanism. This allows them to record their tasks electronically, and tasks for individual team members can be added and printed off as required.
Daily planning	Simple 'to do' lists, which break down work into smaller tasks that can be tackled on a particular day.
Best use of time	Carrying out a task that best fits the time of that particular moment tends to increase overall efficiency. This reduces waiting time, so if a job is likely to take 20 minutes and there is 20 minutes available, then that job is done first.
Handling paper	The four things that can be done with paper that arrives are: act on it, file it, give it to someone else to do, or throw it away. This avoids shuffling papers around the desk and never getting around to completing the work required.
Organisation	This is a technique that has been translated by many businesses into a clear desk policy. Untidy or disorganised desks are banned, and every employee is required to clear their desks at the end of each day, so that they return to an empty desk the following day.
Routine	Even routine tasks, such as filing, have to be carried out as they will help manage time more effectively. Material that needs to be read but does not need action should be skim-read and then set aside, rather than kept on the desk.
Meetings	Meetings need to be as effective as possible, with agendas to keep discussions on topic, decision-making, accurate recording of what has been decided, monitoring and producing accurate minutes.
Information	Techniques tend to revolve around sharing information, so that all who need access to it have it. This means having a standardised way of saving and storing information, whether it is in print or electronic form.
Procrastination	This means putting off tasks until they are unavoidable. The simple way to deal with this is to set deadlines by which goals should be achieved. Businesses also use intermediate goals, or milestones, to signal progress.
Saying no	Many managers are overcommitted because they don't turn down requests to carry out particular tasks. It is important that they focus on their goals and follow their own priorities first in order to remain efficient.

URGENCY

HIGH ←———————————————————→ LOW

IMPORTANCE

HIGH

Quadrant 1 URGENT AND IMPORTANT 'FIRE-FIGHTING'	**Quadrant 2** IMPORTANT BUT NOT URGENT 'QUALITY TIME'
Quadrant 3 URGENT BUT NOT IMPORTANT 'DISTRACTION'	**Quadrant 4** NEITHER URGENT NOR IMPORTANT 'TIME-WASTING'

LOW

Time management grid

The time management grid cross-references urgency and importance. On the left-hand side tasks are urgent, on the right-hand side less urgent, at the top they are important activities and at the bottom less important. This provides us with four quadrants:

- Quadrant 1: urgent and important – these need to be dealt with immediately.
- Quadrant 2: important but not urgent – these activities need to be thought through and given time.
- Quadrant 3: effectively distractions – these need to be dealt with immediately, but they are not actually important, such as an unwanted telephone call.
- Quadrant 4: neither urgent nor important – these waste time and often do not achieve anything.

The tool aims to assist managers in maximising quadrant 2 time and to reduce time spent in quadrant 3 and eliminate quadrant 4 activities.

Time studies

Effectively time studies owe much to time and motion studies that were developed by Frank and Lillian Gilbreth. Time studies involve the identification and measurement in time of each of the sub-elements of a particular job in order to discover how long the whole job takes to be completed. Often time studies can be used as a means by which productivity payments and other performance-related pay is determined.

They developed a view of management that was contemporary with, but independent of, that of F.W. Taylor. They analysed the components of a specific job, breaking down each activity into component parts. They then judged the most efficient means of carrying out each of those components, added the ideal times assigned to each of these components and arrived at an aggregate time for the whole activity.

During his research, Taylor began with the assumption that employees only work for money. He developed a series of work study

techniques which he considered would enable employees to reduce the amount of time it would take to carry out different tasks, leaving the planning and organisation of tasks for the managers and supervisors. He believed that encouragement to work harder and the promise of additional benefits, such as money, as a reward for this would make employees sufficiently motivated to work harder.

Taylor, however, was proved wrong. He discovered that employees would only work harder when they were being supervised, but would return to their normal pace of work once the supervision was removed. Since Taylor's writing on 'scientific management', much emphasis has been placed on job design. Henry Ford developed Taylor's principles into what has become known as 'Fordism'.

Question

Using the Internet, find out ways in which you could manage your own time more effectively throughout your course of study. How transferrable are these skills to business situations?

Critical path analysis

Critical path

A critical path is the longest possible path through which a project has to pass in order to be completed. A critical path identifies crucial activities in the stages of dealing with, or managing, a particular project, identifying in effect the worst case scenario in order to make a clearer estimation of the time a project will take to complete. The critical path aims to focus the organisation's attention on these activities, which are essential to ensure the completion of the project.

Critical path method (CPM)

As opposed to backward scheduling, the critical path method begins with the start time for a particular project. It then proceeds to identify the earliest possible start times and finish times for each activity that is required to complete the overall project. Once this has been completed, the CPM seeks to work backwards from the date by which the project needs to be completed and amends the start times of all the activities in relation to this date. The critical path is the

pathway which has the minimum amount of slack time. This critical path is then given a priority in terms of attention and allocation of resources, aiming to reduce the overall project time.

The CPM should also assist the business in being able to identify aspects or activities in the process which can either be rolled together or speeded up in order to have a positive impact on the overall project completion time.

Critical chain

A critical chain is a means by which an organisation can look at the full duration of a particular project. It can be considered to be more all-inclusive than a critical path. The critical chain not only addresses the issues that a critical path considers, but it also takes into account any factors relating to the supply of products or components prior to the commencement of the production process itself. A critical chain would consider the start and finish times, as well as any slack periods. The longest total time through these stages is known as a critical path. The critical chain seeks to assign the resources

required for each part of the process and recognises the fact that the next stage cannot be undertaken until the resources required for that task are made available. The critical chain then identifies all the stages in the process until the schedule has been completed. In this respect, a critical chain is somewhat longer than a critical path. In addition, the critical chain incorporates time buffers, which aim to protect the activities on the critical chain from beginning later than is desirable.

Alongside a critical chain, a non-critical chain could also be constructed, which ensures that activities which could have an impact on the critical chain are planned in such a way that they do not interrupt the critical chain.

Taking critical path analysis one stage further – an example

A business identifies the seven stages involved in setting up a new training programme, and the estimated length of time needed for each task:

A plan the training programme (4 hrs)

B make a training DVD (6 hrs)

C design and write the training pack (7 hrs)

D show the DVD to selected representative employees (8 hrs)

E test the suitability of the training pack (10 hrs)

F present the training programme to the board of directors (9 hrs)

G announce the training programme to the staff (5 hrs)

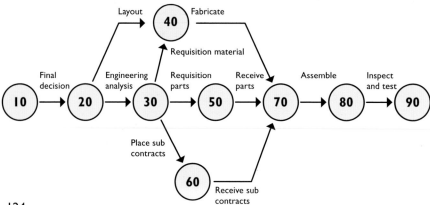

Figure 1

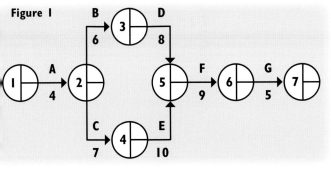

Figure 2

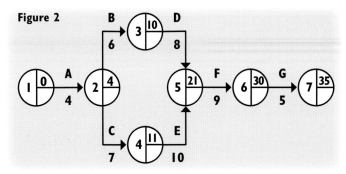

Figure 3

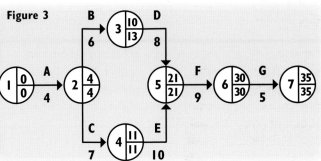

Figure 4

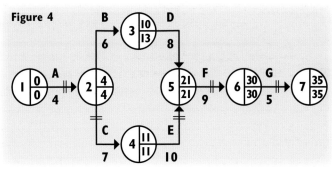

These activities can be shown on a network:

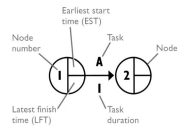

The training programme network shows the order in which the tasks can be completed (**Figure 1**).

If the earliest start time (EST) for A is 0, then B and C cannot start for 4 hours (0+4).

These figures are shown in the top right-hand corner of nodes 1 and 2.

Task D cannot start until A and B have been completed; this takes 10 hours (0+4+6), which is shown in node 3.

Task E cannot start until A and C have been completed; this takes 11 hours (0+4+7), which is shown in node 3.

Task F cannot start until E and D are completed, the EST for task F is 21 (0+4+7+10).

It is important to choose the longest route when calculating the ESTs. The route A, B, D is only 18

(0+4+6+8). The EST of the longer route is shown in node 5 (**Figure 2**).

The next step is to calculate the latest finish time (LFT) of each task without extending the whole project.

We start at node 7 and work back.

Task G must be completed by the 35th hour and this is shown in node 7.

To calculate the LFT for task F, we subtract the time it takes to complete task F from the previous LFT (35−5=30) and place it in node 6.

When we choose between two LFTs, such as for task A, we choose the route that gives the lowest LFT, in this case 4 (11−7) rather than 7 (13−6) (**Figure 3**).

Once all the LFTs have been identified it is possible to outline the critical path. This can be drawn through all of the nodes where the ESTs and the LFTs are the same.

This means that there can be no delays between completing the previous tasks and starting the next one without prolonging the advertising campaign.

The critical path in this case is A, C, E, F, G, shown by striking two short lines across the critical activities (**Figure 4**).

B and D could be delayed for up to three hours and would not affect the task – this is called the float. The total float is found by subtracting the EST and the duration from the LFT, so for task B it would be 3 (13−6−4), this is the total float up to that activity. The free float is found by subtracting the EST at the start of the task and the duration from the EST at the end, so for task B it would be 0 (10−6−4).

Task	Duration	EST	LFT	Total float	Free float
A	4	0	4	0	0
B	6	4	13	3	0
C	7	4	11	0	0
D	8	10	21	3	3
E	10	11	21	0	0
F	9	21	30	0	0
G	5	30	35	0	0

Question

What do you think are the key advantages and disadvantages of critical path analysis? (*6 marks*)

Time management of resources

LEARNING OBJECTIVES

▶ Lean production
▶ Just-in-time production
▶ Kaizen

Lean production

Lean production/manufacturing is an approach based on the Toyota Production system. An organisation takes a number of steps to assist in ensuring that its manufacturing activity focuses on five key concepts:

- Value is centred on customer needs. The business initiates activities only when customers demand them.
- Value creation – which occurs along a series of steps and is known as the value stream. This is achieved through a closely synchronised flow of the organisation's activities.
- Continually making improvements within the production process in order to maintain customer service and strive for perfection.
- Waste reduction
- Engagement of employees

Central to an organisation adopting the lean production/manufacturing approach is the question of waste reduction and a high level of engagement of all company personnel in implementing and improving the manufacturing process.

The benefits available to an organisation adopting the lean production/manufacturing process are high. It is claimed that organisations have achieved benefits of 80% reduction in **cycle time**, 50% reduction in **lead times**, and 50% reduction in the levels of their **inventory**, and an increase in customer response rates, as well as an increase in quality.

Just-in-time production (JIT)

JIT is a philosophy developed in Japan emphasising the importance of deliveries in relation to the process of small lot-sizes. The philosophy emphasises the importance of set-up cost reduction, small lot sizes, pull systems, level production and importantly, the elimination of waste.

JIT is designed to allow the achievement of high-volume production, while ensuring that minimal inventories of raw materials, work-in-progress and finished goods are held by the business. Parts arrive at the manufacturing plant from suppliers, just in time to be placed in the manufacturing process. Then, as the products are processed along the line, they arrive at the next workstation just in time, thereby moving through the whole system very quickly.

JIT relies on managers ensuring that manufacturing waste is kept to a minimum and that nothing is made or brought on to the premises that is not immediately required. JIT requires precision because the right part needs to be in the right place at the right time. Waste is described as being the results from any activity that adds cost without adding value (which includes moving and storing).

JIT is also known as 'lean production' or 'stockless production', and the theory is that it should improve the profits and the returns on investment by the following means:

- Reducing inventory levels
- Increasing the inventory turnover rate
- Improving product quality
- Reducing production and delivery lead times
- Reducing other costs (machine set-ups and equipment breakdown)

JIT also recognises the fact that any underutilised capacity can be used to build up a small stock of products or components (buffer inventories) in order to assure that in the event of a problem the production process will not be interrupted.

JIT is primarily used in manufacturing processes which are repetitive in nature and the same products and components are used and produced in relatively high volumes. Once the flow has been set up, there should be a steady and even flow of materials, components and finished products passing through the facility. Each work station is linked in a similar way to an assembly line (although the exact layout may be a jobbing or batch process layout). The goal is to make all queuing equal to zero and to achieve the ideal lot size per unit of production.

Muda is a Japanese word that translates as waste, useless or futile, and the term refers to any activity carried out by an organisation that does not add value. In other words, anything the customer is not prepared to pay for.

The term Muda was originally part of a trilogy:

- Mura (imbalance)
- Muri (overload)
- Muda (non-value-added)

Just-in-time management regards items that are bought but not being used as waste, even if they are regarded as an asset of the organisation, because they add no value to products that are known to be required by customers.

Over-production, waiting, conveyance, processing, inventory, motion, and correction can all contribute to Muda, which can be found throughout an organisation or its production process.

INTERNET RESEARCH 🔍

The Lean Enterprise Institute can be found at www.lean.org and the website of the Kaizen Institute is at www.kaizen-institute.com/kzn.htm.

Kaizen

Kaizen is a Japanese management term referring to gradual, but orderly, continuous improvement. The kaizen business strategy seeks to involve individuals from across the organisation at any level.

The goal is to work together in order to achieve improvements without having to make large capital investments. Each change or improvement collectively complements and moves the process onwards.

Kaizen requires a culture of sustained continuous improvement, while focusing on the elimination of waste in areas, systems and processes of the organisation. Above all, the cooperation and involvement of all the employees is vital to the overall success of the philosophy.

KEY TERMS

Cycle time – the length of time required to complete a product, from the start time to the moment it rolls off the production line.

Lead times – usually the length of time an organisation takes to produce a product from receiving the order.

Inventory – another term used to describe stock level.

CASE STUDY THE RISE OF LEAN PRODUCTION

Fifty years ago General Motors (GM), Ford and Chrysler dominated the car industry worldwide. GM made half the cars in the US and employed half a million workers. Twenty years ago their market share began to plummet and leaner producers, like Toyota, arrived on the scene. GM and Ford cut thousands of jobs and closed plants, while Toyota opened a new one every year. Just ten years ago GM would have taken around 48 hours to produce a car, while Toyota took just 30. GM learned the lesson the hard way and in the past twenty years has reduced the lead time to just thirty-five hours, while Toyota has maintained its 30-hour average. Ford and Chrysler have responded similarly.

Questions

1 In a lean production factory how are the workers organised? (*4 marks*)
2 Why is it important for a lean production factory to have long-term relationships with its suppliers? (*4 marks*)

Case studies, questions and exam practice

CASE STUDY ROJEE TASHA STAMPINGS LTD

Company profile

- Country: India

- Turnover: US$1.0 million

- No. of employees: 23

- Products: Stamped metal components and sub-assemblies for automobiles

- Customers: Domestic manufacturers of commercial and passenger vehicles

- Technology: Own

- Certification: ISO 9002

Improvements achieved (within 6 months, without any capital investment):

- Turnover: increased by 36%
- Production space: increased by 43%
- Machine downtime: reduced by 100%
- Lead time: reduced by 50%
- Product rejection by customer: reduced by 50%
- Changeover time for press machines: reduced by 80%
- Staff training investment: substantially increased
- Workforce flexibility: increased by 100%
- Productivity awareness: increased dramatically
- Quality awareness: increased
- Staff motivation: improved significantly

Implementation of lean manufacturing involved non-capital changes by using world-class manufacturing (WCM) methods such as single minute exchange of die (SMED), 5S activities (Sort – Straighten – Sweep – Standardise – Self-discipline), variations of the Kanban system and other recognised methods of generating productivity gains.

A number of improvements in time utilisation were achieved. The reduction in set-up time was achieved through the introduction of single minute exchange of die (SMED) method and preparation of standard operating procedures. In a practical example, workers on two press machines broke down the entire changeover process into small activities in order to determine the time wasted for adjustments and readjustments. As a result of this exercise, the changeover time was reduced by 80% (from 62 minutes to 13 minutes), with a similar

result obtained in the case of the second press machine. This, together with a 30% improvement in achievement against takt time contributed to a 50% cut in through-put time.

A major concern of the company was machinery breakdown. A maintenance worker was recruited, which dramatically reduced response time to machinery breakdown, and resulted in a successful implementation of a preventive maintenance programme. The company engineers were trained on error-proofing. This paved the way for the identification of 10 major quality-related issues and for consequent recommendations for action covering various production areas.

The company formalised its training activities. It has established technical training schedules that reflect its development plan. Engineers and workers have become acquainted with world-class manufacturing

(WCM) methods such as SMED and have formed teams with specific problem-solving tasks. After six months of training, nine machine operators became multi-skilled, ready to train new recruits. In conjunction with 5S activities and the application of error-proofing methods, extensive training also contributed to gains in product quality and the consequent 50% remarkable cut in the volume of products returned by customers.

Significant improvements have been achieved through enhanced awareness and corrective measures in the area of production efficiency. A number of contributions came from improvements and the planning and strategy-formulation stage. For example,

the company adopted strategies for improving time utilisation and reducing reject and rework volumes, as well as for maintenance and 5S activities.

Source: adapted from UNIDO Partnership Programme

Questions

1 How was the business able to introduce leaning manufacturing without any real capital investment? (*12 marks*)
2 What is meant by 'takt time' and 'kanban'? (*4 marks*)

TOPIC 5 HUMAN RESOURCE STRATEGIES

Introduction

The final part of *Strategies for success* is the topic of human resource strategies. Again it builds on material you will have covered in AS Business Studies, as it looks at the strategies that are available to businesses in managing their human resources.

Without exception, human resources are the single most important asset that a business or organisation controls. This is regardless of whether the business is capital-intensive or labour-intensive. All businesses need to match their workforce skills, size and location to their needs. They need to make full use of their workforce's potential, and in order to ensure long-term success and prosperity, a good relationship between the employer and the employee is essential.

The first focus area looks at human resource objectives and strategies. Specific objectives can include matching the workforce to the business's needs, minimising costs, making sure that the workforce operates to its full potential, and maintaining good relations. There are different ways in which businesses can achieve these objectives and these are often referred to as either hard or soft HR strategies.

The second focus area looks at developing and implementing workforce plans. We will consider the components of workforce plans and how

internal and external influences affect not only the workforce plan, but also how it is implemented and its chances of success. There are a number of issues involved in implementing workforce plans, including the relationship between the employer and the employees, the costs involved, the training needs of both management and employees, and the business's overall corporate image.

The third focus area looks at competitive organisational structures. Many of the concepts related to organisational structures were covered in AS Business Studies – such as centralisation and decentralisation, de-layering, and flexible workforces. We will examine how these moves to make a business more competitive can be implemented and how they operate in practice.

The final focus area examines effective employer and employee relations and how communication is an important aspect of this relationship. We examine the various ways in which the views, wishes and overall objectives of employees can be represented to the management of the business and the advantages and disadvantages of each. These might include works councils, trade unions and employee groups. This focus also examines ways in which both employers and employees can either avoid or resolve potential industrial disputes.

FOCUS ON HUMAN RESOURCE OBJECTIVES AND STRATEGIES

- HR objectives ▶ page 132
- Internal and external influences on HR objectives ▶ page 134
- HR strategies ▶ page 136
- Case studies, questions and exam practice ▶ page 138

FOCUS ON DEVELOPING AND IMPLEMENTING WORKFORCE PLANS

- Components of workforce plans ▶ page 140
- Assessing internal and external influences on workforce plans ▶ page 142
- Issues in implementing workforce plans ▶ page 144
- The value of workforce planning ▶ page 146
- Case studies, questions and exam practice ▶ page 148

FOCUS ON COMPETITIVE ORGANISATIONAL STRUCTURES

- Factors determining choice of organisational structures ▶ page 150
- Adapting structures to improve competitiveness (1) ▶ page 152
- Adapting structures to improve competitiveness (2) ▶ page 154
- Adapting structures to improve competitiveness (3) ▶ page 156
- Case studies, questions and exam practice ▶ page 158

FOCUS ON EFFECTIVE EMPLOYER/EMPLOYEE RELATIONS

- Managing communications with employees ▶ page 160
- Methods of employee representation ▶ page 162
- Avoiding and resolving industrial disputes ▶ page 164
- Case studies, questions and exam practice ▶ page 166

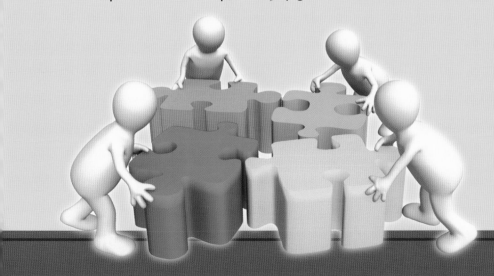

HR objectives

LEARNING OBJECTIVES

- ▶ HR objectives
- ▶ Matching workforce skills
- ▶ Size, location and business needs
- ▶ Workforce potential
- ▶ Minimising labour costs
- ▶ Maintaining good relations

HR objectives

One of the main objectives of human resource management (HRM) is to ensure that staffing and training in particular help increase performance levels and productivity. It tracks data on employees, such as their abilities, skills, personal histories and payroll records.

The most important objective, however, is to provide an efficient and effective back-up system to ensure that issues such as pay, benefits and treatment are fairly and handled consistently throughout the organisation. This ensures continuing good relations between management and the workforce.

A key objective is to ensure that there is a complete and comprehensive policy framework in place to deal with all employee matters. Increasingly, issues such as equity and diversity have become major objectives, and procedures have had to be put in place to deal with harassment and grievances.

It is important to remember that Human Resources is closely related to other strategic objectives of the business and HR is a major part of the policy-making, the planning and the coordination of the organisation as a whole.

The principal role of HR, in terms of objectives, is to stimulate the development of individuals and groups to be in the best position to meet the needs of the organisation. A successful business needs effective performance management systems, at departmental, team and individual levels. As we will see, this will involve personal development plans, appraisals, career planning, training events and a host of other initiatives. Increasingly, Human Resources can use technology to assist it in gathering data and monitoring and controlling overall performance.

Matching workforce skills

An important function of Human Resources is to determine the skills available in the current workforce and to identify skills that are needed to carry out jobs within the organisation. The analysis will help to identify where skills do not match, particularly in cases where jobs are changing. A starting point is often the job description, which would contain information about the manual and mental skills required to carry out the job. Ultimately this should assist human resource managers in identifying the correct mix of employees to do particular jobs.

Size, location and business needs

Human resource management must be in a position to be able to respond to the changing needs of the organisation. Particular pressures will be placed on Human Resources as a business grows or diminishes. In the first instance, the objective will be to attract suitable candidates who can readily fill newly created posts. When a business is downsizing, it also needs to identify job roles that could be sacrificed without having a massive detrimental impact on the operations of the organisation.

Increasingly, businesses operate on multiple sites, which brings in another key consideration and set of objectives for HR. Particularly difficult is the problem of dealing with employees in remote locations, specifically in overseas operations. HR may have to allocate new resources to setting up sub-offices staffed with employees who are aware of current labour markets and relevant rules and regulations.

Workforce potential

Before the arrival of performance appraisals, work measurement was a major way of judging the potential of the workforce. It evaluated employees on an individual basis, identifying essential performance criteria related to specific job roles. Common standards of performance were established and then individuals

were tested against those standards. As job roles have become more complex, ensuring that the workforce potential is being achieved has become a difficult task. A key objective, however, is still to try to ensure that the workforce is operating at optimal levels. This can be achieved by installing relevant management systems, supervision and training programmes to ensure that employees remain fully conversant with systems, processes, technology and other issues that could affect their job roles.

Minimising labour costs

As with any area of business operations, the minimisation of costs is an essential driver in decision-making. However, in the vast majority of cases, the salary and wage bill of an organisation is its largest single cost. It is expensive to recruit, train and retain suitable employees. This is increasingly difficult when there is a limited number of skilled employees available due to the fact that unemployment levels are particularly low. This means that businesses have to offer highly competitive payment and benefit packages in order to attract the best possible employees.

It is a major concern for businesses that are labour-intensive, as they will need highly skilled employees. It is not so much of a problem when the business is capital-intensive; as many of the tasks and duties that need to be carried out can be easily passed on to new recruits, and training will be fairly straightforward.

Maintaining good relations

Another key objective of Human Resources is to ensure that there remains a high level of cooperation and trust between the employer and the employee. This means managing the relationship on both a group and an individual basis. The business needs to ensure that it has transparent policies that are universally applied to all employees, regardless of their position in the

organisation or the number of years that they have worked for the same employer.

Employees are traditionally concerned with wages and salaries, working conditions, job security and other benefits. In some organisations the key negotiating vehicle is a trade union, which uses what is known as collective bargaining.

It is usually not in the interests of either the employer or the employees for misunderstanding and disagreement to escalate into a major industrial relations problem. An HR objective is, therefore, to minimise the number of industrial disputes, days lost due to industrial action or grievances brought against the employer. In order to achieve this, a business will usually use appraisal questionnaires, attitude surveys and meetings, in order to gauge employees' reactions to the organisation's policies.

Internal and external influences on HR objectives

Internal influences

There can be an enormous number of internal influences on HR objectives. The main influence derives from the overall mission, objectives and strategic plan of the organisation. This is of considerable importance, because the strategic plan is the key driver of the organisation. It determines what the business wishes to achieve in the near future and outlines the steps needed to reach that goal. This inevitably impacts on HR objectives in terms of recruitment, training and retention. It will also impact on HR objectives relating to pay scales, the likely future needs of particular skills and expertise and the long-term management of existing employees.

Beneath the strategic plan are independent but reliant divisional and departmental plans. Each of these areas of the business will have its own specific objectives, into which Human Resources will be required to fit. Over and above the influence of these internal plans is the constant battle to secure sufficient resources in order to ensure that future staffing needs are met in terms of recruitment and training. HR objectives, therefore, are reliant on being able to secure sufficient resources in order to achieve each independent goal.

Human Resources also has to contend with the varying demands of different managers and employees, who require training and staff development as they proceed along their own career paths and require preparation for future roles. An HR objective may be to provide the necessary training and support network, but it will not know with any certainty the extent of those demands.

Most businesses are in a constant state of flux and undergoing internal organisational change. This makes long-term human resource objectives difficult to establish and to maintain, as they may not be fully in line with the direction of the business, due to organisational changes.

In addition to requiring training and support, managers also need constant guidance and advice on a variety of issues, relating to handling employee situations. Some of these may be internally generated problems, while others, as we will see, may be the result of an external influence.

External influences

In recent years, the European Union has had an enormous impact on human resource management. There was, of course, an existing framework of employment law, which governed the key relationships between employers and employees. However, as part of Britain's commitment to the European Union, the government is obliged to accept, adopt and apply EU-wide law in order to **harmonise** the employer/employee relationships across Europe. This has had an increasing impact on working conditions, employee relationships and employee rights.

FOR EXAMPLE

The introduction of the minimum wage was a European-wide initiative and can be seen as being at variance with the key HR objective of minimising labour costs.

KEY TERMS

Harmonise – make legislation and regulations common in all European countries.

Employee representation – a system that allows employees to have a direct influence on the decision-making within an organisation.

The introduction of new rules and regulations concerning the relationship between employers and employees has meant that Human Resources staff have had to adapt quickly to these changes and be in a position to provide guidance and advice to managers. These rules cover benefits, health and safety, working hours and other issues such as flexible working and employee representation.

Increasingly HR objectives are also affected by the competition and the market itself. When there is high unemployment, a business will generally have the pick of the widest possible range of potential employees. However, as employment rises, the available pool of potential candidates dwindles, making it far more difficult to attract and recruit suitable employees. This is against a backdrop of businesses continuing to expand and requiring more employees, but they are required to compete for those employees with their rivals. This has had a marked impact on HR objectives, and means that the business needs to be far more proactive in finding suitable candidates, securing them as employees and then ensuring that they retain them. The continuing danger is, of course, that their key employees are recruitment targets for their competitors.

FOR EXAMPLE

A growing trend in Human Resources is the head-hunter. Head-hunters seek out well-qualified and experienced people currently working for a particular business. They then approach them and try to persuade them to move to a rival business. The head-hunter receives a premium payment from the recruiting business for securing the skilled employee.

CASE STUDY PROBLEMS, PROBLEMS, PROBLEMS

A recent survey showed that private-sector employees were more likely to encounter recruitment problems than public-sector organisations, with 77% in the private sector saying they had difficulties compared to 73% in the public sector. The manufacturing and production sector was the least likely to encounter difficulties, with only 65% claiming recruitment problems. Larger businesses had more recruitment problems than smaller ones. In businesses with over 1,000 employees 75% had recruitment problems, compared to 68% of employers with fewer than 250 staff. One of the problems was that employers had tried to cut their recruitment costs. Public-sector employers were the most likely to do this. Smaller businesses were far less likely to take measures to lower recruitment costs, knowing that it was difficult for them to find staff in the first place. In terms of priorities, dealing with new legislation was a considerable concern. Many businesses struggled to ensure that training was maintained, others cited their key objectives as being absence management, employee retention, recruitment and salary reviews.

Questions

1 Why might larger businesses find it more difficult to recruit than smaller ones? (*6 marks*)
2 What do you think is meant by the term 'absence management'? (*4 marks*)

HR strategies

LEARNING OBJECTIVES

► Human resource accounting
► Human resource audit
► Human resource information system
► Human resource plan
► Hard and soft HRM

Human resource accounting

The term 'human resource accounting' refers to the systematic recording, measurement and analysis of all the costs involved in the department's activities. In addition to identifying the costs, the financial benefits to the organisation will also be calculated. The costs and financial benefits will include:

- the recruitment and utilisation of human resources
- an estimation of training costs
- an assessment of the effects of training programmes
- an assessment of the effects of staff development programmes
- an investigation into the consequences of wage and salary increases
- an investigation into the consequences of the introduction of incentive schemes
- any other financial implications connected to the continued utilisation of human resources.

Human resource audit

A human resource audit examines and reviews an organisation's policies, procedures and practices across the human resource function. Typically, elements included in a human resource audit are:

- personnel policies
- review of personnel files
- performance appraisal
- evaluation processes
- termination processes, including exit interviews
- compliance with employment law
- recruitment procedures

- review of benefits and compensations
- review of employee status and classifications
- review of job descriptions and job specifications

Human resource information system

Human resource information systems, or HRIs, are gradually beginning to replace fully manual or part-computerised and part-manual systems used by human resource departments. Despite the availability of complex, integrated HRI systems, many businesses still retain a form of paper records. Most of these are gradually moving across to scanned documents which are stored electronically, rather than retaining the originals.

One of the biggest advantages of using an HRIS is that the system can be used with an integrated payroll. In this way, common data needs to be entered only once and can be maintained by either Human Resources or payroll.

Other businesses opt for stand-alone HRIS, which means that it is sometimes difficult to coordinate with payroll.

Clearly, a decision whether to purchase an HRIS very much depends on the nature of the business and its present capacity to deal with human resource issues, and, indeed, whether it wishes to integrate this into a payroll system. Generally, basic systems can be purchased for a little in excess of $300, while a larger organisation, which has several thousand employees, may find that the cost is actually closer to $1 million.

BOOK RESEARCH

Jeffrey Pinto and Ido Millet, *Successful Information System Implementation: The Human Side*, Project Management Institute, 1999.

One of the inherent problems with any proprietary HRIS software is that it will not necessarily reflect a business's needs and will therefore need to be configured or customised specifically for the task the business requires it for. Most software vendors will offer support but, in the longer term, businesses realise that in-house support is essential to maintain the system.

HRIS can handle pay, benefits, applicant tracking, recruitment, time and attendance, skills inventories, health and safety, compensation and retirement plans.

Human resource plan

A human resource plan is the HR department's forecast of the number and type of employees required in the future and its anticipation of how likely this need is to be realised. The current human resources will be compared with future likely needs, and programmes will be set up for recruitment drives, training, the possible redeployment of current employees, or redundancies. This planning process can assist human resource management in:

- recruitment
- the avoidance of redundancy or plans for redeployment
- training
- professional development needs
- estimating the costs involved in supplying the required number of employees
- ensuring productivity targets are met
- ensuring other resources, such as accommodation, are available when needed

Clearly, a human resource plan needs to be continuously monitored and readjusted as company objectives change or are affected by unforeseen internal and external considerations. Most organisations would produce both a short-term plan (usually up to 1 year ahead), and a longer-term plan (usually 5 years ahead) to include the following considerations:

- organisational objectives
- human resource objectives
- current utilisation of human resources
- internal organisational environment
- external environment
- the potential supply of labour

Planning for resource implications gives an organisation the ability to cope with human resource consequences of any possible change in circumstances. It could also assist in developing new and improved methods of managing employees in order to avoid labour shortfalls or surpluses in the future. Duplication of effort among the different sections of the organisation can also be avoided, provided the planning has improved the coordination and integration of employees.

Hard HRM

The fundamentals of hard management can be closely associated with a quote by Peter Drucker: 'Doing the right things is more important than doing things right.' This seems to be the fundamental ethos behind hard management, in as much as the

primary role of all private businesses is to be competitive and to produce a profit. All other considerations, as far as hard management is concerned, are subservient to this.

Hard management, therefore, covers all areas of the business, including human resources. Rather than focusing on employee job satisfaction, motivation or even employee retention, the drive is to achieve a competitive advantage, make the best return on investment and meet or exceed the organisation's objectives. Proponents of hard management believe that if this holistic approach is adopted, then management will do the right thing, which may mean that particularly valued employees are not only well rewarded but also well treated. Hard management is to be distinguished from soft management in that the latter puts human resource factors on an equal basis with other objectives and strategies of the business.

Soft HRM

Soft human resource management, as the term infers, places an emphasis on employees and motivation as a means by which productivity and performance may be achieved. The system relies on the proactive use of the human resource department to develop, encourage and support employees.

> **Questions**
>
> How might a human resource plan ensure that HR objectives are met? (*12 marks*)

Case studies, questions and exam practice

CASE STUDY HR AND MERGERS

Too often, mergers and acquisitions are arranged without reference to the HR team. The latter then has to find ways to deliver head-count reduction, and higher productivity through synergy, while ensuring that the company has the right skills to take the new organisation forward.

The capacity to do this varies enormously from organisation to organisation. Some companies have a highly skilled HR team, which is used to working at a strategic level alongside the business. Others have little more than a small personnel function dealing with contracts and pay.

The areas that HR will have to deal with are outlined below. This will have an impact on the employment relationship and upon subsequent employee commitment to the business.

Mergers can provide an opportunity for the HR team to claim a strategic place in the organisation. It is a time to demonstrate that the function can support strategic goals and be instrumental in delivering a high-performance organisation.

One chief executive recognised the value of HR when he arrived in a newly acquired organisation for the first time to meet his new employees with a well-prepared, five-year business plan. He soon realised that staff were not interested in detailed plans for the organisation but only in decisions that related to their jobs and security. The CEO rang Head Office and asked the HR director to join him to deal specifically with the human resource issues.

HR should be able to provide the bridge between the business needs and the employees. While the senior

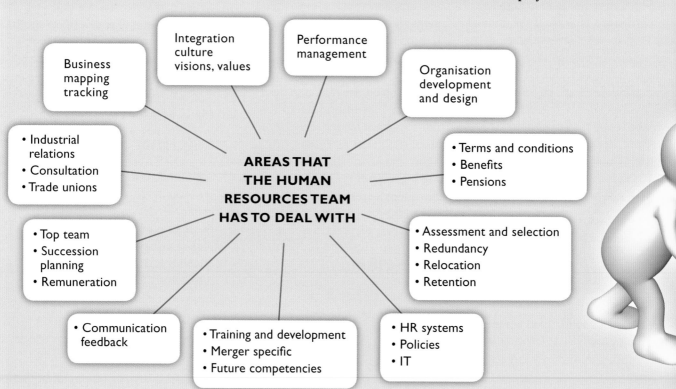

Integration culture visions, values

Performance management

Business mapping tracking

Organisation development and design

- Industrial relations
- Consultation
- Trade unions

AREAS THAT THE HUMAN RESOURCES TEAM HAS TO DEAL WITH

- Terms and conditions
- Benefits
- Pensions

- Top team
- Succession planning
- Remuneration

- Assessment and selection
- Redundancy
- Relocation
- Retention

- Communication feedback

- Training and development
- Merger specific
- Future competencies

- HR systems
- Policies
- IT

team may have exhausted its energies in 'doing the deal', HR needs to plan the longer-term strategy for delivering the deal. Research found that organisations that were strongly HR led, anticipated and overcame many of the integration stumbling blocks that beset other mergers. Some HR teams raised their standing within the organisation so that they became key players in subsequent merger discussions.

HR may be viewed by the business as dealing with 'soft' issues, but the 'hard' issues can be at risk of taking over completely as beleaguered staff deal with contracts, rewards systems, benefits and pension schemes. Research also suggests that over 75% of HR time is spent on fewer than 5% of the employees. These can include staff in outposts on irregular contracts. As with other aspects of merger management, excellent project

management skills are a great asset for the HR team. Dividing the work up in terms of accountability and delivery against a strict timetable is a valuable exercise, particularly where joint project groups from both organisations can demonstrate integration principles in their own roles.

While the 'hard' HR issues can risk taking over in terms of time and energy, HR professionals should maintain the 'body' but also keep an eye on the 'soul' of the organisation. This is a demanding and often emotionally draining process while HR personnel themselves may not be certain of their own future.

Source: adapted from 'Reaping the Benefits of Mergers and Acquisitions'

Questions

1 What is meant by 'find ways to deliver head-count reduction, and higher productivity through synergy, while ensuring that the company has the right skills to take the new organisation forward'? Is this a hard or soft HR job? (*8 marks*)

2 Why might employees be more concerned with job security in situations such as this, rather than with the reorganisation of the business itself? (*4 marks*)

Components of workforce plans

What is workforce planning?

An effective workforce plan is an essential tool to identify appropriate workload staffing levels and justify budget allocations so that organisations can meet their objectives. Workforce planning has many definitions, but one of the most useful describes it as: 'Workforce planning is a systematic process for identifying the human capital required to meet an organisation's goals, and developing the strategies to meet these requirements.'

This definition covers what many consider to be the key elements of workforce planning. However, it also tends to involve the following:

- A systematic process that is integrated, methodical, and ongoing.
- Identifying the human capital required to meet organisational goals. This consists of determining the number and skills of workers required and where and when they will be needed.
- Developing the strategies to meet these requirements, which involves identifying actions that must be taken to attract (and retain) the number and types of workers the organisation needs.
- Effective workforce planning is a continuous process that ensures an organisation has the right number of people in the right jobs at the right time.

Why is workforce planning important?

Workforce planning provides managers with a strategic basis for making human resource decisions. It allows managers to anticipate change rather than be overcome by events, as well as providing strategic methods for addressing present and anticipated workforce issues. Organisational success depends on having employees with the right competencies at the right time. Workforce planning provides managers with the means of identifying the competencies needed in the workforce. This means they will not only have the right mix for the present, but also for the future. It also allows for the selection and development of the workforce for those future needs.

WORKFORCE PLANNING IN CONTEXT

What is in a workforce plan?

Strategic planning sets organisational direction and measurable objectives. These goals and objectives not only provide the basis for determining necessary financial resources, but also the basis for workforce needs. If the right people with the right competencies are not in place, it is difficult to effectively achieve the organisation's strategic goals and objectives. The workforce plan aims to highlight the people factor in achieving results. Workforce planning requires effective management leadership and cooperative supportive efforts of staff in several functional areas. Strategic planning, budgeting and human resources are key elements in workforce planning. Human Resources provides the necessary tools for identifying needed competencies and for building the future workforce through strategic recruitment, training, development, and retention techniques.

Strategic plan and scorecard

- Vision, mission, goals and objectives
- Performance measures
- Key future functional requirements

Workforce planning

- Present and future staffing profiles and projections
- Gap analysis
- Workforce strategies

Human capital

- Recruitment, development and retention of critical competencies

Results

- Value and benefit
- Customer
- Financial
- Key business processes
- Internal capacity

The first key step is to outline a workforce planning model. This diagram shows a typical planning model.

Phase I
SET STRATEGIC DIRECTION
Determine future functional requirements through the organisation's strategic planning and budgeting process

Phase IV
MONITOR, EVALUATE, REVISE
Assess what's working and what's not working

Make adjustments to the plan

Address new workforce and organisational issues

Phase II
WORKFORCE ANALYSIS/STRATEGIES
Step 1: Demand forecast
future workforce profile needed

Step 2: Supply projection
present workforce profile

Step 3: Gap analysis
discrepancy between demand and supply

Step 4: Strategy development
solutions to close gaps

Phase III
IMPLEMENT WORKFORCE PLAN
Communicate workforce plan

Implement strategies to close gaps – examples include: success planning, target recruitment, training programmes, restructuring, retention strategies, etc.

EXPLANATION OF PROCESSES

Phase I
Workforce planning is a natural complement to strategic planning since it is through the workforce that the objectives of the strategic plan will be achieved. Workforce planning cannot be effectively accomplished unless a meaningful strategic plan has been prepared for the organisation. A useful guideline in determining planning levels is to ensure that the outcomes of workforce planning will relate directly to the organisation's strategic plan. As such, the level of analysis should be at least equivalent to that of the strategic plan, and preferably carried out at functional level where the front-line effects will be felt.

Phase II
The demand forecast deals with the workforce that will be needed to accomplish future functional requirements and carry out the mission of the organisation. The supply projection step involves: 1) developing the present workforce profile, and 2) projecting that profile into the future, as though either no management action was taken to replace attrition or develop existing staff, or if only the normal course of action continues. Gap analysis is the process of comparing the workforce demand forecast to the workforce supply projection. The expected result is the identification of gaps and surpluses in staffing levels and competencies needed to carry out future functional requirements of the organisation. The final step in the workforce analysis phase involves the development of strategies to address future gaps and surpluses. There is a wide range of strategies that agencies might use to attract and develop staff with needed competencies and to deal with excesses in competencies no longer needed in the organisation.

Phase III
The workforce plan should be implemented in connection with the requirements of the organisation's strategic plan. If the strategic plan timetable changes – due to unanticipated customer, leadership, or legislative changes – adjustments to the workforce plan strategies may be needed.

Phase IV
Evaluation and adjustments are implicit in workforce planning or any good planning and project-management process. If an organisation does not engage in a systematic review of its workforce planning efforts, it runs the risk of not responding to changes that occur incrementally from within or unanticipated external impacts.

Question
An organisation's vision, mission, and measurable goals and objectives drive the identification of future functional requirements. In turn, those requirements drive the analysis and elements of the workforce plan. Discuss. (*18 marks*)

Assessing internal and external influences on workforce plans

LEARNING OBJECTIVES

▶ Roles and responsibilities
▶ Building support for the plan
▶ Factors that affect workforce planning
▶ Workforce analysis matrix

Roles and responsibilities

When employees are involved in the workforce planning process, they help to accept the plan and promote it to other employees. There are several roles and responsibilities:

- **Senior managers** are responsible for recognising the need for workforce planning, demonstrating commitment, and providing the resources to make it happen.
- **Line managers** should serve on workforce planning teams. Managers are also responsible for using workforce planning as a process for aligning people actions, such as recruitment and training, with strategic goals and objectives.
- **HR professionals** should serve on workforce planning teams and provide support and workforce data. They should also work closely with line managers in developing and implementing workforce plans.
- **IT professionals** should serve on workforce planning teams, especially if the process is being automated.
- **Strategic planners** should serve on workforce planning teams to ensure linkage between the strategic plan and the workforce plan.
- **Budget analysts** should serve on workforce planning teams to ensure linkage between the budget and workforce planning.

Building support

Gaining and maintaining management and staff commitment to the workforce planning process is vital to develop an effective workforce plan. Therefore, organisations should work hard from the outset to gain commitment, using some of the following techniques:

- Obtain support from senior management within the business. It is important that senior managers understand the value of workforce planning as their commitment can determine its success or failure. Understanding the factors that affect the organisation's future operations and competition will help convince senior leaders of the need for workforce planning.
- Communicate benefits and results of workforce planning to managers and workers. Management should be involved in understanding the link between workforce plans and the budget, and workers need to understand how workforce planning affects them and the business.
- Establish a team of dedicated and knowledgeable employees from different functional areas and organisational levels. Trust for the workforce plan can be achieved by involving employees in the planning process.
- Automate the process so that data can be easily stored and retrieved, thereby simplifying the process. The more simple the process, the more involvement and acceptance organisations will have from those who are participating in it.
- Develop and implement a plan to ensure accountability within each participating division of an agency. This will help to ensure success of the strategies within the plan and hold those who are not meeting the goals accountable.
- Seek continuous feedback for improvements to the process. The workforce planning process should be continually reviewed and refined to ensure effectiveness and continuous improvement.

Factors affecting workforce planning

The table at the top of the opposite page summarises the major factors that could have an impact on the workforce planning process.

Workforce analysis matrix

The second table opposite shows task requirements and which of the key internal stakeholders are likely to have an influence on the process.

Other key influences

Perhaps one of the other major influences on workforce planning is the labour environment itself. The business will need to take into account the changes in the size of the labour force, the major population and employment trends (such as increased numbers of women wanting part-time work). These factors will have an impact on the business's ability to recruit.

Driver of change	Area of impact on future workforce needs				
	Employees needed (workload)	Demographics	Geographical location	Occupational competencies	General (core) competencies
Demographic trends (e.g. aging workforce, more minorities and women, etc.)		X			X
Programme strategies that affect staffing (e.g. expanding programme coverage)	X		X	X	
Diversity goals		X			X
External mandates (e.g. departmental initiatives and new legislation)	X	X	X	X	X
Special programmes (e.g. quality improvement initiatives)	X	X	X	X	X
Cyclical workload factors	X		X	X	X
Evolution of jobs from defined duties and roles (i.e. specialists to generalists)					X
New technology, different work process, and workflow	X		X	X	
Budget constraints	X		X	X	X
Growth of team-based organisations					X
New organisational designs to provide better, faster, and cheaper delivery of services	X		X		

Activity	Input	Output	Participants
Supply analysis	Workforce levels, demographic information, hiring and turnover trends Workforce skills/experience data collection	Current workforce profile (include relevant information about number of workers, salary, skill assessment, classification, tenure, supervisory ratio, and diversity) Trends/predictors (turnover, retirement rates, and replacement patterns) Workforce skills inventory	Programme managers, supervisors, and staff; HR staff
Demand analysis	Management assessment of organisation direction and budget plans Analysis of jobs needed Analysis of skills needed	Future workforce profile (include relevant information about types of jobs needed, number of workers needed, and worker skills needed)	Executive management; planning and budget staff; programme managers and supervisors; HR staff
Gap analysis	Supply analysis and demand analysis summaries	Analysis of difference between present workforce and future needs; establish priorities for addressing change	Programme managers and supervisors; HR staff
Strategy development	Gap analysis summary	Develop strategies for workforce transition	Executive management; programme managers and supervisors; HR staff

The actual overall business objectives will also influence the plan, particularly if different parts of the organisation have their own major objectives. The business might also consider the fact that in the future it may choose to change the types of products or services that it offers, or the markets in which they are sold and how they are distributed.

Location factors are also significant, such as where the main business is located and whether there are different parts of the organisation located elsewhere. It very much depends on how the business is organised. If the different locations are mutually dependent, location issues can affect the whole organisation. Specialist skills may be needed in particular locations and the business needs to be aware of this.

Timetables can also impact on the plan. The strategic needs of the business may require long- or short-term solutions. If the business is expanding rapidly, then the workforce needs may be more pressing than in an organisation that is growing slowly.

Question

Suggest four ways in which a business could forecast future workforce demands. (*8 marks*)

Issues in implementing workforce plans

Workforce planning in context

It is important to appreciate that workforce planning cannot take place in isolation; it needs to be part of a broad strategy that seeks to react to both internal and external pressures in the present and in the future.

The following diagram illustrates the idea that the strategic planning process – of which workforce planning is an important element – responds to a range of specific issues.

The strategic planning process aims to engage all levels of the workforce, to capture accurate information from them and to ensure the implementation of workforce plans and workforce development initiatives. The design of methodologies that support the linking of workforce development with business development is a major feature of this process.

Key issues in implementing workforce plans

The lessons about workforce planning and development that emerge from businesses, experiences are transferable across industries, sectors and organisations. Each of these lessons can also be regarded as a critical success factor.

• *It is important to link workforce planning and development into core business planning and reporting cycles.*

Sustainable workforce development outcomes are achieved by integrating workforce planning methods and practice into normal business planning cycles. Businesses find that it is also important to demonstrate the value of workforce planning and development for achieving business goals. For example, a business could integrate workforce planning methods into normal business planning cycles by designing a process that required individual divisions to incorporate specific workforce planning interventions into business plans, and to report on these within overall planning cycles. Key performance indicators can be developed to monitor progress for each component of the workforce plan. As an alternative, executive and senior management could be required to present a business case for undertaking a workforce planning project that includes a risk assessment associated with not undertaking workforce planning.

• *Good practice in workforce planning and development identifies the needs of employers and employees, and generates strategies that simultaneously meet the needs of both.*

This highlights the importance of workforce development in building 'learning organisations' in order to meet change-based challenges while simultaneously enabling employees to build their skills and qualifications. It includes the development of individual training and career plans designed to meet both employee and employer needs as part of an overall learning strategy. Some businesses will use organisation-based workforce planning and development that is designed to promote a commitment to lifelong learning and to enabling ongoing work-related learning.

• *Partnerships play a key role in effective workforce planning and development.*

Many of the issues addressed through workforce planning are complex and require multiple solutions and actions, a range of skills, and networks of influence. Consequently, there are usually a number of different stakeholders involved in the workforce planning and development process. This demonstrates the importance of different roles and responsibilities being clearly defined, and processes established to enable a collaborative approach.

• *Good practice in workforce planning and development draws on a range of methods.*

It is important for the organisation to appreciate that it may not get the planning system right first time but that it will need to learn from experience and from the experiences of other organisations that have used alternative approaches

• *Handling ageing workforces and skill gaps.*

Attracting and retaining a skilled workforce, and good practice in building workplace environments, are facilitated by flexible working conditions that enable work-life balance across the different life phases of employees, and during the transitions from one phase to another. Some organisations will gear their workforce planning to address workforce challenges through a whole-of-life approach to employment and workforce development.

• *Workforce planning and development practitioners play a critical role by sharing their expertise and transferring learning.*

Expert workforce planning and development practitioners were found to have played a key role, with the most sustainable impact being achieved when their methodology can be transferred to the organisation as a whole. This transfer needs to be targeted to management, in particular those with responsibility for implementing a workforce plan and for interpreting findings.

• *Good practice in workforce planning and development involves engagement of the workforce in the process, particularly in relation to data-gathering and developing action or implementation plans following data analysis.*

Workforce planning requires the participation of all workforce members, both in obtaining an accurate and complete workforce profile and other supply data, and in implementing the final plan. Specific strategies include identifying people in the workforce to act as 'messengers' or 'champions'. Their role includes encouraging other workforce members to participate in the data-collection and planning processes, and acting as a liaison point between those driving the process and the rest of the workforce. The implementation of the final workforce plan can be structured to further the engagement process (for example, through workshops that enable the workforce to develop an implementation plan and process).

CASE STUDY NO HR?

Talent acquisition and recruitment are rated some of the most important strategic issues (second only to sales growth for business leaders) facing companies today. When it comes to future workforce challenges, retention comes in first for both line managers and HR leaders. What's more, 90% of respondents report that they currently have plans to address critical workforce challenges (88% indicate that they have a plan to address attracting and recruiting qualified talent). In addition, 80% of all respondents report that they are currently in the process of changing their workforce composition – the mix of employee type (64%), job redesign (57%), outsourcing (44%), and offshoring (40%). This is significant, because both groups of respondents fully recognise that the right human capital is vital to achieving the expected business return – and acquiring the right human capital can be a challenge in the current and forecasted business environment.

However, when it comes to who develops strategy and who implements it, an interesting pattern emerges. Twenty-three percent of business leaders and 19% of HR leaders see HR as not involved in developing strategy, or only involved in helping to implement strategy. This finding is significant – nearly 25% of companies are not

involving HR in strategic plan development. In addition, when asked if HR was primarily responsible for developing workforce plans, HR claims more responsibility than business leaders would give them credit for. Fifty-six per cent of business leaders claim that HR is primarily responsible for workforce plan development, while 75% of HR claims primary responsibility.

A factor that affects both the strategy and working relationship between business and HR leaders is that many business leaders feel that HR staff lack the necessary business acumen to take an active role in developing strategy. In fact, only 55% of business leaders rate their HR partners as 'well versed' in financial acumen, while 80% of HR rate themselves so – a significant gap in perceived skill. In turn, HR feels business leaders understate the value of HR and should do a better job with proactive planning.

Source: adapted from Vertitude

Question

Why might it be the case that HR is not as closely involved in workforce planning as we would imagine? (*10 marks*)

The value of workforce planning

Benefits of workforce planning

Workforce planning provides organisations with many benefits:

- It allows for a more effective and efficient use of workers. This will become increasingly important as some organisations find themselves having to do the same amount of work or more with fewer staff members.
- It helps ensure that replacements are available to fill important vacancies. Filling vacancies is especially critical as organisations face an increasing number of workers eligible for retirement, combined with labour market shortages.
- It provides realistic staffing projections for budget purposes. Realistic projections are very helpful when justifying budget requests.
- It provides a clear rationale for linking expenditures for training and retraining, development, career counselling, and recruiting efforts.
- It helps maintain or improve a diversified workforce.
- It helps an organisation prepare for restructuring, reducing, or expanding its workforce.

In many respects, the precise benefits will depend on the size and type of business or organisation in question; however, the following list outlines the most common advantages of workforce planning:

- Understanding the skills needed for the future.

- Managing employment expenditure by anticipating changes.
- Ensuring that sufficient and appropriate training and development is provided.
- Coping with peaks and troughs in supply and demand for different skills.
- Delivering improved services by linking business strategy to people plans.
- Retaining employees and identifying longer-term workplace requirements.
- Implementing diversity policies effectively.
- Manage staff performance and sickness levels.

Workforce planning as a broad approach to human resource planning

Workforce planning and development framework

A workforce plan can provide a workable framework and set of solutions to the human resource needs of an organisation. A good workforce plan can ensure that the business has the right people in the right place at the right time. The plan is divided into two sections.

The first section is a snapshot of your part of the organisation. It includes the number of employees, the gender and ethnic breakdown, age profile, turnover and sickness rates. This information will be available in reports from HR. The snapshot will help identify any issues that

need to be addressed – e.g. high levels of turnover or sickness, a skewed age profile, etc.

The second section is a series of questions that will challenge the organisation to consider how it needs to develop its workforce. There are prompts within the following question areas:

- recruitment issues
- retention issues and succession planning
- service issues – will the service change and therefore require new skills?
- new roles and working practices
- organisation development
- skills and competencies which need to be developed.

An outcome of this part of the section is a training and development plan for the business. This is a document that identifies broad themes rather than individual training needs. Within the training and development plan it is possible to identify:

- development needs for the organisation
- how development will be achieved
- how development will be evaluated
- implications for the training budget.

An example of how the organisation can use the basis of the workforce plan in a broader context is summarised in the table on the opposite page.

Current recruitment and retention issues

Recruitment
- Which are the 'difficult to recruit' posts?
- Why are these difficult?
- What are the current skills shortages?
- What is the impact of recruitment problems on the organisation?

Retention
- Where is turnover particularly high?
- What specific skills are being lost?
- What factors cause turnover?
- What is the impact of high turnover on the organisation?

Future workforce requirements

Organisational issues
- Modernisation requirements
- Impact of legislation
- Demographic changes that impact on service
- Best-value reviews
- Service plans and developments
- Changes to systems and processes

Staffing numbers
- Planned changes
- What is the short-, medium- and long-term impact?

New roles/working practices
- New models of service delivery e.g. outsourcing
- Specialist staff, generic roles, support roles, breaking down departmental boundaries
- Contracts/annualised hours/shift patterns
- Home-working/flexible working

New skills/competencies
- Competencies identified e.g. customer focus/ teamworking
- Professional skills updating
- Technical skills
- IT skills
- Management competencies

Training and development implications

- Development needs
- Who is affected?
- How will development be achieved?
- Who is responsible for organising it?
- What benefits are anticipated?

Source: adapted from New Forest District Council

CASE STUDY POOR PLANNING

Poor NHS workforce planning by the government a few years ago has led to the current climate of staff cutbacks and redundancies, according to workforce experts. The government should have warned the NHS to start trimming its growing staff back in 2004.

John Sargent, a workforce development consultant and former chief executive of the Greater Manchester Workforce Development Confederation, told the MPs that warnings could and should have come sooner. He said, 'The [health] department has an important role – a key leadership role – but all of us knew back in 2004 that a comprehensive spending review was coming, and most people can guess roughly what it might be like. It certainly won't be the growth in money terms of 7.3% that we've seen. Now when you bear in mind there is a four year lead-in time to get more nurses registered, and more for doctors, then there's a very strong argument that, back in 2004, the department should have been anticipating the most likely scenarios within the next spending review. The commissioning changes should have been flagged up in 2004, and reductions should have been occurring from 2005 onwards in anticipation of the next spending review.'

Anne Rainsberry, director of people and organisational development at NHS London, the strategic health authority for London, said that some areas of the country had been under pressure to meet the health department's national targets, felt by some authorities to be sometimes unaffordable. 'My view would be that the department could strengthen its expertise in the area of strategic workforce planning, and that would be most welcome,' she said.

The effect of government policies was also a problem, said Trish Knight, director of workforce development and commissioning at the Leicestershire, Northamptonshire and Rutland Healthcare Workforce Deanery. 'In some of [the health department's] policies they haven't really considered the financial implications of the workforce,' said Ms Knight. 'If you take the example of [the white paper], "Our Health, Our Care, Our Say", it is an excellent policy document, but what does that mean, not just in workforce terms, but in the finances of the workforce?'

Question

How might the fact that the workforce planning is affected by an external finance provider (in this case the government) make the planning process far more complicated? (*12 marks*)

Case studies, questions and exam practice

CASE STUDY WORKFORCE ANALYSIS

Analysis of workforce data is the key element in the workforce planning process. Workforce analysis frequently considers information such as occupations, skills and experience, retirement eligibility, diversity, turnover rates, and trend data. Questions organisations should consider include:

- Are there certain occupational groups with increasing worker turnover?
- Can factors influencing turnover be identified?
- Has turnover reduced the skill set of a certain occupational group?

Step 1
SUPPLY ANALYSIS

Consider:
- Staffing levels
- Workforce skills
- Workforce demographics
- Employment trends

Step 2
DEMAND ANALYSIS

Identify:
- Workforce skills to meet projected needs
- Staffing patterns
- Anticipated programme and workload changes

Step 3
GAP ANALYSIS

- Compare supply analysis with demand analysis to determine future gaps (shortages) and surpluses (excesses) in the number of staff and needed skills
- Identify future changes in workforce demographics
- Identify areas in which management action will be needed to reach workforce objectives

Step 4
STRATEGY DEVELOPMENT

Plan:
- Recruiting
- Succession
- Employee development and retraining
- Work/organisation change

Supply analysis focuses on the specifics of an organisation's existing workforce and projects future workforce supply. This step involves (1) creating a current workforce profile, (2) reviewing trend data, and (3) projecting future workforce supply.

Demand analysis identifies the workforce needed to carry out the mission of an organisation. The focus of this step should be on the functions that an organisation must perform and not just on the people. One reason this step is separated from the supply projections is to ensure that changes in functions are considered. These changes might have a significant impact on the size and kind of workforce that will be needed in the future. Two ways to determine future functional requirements are through environmental scanning and organisational analysis.

Gap analysis is the process of comparing the workforce supply projection with the workforce demand forecast. An analysis should consider the composition of the workforce, including demographic characteristics, geographic location, size, and employee skill level. The organisation will eventually establish workforce strategies based on the results of this analysis.

The final step in the workforce analysis phase involves the development of strategies to address future gaps and surpluses. Strategies include the programmes, policies, and practices that assist organisations in recruiting, developing, and retaining the critical staff needed to achieve programme goals. A wide range of strategies exists for attracting and/or developing staff with needed skills and dealing with workers or skills no longer needed in an organisation.

Source: adapted from the State of Texas

Questions

1 Suggest SIX ways in which an organisation could analyse its existing workforce. (*6 marks*)
2 What is meant by environmental scanning and organisational analysis? (*4 marks*)
3 Explain the two possible outcomes of gap analysis. (*8 marks*)
4 Suggest FOUR factors that could influence or have an impact on strategy. (*8 marks*)

Factors determining choice of organisational structures

Organisational culture

The first way in which the organisational structure of a business can be influenced is by its organisational culture. Various classifications of an organisation's culture were suggested by researchers including Harrison, Handy, Deal and Kennedy, and Quinn and McGrath. Over time, these classifications have become more developed, making it possible to approach them in broad terms only.

In 1972 Harrison suggested four main categories of organisational culture – power, role, task and person. Charles Handy reworked Harrison's theory and identified them as described in the table below.

Quinn and McGrath also identified four different organisational cultures, shown in the table on the right.

Culture	Description
Rational	The rational culture is firmly based on the needs of a market. The organisation places emphasis on productivity and efficiency and encourages management to be goal-orientated and decisive. All activities are focused on tangible performance and employees are rewarded on achievement.
Adhocracy	This type of culture is an adaptive, creative and autonomous one where authority is largely based on the abilities and charismatic nature of leaders. These organisations tend to be risk-orientated and emphasis is placed on employees' adherence to the values of the organisation itself.
Consensual	These types of organisation are often concerned with equality, integrity and fairness, and much of the authority is based on informal acceptance of power. Decisions are made by collective agreements or consensus and dominant leaders are not often present. Morale is important, as is cooperation and support between employees in order to reach organisational objectives. Employee loyalty is high.
Hierarchical	This type of culture relies on stability and control through the setting of rigid regulations and procedures. Decisions are made logically on facts alone, with the management tending to be cautious and conservative. The employees are strictly controlled, with management expecting obedience.

Culture	Description	Culture	Description
Power	This type of culture is based on trust and good personal communication. There is little need for rigid bureaucratic procedures since power and authority rests with only a few individuals. The power culture is dynamic in that change can take place quickly, but it is dependent on a small number of key, powerful individuals. This culture tends to be tough on employees because the key focus is the success of the organisation, often resulting in higher labour turnover.	Task	This type of organisational culture relies on employee expertise. The matrix structure tends to prevail, with teams of individuals specialising. These organisations tend to be flexible, with individual employees working with autonomy, allowing fast reaction to changes in the external environment and having set procedures in place to address these.
Role	This type of culture tends to be bureaucratic in nature, thus requiring logical, coordinated and rational processes with heavy emphasis on rules and procedures. Control lies with a small number of employees who have a high degree of authority. They tend to be stable organisations, operating in a predictable environment with products and services that have a long lifespan. Not considered to be innovative organisations, they can adapt to gradual, minor change, but not radical ones.	Person	This type of culture relies on collective decision-making, often associated with partnerships. Compromise is important, and individuals will tend to work within their own specialist area, coordinating all aspects and working with autonomy, without the need to report to other employees.

It should be remembered that no one organisation fits neatly into any one of the categories mentioned and the majority are too complex to be categorised generally. The classifications should be regarded only as a reference point for comparison of extremes.

Organisational mapping

Organisational mapping seeks to identify the tasks and functions carried out by each individual employee to act as a means by which under- or over-commitment of individuals can be identified. The process begins with assigning a number to each task. It also requires the name of the responsible individual and the estimated time required to perform the task, usually expressed as either hours or weeks. Once this has been carried out, it is possible to add up the projected time for the completion of all necessary tasks for each individual, which will produce either a negative or a positive number. The process should then reveal where key employees are over- or under-committed. Typically, the organisational mapping is displayed as a traditional organisational chart, which details the over- or under-commitment.

For more on flat and hierarchical structures see Adapting organisational structures to improve competitiveness (2) on pp. 154–5.

Organisational structure

The organisational structure of a business details the hierarchical levels in the case of a horizontally organised entity. Organisational structure can also be vertical by function or operation and indeed by use of a matrix. Traditionally, organisational structures kept functional areas separate, each having their own hierarchical levels. Increasingly, however, businesses have reduced the number of management layers and reorganised their businesses into operational units. Each operational unit will have access to marketing and production and other specialists in the form of a matrix.

A functionally based organisational structure is designed around specific sections of the organisation, usually those that produce, market and sell the organisation's product or service. Functional structures can be a substructure of hierarchical or flat structures and can be similarly controlled by a managing director, supported by relevant senior function or departmental managers. The creation of positions and departments around specialised functions is an integral part of the

BOOK RESEARCH

Jon Sutherland and Diane Canwell, *Organisation Structures and Processes*, Pitman Publishing, 1997 and 2007.

functional structure. There will be common themes, in terms of function or process within each department, enabling management to concentrate on specific issues within their own technical area of expertise.

The use of a matrix organisational structure allows the opportunity for teams to be developed in order that particular tasks can be undertaken. Matrix structures often develop in stages, with the first being the establishment of temporary teams, which, having studied a particular problem and suggested recommendations, might be considered significant enough to be retained on a more permanent basis. These teams will consist of a number of different individuals from the different functions of the organisation.

Question

To what extent does Charles Handy's theory explain how organisations choose to structure themselves?
(*12 marks*)

Adapting structures to improve competitiveness (1)

LEARNING OBJECTIVES

▶ Centralisation
▶ Decentralisation
▶ Delegation
▶ Empowerment
▶ Autonomy

Centralisation

Centralisation is a measure of how concentrated the decision-making processes are within an organisation. The greater the concentration, the more centralised the organisation is considered to be.

Advantages of centralised structures for organisations

- Senior managers enjoy greater control over the organisation.
- The use of standardised procedures can results in cost savings.
- Decisions can be made to benefit the organisation as a whole, whereas a decision made by a department manager may benefit their department, but disadvantage others.
- The organisation can benefit from the decision-making of experienced senior managers.
- In difficult times, the organisation will need strong leadership and pull in one direction. It is believed that strong leadership is often best given from above.

Decentralisation

Decentralisation involves a gradual dispersal of decision-making control across an organisation. Integral to the dispersal of decision-making is the movement of power and authority from the higher levels of management, or a single headquarters unit, to various divisions, branches, departments or subsidiaries of the organisation. At its very core, decentralisation implies delegation – transferring the responsibility and power from senior management to lower-level individuals. The purpose of decentralisation is to encourage flexibility and, above all, to assist faster decision-making which, in turn, means faster response times.

Decentralisation is also strongly associated with the concept of empowerment, affording to frontline staff the power, authority and responsibility to make immediate decisions without reference to senior management.

Advantages of decentralised structures for organisations

- Senior managers have time to concentrate on the most important decisions (as the other decisions can be taken by people lower down the organisation structure).
- Decision-making is a form of empowerment. Empowerment can increase motivation and therefore mean that staff output increases.
- People lower down the chain have a more detailed knowledge of the environment they work in and the people (customers and colleagues) they interact with. This knowledge, skills and experience may enable them to make more effective decisions than senior managers.
- Empowerment will enable departments and their employees to respond faster to changes and new challenges, whereas it may take senior managers longer to appreciate that business needs have changed.
- Empowerment makes it easier for people to accept and make a success of more responsibility.

Some organisations may also decide that a combination of centralisation and decentralisation is more effective. Functional areas

FOR EXAMPLE

An example of a decentralised structure is Tesco the supermarket chain. Each store of Tesco has a store manager who can make certain decisions concerning their store. The store manager is responsible to a regional manager.

such as accounting and purchasing may be centralised to save costs, but recruitment may be decentralised, as units away from head office may have staffing needs specific to them.

Some organisations implement vertical decentralisation which means that they have handed the power to make certain decisions down the hierarchy of their organisation. Vertical decentralisation increases the contribution to decision-making of those at the bottom of the chart.

Horizontal decentralisation spreads responsibility across the organisation. A business might decide to use this for the implementation of new technology across the whole business. This implementation will be the sole responsibility of technology specialists.

Delegation

Delegation is not only an issue for management, but also of considerable importance to Human Resources, as it involves the active use of the skills and experience of employees in subordinate positions. Delegation usually begins with the identification of an individual suitable to perform a particular task. This person needs to be prepared and, above all, given the authority to carry out the job properly.

Delegation means that the manager needs to support and monitor the progress and, once the task is completed, to acknowledge that the job has been completed successfully. Delegation is a means by which pressured key members of staff can reduce their workload in the certain knowledge that vital tasks will still be performed. It is not always possible to delegate all tasks to other individuals, but delegation can mean greater efficiency, increased motivation, skill development and, above all, a more equitable distribution of work throughout a team.

BOOK RESEARCH

J.K. Smart, *Real Delegation: How to get people to do things for you and do them well*, Prentice Hall, 2002.

Empowerment

Empowerment of an individual employee means allowing them to control their contribution to the organisation. This means that they are given the authority and responsibility to complete tasks and attain targets without the direct intervention of management. The benefits of empowerment to the organisation are that it reduces the importance of repetitive administration and the number of managers required at the various levels of the structure. By streamlining management levels, the effectiveness of communication often increases. From an employee's point of view, empowerment increases their creativity and initiative, as well as their commitment to the organisation, by allowing them to work with autonomy.

Autonomy

Autonomy is a measure of an individual's independence within their job role. Autonomy implies that within the context of their work, an individual has a degree of control over what they do, the order in which they do it and the processes involved in carrying it out. Autonomy also suggests that aside from not requiring close supervision or management in order to carry out the function, the individual may have a larger influence over their own working environment. Truly autonomous workers, therefore, are those who are enabled by offering alternative work arrangements or a form of remote working, such as telecommuting or teleworking.

CASE STUDY NATIONAL TRUST CATERING

The National Trust's catering department, which is responsible for the running of around 150 restaurants at Trust-owned properties across the country, has a significant challenge in coordinating the supply and collation of information that can help improve profit margins. Not only are the restaurants widely spread geographically, but each site is encouraged to purchase locally sourced produce and ingredients in keeping with the culture of the Trust.

Hosted centrally by the National Trust, Saffron Spice is accessed through a password-controlled website by both head office and selected personnel at the restaurant sites. In this way, catering managers can record information – such as stock usage, purchase invoices and sales data – simply by logging onto the Internet and uploading the data, which is then routed directly back to head office.

Crucially for the National Trust, the move to a centralised structure needed to avoid imposing a rigid process that would run counter to the local sourcing of food products and individual pricing structure. Saffron

Spice is designed to enable this flexibility, while also arming area managers and a central catering team with information that will aid negotiations with suppliers.

It is hoped that Saffron Spice will introduce the degree of flexibility that the National Trust needs, while at the same time improving the knowledge of the cost and pricing relationship at catering manager level, sharing best practice. For instance, if a certain dish is achieving a higher margin in one restaurant compared with others, the new system will be able to spot any such opportunities more easily. It will also be possible to check more readily that the National Trust's food-sourcing policy and buying guidelines are being followed.

Source: adapted from Fretwell Downing Hospitality

Question

Why has the National Trust chosen to centralise in this way? What degree of autonomy has remained and why? (*12 marks*)

Adapting structures to improve competitiveness (2)

LEARNING
OBJECTIVES

▶ Flat structures
▶ Hierarchical structures
▶ Chains of command
▶ Spans of control

Flat structures

A flat organisational structure is a hierarchical structure in the sense that it is in the shape of a pyramid, but it has fewer layers. If necessary, a hierarchical structure can be de-layered in order to create a flat structure. The de-layering process often allows decisions to be made more quickly and efficiently because the layers are able to communicate more easily with each other. This enables the organisation to be less bureaucratic, and is a simpler structure often used by organisations operating from a single site. The directors and other major decision-makers are more available for consultation with employees, who are likely to feel more a part of the process. This encourages motivation, particularly among junior managers, who may be given more responsibility through delegation from the senior management level of the structure.

Hierarchical structures

A hierarchical organisation structure is best imagined by using the image of a pyramid. At the top are the major decision-makers, who are few in number, and further down the pyramid, the shape of the organisation broadens as more employees become involved at the lower levels. At the base of the pyramid are the majority of the workers.

Power, responsibility and authority are concentrated at the top of the pyramid and decisions flow from top to bottom. An organisation would choose this form of structure when decisions need to be made by those who have the necessary expertise and experience, as well as the authority to ensure that decisions are implemented.

The most common version of this form of structure is the steep pyramid, where there are many different layers of management, possibly within an organisation that operates in several different locations, needing to fulfil different administrative functions, or in organisations that are of a complex nature for other reasons.

There are some disadvantages for those lower down the hierarchical structure in that, if the pyramid is too multilayered and complex, they often find difficulty in understanding how and why decisions are made. The organisation may also find that it is too bureaucratic in nature, the result being that the decision-making process becomes too complicated and time-consuming because there are too many layers involved.

Chains of command

The chain of command within an organisation is typically associated with a business that has a hierarchical structure. The chain of command is the formal line of communication, beginning with the board of directors, or managing director, who then passes instructions down to departmental managers, section heads and then to individual employees. The chain of command typifies a pyramid-shaped organisation, where the lower down the pyramid the individuals are, the more they will have to be informed of decisions and instructions. Effectively, the chain of command of the board of directors or the managing director encompasses every individual beneath them in the hierarchical structure. Similarly, the chain of command of a section head is merely the immediate employees who work under that individual's supervision. The term 'chain of command' is closely associated with 'span of control'.

Spans of control

The span of control is the number of subordinates for whom a manager has direct responsibility. The ideal number frequently quoted is between five and nine individuals under the control of one manager. Beyond this it becomes increasingly difficult to react or respond to their specific needs. Span of control, therefore, implies that additional levels of hierarchy need to be inserted, both above and below each manager, in order to reduce the span of control to a manageable level.

In 1916, Henri Fayol, a French industrialist, wrote his views and theories about the problems commonly encountered by organisations. His view was that many of the root causes of industrial failure were down to management

BOOK RESEARCH

Doede Keuning and Wilfred Opheij, *De-layering organisations: How to beat bureaucracy and create a flexible and responsive organisation*, Pitman, 1994.

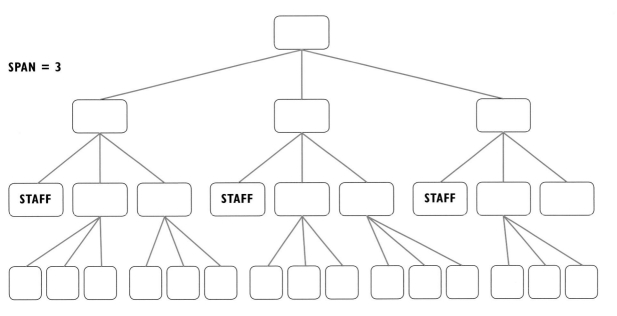

SPAN = 3

and personnel. Fayol was a 'top-down' theorist who believed that change must begin with the board of directors or the managing director.

Fayol began by identifying the three main aspects of management, which are:

- the activities of the organisation
- the elements of management
- the principles of management

Fayol identified the six main categories of activities in an organisation as being:

- *Technical activities* – including production, manufacture and adaptation
- *Commercial activities* – including buying, selling and exchanging
- *Financial activities* – including the seeking of finance and deciding the best use of that finance
- *Security services* – including the protection of the organisation, its employees and its property
- *Accounting services* – including the production of balance sheets, costings, statistical data and stock inventories
- *Managerial activities* – including forecasting and planning, organisation, giving instruction, coordinating and controlling employee activity

Fayol then identified 14 elements and principles of management which were key qualities and functions:

- *Division of work* – ensuring that all employees know what their duties are
- *Authority* – the ability to give clear, complete and unambiguous instructions
- *Discipline* – to be rigid and firm when appropriate but always to ensure understanding
- *Unity of command* – to ensure that all aspects of management within the organisation are uniform
- *Unity of direction* – to ensure that the business has a clear corporate strategy
- *Subordination* – the ability to put the organisation first and personal needs and commitments second
- *Remuneration* – the need for a fair wage for a fair day's work
- *Centralisation* – to ensure that tasks are concentrated and not duplicated, in order to maintain cost effectiveness
- *Clear scalar chain* – to ensure that all individuals within the organisation know their position (Fayol suggested that this could be achieved through the production of an organisation chart)
- *Internal order* – to strive to avoid internal conflict

- *Equality* – to ensure equal opportunity within the organisation and avoid discrimination by age, sex, sexual orientation, disability or religion
- *Stability of tenure* – to ensure that employees feel that their job is secure and are not concerned about their own security
- *Initiative* – to encourage idea creation and to accept ideas from employees without necessarily engaging senior management input
- *Esprit de corps* – to encourage a company spirit where individuals are proud to support the objectives of the business

Fayol also identified some rules that he considered management should follow. He wrote that an individual who specialises would become more skilled, efficient and effective, but he also considered that the manager should have the ultimate accountability for the employees.

> ### Question
>
> Explain how Fayol's theory could help explain how an organisation chooses to structure itself. (*15 marks*)

Adapting structures to improve competitiveness (3)

Flexible staffing

Flexible staffing aims to provide the business with a responsive approach to the deployment of employees. Flexible staffing implies that the business will have a small number of core employees supported by a number of available either part-time workers or contract workers. Part-time workers' hours can be changed or amended in order to fit with additional pressures of work or demand, while contract workers can be brought in or outsourced from employment agencies. Temporary contracts can be offered to individuals for fixed periods of time, and once the immediate problem period has passed, staffing levels can then return to their normal pattern.

Flexitime

Flexitime allows employees to choose, within set limits, when they wish to begin and end work. They are required to work during core times and must work an agreed number of hours during a given period (usually four weeks). Outside the core times are flexible bands of time during which employees may choose whether or not to be at work. The total period for which the workplace is open is known as the bandwidth. Working out the starting and finishing times of lunch breaks and the maximum and minimum lunch period entitlements also has to be calculated. The employee's hours of attendance are recorded and added up at the end of each period and, within expressed and agreed limits,

employees can carry over any excess or deficit in the number of hours they are required to work. Some schemes allow employees to take excess hours as additional leave, known as flexileave.

Flexitime is typically used for office-based staff below managerial level in both public sector and private sector service organisations. Manufacturing organisations are less likely to operate a flexitime system.

Those carrying out shift work are usually excluded from flexitime schemes, as are senior managers or key personnel. Other groups of workers for whom flexitime systems are rarely an option include those who serve the public during specific organisational opening times.

For employers, flexitime can aid the recruitment and retention of staff. It can also help provide staff cover outside normal working hours and reduce the need for overtime. In addition, flexitime can also improve the provision of equal opportunities to staff unable to work standard hours.

Flexitime can give employees greater freedom to organise their working lives to suit domestic commitments, and travelling can be cheaper and easier if it is outside peak time. However, the use of a flexitime system can result in increased administration costs, including the costs of keeping records, and extra heating and lighting, as well as the issue of how to provide adequate supervision throughout the bandwidth.

An effective flexitime system can be developed if the organisation:

- involves managers and trade union or employee representatives at an early stage, possibly by means of a working group, to plan, implement and monitor the scheme
- ensures supervisors and line managers are kept fully informed on the development of the scheme
- pilots the scheme for a trial period and receives feedback on opinions
- identifies individuals who will participate in the scheme – often it is more appropriate to ask for volunteers rather than to impose compulsion
- ensures there are procedures in place for dealing with medical appointments, absences, etc.
- sets up a system by which employees and line managers can easily record time worked.

Flexiplace

Flexiplace systems allow flexibility in which employees carry out the duties of their job role on behalf of the organisation. Often this will be at home or another remote location linked to the organisation by means of computer networks and telecommunication systems. There are control problems associated with the widespread use of home working as a primary method of carrying out core activities, since there will be a reliance on the various outworkers completing the series of tasks at precisely the right point. At the same time, the organisational structure has to be capable of accommodating the requirement of continuous communication and supervision of remote workers.

An employee could also be required to show flexibility by being geographically mobile. Individuals, particularly those who are involved in maintenance, carry out their duties in a variety of locations, very often in other countries. The flexibility requires the willingness of the employee to travel, and some form of reward from the organisation will then be appropriate in order to compensate the employee for the inevitable disruption to their domestic life.

Compressed working week

The compressed working week is an example of an alternative work arrangement, and is often referred to as a compressed time option. Some businesses will refer to the compressed working week as a 4/10 schedule, which refers to the common practice of employees working four ten-hour days, with the fifth day as leave. Alternatively, the system is referred to as a nine-day fortnight, or 9/80, and in some cases as a 9/8 schedule.

The nine-day fortnight means simply that the employee works for nine working days in each two-week block. A 9/80 schedule refers to a system when employees work for 80 hours over nine days (instead of the normal 10). A 9/8 schedule is more complex, as employees work for nine hours on four days of the week, and for eight hours on the fifth day, or they have a day off.

As far as the US and the UK are concerned, more than 25% of private-sector employers offer compressed working weeks. There are a number of advantages associated with these more complicated work schedules, which tend to be centred on two key areas:

- *Customer satisfaction* – a traditional five-day week schedule often meant that businesses would be required to take on additional staff to cover periods beyond Monday to Friday. There would be associated breaks in production, coverage and consistency in relation to dealing with customers. Equally, for times when the business needed extra coverage, there would be a requirement to pay employees overtime. Using a compressed working week, more employees can be deployed at crucial times of the week and lower staffing levels can be maintained when demand is lower.

- *Employee retention* – it has been a major discovery that a compressed working week is attractive and adds to the retention strategies of a business. A compressed working week offers a degree of flexibility. Guaranteed additional time of sufficient longevity to deal with domestic issues (such as childcare, for example), means that a compressed working week is often attractive to employees with young children, or with other commitments outside work.

The compressed working week, however, does have problems associated with it, specifically with reference to issues of safety and the health of employees. A longer, albeit concentrated, working week does add to the physical strain on employees, as they will inevitably have shorter breaks between blocks of work within a four-day period. Crucial to the imposition of a compressed working week is the requirement for the business to give employees sufficient time to reschedule their personal lives. Providing the imposition is planned before it is initiated, most employees seem to be receptive to the concept of the compressed working week.

> ### Questions
>
> A compressed working week should work for almost any organisation. Discuss.
> (*12 marks*)

Case studies, questions and exam practice

CASE STUDY A NEW WORKING ENVIRONMENT

The Environmental Services Department at Slough Borough Council decided to introduce flexible working, and the team has been able to recruit and retain five new staff that would not have been able to take up the posts previously.

Slough Borough Council was experiencing staff recruitment and retention problems as workers were being attracted by the higher salaries of nearby boroughs that offer London allowances. Around 70 per cent of an Environmental Health Officer's time is spent out of the office, making these posts ideal for a mobile working solution.

Once trade unions had been consulted, WiseWork provided in-depth advice and assistance in setting up a home-working scheme on a six-month pilot basis in the Environmental Services Department. The pilot involved 12 Environmental Health Officers who carry out inspection work within the borough. Although their jobs were already mobile, they were still coming into the office for desk work.

WiseWork provided training for all the staff involved in the pilot to assist them in managing

the culture change of homeworking. Team leaders were helped to learn to fully trust their staff. The pilot proved so successful that the scheme was extended to other Environmental Health Officers and Trading Standards Officers. Now 24 officers (70 per cent of the group) have the ability to work from home.

While neighbouring local authorities are offering financial incentives to attract employees, Slough is able to retain staff by offering flexible homeworking. The employee turnover rate in Environmental Services has dropped to zero and the department has made significant savings in office space.

Staff output has also improved, and those working from home are hitting 100 per cent of their targets compared with 70 per cent for office-based workers. As a result of the benefits enjoyed by Environmental Services, Social Services and Education are now starting their own flexible working schemes.

Digital Steps is a small software developer working in a specialist field where there is a shortage in qualified people. They received an award under the DTI Challenge Fund to review their work-life balance provisions to see if this would help them to recruit more female staff.

Although the organisation already had a flexible approach to working arrangements, which allowed staff to change their hours on an informal basis, WiseWork advised reinforcing this message as the company grew. An Employee Handbook was produced to help existing and new employees to understand the approach to work-life balance.

All employees were interviewed by WiseWork and an employee survey was carried out to find out how staff felt about working for the company, including their views on work-life balance.

Although it was decided not to have a formal 'working at home' policy, the company introduced a flexitime scheme and allows working from home when appropriate. This has been well received by current staff, especially some of the female workers who need more flexibility, and it is a major selling point for the organisation in terms of recruitment.

One of the Digital Steps directors said: 'This project has been invaluable in helping us understand the ambitions of our employees in terms of work-life balance. Through interviews, surveys and focused project teams, we have gained an understanding of their requirements and have been able to make positive changes to address these. It turns out that remarkably small changes can result in significant benefits.'

Source: adapted from WiseWorks, Slough Borough Council and Digital Steps

Questions

1   What were the main reasons why the two organisations wanted to introduce flexible working? (*6 marks*)
2   What were the outcomes for the two organisations? (*6 marks*)

Managing communications with employees

LEARNING OBJECTIVES

▶ Why communicate with employees?
▶ Communication channels
▶ Communication methods
▶ Communication standards
▶ Communication barriers
▶ Engagement

Why communicate with employees?

Effective two-way communication systems can assist in building up a psychological bond where the employees feel that they are valued by their employer, and the employer values the contribution of the employee. Increased employee commitment should lead to improved work performance. It should also mean lower labour turnover, make it easier to recruit and enhance the reputation of the organisation.

According to ACAS (Advisory Conciliation and Arbitration Service), good employee communications and consultation can:

- Improve organisational performance – time spent communicating at the outset of a new project or development can minimise subsequent rumour and misunderstanding.
- Improve management performance and decision-making – allowing employees to express their views can help managers and supervisors arrive at sound decisions which can more readily be accepted by employees as a whole; this may be particularly important at times of emergency or where new practices or procedures are being introduced.
- Improve employees' performance and commitment – employees will perform better if they are given regular, accurate information about their jobs, such as updated technical instructions, targets, deadlines and feedback. Their commitment is also likely to be

enhanced if they know what the organisation is trying to achieve and how they, as individuals, can influence decisions.

- Help develop greater trust – discussing issues of common interest and allowing employees an opportunity to express their views can engender improved management/employee relations
- Increase job satisfaction – employees are more likely to be motivated if they have a good understanding of their job and how it fits into the organisation as a whole and are actively encouraged to express their views and ideas.
- Encourage a more flexible working environment – employers can help to promote a good 'work-life balance' within the organisation by talking to all their staff about developing flexible working policies and practices.

Communication channels

The organisational structure will determine the channels through which communication is regularly made. Communication channels need to ensure that the information flows freely throughout the organisation in order that the right information meets the right person at the right time. Open communication channels tend to take the form of the following:

- noticeboards
- newsletters
- minutes of meetings
- non-confidential internal mail
- multi-user computer systems
- e-mail

Communication channels also have to pass information of a confidential or security-restricted nature and the organisation will restrict the access to this information in a variety of ways, including passwords for computer systems.

Communication methods

An organisation will select the most effective method of communication for transmitting information both internally and externally, taking into account considerations such as speed, cost, feedback requirements or written documentation needs. The following illustration identifies the main methods of communication, in both written and verbal format.

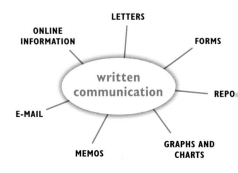

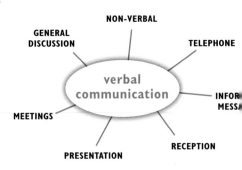

Communication standards

This is a formal protocol, often administered by the human resources department, which applies to internal communications within a business. The communication standards set the rules with regard to the elimination of racial, age, gender or other biases in communications within the organisation.

Communication barriers

A communication barrier is a problem in the communication system or stream which effectively blocks either the communication itself or the understanding of that communication between the relevant parties. Communication barriers can take a number of different forms, such as:

- lack of sufficient or effective training of employees
- lack of information needed to make a decision
- personal relationship problems
- faulty or inadequate systems or procedures

Engagement

The term 'engagement' can actually refer to both employees and customers. Engaged employees are encouraged to use their natural talents in order to assist the business in having a competitive edge. It is believed that, collectively, efforts involving employee engagement can actually assist in the engagement of customers themselves. Employee engagement requires employee understanding, not only of the business but also the management and what both hope to achieve. Managers within organisations must assist employees in realising their expectations, which have been learned by the subordinates as being the primary motivators of the business itself.

Employee engagement, therefore, involves the mobilisation of the talent, energy and resources of employees. If done effectively, employee engagement delivers the following:

- Contributes to the development of a healthy and sustainable business

BOOK RESEARCH

Richard H. Axelrod, *Terms of engagement: Changing the way we change our organisations.* San Francisco, California: Berrett-Koehler Publishers Inc. 2000.

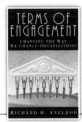

- Assists the business in identifying the needs and the solutions of customers
- Creates opportunities for dialogue with the business's stakeholders
- Provides leverage for the business in the sense that it strengthens relations with stakeholders and leads to partnerships
- Uses resources more efficiently
- Allows for the development of skills and personnel
- Is an asset for leadership and team development
- Assists in bringing any form of corporate culture into sharp focus, building morale, loyalty and pride in the workforces
- Assists in the establishment and maintenance of the business's reputation

CASE STUDY ROTHERHAM METROPOLITAN BOROUGH COUNCIL

Profile: 13,500 staff

Historic Performance: in 2002 the Council was in the 'doldrums', with one star and rated as 'weak' in the Comprehensive Performance Assessment. Only 24% of staff rated morale as 'high'.

Approach: Rotherham's 'Exchange Programme' was runner-up in the 'Improving Business Performance Through Engaging Staff' category of the CIPD People Management Awards. A representative 'Reach-in' panel that gives detailed feedback and quarterly focus groups to handle hot topics, supplemented conventional

methods such as staff surveys and an employee suggestion scheme. Through effective promotion, the number of employee suggestions increased sixfold from 50 per year to 300.

The Council's wider mission to motivate and inspire is encapsulated in its HEART approach:

- Help each other learn and develop
- Empower through open communication
- Appreciate and respect others
- Recognise and acknowledge contributions
- Try new ideas and initiatives.

Impact:

- Staff turnover is down from 18% to 9%.
- Average absence is down from 13.8 days to 9.2 days.
- Rotherham is now a three-star council and rated as 'strongly improving'.
- 65% of staff responded that they are happy at work.

Question

Explain how the HEART approach had an impact on the council. (*10 marks*)

Methods of employee representation

Works council

Although works councils were not legally required in organisations of a certain size in the UK until 2005, they have been required by legislation in many other European countries. The involvement of employees within works councils varies very much, depending on the nature of the organisation, its size and its location internationally. However the scope of their discussion and decision-making can range from the recruitment procedures through to the council's legal right to delay complex issues, such as merger or takeover discussions.

The introduction of works councils has freed management from a number of issues, including the need to gain acceptance, or go through sometimes lengthy negotiation talks with trade union representatives on issues relating to working conditions. Works councils have the power to execute decisions on issues such as overtime and promotion and have proved a positive step in encouraging management to accept ideas and suggestions from employees. This allows change to be introduced within an organisation more easily and the works council members are also able to brief management regarding any issues that may be occurring that could result in some form of conflict within the organisation.

There are some disadvantages, however, in that the decision-making process can be slower, the running of works councils costly, and meetings hostile if not compiled from like-minded individuals.

Employee representation and participation

Employee participation is synonymous with concepts such as employee involvement, commitment, empowerment, participative management, quality circles, team-working and total quality management. Indeed the range of employee participation schemes is vast, but in many organisations they have become a permanent phenomenon.

Despite the criticisms of employee participation or employee involvement – neither of which are new concepts – the rise in human resource management has seen approaches that regard the employee as an asset that can be invested in (training and development) and included in decision-making (leading to employee motivation, commitment and higher performance). Many businesses adopted participative management schemes during the early 1980s. At the same time, businesses were responding to increased competition from various countries, which exposed weaknesses in working practices, output and productivity.

The first Employee Involvement (EI) schemes were quality circles (QCs), but after an initial interest in QCs, they were on the decline by the mid-1980s. The main reasons for the failures were that managers did not have the right training and leadership skills, and ultimately QCs did not have the decision-making power to maintain interest. Team-working became fashionable, with groups of workers taking responsibility for an entire unit of work, with the emphasis on problem solving. Again may attempts failed to succeed against a backdrop of the need for training and the absence of results-centred actions. The team-working fad failed to address the fact that embedded culture cannot be changed without the presence of long-term strategies.

Total quality management (TQM) has proved to be equally unworkable in many organisations as they are too preoccupied with production orientations, and often neglect the other aspects of employee participation (often referred to as soft human resource management) such as true employee involvement and team-work.

Unless there is a strong commitment to employee participation, many of the attempts will inevitably fail, and this is exacerbated by high management turnover. Each new wave of management introduces a new wave of participation, and increasingly, government legislation and economic trends have resulted in an institution of new schemes. Nonetheless, employees are seen to approve of participation schemes, which may in part be explained by higher levels of education and training. Equally, as society has adapted, so legislation to protect employee rights, and steps to increase the democratisation of society, have begun to encourage organisations to treat employees fairly and, above all, the expectation is to work for a business that supports democratic, participative and egalitarian principles.

There are a number of key areas to address as far as the implementation of participation schemes is concerned:

- A willingness by management to concede some of their decision-making power
- Training managers (and supervisors) in participation initiatives
- Having a clear policy regarding the role and power of line managers in relation to senior management and the workforce under their supervision
- Training workers in group-working skills such as presentation, leadership, assertiveness, problem-solving, etc.
- Providing proper feedback mechanisms that clearly indicate the workforce is being listened to
- Implementing group decisions to reinforce the view among the workforce that their contributions are valued
- Recognising that conflicting views have a place in developing initiatives

Employee participation remains at the very core of human resource management as it is clear that if the participation is effectively implemented then the benefits both in terms of empowerment and the ability to manage and control are greatly enhanced. Participation can still be seen as a continuous power struggle between management and employees. Despite failures, many organisations have re-introduced schemes and, gradually, organisational culture is adapting to allow participation to become an integral element of business strategy.

Trade unions

Trade unions protect the interests of their members in areas relating to wages and salaries, working conditions, job security and welfare benefits. They negotiate with management of organisations on behalf of members of the trade union who work for the business. The national committee of the trade union is an elected group of permanent employees who implement the policies of the members. Regional and district committees are formed around the country, with branches in the larger towns, and one union member attached to each branch. Trade union representatives negotiate with the management of an organisation during the documenting and implementation of collective agreements and collective bargaining disputes resolution. They would also be entitled to attend disciplinary and grievance interviews, as well as to be involved in discussions regarding dismissal.

Worker directors

Worker directors are employees, often elected by works councils, to represent employees on the board of a business. Although there is a growing requirement under European Employment Strategy and EU Directives related to European Works Councils to require businesses to have employee representation on boards, there has been considerable opposition for a number of different reasons. Most notably, worker directors are reluctant to make decisions without referring back to their peer groups, thus slowing down the decision-making process. Businesses are also very apprehensive on the question of confidentiality, particularly when worker-directors have access to information which may have a negative impact with those who place them on the board in the first place. Trade unions have, in the past, also been suspicious of worker-directors as they feel that their presence simply confuses the issue as the unions may end up having to fight their own members in the role of a member of the board.

> ### Question
>
> Distinguish between works councils and trade unions.
> (*12 marks*)

Avoiding and resolving industrial disputes

LEARNING
OBJECTIVES

▶ Dispute resolution
▶ Industrial action
▶ Industrial relations
▶ Industrial tribunals
▶ Advisory Conciliation and Arbitration Service (ACAS)

Dispute resolution

Resolving disputes is one of the key functions of human resource management. The first stage of dispute resolution is to try to avoid a dispute in the first place. This should be done through consultation with trade union representatives or employee associations to form an agreement about working conditions. During these negotiations there will be discussions about the formation of a programme or set of procedures that will be followed in the case of a dispute, usually in order to avoid industrial action.

Although the procedures put in place will vary from organisation to organisation, the general content of such an agreement regarding dispute procedures will include the following guidelines:

- The dispute will initially be discussed between the employee and their immediate line manager.
- The employee's trade union representative will be called in to meet the line manager, or a member of middle management, should the initial discussion not resolve the issue.
- The trade union representative will meet with senior managers should there still be no resolution.
- If the dispute remains unsolved, senior national representatives of the trade union will meet with senior managers of the organisation.

The next stage of the dispute resolution could involve the intervention of an independent arbitrator. It should be noted that the majority of dispute agreements contain the clause that no industrial action will be taken until all the stages of the agreement have been undertaken.

Industrial action

Industrial action is often the result of a lack of agreement in dispute resolution. Industrial action can take a number of different forms, all of which will have been the centre of discussions between trade union members, their representative and the management of the organisation. If, after a series of negotiation discussions, there is no resolution to the issue, then trade union representatives have the following options to present to their members:

- To withdraw cooperation with management by ending negotiation and assistance in future dispute resolution and the compilation of agreements until the industrial action issue has been resolved.
- To insist on formal rights – this means that the trade union representative would bring to the attention of management every issue that arises, however trivial. (Normally trivial incidences would have been dealt with in a less formal manner.)
- Withdraw willingness to work overtime – this means that employees would not be prepared to work additional hours to those stipulated as their normal working hours. This form of industrial action can have serious implications to an organisation that relies on employee cooperation to meet production output targets.
- Work a 'go-slow' or a 'work to rule' – this means that employees will continue to adhere to the requirements of their contract of employment, but will not carry out any additional duties, nor respond to urgent requirements or rush jobs as they may emerge.
- Withdrawal of labour – in effect this is strike action. A trade union might call for an unofficial strike, which could be for short periods of time until the dispute is finally resolved. In some cases an official strike is called, usually when the dispute has remained unresolved for a length of time or a collective agreement is thought to have been broken by the employer.

Industrial relations

The term 'industrial relations' has largely negative connotations as it is invariably preceded by the words 'poor' or 'bad'. As a general term, industrial relations refers to the ongoing dialogue or relationship between employers and employees, which may, or may not, involve aspects of collective bargaining, discussions regarding working conditions, rewards, job structures and a variety of other human resource topics. The term also implies an underlying conflict between those

who own and control industry and those who provide the labour in order to fuel it. In most countries industrial relations have had periods during which the relationship between employers and employees (largely represented by trade unions) has been extremely poor, confrontational and irreconcilable on the basis that their objectives are mutually exclusive.

The term 'industrial relations' is also interchangeable in many respects with the term 'labour relations', which again refers to the ongoing attitudes of employers and employees towards one another, and their ability or willingness to cooperate on various matters. There is an underlying suspicion for both parties that decisions and stances are taken without regard to the other's desires.

Industrial tribunals

The exact nature and make-up of an industrial tribunal is very dependent upon the individual country involved. For the most part, however, industrial tribunals are concerned with matters such as unfair dismissal, discrimination or other alleged breaches of employment law that have resulted in the termination of employment or other disciplinary measures taken against an employee. Increasingly, in most countries, as the result of more stringent legislation, industrial tribunals are becoming more legalistic and formal and have begun to adopt an adversarial nature, rather than, as in the past, having been more inquisitorial. Industrial tribunals require both parties to present relevant evidence, including

documentation and witnesses, in order to pass a judgement based on that country's employment law. In Europe, employment law has become standardised as the result of a number of European Directives which, in England, for example, have led to the establishment of Employment Appeal Tribunals. The normal composition of an industrial tribunal is a fully qualified, legal representative, who chairs the tribunal, supported by two lay members, normally nominated one each from an employer organisation and an employee organisation. The industrial tribunal will hear the case, leaving open the option for either party to make an appeal, firstly through an employment appeals tribunal and then, perhaps, a higher court, depending on the complexity of the case.

Advisory Conciliation and Arbitration Service (ACAS)

ACAS operates as a mediator during problems or disputes between employers and employees. Their primary role is to encourage good working relationships between employers and employees and to help set up structures and systems, as well as practically settling disputes. ACAS deals not only with broader

industrial disputes, but also focuses on individual complaints which have been referred to employment tribunals. On average they settle around 75% of cases which have been referred to an employment tribunal, obviating the need for the tribunal to consider the case.

ACAS is involved in four main areas of activity. These are:

- The provision of impartial information and help (on average they take 750,000 calls a year on their helpline).
- The prevention and resolution of problems between employers and employees (ACAS is successful in over 90% of all cases)
- The settlement of complaints about employees' rights (around 70% of potential employment tribunal cases referred to ACAS are resolved by ACAS)
- The fostering of effective working relationships through seminars and workshops. Small businesses in particular are targeted, as well as those without clearly identified human resource management departments.

INTERNET RESEARCH 🔍

For more information about the work of ACAS, visit www.acas.org.uk

Question

Distinguish between the work of industrial tribunals and ACAS. (*12 marks*)

Case studies, questions and exam practice

CASE STUDY NATIONWIDE COMMUNICATIONS

'Effective communication is part of the lifeblood of any major organisation,' according to Tom Harvey, Head of Internal Communications for Nationwide Building Society.

For Tom Harvey, the future of internal communications lies in harnessing the ever-increasing media for communication, and channelling that energy into creating an even stronger brand that does not get diluted by the mass of messages or information.

Technological developments have impacted upon the practice of passing on information; the audience, perhaps once upon a time naturally captive and attentive, has changed. The new audience is challenging, familiar with communications technology and not tied to one organisation for life. A recent HR survey showed that most employees will work for an average of seven employers during their working life.

Within this context of a more flexible labour market, the tasks of the internal communications team within a large organisation are harder and more challenging than ever before. At Nationwide, the tools that are used for internal communications are fairly typical; an intranet, e-mail, some audio/visual presentations for training and explanation, face-to-face communication and the house magazine.

The philosophy at Nationwide is not one of trying to constantly exploit new technology, but to focus on the message being delivered. Harvey argues that the role of

internal communications 'is akin to the narrow part of an hour glass' – there is a vast quantity of information that exists and that could be communicated to staff, but only a small amount makes it through the 'narrow part' to be read.

The trick is to make certain that the filtered information is that which is most likely to draw interest. Nationwide's house magazine, for example, makes use of a very traditional method of communication – a tangible, paper format, and substantial at 32 pages – it is positively supported by 85% of Nationwide's staff and still represents one of the most effective methods of communicating with staff. Its blend of hard business, employee news and entertainment seems a popular format and one that would be hard to improve upon substantially through another medium.

The role of the internal communications manager at Nationwide, however, is more than just a moderator. Raising the brand awareness of employees and ensuring that they are proud to work for their employer makes good business – if Nationwide can use its own staff to advertise its products and make personal recommendations, then it will continue to grow.

If the internal communications manager can orchestrate their team to help foster a sense of belonging and pride within the organisation, the company will be more successful overall. Harvey sees his role as similar to an editor of a newspaper or magazine – each story that is published or delivered within Nationwide is considered

carefully for its audience. Employees, like members of the public, can be turned off by the wrong message. As new forms of communication, both internal and external, have grown, internally communicated messages have to compete with more and more traffic; if there is no appeal, internal communications will simply not be read.

Source: adapted from Nationwide

Question

Suggest the different types of internal communications that could be used in an organisation like Nationwide, and why the nature of the business and its structure requires a range of types to be used. (*12 marks*)

CHECKLIST AND REVISION

CHECKLIST

- [ ] Using objectives and strategies
- [ ] Understanding financial objectives
- [ ] Using financial data to measure and assess performance
- [ ] Interpreting published accounts
- [ ] Selecting financial strategies
- [ ] Making investment decisions
- [ ] Understanding marketing objectives
- [ ] Analysing markets and marketing
- [ ] Selecting marketing strategies
- [ ] Developing and implementing marketing plans
- [ ] Understanding operational objectives
- [ ] Operational strategies: scale and resource mix
- [ ] Operational strategies: innovation
- [ ] Operational strategies: location
- [ ] Operational strategies: lean production
- [ ] Understanding HR objectives and strategies
- [ ] Developing and implementing workforce plans
- [ ] Competitive organisational structures
- [ ] Effective employer/employee relations

MOCK EXAM

INVESTMENT CHOICES

Read the case study and answer all the questions that follow.

Signal Associates is an investment consultancy. It has been approached by a consortium of investors who are looking at two potential investment opportunities and want the consultants' unbiased opinion. The asking price for the investments is £500,000 each. The fund has £490,000 for immediate investment, so a deal will have to be done regarding the asking prices.

The first option is a pub/restaurant and guest house in Norwich, Norfolk. The sales income is £156,000 pa, with a net profit of £22,000 pa. The second is a night club in the centre of the city. It has a sales income of £233,000 pa, with a net profit of £29,000 pa. The investors are looking for a business that provides better than average figures for both ROCE and net profit.

The consultants have compiled market research data on the Norwich area from secondary research sources to begin the process of market analysis.

The current owners of the pub run the business with eight part-time members of staff (four family members plus eight part-timers working, on average, 20 hours per week). The pub is very busy during the week (particularly at lunchtimes) and less busy over the weekend, but the restaurant is popular on Friday and Saturday nights. The guest house business has fallen off over the past three years, largely due to the problem of being able to retain sufficient part-time staff to run the eight-bedroom facility at the back of the property. Staff turnover is around 250% overall. Wage rates paid by the pub average at £10.50, but general catering staff tend to be teenagers and are paid less than this. On average they remain with the business for less than a month.

The night club has a more stable staff situation. It employs six members of staff for the four nights of the week it is open (Wednesday–Saturday). The club has tried to open as a café/bar during the daytime, but has found it impossible to run (due to the size of the property) with fewer than three members of staff. This has meant that the business has never broken even on this part of the operation, so it no longer opens in the daytime. There have been problems with DJs – the four resident DJs no longer attract the numbers of customers – but the owners cannot replace them as they have entered into four-year, one-night guaranteed contracts with each of them (with two years yet to run). Guaranteed payment for the night has, in the opinion of the current owner, made the DJs 'boring, predictable and lazy'.

Appendix A **Industry average ROCE and net profit %**

	Leisure and hotels	Airline	Manufacturer	Retailer	Banking	Refining	Fast food	Professional services
ROCE	5.56%	3.16%	−12.12%	−0.12%	33.63%	16.17%	16.14%	16.29%
Net profit	7.36%	4.05%	−10.48%	1.63%	10.87%	12.63%	7.55%	27.15%

Appendix B

Norwich population

- The population of the Norwich Travel to Work Area, i.e. the area of Norwich in which most people both live and work, is 367,035, and the 1991 figure was 351,340.
- 121,600 people live in the Norwich City Council area.
- Norwich is the fourth most densely populated Local Authority District within the Eastern Region, with 3,179 people per square kilometre (8,241 per square mile).

Norwich workforce

- The workforce of the Norwich Travel to Work Area is 169,627 people. The Norwich City Council area supports around 88,000 jobs.
- One third of Norfolk's working-age population works within the City Council area.
- Approximately 77% of the City Council's working-age resident population is economically active.

Norwich employment profile

- Reflecting the national picture, employment in Norwich is predominantly service sector based
- The business and financial sector accounts for a further 28.7% of employment in Norwich
- 20% of people employed in Norwich work in public services (government, health and education)
- 24% of employment is based in distribution, hotels and restaurants (including retail)
- The manufacturing sector accounts for 11% of employment in Norwich
- Around 5% of people employed in Norwich work in the transport and communications sector and almost 4% work in the construction industry.

Unemployment and deprivation

- Unemployment in the Norwich Travel to Work Area is lower than the UK rate – 2% against 2.3% (June 2005).
- The rate of unemployment in the Norwich City Council area stands at 3.4% compared to a country rate of 2.1% (June 2005)
- The Index of Deprivation, 2004, indicated that Norwich is the most deprived district in the Eastern Region relative to the numbers of people affected by deprivation. On this measure, Norwich is ranked 50th nationally; within the most deprived 20% of areas.

Average earnings

- Average earnings in Norwich are £10.44 per hour excluding overtime, compared to £11.87 in the Eastern Region and £11.96 in UK as a whole.

Appendix C **Location**

Norwich has easy connections internationally and with the rest of the UK:

- Norwich International Airport offers flights to an increasing number of national and international destinations, including four daily (45 minute) flights to Schiphol, in the Netherlands, from where worldwide connections can be made.
- An Intercity rail service operates between Norwich and Liverpool Street in London, with a journey time of 1 hour 54 minutes. There are three trains per hour at peak times.
- There is a direct hourly rail link to Cambridge and the journey takes 74 minutes.
- Recent widening of the A11 has improved links with Cambridge, London and Stansted.

Questions

1 Calculate the ROCE and the net profit margin of the two businesses and compare them to the industry averages. On these figures, suggest which would be the better investment and why. Assume that the purchase price is £490,000 in each case. (*10 marks*)
2 Analyse the market using the data from Appendix B in relation to market potential for the two different businesses. (*30 marks*)
3 Identify areas of market research that may be missing but necessary to complete the market analysis, and make a decision about the optimal location for the two businesses. Also use Appendix C for this question. (*15 marks*)
4 Comment on the current employee relations in the two businesses and suggest how they might be resolved under new ownership. (*15 marks*)

UNIT 4

THE BUSINESS ENVIRONMENT AND MANAGING CHANGE

Introduction

The core themes of Unit 4, the second of the Business Studies A2 units, look at corporate aims and objectives, assessing changes in the business environment and managing change. Again, they are all likely to be issues that focus on larger organisations than you would have studied in the AS Business Studies. But you will still find material that you covered in the AS Business Studies to be very useful and you will also see some recurring themes from Unit 3. The examination itself is one hour and forty-five minutes long. It accounts for 25% of the total A-level mark, and 80 marks are available. It is a two-part examination paper.

Section A asks questions broadly based on prior research, giving a topic with some broad guidelines on what to look for. You should focus on finding out as much as you can, for example, about globalisation, technology, leadership, organisational culture, strategic change or the government's impact on businesses. Try to find useful and quotable real-life business case studies to illustrate your points. The questions you answer in Section A are worth half the marks for the entire paper.

Section B offers a choice of essays. You need to choose only one, which is worth half the total marks on the paper. Remember that this examination paper is likely to draw on any part of the entire A-level syllabus, not just the material that you cover in Unit 4. The examiners will expect a more complex and deeper set of responses from you than they have until this point.

The first section of this unit looks at corporate aims and objectives. It examines mission statements, corporate aims and objectives, strategies and different stakeholder perspectives.

The second section looks at the assessment of changes in the business environment from various perspectives, essentially looking at the relationship between businesses and their external environment, and covering the economic, political and legal, social, technological and competitive environments.

The final section looks at managing change. It begins by examining the causes of change and how a business can plan for change, before looking at influences on the change process – primarily leadership and organisational culture. This naturally leads to the process of making strategic decisions and how information management is important, how different techniques are used for decision-making and what influences those decisions. Finally, it looks at the question of implementing and managing change itself, the techniques that are used and the factors that promote and resist change.

Unlike Unit 3, Unit 4 follows the exact specification of the AQA Business Studies A2 Unit 4. Each of the core themes is examined in detail, broken down into topics and given its own section. The sections comprise a number of spreads, each of which looks at a particular aspect of the topic. On each double-page spread there are either essay questions or mini case studies with extended questions. At the end of each topic there is an opportunity for you to try out a series of questions that are similar to the type that you will encounter in the examination.

At the end of the unit there is a summary of the unit's key concepts, and a full mock examination.

TOPIC 1: CORPORATE AIMS AND OBJECTIVES

▶ page 172

TOPIC 2: ASSESSING CHANGES IN THE BUSINESS ENVIRONMENT

▶ page 184

TOPIC 3: MANAGING CHANGE

▶ page 248

CHECKLIST AND REVISION

▶ page 306

TOPIC 1 CORPORATE AIMS AND OBJECTIVES

Introduction

This is the first of three core themes for the Business Environment and Managing Change unit. Bear in mind that you will not only be examined on material that you cover in this topic, but will also be expected to bring in any other relevant information that you have covered throughout the whole of the course, including the AS units.

Overall, this unit looks at the relationship between businesses and external factors. It is therefore logical to start with corporate aims and objectives. This means identifying what an organisation is attempting to achieve and how this should ultimately help it determine its strategies.

Businesses can often have extremely vague missions, aims and objectives, but the point of the process should be to successively refine those missions and aims into more manageable objectives, and then to create a series of strategies that can help the business achieve them. This is, of course, all against the backdrop of having to take into account differing stakeholder perspectives. We also look at the fact that there may be potential conflict and pressure from different stakeholders, and that this can impact on the decision-making process of the organisation.

This is a relatively short topic, but it is an important introduction to the unit, as it illustrates the fact that, whatever an organisation's corporate aims and objectives may be, they are often bound and restricted by events in the external environment that are beyond their control.

FOCUS ON UNDERSTANDING MISSION AIMS AND OBJECTIVES

- Purpose and value of mission statements ▶ page 174
- Corporate aims and objectives ▶ page 176
- Corporate strategies ▶ page 178
- Differing stakeholder perspectives ▶ page 180
- Case studies, questions and exam practice ▶ page 182

Purpose and value of mission statements

LEARNING
OBJECTIVES

▶ Mission statements
▶ What are the features of a mission statement?
▶ The value of mission statements

Mission statements

In many cases, indications of an organisation's fundamental policy will be contained within a mission statement. A mission statement essentially describes, as succinctly as possible, the organisation's business vision, including its fundamental values and essential purpose. The statement will also refer to its aims for the future, as mission statements tend to be a statement of where a business wishes to be, rather than a description of where it is at the current time. Therefore, though the fundamental ethos of a company is likely to may remain the same, details in a mission statement are subject to periodic change.

A business may choose to incorporate within its mission statement a vision of how it wishes

its employees and systems to respond, react and fulfil the needs of its customers or clients. Human Resources, for example, will seek to match these aspirations by instituting employee development programmes and associated training, in order to fulfil the desires and commitments made in the mission statement.

It has become increasingly popular for organisations to produce mission statements – sometimes called 'visions'. The two terms are similar, but essentially an organisation's vision serves to provide it with the overall frame of reference within which the organisation then creates its mission statement (and selects its goals). Mission statements and goals are difficult to measure. They vary in length, and some are specific and others more general.

What are the features of a mission statement?

A mission statement should describe an organisation's purpose, customers, products or services, market niche, area of operations, business philosophy and basic operations. It should be the most visible and widely publicised element of the organisation's strategic management process. Ideally, it should consist of the following:

- the specification of target customers and markets and the primary customer needs that the organisation aims to satisfy

- the identification of primary products and services, stating which unsatisfied customer needs the business aims to satisfy
- the geographic area in which the business operates
- core technologies used by the organisation
- an expression of commitment to survival, growth and profitability, to explain the organisation's economic objectives
- the key elements of the company philosophy, covering the basic ideas, beliefs, values, aspirations and philosophical priorities of the organisation
- the organisation's self-concept, defining its unique competences or major competitive advantage
- the organisation's desired public image, showing its responsiveness to social, community and environmental issues
- the organisation's concern for employees, illustrating that its employees are a valuable resource.

An ideal mission statement should:

- define what the organisation is and what it aspires to be
- be limited enough to exclude flawed projects and broad enough to encompass creative growth
- distinguish a given organisation structure from its peers
- serve as a framework for assessing current and future activities
- be sufficiently clear and concise to be understood by employees throughout the organisation.

The value of mission statements

In an organisation's desire to identify with as many stakeholders as it can, its mission statement tends to be all-embracing, and it will use bland and abstract words. However, the true value of the mission statement is the extent to which it is actually understood and, crucially, accepted throughout the organisation. In addition to this, the mission statement needs to be translated into meaningful terms and actions by the organisation.

The problem remains that even a well thought through and well-written mission statement is meaningless unless the business practises what it preaches. More importantly, just writing a mission statement achieves nothing if it is too vague or confusing for those who will be expected to use it as a guiding force in their work.

However, as long as an organisation's values and mission are aligned to its actual behaviour, then mission statements can have a powerful impact on the productivity and success of a business.

Harley-Davidson's mission statement:

'We fulfil dreams through the experiences of motorcycling – by providing to motorcyclists and to the general public an expanding line of motorcycles, branded products and services in selected market segments.'

BP Group's mission statement:

'The world's need for energy is growing steadily day by day. Energy and materials, used safely and efficiently, are essential to the prosperity and growth of every country and every region in the world. Sustaining and enhancing our quality of life depends on them. Our goal is to play a leading role in meeting these needs from oil, gas, solar power and petrochemicals without damaging the environment.

Ours is a positive and progressive involvement. Innovation will be the hallmark of the way we work with people, technology, assets and relationships. We will always be constructive, using our know-how to produce constructive and creative solutions to every challenge.

Our success depends on our making, and being seen to make, a distinctive contribution to every activity in which we are involved.'

Examples of mission statements

CASE STUDY TWO SIDES OF THE BRAIN

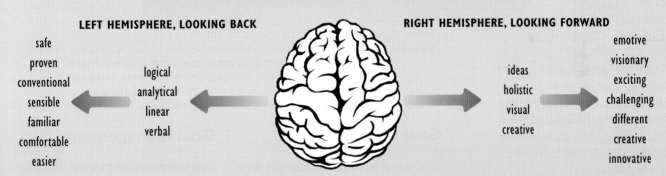

LEFT HEMISPHERE, LOOKING BACK

safe
proven
conventional
sensible
familiar
comfortable
easier

logical
analytical
linear
verbal

RIGHT HEMISPHERE, LOOKING FORWARD

ideas
holistic
visual
creative

emotive
visionary
exciting
challenging
different
creative
innovative

Research into the brain has shown that the brain is divided into two distinct halves. Most people tend to be left-hemisphere dominant. The belief used to be that we are all born one way or the other, but actually we are all born with equal access to left-brain and right-brain activity, and are simply conditioned to use the left more. The result is that not only do most people communicate and think from a limited perspective; they do so without realising that they can create a more balanced approach.

The diagram above illustrates the effect of left-brain and right-brain thinking on an organisation or team. In most organisations, the left brain is the dominant influence in thinking. Education is changing, and business must do the same in order to make mission statements less of an aspiration and more a reality.

The issue is not that there needs to be a full swing from one extreme to the other, but that there needs to be more of a balance between left-brain and right-brain thinking. There will be inevitable risks, and more 'failures', but the benefits will be innovations that lead to success, not stagnation.

Source: adapted from Innerbeat

Question

How might this view of the way in which mission statements are created and written be useful to businesses? *(10 marks)*

Corporate aims and objectives

LEARNING OBJECTIVES

▶ Aims and objectives
▶ Goals
▶ Goal characteristics
▶ Goal management

▶ Goal congruence
▶ Strategic planning
▶ Strategy formulation and thinking

Aims and objectives

An organisation's objectives often derive from, or are the catalyst that helps create its mission statement. Objectives are broad goals or strategies that the organisation seeks to adopt in order to achieve its primary aims. Objectives, by their very nature, are broad and often ill-defined. They merely represent an outline or guideline that suggests the direction in which the organisation intends to move. Broad objectives could include considerably increasing output, launching new products, or providing higher-quality customer service.

Goals

Goals are targets or states that an organisation seeks to achieve over a specified period of time. They need to be attainable but challenging. The management of the process that delivers the achievement of these goals can be a key function of the strategic management process. The criteria or conditions that should be applied to the setting of goals are shown in the table above.

Criteria or condition	Goal description
Goals should be stable over time	Continually changing the goals leads to problems of attainment and possible demotivation. Predetermined goals should be achieved, then amended.
Goals should be specific and clear	Ambiguous goals that are clearly spelled out can be judged more effectively in terms of attainment.
Goals should be linked to reality	Impossible goals, plucked out of the air, require chance or good fortune to secure their attainment. Goals should be linked to the possible and the real state or position of the organisation.
Goals should be over-arching	Goals need to be central to the organisation in that all parts of the business should be able to see their place in their attainment.
Goals should be unique and designed to differentiate	Sharing similar goals with the competition is not an ideal way forward. Some form of competitive advantage over the competition should be sought.
Goals should be linked to actions	The interpretation of the goals at management and employee level should clearly indicate what has to be done in order to attain the goals. In other words, there needs to be a plan to attain the goals, by steps or actions over time.
Goals should infer foresight	Goals should be linked to cause and effect. The organisation should be able to see where it is likely to be once its goals have been attained. Above all, it needs to be ready for that altered state and be prepared to set new goals from that point.

Goal characteristics

Goal characteristics describe the ways in which they are meaningful to the organisation. They should:

- have a precise nature
- address the organisation's key issues
- be realistic, but challenging
- have a definite time frame.

Goal management

Goal management provides managers and employees with the tools they need to establish their individual goals based on objectives and directions.

The goal management process is shown in the following diagram.

LEVEL OF ORGANISATION	HOW?	GOAL OR OBJECTIVE
Board	Goal management	Corporate vision
↓	↓	↓
Senior management	Management by objectives/ project tracking	Corporate goals and objectives
↓	↓	↓
Departmental management/ team leaders	Performance management	Departmental or team objectives
↓		↓
Employees		Individual goals or objectives

Goals congruence

Goal congruence occurs when the objectives of two different stakeholders in an organisation have been met. In other words, the goals or objectives of those two stakeholders, such as the management and the shareholders, have both been reached through the joint or several actions of the two parties.

Strategic planning

A strategic plan is an overarching series of activities that aim to implement and develop a new concept, deal with a problem, or establish the foundation of the business's objectives in the coming period. As the illustration below shows, there is a close relationship between the implementation and the strategic development process.

Strategic planning should, as the diagram illustrates, be a continual process, with the monitoring and control procedures providing the information for the development of the strategic plan and future strategic plans.

Strategy formulation and thinking

Strategy formulation needs to ensure that any planned course of action is consistent with the general strategy of the business and the business's ability to achieve these objectives. Normally, strategic formulation takes place at three different levels of an organisation. These are:

- Corporate level – where strategy formulation is based on objectives and strategies for achieving these objectives.
- Business level – which is often known as competitive strategy formulation and deals with strategy formulation in relation to each area in which the organisation is involved.
- Functional level – which is strategy formulation related directly to ensuring that either corporate level or business-level strategy can be achieved through manipulation of current functional activities.

Strategic thinking is essentially a process in which senior management deals with significant issues and undertakes a decision-making process in order to deal with them. Strategic thinking may involve organisational or personal decisions, the identification and decision-making surrounding an important issue, or simply understanding a situation. Strategic thinking implies the generation of alternatives and the evaluation of these alternatives in an objective manner. It therefore incorporates creative ideas, idea generation, divergent thinking and, above all, logical and rational thought. Typically, strategic thinking would include some, or all, of the following characteristics:

- identifying and then focusing on important issues
- selecting key information
- identifying any linkages, patterns or interactions
- distinguishing cause and effect
- clarifying assumptions
- looking at issues or situations in a broad context
- taking a long-term view
- understanding implications and consequences
- generating alternatives, and objectively evaluating them
- being flexible
- using logical, rational thinking alongside creative idea generation.

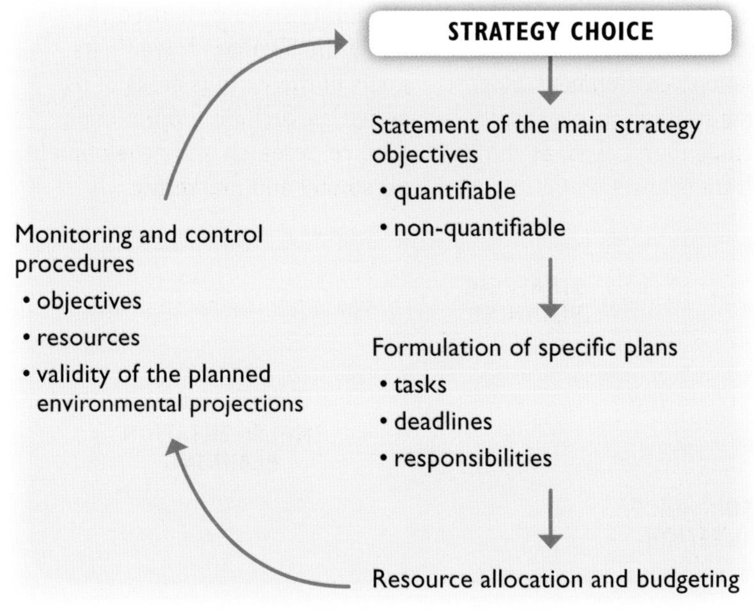

> **Question**
>
> Explain the criteria that should be applied to all organisational goals. *(18 marks)*

For more on stakeholders' perspectives and goals see Differing stakeholder perspectives on pp. 180–1.

STRATEGY CHOICE

↓

Statement of the main strategy objectives
- quantifiable
- non-quantifiable

↓

Formulation of specific plans
- tasks
- deadlines
- responsibilities

↓

Resource allocation and budgeting

Monitoring and control procedures
- objectives
- resources
- validity of the planned environmental projections

Corporate strategies

LEARNING
OBJECTIVES

▶ Strategic management
▶ Strategic management process
▶ Corporate level strategy
▶ Corporate planning

Strategic management

At its simplest, strategic level, management provides an organisation with:

- the ability to determine its long-term direction
- the ability to assess its long-term performance
- the ability to ensure that plans are correctly and expertly formulated
- the ability to monitor and effectively implement plans
- the ability to carry out a continuous evaluation of the business and its performance.

Strategic management seeks to ensure that the missions or objectives of the organisation:

- are translated into objectives (clear and obvious)
- become strategies that can be employed
- lead to goal-setting
- once they have become goals, are superimposed on any project or programme of activities.

Strategic management seeks to integrate the organisational functions and processes into a broad, cohesive strategy. It also seeks to coordinate the various functional elements of the organisation, ensuring that they interact and use their interdependencies in a positive and constructive manner.

Strategic management is, in effect, the process by which the organisation, in a dynamic and, above all, interactive manner, seeks to ensure that the organisation responds to its general environment.

BOOK RESEARCH

Tim Hannagan, *Mastering strategic management*, Basingstoke: Palgrave Macmillan, 2002.

Strategic management process

The strategic management process can be seen as an ongoing management function which involves a complex series of decisions and actions. These decisions and actions aim to:

- formulate strategy
- implement strategy
- monitor and respond to performance measures.

The process itself tends to be forward-looking in the sense that it is concerned with the achievement of objectives, in relation to, and interacting with, the organisation's environment. Most models of the strategic management process include four stages, as shown in the diagram below.

Alternatives could include a distinctly different set of processes, such as:

- environmental scanning
- formulation
- implementation
- evaluation and control.

Any strategic management process, regardless of its configuration, should address the following:

- Where is the organisation at the moment?
- Where does the organisation wish or need to be?
- How will the organisation get there?

Corporate level strategy

Corporate strategy can be seen as the overarching strategy put in place by a business that encompasses the deployment of its resources. Corporate strategy is used to move the business towards its goals in the various areas of its activities, including production, finance, research and development, personnel and marketing.

STRATEGIC PLANNING

IMPLEMENTATION PLANNING

CUSTOMER SATISFACTION

PERFORMANCE EVALUATION

EXECUTION

Corporate planning

As with any level of management, a planning process must be undertaken in order to outline, monitor, implement, continue to monitor and assess the outcomes of any plan. In order to do this, the senior management must first identify and agree performance levels. These may be both operational and financial performance levels. Typically, they will also identify when these particular performance levels should be reached. At corporate level, the planning process can be fairly complex; not only does it have to incorporate a series of both qualitative and quantitative objectives and measurements, but it also has to achieve the overall support of those within the organisation. While there is no definitive model of the corporate planning process, the conceptual model below indicates the overall series of steps that need to be taken in order to achieve a viable corporate level plan.

The business needs to formulate a plan that is in broad accord with the organisation's posture and position, otherwise it will be impossible for the organisation to have any hope of achieving the performance objectives. The planning process should also indicate the journey upon which the organisation is about to embark, in order to achieve the objectives and to achieve its new position and posture in the future. None of this planning can take place without due attention to the organisation's external environment. The organisation needs to analyse the environment and use this information as the basis for its forecasting. It is only then that the business can begin to develop performance objectives and, above all, decide how these performance objectives will be achieved. In other words, the business must apply a series of rational criteria, linked to its current position and posture, in order for the business to move forward. In many respects the model for any planning process is in essence a planning process that incorporates issue management, as can be seen in the diagram below.

This model shows how the business can at first recognise that a decision related to the overall plan has to be identified and then a decision taken on it. The issue cannot be advanced until there is a commitment by the organisation and a policy formulated in order to deal with it. Only at this point can that element of the plan be implemented.

If the policy implementation is satisfactory, then regular feedback and control may reveal new issues for which commitment and policy formulation needs to be developed. It is rare that the implementation policy is a smooth process and there may be a period – which can be called a policy learning phase – where the business and its employees and management gradually incorporate the new policy into their day-to-day thinking. At this stage the detail of the plan can then come into operation, with detailed procedures regarding the new policy. Eventually, the policy will become, in effect, institutionalised and an integral part of the overall business operations. Again, regular feedback and control systems will identify new issues for which policy formulation and implementation will have to follow.

MODEL OF PLANNING PROCESS

Mission statement
↓
Environmental analysis
↓
Senior management decisions
↓
Planning and procedures to implement objectives
↓
Evaluation of performance
↓
Reports to senior management on performance
↓
Revision of policies and plans

CONCEPTUAL PLANNING MODEL INCORPORATING ISSUE MANAGEMENT

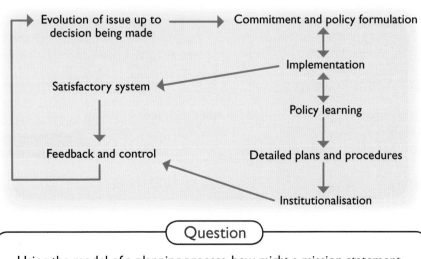

Evolution of issue up to decision being made → Commitment and policy formulation

Satisfactory system ← Implementation

Feedback and control → Policy learning

Detailed plans and procedures

Institutionalisation

Question

Using the model of a planning process, how might a mission statement outlining plans to increase a business's commitment to first-class customer service, be translated into reality? *(12 marks)*

Differing stakeholder perspectives

Stakeholders

A stakeholder is an individual or a group that is either affected by, or has a vested interest in a particular business. Stakeholders can include customers, managers, employees, suppliers and the community, as well as the organisation itself. Each business places a degree of importance on each stakeholder and will attempt to understand what its stakeholders require of it. They will take these views into account when making decisions.

The diagram below illustrates an identification of stakeholders in the case of a public sector organisation, such as a hospital. More complex versions can identify many different stakeholder subsets but the advantage of this type of illustration is that it shows the way that different groups tend to pull the organisation in many different directions. Often, as in this example of a public sector organisation, service users will want to see more money spent, whereas central government will want to see less.

FOR EXAMPLE

Taking the example of a public sector organisation and its stakeholders a little further, we can see in the following diagram the relative position and influence of the different stakeholder groups in relation to a proposed change project.

Although the diagram is not exhaustive, it shows the starting point that a local authority or a hospital, for example, would take in seeking to develop a new project. In this case, we have chosen a proposed drop-in centre.

Using this type of analysis allows the organisation to establish precisely what is needed in order to influence change. From the diagram, it is clear to see that stakeholder perspectives need to be adjusted to the right. In other words they have to be shifted to, at worst, a neutral stance and ideally a committed stance to the project. The same sets of conditions apply to business organisations that obviously have some of the same

stakeholders. There will also be specific others, such as the owners or shareholders, with a high influence.

The relationship between a major stakeholder and the business needs careful management. In the private sector, customers are usually willing purchasers of products and services. In the public sector, the relationship with customers or clients is very different. Some may be enthusiastic users of a service, others will simply have no choice, while another group may be reluctant or have to be coerced into using the service.

FOR EXAMPLE

If you were caught speeding on a motorway and stopped by the police, you might well receive a customer satisfaction questionnaire in addition to a fine. The questionnaire would not ask if you enjoyed being stopped and fined and whether they could count on you speeding again in the future, but it would focus on how you were dealt with, whether you understood why you were stopped and whether the correct procedures were followed.

Stakeholder analysis

Stakeholder analysis refers to a range of tools and activities that aim to identify and describe the stakeholders of a business under the following criteria:

- the attributes
- their interrelationships
- their interests related to given issues
- their interest and influence over given resources.

Stakeholder analysis takes place for a variety of reasons, including:

- to empirically discover the existing patterns of interaction and interrelationships
- to improve interventions
- to provide a management approach to policy making
- To provide a prediction tool.

In essence, stakeholder analysis attempts to identify the key 'actors' in the system and assess their respective interests within it. Stakeholder analysis also therefore helps a business understand what can often be a complex and potentially turbulent business environment. There is a notion that the management of the organisation has a desire to, in some way, manage a stakeholder relationship. Typically, stakeholders are described as either internal or external, as can be seen in the table below.

There are also groups straddling the divide between internal and external, including the following:

- customers
- vendors
- suppliers

Stakeholder analysis seeks to identify the following features of stakeholder groups:

- the relative power and interest of each stakeholder
- the importance and influence of each stakeholder
- the multiple interests that they have, or indeed multiple roles
- the networks and coalitions to which they belong.

A flexible set of steps to accomplish stakeholder analysis would therefore include:

- an identification of the main purpose of any analysis
- a development of the organisation's understanding of the stakeholder system and decision-makers in that system
- an identification of the key stakeholders related to the organisation
- an identification of stakeholder interest, their characteristics and their sets of circumstances
- an identification of any patterns of interaction between stakeholders
- a definition of any options for the organisation.

In order to assess the relative power and participation of any potential stakeholders, a model of stakeholder involvement can be constructed, as can be seen in the following diagram:

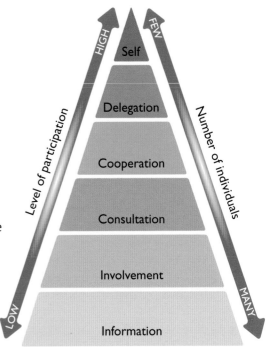

This model reveals that the larger groups, such as consumers, although significant in number, are not overly involved in an organisation. Meanwhile, stakeholders, such as the board of directors, although fewer in number, are closely involved.

Stakeholder analysis may be undertaken for a variety of reasons. Proactive stakeholder analysis is relevant when there is no immediate crisis between the stakeholders and the organisation, while reactive stakeholder management may be prompted in reaction to a conflict or dispute.

Internal stakeholders	External stakeholders
Management (both direct and functional)	Government (regulators, legislators, legal systems, courts, political parties)
Employees (groups, teams and unions)	Competitors
Sponsors	Community (special interest groups, local population)
Owners (stock or shareholders, board of directors, venture capitalists, finance providers)	Media (radio, television, Internet data services and newspapers)
Functional departments (accounts, HRM, engineering, marketing, etc)	

Question

How might a business go about identifying its stakeholders, their influence and their attitude to future plans? *(18 marks)*

Case studies, questions and exam practice

CASE STUDY 'TOTALLY GREENWICH' CAR FREE WEEKEND

The 'Totally Greenwich' Car Free Weekend event reached a number of objectives for a wide range of stakeholders, all of whom benefit from the successful outcome of this initiative.

The main objectives of the event were to:

* reduce traffic and pollution, and improve air quality
* increase visitor spend in the area
* target new visitor audiences to Greenwich
* promote shoulder seasons
* raise awareness of the destination to attract repeat visitors
* plan for environmental improvements.

The event involved localised street closures and celebratory activities such as carnival parades, street theatre and interactive displays and was in support of the annual 'In Town Without My Car' European initiative also known as Car Free Day. This coincided with other popular events such as London Open House and the Greenwich Riverfront Jazz Festival, forming a weekend of 'festival' activity, and was a main component of the regional tourist board's (Visit London) widely publicised September events programme. Car Free Day activities took place in the heart of the Maritime Greenwich World Heritage Site, on a major transport artery into central London. This entire area incorporates many shops and restaurants, the busy

covered market, and numerous attractions, and was therefore organised by Greenwich Council in partnership with a wide range of transport providers, businesses and community organisations. Consultation was carried out through the area traders association, the business development unit, the World Heritage Site forums, the town centre agency and the local attractions group. Homes and businesses located within the area were given advance notice of the road closure and the possible impact on traffic movement, with an opportunity to get involved in the planning. The Council's newspaper, mailed to every home in the borough, was also used for promotion and to encourage local involvement.

Key findings from the event

- 86% of businesses felt that visitor numbers had increased on the day.
- The majority of business premises (66%) saw an increase in sales.
- 80% of businesses stated that they would like to see the initiative repeated.
- Car Free Day influenced 51% of people questioned to visit Greenwich on that particular day.
- 62% of people stated they were planning to shop or visit the bars/restaurants.
- 68% of people stated that they would be 'very likely' to make a repeat visit.
- The majority of businesses and residents felt possible part-pedestrianisation of Greenwich town centre to be a good idea.

Visitor, business and resident surveys were conducted to gauge awareness, satisfaction, and commercial success. Surveys monitoring environmental effects such as traffic and air quality were undertaken and used as evidence to support environmental improvements. The impact of this event was wide, with a diverse range of stakeholders involved. Therefore, it is vital that the results of the evaluation are widely reported back to stakeholders each year, helping to demonstrate the success to local businesses and residents, and encourage support for future events.

Source: adapted from Greenwich Council

Question

Identify the stakeholders in this case study and comment on their likely perspectives. *(12 marks)*

TOPIC 2 ASSESSING CHANGES IN THE BUSINESS ENVIRONMENT

Introduction

This is the second of the three core themes for the Business Environment and Managing Change unit. In this part of the unit we examine the relationships between organisations and their external environment. There are a wide variety of opportunities and threats that are created in the modern business environment. The business needs to be able to acquire, assemble and manage information about the changing environment and then communicate that information to those who must make a decision and assess its impact on the organisation.

There are five different parts to this topic. The first focus area looks at the relationship between the business and the economic environment. You will not need to know too much in terms of pure economics, but you will be introduced to concepts such as the business cycle, interest rates, exchange rates, inflation, unemployment, economic growth, globalisation and emerging markets.

The second focus area looks at the political and legal environment. It considers how the government intervenes in the economy, typical government economic policies, and political decisions that affect trade and access to markets. This focus area also looks at the impact of legislation and evaluates how businesses respond to a changing political and legal landscape.

The third focus area examines the business and the social environment. It considers demographic and environmental issues and the nature of corporate social responsibility. This is followed by the short, fourth focus area, which examines the technological environment, how businesses respond to technological changes, and how this can affect the culture, processes and systems of a business.

The final focus area looks at the competitive environment in a broader sense. It examines new competitors, dominant businesses, changes in the buying power of customers and the selling power of suppliers.

FOCUS ON THE ECONOMIC ENVIRONMENT

- Impact of the competitive environment ▶ page 186
- The structures of markets and industries ▶ page 188
- The business cycle ▶ page 190
- Interest and exchange rates ▶ page 192
- Inflation and unemployment ▶ page 194
- Economic growth ▶ page 196
- Growth of global markets ▶ page 198
- Evaluating strategies to respond to change ▶ page 200
- Case studies, questions and exam practice ▶ page 202

FOCUS ON THE POLITICAL AND LEGAL ENVIRONMENT

- Government intervention in the economy ▶ page 204
- Tax and subsidy ▶ page 206
- Monetary and fiscal policy ▶ page 208
- Supply side policies ▶ page 210
- Political decisions affecting trade and access to markets ▶ page 212
- Impact of legislation: employment law ▶ page 214
- Impact of legislation: consumer protection ▶ page 216
- Impact of legislation: health and safety ▶ page 218
- Business responses to a change in political and legal environment ▶ page 220
- Case studies, questions and exam practice ▶ page 222

FOCUS ON THE SOCIAL ENVIRONMENT

- Changes in the social environment: demographic factors ▶ page 224
- Changes in the social environment: environmental issues ▶ page 226
- The changing nature of the ethical environment ▶ page 228
- Social environment and corporate responsibility ▶ page 230
- Case studies, questions and exam practice ▶ page 232

FOCUS ON THE TECHNOLOGICAL ENVIRONMENT

- Effects of technological change ▶ page 234
- Responses of businesses to technological change ▶ page 236
- Case studies, questions and exam practice ▶ page 238

FOCUS ON THE COMPETITIVE ENVIRONMENT

- Changes in the competitive structure: new competitors and dominant businesses ▶ page 240
- Changes in the competitive structure: customers and suppliers ▶ page 242
- Evaluating responses to a change in the competitive environment ▶ page 244
- Case studies, questions and exam practice ▶ page 246

Impact of the competitive environment

Impact of economic factors

An organisation's macro environment consists of nonspecific aspects of the organisation's surroundings that have the potential to affect its strategies. Macro-environmental variables include socio-cultural, technological, political-legal, economic, and international variables. In this focus area we will be looking at the economic factors.

Economic factors refer to the character and direction of the economic system (or systems) within which the business operates. Economic factors can include:

- balance of payments
- the state of the business cycle
- the distribution of income within the population
- governmental monetary and fiscal policies.

It is important to remember that economic factors and their impact may differ between sectors and industries. Some of these factors will be dealt with in the next focus area.

You will recall that the balance of payments of a country refers to the net difference in value of goods bought and sold by individuals and organisations of the country. To decrease the value of goods imported into a country, it is common practice to construct barriers to entry for particular classes of products. Such practices reduce competition for firms whose products are protected by the trade barriers. This is not an option when Britain deals directly with another EU country.

The business cycle is another economic factor that may influence the operation of an organisation. Purchases of many durable goods (such as appliances, furniture, and vehicles) can be delayed during periods of recession and depression, as can purchases of new equipment and factory expansions.

Economic downturns result in lower profits, reductions in employment, increased borrowing, and decreased productivity for businesses adversely affected by the recession. Positive consequences of recessions can include reductions in waste, more realistic perceptions of working conditions, exit of barely efficient businesses, and a more efficient system overall.

Some organisations may actually benefit from an economic downturn. Postponed purchases may result in the need to service existing products. A customer choosing to keep a used car rather than buying a new one will have to have it repaired, thus creating an increased demand for car mechanics and replacement parts. Limited job opportunities during downturns also encourage individuals unable to get satisfactory jobs to consider returning to education or joining the armed forces.

The distribution of income often differs between economic systems. Two countries with the same mean or average (per capita) income levels may have completely different distributions of income. The majority of people in the United States, for example, are considered middle income, with only a relatively small number having exceptionally high or low incomes. Developing countries, on the other hand, tend to have a combination of extremely wealthy and extremely poor people; few can be considered as middle income. The mean income in the developing country and the United States may appear to be the same, but the opportunities to market products to the middle classes are much better in the United States.

Transfer payments are designed to change the distribution of income in a country through social security, tax credits or welfare payments. They aim to provide money to individuals in lower income brackets to enable them to purchase goods and services that they could not otherwise afford.

As we will also see, monetary and fiscal policies aim to influence business operations. Essentially, monetary policy aims to affect the supply of money and interest rates, while fiscal policies centre on purchases or investments made by the government.

THREAT OF NEW ENTRY
- Time and cost of entry
- Specialist knowledge
- Economies of scale
- Cost advantages
- Technology protection
- Barriers to entry, etc.

COMPETITIVE RIVALRY
- Number of competitors
- Quality differences
- Other differences
- Switching costs
- Customer loyalty
- Costs of leaving market, etc.

SUPPLIER POWER
- Number of suppliers
- Size of suppliers
- Uniqueness of service
- Ability to substitute
- Cost of changing, etc.

THREAT OF NEW ENTRY

SUPPLIER POWER   COMPETITIVE RIVALRY   BUYER POWER

THREAT OF SUBSTITUTION
- Substitute performance
- Cost of change

THREAT OF SUBSTITUTION

BUYER POWER
- Number of customers
- Size of each order
- Differences between competitors
- Price sensitivity
- Ability to substitute
- Cost of changing, etc.

FOR EXAMPLE

The government decides to allocate considerable spending to the armed forces to purchase new weapons and equipment. This is a fiscal policy, as the government allocates contracts to manufacturers to provide the goods. Had the government decided to spend the money on education and training, then this would have constituted a transfer payment and the beneficiaries of the fiscal policy would have been schools and colleges as well as private training agencies. Spending in one area means that other businesses and organisations lose out and may have to cut their budgets.

Porter's Five Forces

Porter's Five Forces (illustrated above) is a simple but powerful tool for understanding where power lies in a business situation. It is important in helping to understand the competitive environment. It shows where the power lies, allowing a business to take advantage of strength, improve a position of weakness and hopefully avoid making mistakes.

The tool assumes that there are five important forces that will determine the competitive power in a situation, explained in the table below:

Power	Explanation
Supplier power	This looks at how easy it is for suppliers to drive up prices. It is dependent on the number of suppliers of each key input (e.g. a component or raw material); how unique that product or service may be; their strength and control over the market and the cost to users of switching between them. The fewer suppliers, the stronger each supplier will be.
Buyer power	This is how easy it may be for buyers to drive the prices down. It is dependent on the number of buyers, the importance of each individual buyer to the business and the cost of switching to someone else. If the business deals with a few powerful buyers then it is often able to dictate terms.
Competitive rivalry	This looks at the number of competitors and their capability. A business in a market where there are several competitors offering equally attractive products and services, will be unlikely to have a great deal of power. If suppliers and buyers do not get a good deal from one business, they will go elsewhere. However, if the business can offer something others cannot, then it is in a far stronger position.
Threat of substitution	This looks at how easy it is for customers to find another product or service that broadly does what the business offers. Even unique products and services can be substituted. For example, a unique software product that automates a production process may be substituted by carrying out the process manually or by outsourcing it. If substitution is easy and viable, this weakens the business.
Threat of new entry	Finally, power can be affected by the ability of another business to enter the market and compete with the existing businesses supplying that market. If the existing businesses do not have economies of scale or protection for their key technologies and processes, then a new competitor can quickly enter the market and weaken their position.

Question

To what extent does Porter's Five Forces model explain the nature of a competitive market?
(18 marks)

The structure of markets and industries

Degrees of competition

In any market there is a set of circumstances that effectively determines the level of competition, the actions of a business in that market and the reactions of the buyers. In an ideal and theoretical world, there is perfect competition. In this market, all the businesses are efficient and producing at the lowest cost, as only the most efficient of businesses can survive in this market. The customers are free to choose what they want, only constrained by their level of income. Because there is a high level of competition in the market, the prices are kept low, but quality remains high. The key features of the market with perfect competition are shown in the following table.

Feature	What does it mean?
Homogeneous products	It is difficult to tell the difference between the products and services sold by the competitors in the market.
Easy entry and exit	It is relatively easy for new competitors to enter the market, and it is easy for a business to decide to leave the market and stop competing.
Large numbers of sellers and buyers	The buyers have access to the widest range of sellers and there are many buyers interested in the products and services offered.
Buyers have access to all necessary information	It is easy for the buyers to find out about the products and services sold in the market and they can also find out which offers the best value for money.

Having established the ideal type of market, it is now possible to compare that type of market with other more extreme versions of markets. This means that we can now identify the characteristics of these markets, in the table below.

Perfect competition	Monopolistic competition	Oligopoly	Monopoly
Homogeneous products	Differentiated products	Differentiated products	No substitute products
Free entry	Free entry	Barriers to entry	Barriers to entry
Many sellers	Many sellers	Many sellers	Single seller
Businesses are price takers	Businesses are price takers	Businesses are price makers	Businesses are price makers
Example – most markets	Example – football shirts from different clubs and markets where branding is important.	Example – where the markets are dominated by a handful of businesses, such as the chocolate market in Britain, which is dominated by Cadbury's and Nestlé, the businesses constantly copy one another and avoid competing on price.	Example – where there is only one option available in the market. This is rare, but may include regional transport services and certain pharmaceutical products.

Unfair competition

Due to the differing nature of markets, sometimes the situation may indicate that there is unfair competition. In a market that has an oligopoly, there may be an agreement between the businesses to charge similar prices. This is not strictly illegal, but it may be investigated if there is a complaint. When businesses enter into an agreement to share the market, then this is considered to be a restrictive practice. These businesses will agree not to compete with one another in particular geographical areas.

Cartels are an illegal form of agreement. In this agreement, the businesses undertake to limit the chances of new competitors entering the market, and may also keep a close control on supply so that prices are kept artificially high. Governments will tend to act against businesses using illegal practices that amount to unfair competition.

Market failure

Market failure takes place when the production or supply of products and services leads to either over-production or under-production, in other words more or less than the consumers actually demand. Market failure can occur in various different ways, including the following:

- Pollution can be seen as market failure – producers may create pollution, and fail to pay the full costs of dealing with it so that it is passed on to consumers and to society to deal with. In an ideal situation, if pollution were unavoidable, then the full costs of the pollution would be passed on to the consumers, the price would rise, and the demand for it would fall so that fewer products would need to be made.
- In a market with a monopoly there is market failure – the producer can make fewer products, but still charge high prices for them, as the prices are often higher than would be acceptable in a market with more competition.
- Market failure often involves unfair competition – railway passengers pay the full cost of their travel, while car users are subsidised. Rail travel is seen as cleaner and less polluting, while road travel is polluting and a threat to the environment. Road construction is funded through taxation and car users only pay road tax and taxes on the fuel they use.
- Market failures are inevitable – this is true, but in free markets, the chances are far lower and the worst excesses and consequences of market failure can be offset by government intervention through law and regulation.

CASE STUDY SUPERMARKET PRICE FIXING

In April 2008, The Office of Fair Trading (OFT) alleged that tobacco firms and supermarkets were engaged in unlawful practices linked to retail prices for tobacco. Eleven retailers were named including Asda, Sainsbury's and Tesco. One of the allegations was that retailers and tobacco groups arranged to swap information on future pricing. A separate allegation was that there was an understanding that the price of some brands would be linked to rival brands.

'For markets to work well for consumers, it is a fundamental principle that pricing decisions should be made independently,' said OFT chief executive John Fingleton. 'If we find evidence of anti-competitive activity, we are prepared to use the appropriate powers to punish the companies involved and to deter other businesses from taking part in such behaviour.'

Question

Find out what the allegations were that were made against supermarkets regarding dairy price fixing. What was the outcome? *(12 marks)*

The business cycle

LEARNING
OBJECTIVES

▶ Cyclical changes
▶ Phases of the cycle
▶ How businesses are affected
by the cycle

Cyclical changes

The business cycle is the regular pattern of fluctuations in economic activity. There is a usual pattern of bust, recovery, boom and recession. A country's levels of economic growth, employment and inflation are all directly affected in each phase of the business cycle, which also has an impact on business earnings and cash flows. The occurrence of business cycles is not always regular and predictable. For this reason it is difficult to forecast the business cycle. Various commentators cite developments and indicators as causes of the business cycle. The most common ones are:

- over-investment
- under-consumption
- fluctuations in output
- the interaction of the **multiplier** and **accelerator**
- war
- international politics.

KEY TERMS

Multiplier – the relationship between spending and consumption. It is also referred to as expenditure multiplier. Spending will trigger the national income. Expenditure multiplier does not differentiate between consumption and investment spending. This is called the multiplier effect.

Accelerator – each level of output needs a specific amount of capital. If output (and the capital required to buy the necessary machinery) is expected to rise, the amount of capital within an economy will also increase.

FOR EXAMPLE

The following two charts look at the US Gross Domestic Product from 1930 to 2002 and the actual effect on the trade cycle. They highlight the recessions and the phases of the business/economic cycle.

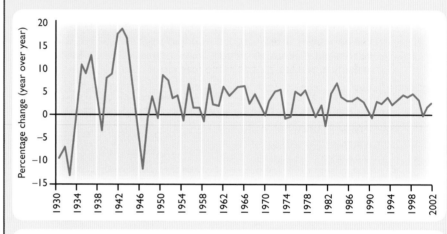

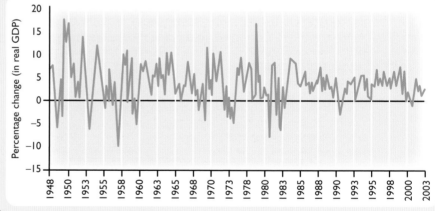

Phases of the cycle

As we have seen from the example of the US economy, the theory is that the business cycle has a recurrent sequence of events every nine or so years. In fact, the business cycle is far less easy to predict, and government policies tend to smooth out the peaks and troughs, or at least go some way to ensuring that the periods between recessions are extended.

The British government suggested that the last cycle began in 1997 or 1998. Using the business cycle, this would predict a recession beginning in 2006 or 2007; in fact it took until 2008–09 for a full-blown recession to develop.

The phases of the cycle are outlined in the table opposite.

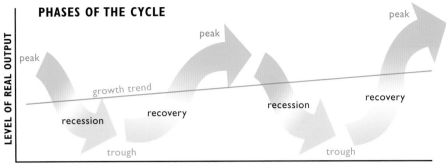

PHASES OF THE CYCLE

Phase	Typical characteristics
Recession	A recession will usually begin with falling sales. Businesses react by increasing their marketing. There will be increased competition for the falling demand and customers will be price sensitive. Businesses will cut output and this will lead to increases in unemployment. Businesses will tend not to make serious investments and any investment involving increased capacity will be shelved. The prospects will be gloomy and there will be relatively low levels of capacity utilisation. Businesses will begin to make financial losses, and some may close.
Recovery	Businesses react to recovery in a hesitant and cautious manner, as they are not sure whether this is a signal that demand will continue to increase. Expectations will still be low and businesses will be reluctant to make serious investments. Unemployment will not improve until it becomes clear that demand is increasing and this increase is sustainable. For these reasons recovery can take a long time. There will be spare capacity and output can be increased quickly. Businesses will begin to use their underutilised capital equipment to increase their output, and only when they have reached full capacity utilisation will they consider making expansion investments.
Boom	As the economy comes out of recovery and demand continues to increase, investment increases and suppliers find it increasingly difficult to satisfy the requirements of businesses. Most of the best skilled labour has already been taken on, so businesses struggle to recruit and are working at full capacity. In order to attract skilled labour, wages have to increase quicker than inflation, prices rise and increased level of demand continues, despite higher prices. There is usually inflation in this period, as there is a continual rise in the level of prices. In some cases the boom overheats, which means that the economy is growing too fast. In many cases there are situations when businesses cannot cope with the level of demand. There is a shortage of capacity and businesses are using all their resources. The economy is reaching full capacity output but is constrained by supply, making costs rise. This causes inflation to accelerate and the government usually responds by increasing interest rates.
Downturn	Rising costs tend to discourage continuing growth. Profitability will be reduced and it will be less attractive to make investments. Rising interest rates tend to stop businesses and consumers from spending. Businesses that have borrowed money in order to invest will now be paying higher interest rate charges. As a result there will be less money available and demand will fall. Businesses cut back their investment plans and some employees become jobless. Cuts in their income further reduce the amount of money available, signalling another drop in demand. Once demand falls, reduced real incomes make demand fall even quicker. Consumers and businesses draw on their past savings to try and stabilise the situation.

How businesses are affected by the cycle

The different stages of the cycle can affect businesses in a variety of ways. Even when there is a drop in income, some products and services still continue to be purchased, such as basic food items, whereas high-tech equipment and machinery for manufacturing may be one of the first to notice a drop in demand.

If a business can survive a recession then it will usually emerge stronger than ever before. It will have had to continue to compete with reduced investment, resources and employees. In other words, it will probably have become far more efficient. It should, therefore, be in a better position to take advantage of the recovery situation when it arrives.

Businesses often try to survive recessions by diversifying, so that they are not over-reliant on a single product or service, which could be more drastically affected by a drop in demand.

Difficult times mean that businesses often turn to tackling problems that should have been solved before a downturn or recession, such as de-layering or cutting back on wastage. Businesses will use contingency planning to try to handle the unpredictable effects at stages of the cycle.

> **Question**
>
> What is the role of investment in the business cycle?
> *(12 marks)*

For more about contingency planning see Contingency planning on pp. 264–5.

Interest and exchange rates

Interest rates

Interest rates can affect businesses in a number of different ways, not only by their rise or fall. In fact, small increases or decreases will have very little impact. A change in the interest rate could obviously have an impact on whether a business decides to make an investment. If interest rates are rising, then investment may be postponed.

Interest rates also affect a business's customers. Increased interest rates may mean that customers decide to save rather than spend. They are attracted to saving because of the high interest rates and dissuaded from purchasing because of the high cost of borrowing the money to make the purchase. If interest rates fall, however, consumers will be less inclined to save and more inclined to spend.

Interest rates also have a direct impact on the value of the currency. Rising interest rates will tend to cause rises in the exchange rate, whereas falling interest rates will usually cause the currency to decline and make it more difficult for British businesses to sell their products into overseas markets. There is a close relationship between interest rates and exchange rates, as can be seen in the table above.

Rising interest rates	Falling interest rates
British interest rates rise higher than those of other countries.	British interest rates fall compared to other countries.
Foreign investors are attracted to Britain as a result of the high interest rates offered for investment.	Britain is less attractive to overseas investors because higher interest rates are available elsewhere.
Foreign investors purchase sterling in order to make investments in Britain.	In order to make those investments in other countries, foreign investors sell sterling.
The demand for sterling increases so the price of sterling, or the exchange rate, rises.	This means the supply of sterling increases, so the price of sterling, or the exchange rate, falls.

Exchange rates

Exchange rates directly affect British businesses in two different ways:

- When British businesses are selling abroad, the revenue they receive from those products and services is affected by the exchange rate.
- When British businesses purchase raw materials, components or finished goods from abroad the price paid is affected by the exchange rates.

When exchange rates fluctuate, there is uncertainty about how much a British business is paying for purchases made overseas and how much it is receiving for products and services sold overseas.

FOR EXAMPLE

A British business agrees to export products to Australia. The contract is signed and the payment will be made in Australian dollars. In the time that elapses between the contract being signed and the invoice received, sterling rises in value against the Australian dollar. This means that the Australian dollar payment is actually worth less when it is paid to the British exporter.

Even insisting that payment is made in a domestic currency does not protect an exporter. If a British business sells products abroad and is paid in sterling, then, when sterling increases, the overseas customer will find that the products are more expensive in their own currency. This could affect the British business because the foreign customers may actually cut back on their purchases.

Businesses can respond to changes in exchange rates by dropping prices to offset the negative impact of a rise in the exchange rate. Some businesses will try to avoid exchange rate uncertainty by actually fixing the exchange rate for a future date. They agree between themselves and the overseas customer or supplier what the exchange rate will be when the payments fall due.

Some businesses will choose a different approach. Some Japanese companies, for example, have located in Britain in order to avoid complications with fluctuations in the exchange rate, although this has not protected them from fluctuations in the exchange rate between sterling and the Euro. Unsurprisingly, businesses such as these are strongly in favour of Britain adopting the Euro.

For many businesses, selling products and services abroad is essential as it offers a clear opportunity to expand. However, there are always more uncertainties in export markets. If the exchange rates are not in the British business's favour then it will have to fight very hard to remain competitive.

A business that is exporting when there is a fall in the exchange rate has a very definite advantage. The value of its products in sterling will rise if the foreign currency price remains the same. The business could leave the price at the same level and take higher profits, or it could cut prices and aim to gain greater market penetration through increased sales.

Rising interest rates also give businesses a dilemma. They need to make an assessment of how higher prices will affect sales. If they think that overseas markets will simply switch to substitute products and services, then the business will have to accept lower profit margins and drop the price. It is difficult to remain competitive when exchange rates are rising.

CASE STUDY EXCHANGE RATE WINNERS AND LOSERS

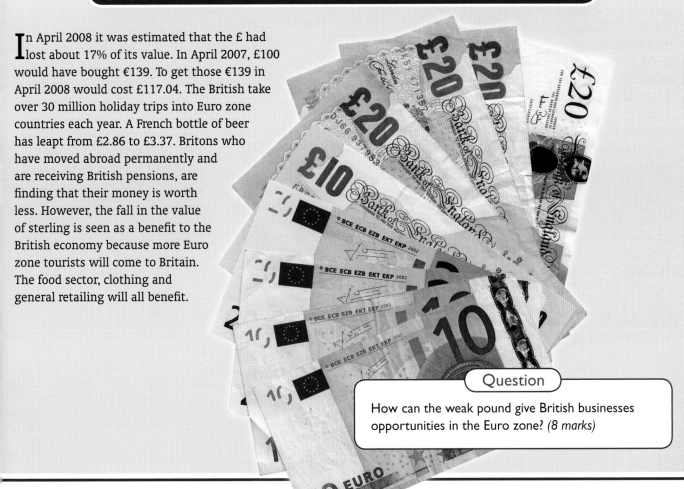

In April 2008 it was estimated that the £ had lost about 17% of its value. In April 2007, £100 would have bought €139. To get those €139 in April 2008 would cost £117.04. The British take over 30 million holiday trips into Euro zone countries each year. A French bottle of beer has leapt from £2.86 to £3.37. Britons who have moved abroad permanently and are receiving British pensions, are finding that their money is worth less. However, the fall in the value of sterling is seen as a benefit to the British economy because more Euro zone tourists will come to Britain. The food sector, clothing and general retailing will all benefit.

Question

How can the weak pound give British businesses opportunities in the Euro zone? *(8 marks)*

Inflation and unemployment

Inflation

Inflation is a general and sustained increase in an economy's pricing levels. It is usually caused by an excess demand within the economy, and may also lead to a devaluation of the country's currency. Inflation is measured in the US by the Consumer Price Index (CPI) and similar measures in other countries. It can also be measured by inflationary indicators such as the Producer Price Index which is prepared by the US Bureau of Labor Statistics.

Inflation is typified by a persistent rise in both prices and wages. As wages rise, production costs increase, thereby leading to a further rise in prices. In effect, if not controlled, then the economy can find itself in an inflationary spiral in which the rate of inflation increases at such a speed that it becomes almost impossible to control without significant restrictions on the supply of money and a major devaluation of the currency.

Inflation can be caused by a wide variety of different situations, such as a rapid increase in the money supply. This was a suggestion made by the US economist, Milton Friedman. Monetarists such as Friedman believe that inflation can be completely controlled by a strong grip on the money supply. Other approaches, such as that suggested by John Maynard Keynes, involve a rigid incomes policy to maintain low inflation and low unemployment.

Countries such as the US and the UK have experienced a broad range of inflation from virtually zero to in excess of 23%. However, it is generally considered reasonable and controllable to expect an annual inflation rate of between 2% and 3%. In the diagram below we can see two sets of figures, the CPI (Consumer Prices Index) and the RPI (Retail Prices Index). The Bank of England uses the CPI as its inflation target, while the

RPI is used to calculate increases in pensions and other state benefits. The Office of National Statistics collects about 120,000 prices every month for a 'basket' of about 650 goods and services. The change in the prices of those items is used to compile the two main measures of inflation.

Inflation has remained comparatively low in Britain over the past few years, which has made it easier to control costs and for businesses to establish their pricing strategies. Providing Britain's inflation remains low compared to that of its key rivals, British businesses will have a competitive advantage. Overseas businesses facing higher inflation levels have to respond by increasing their prices in order to maintain their profit margins.

Another key advantage of stable inflation rates is that a business can forecast its sales with more accuracy, as it will have a clearer understanding of demand.

Inflation can be caused by high levels of demand and businesses will tend to expand to meet higher levels of demand. There are two elements affecting demand in this equation:

- High demand causes inflation through what is known as demand-pull inflation.
- Inflation can be fuelled by demands for higher wages, which is known as cost-push inflation.

The government has to ensure that it keeps both of these potential inflation-creating situations under control.

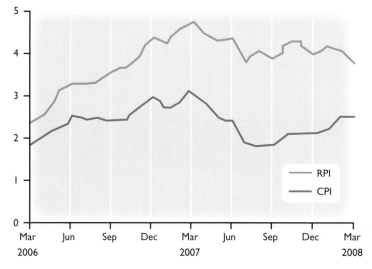

Source: National Statistics

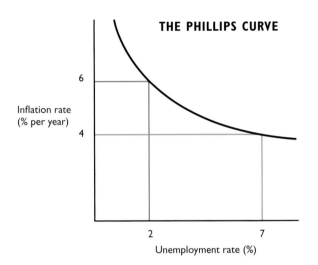

Unemployment

After the early 1990s, unemployment fell steadily from a peak of three million. It fell back to 1.5 million, but by late 2008 to early 2009 it began to rise once again. This is a comparatively low level of unemployment and with it there are new problems and challenges for businesses. With unemployment so low, businesses find it difficult to fill particular job vacancies, owing to the lack of available skilled labour. As an interim measure the government has encouraged overseas workers coming to Britain to fill vacancies that cannot be filled by British citizens. This has been particularly notable in the National Health Service.

Both businesses and the government can respond by encouraging increased specialist training in schools and colleges. Businesses can also respond by switching from labour-intensive production and servicing to more capital-intensive methods. This has the additional advantage of encouraging businesses to make

investments that will mean that they will be more competitive on the international stage in the future. Some businesses have taken an even more drastic step and have chosen to relocate outside Europe, where there are significant pools of skilled labour available to them. The added advantage is that this skilled labour in countries such as India or China is far cheaper.

While businesses struggle to find skilled labour it does mean a boom time for businesses that provide training courses and for recruitment agencies. Their skills and expertise are in great demand by British businesses.

In April 2008 employment in Britain was the highest since records began in 1971. There were 29.5 million people in work. Nonetheless, some parts of the British economy were not faring so well. Employment in the manufacturing sector had by this stage fallen to its lowest figure since 1978.

Inflation and unemployment

One of the key goals is to try to keep both inflation and unemployment low. However, the economist A.W. Phillips discovered a sinister relationship between inflation and unemployment. He suggested that, as more people work, so the national output increases. This causes wages to increase. As a result, consumers have more money and spend more. This leads to consumers demanding more products and services, which in turn causes the prices of products and services to increase. In other words there is an inverse relationship. Inflation rises as unemployment falls, and inflation falls as unemployment rises.

Phillips summarised his work in what has become known as the Phillips Curve, illustrated in the diagram above.

Obviously, this Phillips Curve is just an example and the actual Phillips Curve for any particular country will depend on the number of years that it aims to represent. Both inflation and unemployment rates are shown as percentages.

There is one particular problem with the Phillips Curve and that is that it does not explain periods of high inflation and high unemployment, known as stagflation.

> **Question**
>
> What particular problems might be encountered when using the Phillips Curve? (12 marks)

195

Economic growth

LEARNING OBJECTIVES

► Growth level versus growth rate
► Increased productivity
► Requirements for growth
► Standard of living
► Convergence

Growth level versus growth rate

It is important to note that there is a distinction between growth level and growth rate. Growth level is the long-term rate of growth and is the starting value of whatever is growing. Growth rate is the change in growth level from year to year and is a short-term rate of growth.

The most important part in increasing overall economic productivity is the growth level. The growth level shows where the economy is relative to its long-term positioning. If, for example, the economy grows at around 2% a year, then this is the economy's growth level. If the economy grows at an increased level, for example 5%, then the 3% difference between this and the growth level is the growth rate.

An economy that has a low growth level will not grow a great deal in the long term, even if there are periods of high growth. If, over a 25-year period, an economy has a steady growth level of 3%, then it will have outgrown an economy that has an unpredictable growth rate, but a growth level of 1%.

The distinctions are important because government policy aims to create desirable short-term effects and desirable long-term effects. Governments need to make sure that there is not a trade-off between policies that affect the growth level and those that affect the growth rate.

FOR EXAMPLE

A business has 50 production lines producing fresh sandwiches. The business wants to increase its output so it decides to purchase five new sandwich production lines. The level of growth is 50, as this is the number of production lines that the business had. The growth rate is 10% from one year to the next because the capital being used by the business has increased by 10%.

Increased productivity

When looking at whether an economy is growing in the long run, it is important to look at how output is actually created. All businesses use a combination of labour and capital. Labour is, of course, the employees who produce, manage or process production. Capital incorporates the ideas needed for production, as well as the machines that are physically used for that production. Labour in effect utilises the capital in the production process, so, for example, when workers make cars they use capital tools and assembly lines to create a finished product.

In order to increase productivity, employees need to be able to produce more output and this is known as labour productivity growth. Increased spending on capital can assist this by either making it easier to produce more products or to ensure that the level of quality increases.

Requirements for growth

Increasing capital, both human and physical, is the only sure way of increasing productivity growth in the long term. One way to directly increase the amount of capital in an economy is to increase the spending on capital.

Businesses will purchase new machinery and tools and they will also pay for training for their employees. However, in order to fund much of this investment they need to find someone willing to lend them sufficient money for their capital expenditure.

There is always a balance between the amount of money being saved in a country and the amount being spent. After all, the amount of money being saved directly affects the amount of money available for capital expenditure. Britain and the US, for example, have low savings rates, whereas countries like Japan have high savings rates.

Standard of living

We have seen that labour is required to ensure increased productivity. However, it would appear that if productivity increases there is actually less need to take on more employees because less labour is required to produce the same amount of output. Historically, this does not seem actually to be the case. Increased productivity seems to have a positive impact on the economy as a whole. As productivity increases it is often the case that there are more products and services available and more markets wishing to purchase them. As production becomes less expensive, due to efficiency, the quantity demanded increases. So, in effect, increases in productivity are offset by increases in demand, meaning that jobs are not lost.

If a country lags behind in terms of productivity it will tend to have lower wages and lower living standards than a country that has high productivity. The country that lags behind has to price its products competitively on the international market and the only way it can do this is to keep wages low.

You may have seen ways of comparing the standard of living or the prosperity of people living in different countries around the world. The simple equation is to divide the gross domestic product (GDP) by the total number of people in the country. This gives an average amount of income that each member of that population theoretically earns. The higher the figure, the greater the prosperity and the better the standard of living in the country. In developing countries this GDP per capita is extremely low, whereas in countries like the US it may be in excess of $25,000.

Convergence

In industrialised countries we see productivity and GDP per capita increasing. In fact, in industrialised countries these two measures are very similar and this suggests that through economic growth the countries have reached a convergence, where they have a common level, or similar level, of prosperity.

Convergence does not occur in every country – some countries will choose to spend funds on infrastructure, technology or education, all of which will ultimately assist them in ensuring that productivity and GDP per capita continue to rise. Some countries do not have a solid infrastructure or an educated population, and worse still they have unstable governments. In these situations they cannot hope to gain convergence.

> **Question**
>
> How useful is GDP per capita as a measure of economic growth? *(12 marks)*

Growth of global markets

Globalisation

Globalisation has many connotations, both positive and negative. In terms of international trade, the term refers to the situation which now presents the world with the fact that individuals, businesses and governments have become increasingly dependent upon one another and integrated with one another.

As far as business is concerned, the opportunities are enormous, with new markets opening up, access to different workforces, business partners, raw materials, components, products and services. Hand in hand with these opportunities are increased competitive threats.

The term 'globalisation' probably came into existence in the early 1980s when there was a rapid increase in the growth of international trade and the flow of capital around the world. The negative connotation with regard to globalisation has come from the increase in income inequality between the richest nations in the world and the poorest. The growth of globalisation has also seen the diminishing power of the governments of the lesser developed nations in comparison to vast, multinational businesses. In essence, globalisation implies international integration through a process of free trade, deregulation and liberalisation of trade.

BOOK RESEARCH

Stephanie Lawson, *The New Agenda for International Relations: From Polarization to Globalization in World Politics*, Cambridge: Polity Press, 2001.

Global manufacturing

Global manufacturing refers to situations when an international business chooses to consider the various and alternative factors, both advantageous and disadvantageous, of various countries before deciding on where it will manufacture products. Each country has a range of radically different political economies, national cultures, technological expertise and other externalities. Technological factors, for example, could include the costs of setting up manufacturing facilities. Product factors could include the transportation costs, which would be expressed in a value-to-weight ratio. Location issues revolve around decisions about whether to centralise or decentralise manufacturing. All these considerations involve trade-offs, and no single location would necessarily be ideal or clearly better than any other choice. It is clear, however, that with careful and prudent management, overseas manufacturing facilities, even from a low base start, can be capable of replicating the same levels of efficiency as a home production unit. Increasingly international businesses are looking to establish

overseas manufacturing units as centres of excellence. With the assistance of local management, factories can be upgraded over a period of time. For international businesses that manufacture in a variety of different overseas environments, it is often a question of determining how much of the final product is actually manufactured as components and what is bought from outsourced organisations. International manufacturers will seek to be strategically flexible by subcontracting work to various foreign countries. Vertical integration through strategic alliances can also assist an international business in gaining the greatest potential benefits from its involvement with overseas manufacturing facilities.

Increasingly, information technology is providing a means by which ever more remote cooperative manufacturing units can work together in terms of inputs, production schedules and information flow and output targets.

McDonaldisation

McDonaldisation originally referred to technological advances in the preserving and storing of foodstuffs and the growing ownership of automobiles during the 1950s, coupled with the development of US suburbs which transformed the way in which Americans shopped and ate. The larger supermarkets in the US succeeded in overwhelming many smaller and longer established businesses, a trend which has been replicated in many other countries. The emphasis of service had moved from quality to price and efficiency. The key characteristics of McDonaldisation are:

- *Efficiency* – consumers could obtain what they needed very quickly, with very little effort on behalf of the business. Employees could perform their tasks more easily and, above all, more quickly, thus serving customers more efficiently. Coupled with this increase in efficiency, the quality aspects lessened, particularly given the fact that technologies

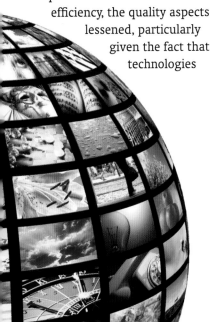

that do not require the input of humans performed many of the tasks.
- *Control* – McDonaldisation radically changed the way in which employees were treated and expected to behave, as well as the way in which customers were expected to interact with the business. For very much the first time customers queued up at a counter to collect their food and cleared tables after they had finished eating.
- *Predictability* – this was important as consumers knew exactly what they were purchasing – the product was identical no matter which outlet the customers visited. This meant that McDonaldised businesses could more easily sell their business as a franchise operation.

McDonaldisation has spread across the globe, not simply in the retailing of hamburgers and related products. The concept now revolves around the idea that the consumer can purchase standardised items at relatively low prices and that the quality of products does not differ significantly in the various outlets scattered around the world. Given that there is a far great availability of products and services on the global market, McDonaldisation is said to have been an integral part of making these goods available to larger proportions of the population. Consumers, by

BOOK RESEARCH

George Ritzer, *The McDonaldization of Society*, Thousand Oaks, California: Pine Forge Press, 1996.

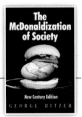

purchasing standardised products, are able to obtain what they perceive they need without very much delay. Convenience and uniform quality has competed well against other economic alternatives, notably higher priced customised products and services. In settling for standardised products, individuals in different countries around the world can now afford products and services which hitherto they could not afford.

McDonaldisation has been seen to be an ideal solution in providing faster, efficient products and services to a working population that has considerably less free time than in the past. McDonaldised products provide a familiar, stable and safe alternative to taking risks in purchasing unknown products. It has also been a feature of McDonaldisation that consumers can compare competing products more easily.

> **Question**
>
> To what extent is McDonaldisation just a feature of globalisation? *(18 marks)*

Evaluating strategies to respond to changes

Business strategies and options

As we have seen, a business's strategy is a means by which the business aims to achieve its corporate objectives. A business may have a variety of strategies that may be put in place to take advantage of specific economic factors, or have been created to respond to these economic factors. The following table outlines the key challenges and responses.

Responding to the market

The precise response to the market would depend very much on the degree of competition and the trends in that market. A business will always seek the opportunity to differentiate its products and services from that of the competition, and to find ways to inform potential customers of the advantages of choosing them rather than purchasing a competitor's products and services.

Responding to the business cycle

One way in which businesses often try to respond to a recession is to diversify. It also gives them the necessary impetus to tackle any systemic organisational problems, which should mean that they are a more efficient organisation once the recession has ended.

During a recovery, investment and increased production will be hesitant, as the business will be unsure whether or not the recovery is sustainable. During a boom time the business will attempt to reach as close to total capacity utilisation as possible, in order to maximise profit. When a downturn occurs the business may begin reducing its output and taking precautionary steps to reduce costs in case the situation spirals into a recession.

Challenge	Problems	Possible responses
Business cycle	Recession, recovery, boom, downturn	Dependent on stage of the business cycle
Unemployment	Skill surplus and reduced customer spending	Retain key employees and seek new markets for products and services
Labour market	Surplus or shortage of skills	Offer better financial and non-financial package to attract key workers
Exchange rates	Sterling valued higher or lower than before	Ensure that effect of exchange rate changes does not adversely affect profits
Interest rates	High or low interest rates, or rising or falling interest rates	If interest rates are high or increasing, then cut back on investments. If they are low or falling, consider investments.
Inflation	Price increases and trends in price changes	Control costs if prices are rising slowly, ensure sales forecasts are accurate

Ideally, businesses would like to be price makers, rather than price takers, although this is not always a viable option.

Responding to interest and exchange rates

The prevailing interest rate will have a marked effect on a business's willingness to borrow money, and this will directly impact on investment and expansion. When interest rates are high, or appear to be moving upwards, then investment plans will usually be shelved or postponed. The business also needs to be aware that it will affect customer spending: customers may delay purchasing products and services, so the business will expect to see demand fall and will cut production or output to match.

If interest rates are falling or are low then a business will take advantage of the lower cost of borrowing to make investments and to expand. They will also step up production to match increased demand from customers.

If sterling has a high value compared to that of foreign currencies then it is difficult for British businesses to export abroad, but it is cheaper for them to import foreign goods. If sterling is low then British products and services appear cheaper to overseas markets and more export sales can be achieved. On the other hand, it makes importing overseas products and services less attractive, as they are more expensive.

To respond, businesses will try to predict fluctuations in the exchange rate and also try to negotiate contracts that are quoted in sterling, rather than an overseas currency.

Responding to inflation and unemployment

If inflation is rising, then it is difficult to control costs and this means it is difficult to maintain profit margins, particularly if the business does not increase its prices, which would further fuel inflation. High inflation also makes sales forecasts somewhat unpredictable, as it is difficult to gauge their actual value, particularly if they relate to a period too far into the future.

Low inflation will attract overseas investment and business confidence. If inflation and prices are relatively stable then British businesses will tend to expand their capacity through investment and be willing to develop new products and services, as this stability removes much of the risk.

A business will be much more cautious when there is higher inflation, as the precise effects will be difficult to predict. Prices are constantly changing and the business will need to be aware of the fact that a responsible government will make changes in its economic policy to try to control inflation.

KEY TERMS

Income elastic – these are products or services, such as cars and overseas holidays, whose sales are linked to a customer's available funds. They are more likely to be purchased when a customer has excess income, but their sales will fall when income levels drop.

Responding to economic growth and the global market

Economic growth provides businesses with enormous opportunities. There will be high levels of consumer spending, which will encourage existing businesses to expand and new businesses to set up. There will be higher sales and increased profits and there will be particular expansion for businesses that sell income elastic products. These positive points imply continued business growth, profit and investment. However, there will be shortages of labour and other resources, meaning that businesses will have to respond by paying higher wages and coping with increased costs and then have to increase their prices, which could cause inflation and uncertainty.

Businesses will also have to respond by ensuring that their management and employees are given full support during growth periods, as their workloads will be increased. Businesses will have to put in place clear decision-making processes, quality control and coordination procedures, as all these issues will be under threat with the business working at full capacity.

Question

Rapid rates of economic growth bring very few benefits to a business and an enormous number of problems. Discuss. *(15 marks)*

Case studies, questions and exam practice

CASE STUDY NIKE

Nike is based in Oregon in the United States. It has over 29,000 direct employees around the world, but this is really no indication of the true number of people employed due to business generated by Nike. It is estimated that a further 650,000 people are employed in the manufacture of Nike products. It should be noted, however, that this manufacturing work is completed by companies under contract to Nike – they are not actually employees of the business.

The simple beginnings of the company disguise the complex structure which is in operation today. Nike is an enormous company which has grown from annual sales of US$8,000 in 1962 to the US$15 billion that it earns today. After starting out importing shoes from one manufacturer, today they organise the production of a complete line of sporting apparel; from shoes to ice skates, and from track suits to team jerseys.

Like any multi-national company, Nike used the process of globalisation because the managers felt that the company could benefit by doing so. However, it is worth noting that the company actually started out as a global network; the very first shoes that they sold were made in Japan, and imported into the United States. Today, the global reach of Nike is much more significant. They have manufacturing operations in 45 countries, and their products are sold in almost every country in the world. This sort of expansion cannot happen without a detailed plan, and a plan needs to be 'sold' to the decision-makers if it is to be accepted.

For company reporting purposes, Nike divides the world into four main sections. Some of the pertinent details about each section are shown in the table.

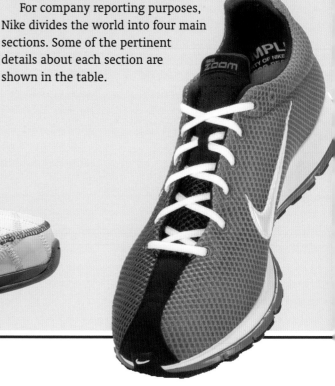

Region:	The USA	Europe, the Middle East and Africa	The Asia Pacific Region	The Americas (other than the USA)
Direct employment	14,000	6,000	3,282	1,076
Factory base	There are no factories operating in the USA	There are 104 factories employing a total of 29,242 workers	There are 252 factories employing over 550,000 workers	There are 137 factories employing a total of 44,600 workers
Countries	The USA	Countries include: Austria, Bulgaria, Croatia, Hungary, Ireland, Israel, Italy, Norway, South Africa, Slovenia and the United Kingdom	Countries include: China, Indonesia, Hong Kong, India, Japan, Korea and New Zealand	Canada, Mexico, Brazil, Argentina and Chile
Revenue (2006)	US$5.7 billion	US$4.3 billion	US$1.0 billion	US$236 million

Over 600,000 people are working in factories that operate specifically to make Nike clothing and footwear. There are very few companies in the world that can claim to have so many employees in so many countries.

Questions

1 Give reasons why Nike's managers could justify globalisation? *(15 marks)*
2 Nike is committed to making investments in the future of the countries in which it operates. Suggest how it might do this and why. *(8 marks)*

Government intervention in the economy

Key priorities

Although Britain is no longer considered as a separate economic entity in the world, successive British governments have wrestled with the problems of trying to manage employment, levels of production, prices and exports and imports. Britain is now part of the European Union, and an integral part of the EU economy. It is also a major player on the world stage and has an impact on the world's economy.

Decisions made by the government aim to manipulate the economy so that inflation does not rise out of control; so that the economy enjoys a steady and sustained growth; so that there is a low rate of unemployment and so that we do not consistently purchase more products and services from abroad than we sell abroad.

We have just quickly outlined the four key priorities that have remained at the heart of most government intervention into the economy for the past 60 years or so. They remain key elements of all government thinking, legislation and policies relating to the economy.

- *Price* – it is in the interests of the economy to have stable pricing as this is a clear indicator of the government's ability to control inflation. As we have seen, it is usually measured using the Retail Price Index. At times, Britain has suffered from high rates of inflation. Although there is dispute about the current rates, they are believed to be below 3%. By having a lower rate of inflation than other countries, British businesses have a potential price advantage.

- *Growth* – steady and sustained economic growth in the economy suggests gradually increasing levels of production or output. This is not only good for British businesses, as they enjoy increased incomes, but it is also valuable to the broader economy, as it provides work and customers for raw materials, components and finished goods. Ideally, the British government aims for a year-on-year economic growth rate of about 3%–4%, which is considered to be both steady and sustainable.

- *Employment* – ideally, unemployment would be virtually non-existent. However, there will always be a certain percentage of the population that is unemployed, albeit a comparatively low figure compared to the three million or more people out of work in Britain around 25 years ago. In terms of the economy, high unemployment means wasted labour resources and it also represents a drain on the economy, as these individuals will have to be financially supported by those in work.

- *Balance of trade* – the balance of trade represents the difference between the value of products and services sold to overseas countries and the value of products and services imported by Britain from overseas sources. A 'deficit' indicates that more is being imported than exported, whereas a 'surplus' describes the reverse. Ideally, the balance of payments or trade should be about equal.

Trade-offs and responsibilities

Although the government itself has primary responsibility for handling the economy and intervening when it thinks it necessary, the Bank of England also has a key role to play, because since 1997 its Monetary Policy Committee has had the responsibility for setting interest rates in Britain. Its task is to not only assist the government in meetings its inflation targets, but also to ensure that there is sustained growth in the economy.

It is not always possible for a government to ensure that the four key objectives are being met. In order to achieve continued economic growth and high levels of employment, price stability is important because inflation can contribute to poor economic performance. But being able to achieve all the objectives at the same time is not straightforward. By focusing on one objective the others become more difficult to achieve. High growth and low unemployment can cause inflation, as well as shortages in raw materials and skilled labour, which means that prices are forced up.

Low unemployment also means that people have more money to spend, which means they are tempted to purchase products brought in from abroad, which in turn causes balance of payments problems.

For more on the impact of interest rates see Monetary policy on p. 208.

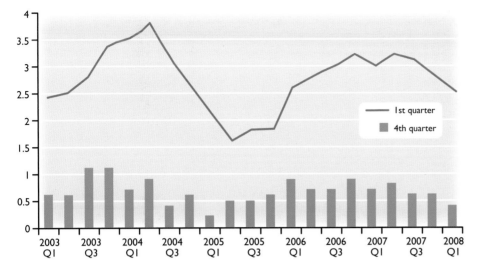

◀ GDP Growth

UK economy rose by 0.4% in Q1 2008. GDP increased by 0.4% in the first quarter of 2008, compared to 0.6% in the previous quarter. There was a deceleration in both production and service industries compared with the fourth quarter of 2007.

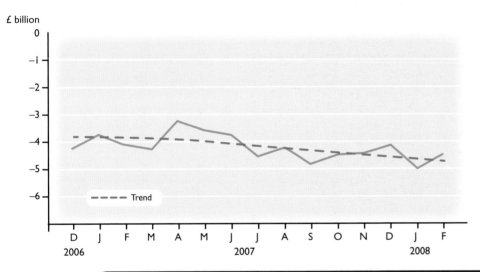

◀ UK Trade

Deficit narrowed to £4.4 billion in February. The UK's deficit on trade in goods and services was £4.4 billion in February, compared with the revised deficit of £5.0 billion in January (originally published as a deficit of £4.1 billion). The surplus on trade in services was £3.0 billion, compared with a surplus of £2.9 billion in January.

CASE STUDY PRODUCTIVITY GROWTH DECREASES

In the fourth quarter of 2007, whole economy productivity growth (measured by output per worker) was 1.7% compared with the same quarter a year earlier, down from a growth of 2.3% in the previous quarter. The decrease in annual productivity growth was due to a decrease in the growth rate of output and an increase in the growth rate of whole economy workers.

The alternative measure of productivity – output per hour worked – showed that whole economy hourly productivity grew by 1.9% in the fourth quarter of 2007 compared with the same quarter a year ago, up from 1.8% in the previous quarter.

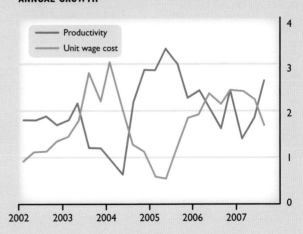

WHOLE ECONOMY PRODUCTIVITY AND UNIT WAGE COSTS, ANNUAL GROWTH

Question

What does the graph tell us about manufacturing productivity and unit wage costs? *(12 marks)*

Tax and subsidy

Taxes

Taxation policy has a direct impact on the level of economic activity. Businesses are taxed in exactly the same way in which income is taxed. Businesses pay corporation tax on their profits. This is a form of direct taxation.

The taxation burden overall has another marked impact on the businesses, as tax is also levied on potential customers' incomes or profits, which means that higher taxation reduces the amount of available consumer spending. Businesses that are most immediately affected by tax increases are those that usually supply luxury goods, while businesses that supply basic items may be relatively unaffected by changes in taxation.

Rather like the community charge, businesses also pay a business rate to their local authority, which is based on the value of the property that is owned by the business. This money is ploughed back into the local economy to supply services. Businesses also pay indirect taxation, known in Britain as Value Added Tax (VAT). Changes in this form of taxation can also have a drastic impact on the level of economic activity. Increasing VAT would undoubtedly cut consumer spending and thus the level of economic activity, although the precise effects will be related to whether the products or services being sold are price sensitive.

Increasing indirect taxation is also inflationary, as it pushes up prices by increasing costs. Each time products or services pass along the supply chain in exchange for money, VAT is paid on those products and services, based on their current value. Businesses pay the balance between the VAT they have paid out and the VAT they have collected.

Subsidies

Subsidies are payments made by the government in order to support a particular sector of the economy or a specific industry. Subsidies will have an effect on the competition, market power and entry into the market. Subsidies usually take the form of grants or tax breaks in order to reduce a business's costs so that it can continue to operate with the support of the government funds.

Subsidies often distort competition because they cause businesses to set output and pricing levels at inefficient levels. They keep inefficient businesses in the market; they discourage entry by efficient businesses and effectively encourage entry by inefficient ones. The Office of Fair Trading, for example, believes that they also distort investment, research and development.

Again according to the Office of Fair Trading, subsidies also distort competition, which suggests that governments should look at the effects of subsidies before introducing schemes. They believe that there is minimal distortion in prices and output, but subsidies do have an

impact on capacity decisions.

Subsidies also aim to protect employment in particular regions, which effectively ties businesses to retaining employees for fear of losing their subsidies if they were to reduce their workforce.

A wide variety of different businesses receive government subsidies. Subsidies are available for research and development in energy, for farms, for exports, for areas with high unemployment.

Even in Europe there are subsidies. Through the Common Agricultural Policy the EU subsidises tobacco growing with around £700 million per year. Most government subsidies, however, require EU agreement, as unfair subsidies are seen to distort the markets and to be unfair to competitors. In effect, inefficient businesses receive funding in order to compete with more efficient businesses. Under normal circumstances, without the subsidies the inefficient businesses would either have to significantly restructure or they would be forced out of business.

FOR EXAMPLE

Farm subsidies in the European Union are in excess of €40 billion. This not only subsidises inefficient farming methods, but also rewards large businesses such as Nestlé with subsidies to send surplus butter and milk to developing countries, such as Bangladesh. EU farming subsidies in Britain are worth over £2 billion per year. However, the largest and richest farmers receive the largest subsidies, and according to recent figures the 100 farmers at the bottom of the list received less than £25 each in subsidies.

CASE STUDY BRITISH AIRLINES – TAXED OR SUBSIDISED?

The industry is often accused of being subsidised or under-taxed. The actual tax and subsidy position of aviation in the UK is as follows:

- *VAT* – air travel, like all UK public transport modes is zero-rated for VAT.
- *Fuel Tax* – airlines pay no fuel tax, and other public transport modes are treated in a similar way. Diesel trains pay 6.44p per litre red diesel rate, and buses get a fuel duty rebate that results in an effective tax rate of less than 10p per litre. Rail is exempt from the climate-change levy.
- *Air Passenger Duty (APD)* – unique to air travel, APD collects over £900 million per annum. This is equivalent to over one-and-a-half times the carbon cost of the flights on which it is levied. No income from this environmental tax is used to address environmental challenges and it is a very inefficient and ineffective approach to dealing with issues like climate change.

Subsidy and infrastructure

- Air travel pays for its entire infrastructure – on the ground and in the air.
- Aviation receives no subsidy from the taxpayer, with the very small exception of regional assistance to some parts of the UK including the Highlands and Islands services in the north of Scotland.
- Other public transport modes receive billions of pounds subsidy each year. Rail received £4.5 billion in 2005/06, with £15 billion planned over the next three years.
- Buses receive about £1.2 billion of subsidy per year.

Question

Using the information in the case study and your own research, comment on the British airline industry in terms of its size, support for other businesses and competitiveness. *(12 marks)*

Monetary and fiscal policy

Monetary policy

The primary objective of monetary policy is to control inflation. A country would set a target for inflation and attempt to ensure that it does not deviate to any degree from this target. Since the UK left the exchange rate mechanism in September 1992, UK monetary policy has involved the use of manipulating interest rates to control the level of inflation.

As the term suggests, monetary policy is a means by which the government controls the money supply. Adopting a monetarist policy relies on the belief that in controlling the money supply price levels are also controlled. There are close links between interest rates, the money supply and the exchange rate. At times when the UK was tied to a fixed exchange rate system, both the rate of interest and the money supply had to be adjusted in order to maintain a fixed exchange rate. During the period between 1990 and 1992, when the UK was part of the Exchange Rate Mechanism (ERM), the government effectively lost control of interest rates and the supply of money.

Monetarists realise that it is notoriously difficult to control interest rates, money supply and exchange rates simultaneously. In May 1997 the then Labour Chancellor, Gordon Brown, made the Bank of England independent, setting up the Monetary Policy Committee (MPC), effectively taking the government and the Chancellor out of the decision-making loop with regard to interest rates.

BOOK RESEARCH

Walsh, Carl, *Monetary Theory and Policy*, Cambridge, Massachusetts, MIT Press. 2003.

Monetary policy will seek to alter interest rates, control the money supply or manipulate the exchange rate. The following table outlines one major aspect of monetary policy – manipulation of the interest rates – and also indicates its impact on other key economic variables.

	Rising interest rates	Falling interest rates
Government objectives	Reduce consumer spending, limit inflationary pressure, slow economic growth, increase imports by creating a deficit	Reduce unemployment, increase production, promote exports by reducing the value of sterling, increase economic growth
Likely outcome	This should dampen down an economic boom	Reduced interest rates help the economy recover from a slump
Implications	Businesses see falling sales, increased demand for credit; businesses cancel or postpone investment; businesses reduce borrowing; value of sterling increases prices of exports and reduces import prices	Demand and sales increase; production is stimulated by increased employment; export sales increase; imports become less competitive; businesses increase investment
Effect on unemployment	Unemployment increases, production declines	Unemployment falls, economic activity increases
Effect on inflation	Demand and output fall, reducing inflationary pressure	Increased output and spending fuels inflation
Effect on economic growth	Businesses cut output and investment; spending declines and growth slows	Cheaper borrowing encourages investment and consumer expenditure so economic growth is stimulated
Effect on exchange rates	Sterling rises in value	The value of sterling falls
Effect on balance of payments	Imports fall, improving the current account balance	Increased spending brings in imports causing a current account balance deficit

Fiscal policy

As we have seen in the previous spread on tax and subsidy, fiscal policy is about the government's expenditure and taxation policies. Broadly, the government can take two different approaches to its fiscal policy:

- *Expansionary fiscal policy* – this means that the government decides to either cut taxation or increase government expenditure by borrowing, which is known as the Public Sector Borrowing Requirement. The alternative is to use surplus funds that it has retained from previous years. Expansionary fiscal policy aims to increase the level of economic activity. It should result in increased output and spending, and lower unemployment, but there will be increased inflationary pressure and a larger number of imports.

- *Contractionary fiscal policy* – the government achieves this by reducing its own spending or increasing taxation. In some cases it will choose to do both at the same time. The policy aims to reduce the level of economic activity, and should mean that output reduces, spending falls and more people become unemployed. It should curb inflationary pressure and consumer spending on imported goods.

The other important aspect of fiscal policy involves precisely where the government chooses to spend its money. Broadly speaking, it has two options. It can either make transfer payments or make investments on the infrastructure. The consequences of these choices are detailed below:

- *Transfer payments* – including payments to the unemployed, the low-waged and those of pensionable age. The net effect of changing the level of transfer payments is seen almost automatically. If increased payments are made then these individuals will be able to spend more, and this money will filter straight back into the economy. If benefits are lower, the recipients will have to cut back almost immediately. More often than not, increases in these payments see increased demand for food, fuel and public transport.

- *Infrastructure payments* – effectively the government makes investments on housing, roads, and other infrastructure projects, such as flood defences. These immediately impact on businesses providing construction services. They will also assist in cutting costs for other businesses. For example, new flood defences could cut the insurance premiums for businesses in flood areas, or a new road could cut transport costs. These are usually considered to be longer-term investments and take longer to have any direct impact on economic activity.

In recent years the government has not favoured fiscal policies, but has preferred to use monetary policy as the means by which to manipulate economic activity and control variables, such as inflation and interest rates. In fact there has been a trend for public expenditure to fall in relation to GDP in the past few years.

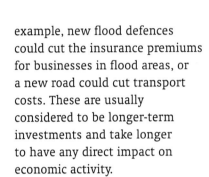

> ### Question
>
> There is very little difference between monetary policy and fiscal policy. Discuss. *(12 marks)*

Supply side policies

What are supply side policies?

Supply side policies aim to improve the supply side potential of an economy, in order to make markets and industries more efficient and therefore help national output to grow at a faster rate.

Governments will use supply side policies in order to try to achieve sustained economic growth without the danger of inflation increases. The problem is that for the policies to work there has to be a high level of aggregate demand. This is necessary so that the productive capacity of the economy can be utilised.

There are many benefits to supply side policies, as we will see, but broadly there are four key benefits:

- Inflation should be lowered because by making the economy more efficient there will be a reduction in cost-push inflation.
- There should be lower unemployment because these policies can tackle all the different types of unemployment and actually reduce the natural rate of unemployment.
- There should be improved economic growth because aggregate supply will have increased.
- There should be improved trade and balance of payments because businesses will be more competitive and they will be able to export more.

Supply side policies tend to focus on the product markets, where products and services are purchased and sold, or the labour market, where labour is bought and sold.

What are supply side policies for product markets?

Most of the supply side policies aim to free up the market to work more efficiently by reducing government interference. They also aim to increase competition and, as an additional aim, increase productivity.

Policy	Outcome and example
Privatisation	This involves the selling of state-owned assets to the private sector, as the argument is that the private sector can run the businesses more efficiently because they are concerned with making profit, and will aim to reduce costs and develop better services. Examples include the privatisation of British Telecom and British Airways. However, the failure of the privatised business, Railtrack, led this side of the railway business to be brought back into public ownership with the creation of Network Rail.
Deregulation of markets	This involves reducing barriers to entry into markets in order to make the markets more competitive. British Telecom used to hold a monopoly position in telecommunications, but now there are many other telecommunications providers. This has led to lower prices and, arguably, a better service.
Tough competition policy	The theory is that greater competition forces businesses to use their resources more efficiently, which means that costs are reduced and consumers benefit from lower prices. Governments have introduced a number of policies to prevent anti-competitive practices, including price-fixing cartels.
Commitment to international trade	If businesses in different countries can compete more freely, then costs should be driven down and consumers will enjoy lower prices. There is free trade throughout the European Union with no trade barriers, and this has been extended to a liberalisation of trade across the world. Britain is part of the World Trade Organisation, which aims to liberalise international trade.
Encouragement of	Governments promote an entrepreneurial culture and provide resources to encourage new business start-ups. These businesses have the potential to become far larger and add to national output, as well as employing more people and coming up with innovations that can be transferred to other sectors. Examples include loan guarantees for new businesses and regional policy assistance.
Capital investment and innovation	If businesses spend money on capital projects they will add to aggregate demand, so the government allows tax relief on research and development projects and cuts corporation tax to encourage investment. Enterprise and innovation is essential to improving economic performance.

What are supply side policies for labour markets?

Supply side policies in this area relate to the quality and quantity of the supply of labour. In addition to this, they aim to make the labour market more flexible, in order to better serve the demands of employers.

There have been enormous changes in the laws regarding trade unions, and many traditional legal protections have been removed, including the ways in which industrial action can be taken and the use of restrictive practices. There has been a marked downturn in the number of strikes, and industrial relations have improved.

Governments can also choose to spend money on education and training. This aims to increase the skills within the workforce and improve employment prospects. In effect, government spending aims to improve workers' human capital. Industry has tended to move away from manual skills, instead using education and training to transform manual workers into employees able to use a broad range of mental skills. Improved training also allows for occupational mobility, and this reduces the problem of structural unemployment, which occurs when there is a permanent contraction of a particular industry or demand for a particular skill.

Tax reforms are also used. Lower tax rates provide short-term boosts to demand, as they encourage employees to work longer hours or to seek better-paid work.

Have Britain's supply side policies worked?

The following table outlines the key successes and failures of supply side policies:

Yes, it has worked	No, it has not worked
There has been sustained economic growth, and Britain has broadly coped with the global economic downturn.	Productivity is still comparatively low compared to main competitors.
There have been sustained falls in unemployment and Britain has a record level of employment.	The balance of payments is still in deficit, which suggests that British businesses are not as competitive abroad as they could be, but it is now again on the increase.
The policies have been able to offset the possible trade-offs between falling unemployment and low inflations – two key government objectives.	The underlying rate of economic growth is slower than many of Britain's key competitors.
The service sector in particular has grown enormously and continues to grow.	British manufacturing has suffered from at least three slumps or recessions in the past decade or so.
British employees are some of the most flexible in the developed economies and there is a high level of occupational flexibility.	There is under-investment in public sector services and a falling share of GDP is allocated to research and development.

> ### Question
>
> Do supply side policies work? Discuss. (12 marks)

Political decisions affecting trade and access to markets

LEARNING
OBJECTIVES

▶ British trade and investment
▶ Trade liberalisation
▶ Key trade issues
▶ Europe and enlargement

British trade and investment

Britain is the eighth largest exporter of goods, and the second largest exporter of services in the world. Exports account for a quarter of Britain's GDP, and Britain now has the highest ratio of inward and outward investment to GDP of any leading economy.

Maximising trade is in the economic interests of the country for the following reasons:

• it means lower prices and wider choice
• it benefits industry through access to competitive sources of materials and components
• it stimulates competition and innovation
• it helps generate resources to promote higher levels of employment and environmental protection.

Trade liberalisation

In the aftermath of the Second World War, the General Agreement on Tariffs and Trade was drawn up. This aimed to liberalise trade throughout the world, and since then the average industrial tariffs of developed countries have fallen from around 40% to less than 5%. Over the same period of time world trade has increased twentyfold and world incomes sixfold.

> ### KEY TERM
>
> **Tariff** – a tax on products, raw materials and commodities that have been produced abroad.

There is still room for continued advances. In the Organisation for Economic Cooperation and Development (OECD) countries (30 countries, including most of Europe, North America and some other countries), tariffs higher than 15% still exist in clothing, footwear and motor vehicles. In non-OECD countries up to three-quarters of all imported products have tariffs.

Trade barriers can be seen to distort domestic markets by pushing up prices and protecting inefficient sectors of the economy from foreign competition. Effectively they penalise foreign producers and encourage inefficient allocation of resources.

Developing countries are gaining much from trade liberalisation and it is seen as a means by which poverty can be reduced across the world.

Key trade issues

Britain is a member of the World Trade Organisation (WTO), which has a membership of around 146 countries. It is used to deal with trade disputes, handle trade negotiations and provide technical assistance. Effectively it deals with the rules of free trade between different countries. The WTO and Britain, among others, are concerned about three key issues regarding free trade:

• Anti-dumping – this is when imports are brought into the market and sold at less than their normal value, which damages the domestic industries.
• Industrial tariffs – which are levied on particular countries to protect industry.
• Technical barriers – this is when the country applies technical regulations or standards to restrict or impede international trade.

There are many key trade issues. An anti-dumping agreement was made in 1994 and agreements have also been made against governments subsidising their own industries to make them artificially competitive against overseas competitors. Negotiations are ongoing regarding environmental concerns and Britain's approach is that trade rules should not block legitimate environmental regulation and that sustainable development is the way forward.

The government department for Business Enterprise and Regulatory Reform (BERR), along with UK Trade and Investment (UKTI), monitor potential trade barriers to British businesses. More broadly, the European Union and the World Trade Organisation also seek to ensure that market access is not impeded throughout the world, particularly if the countries have already agreed to follow the WTO's guidelines.

INTERNET RESEARCH 🔍

BERR's website is at www.berr.gov.uk.

The World Trade Organisation's website is at www.wto.org.

The European Commission's website is at www.ec.europa.eu. Follow the links to the EU and the world and the external trade page.

The Department for International Development's website is at www.dfid. gov.uk.

Much of Britain's trade policy is now linked to broader policies and agreements made within the EU. Certainly the single market within the EU has had a massive impact on trade and the intention is to broaden the benefits of this free trade to other parts of the world. Broadly speaking, the policy is towards open and fair international trading. This means removing tariff or non-tariff barriers, sweeping aside anti-competitive practices and then opening up markets to cheaper supplies of raw materials and components.

The British government recognises the importance of trade and has set two key objectives that aim to reduce global poverty and improve British competitiveness and market access. To this end, a new cabinet committee on trade has been created, in order to give strategic direction and oversight to British trade policy. It is chaired by the Secretary of State for the Department for International Development (DFID).

Europe and enlargement

As of 1 January 2007, there were 27 members of the European Union. This has grown significantly since the original six members back in the 1950s. Britain joined the European Union in 1973. At present there are three more candidate countries; Croatia, Turkey and the Former Yugoslav Republic of Macedonia. Other parts of the former Yugoslavia and Albania are potential candidate countries.

The process of gradually accepting new member countries is known as enlargement. It is a long and complex process and requires the countries to satisfy a number of conditions. Today's EU, with its 27 member states, has a population of around 500 million. It is the world's largest economic zone and effectively there are no trade barriers or constraints to trade. The whole of the EU is an internal market, in which industries from different countries can freely export and import without imposing any barriers to trade. This has offered British businesses enormous opportunities, but it has also meant that they face direct competition from more efficient businesses in other parts of the European Union.

Over time, industry has begun to specialise and to concentrate in particular areas of expertise around Europe. Effectively this means that particular countries focus on their strengths, while their weaker sectors flounder due to competition and are forced to either downsize or close. This process is expected to continue for several more decades. Opening up the British market to EU-based competitors has been the price that has to be paid for opening up European markets to British industries.

Question

Outline the key advantages and disadvantages to Europe and industry of the enlargement of the European Union.
(18 marks)

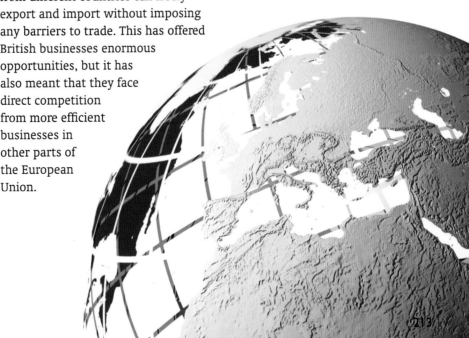

Impact of legislation: employment law

LEARNING OBJECTIVES

▶ Observance of employment legislation
▶ Employment Act 2002
▶ Equal Pay Act 1970
▶ Sex Discrimination Act 1975
▶ Race Relations Act 1976
▶ Disability Discrimination Act 1995
▶ Age discrimination

Observance of employment legislation

Employment legislation is probably the fastest moving aspect of human resource management. New legislation is always in the pipeline and with the added complication of adopting European regulations, which have an impact on existing British law, it means that mistakes and misunderstandings are more than possible.

Employment Act 2002

The Employment Act 2002 was an incredibly important piece of legislation. It brought about major changes to the dispute resolution process. It also improved the rights of working parents. Finally, it put a process in place for more equality in pay between men and women who performed similar work.

Equal Pay Act 1970

The Equal Pay Act made it unlawful for employers to discriminate between men and women in terms of their pay and conditions. Discrimination could be identified when men and women were doing the same or very similar work, but were being paid or treated in different ways.

When the Equal Pay Act was first introduced in 1970 the pay gap between men and women stood at 37%. Five years later it had closed to 30%. The Equal Pay Act extends to requiring equality in the contract of employment. It covers pay, conditions, bonuses, holidays and sick leave. The act has also been extended to require employers to give equal pay in redundancy, travel, pension contributions and pension benefits.

The key to the Equal Pay Act is comparable work. If an individual believes that they are being treated or paid less well than an individual of the other gender they need to find a comparator. This needs to be a person that does a similar job and has similar status in the business. They can, of course, compare themselves to the person who held their position before. If it can be proved that another individual or the previous post holder had better working conditions and better pay, then there is a right to claim that the business has broken the Equal Pay Act.

The individual making the complaint has to use an Equal Pay questionnaire as their first port of call and then refer the case to an employment tribunal if the employer does not accept their claim.

Sex Discrimination Act 1975

The Sex Discrimination Act can be seen as a partner to the Equal Pay Act, as it also considers discrimination on the grounds of gender. It is unlawful for an employer to discriminate on the grounds of gender in training, education, facilities, services and premises.

There are two different types of sex discrimination, known as direct and indirect discrimination. Direct discrimination takes place when an individual is or would be treated less favourably than someone else on the grounds of his or her gender. To prove direct discrimination, it has to be shown that:

- the treatment was less favourable than the treatment that would have been given to a person of the opposite gender
- the treatment given was less favourable because of the gender of the person involved.

A European Directive broadened indirect discrimination in October 2001. It now means that indirect discrimination can be proven when:

- a practice puts or would put one gender at a particular disadvantage compared to the other gender

- a practice puts an individual at a disadvantage
- the employer cannot show that the practice is for a sound and legitimate reason.

The Sex Discrimination Act also covers harassment and sexual harassment. Harassment is described as unwanted conduct that takes place on the grounds of an individual's gender. The behaviour will have to have the effect of violating a person's dignity, intimidating them or degrading them.

Sexual harassment is any form of verbal, non-verbal or physical conduct of a sexual nature. Again it must be proven that the harassment intended to violate someone's dignity, intimidate him or her or humiliate him or her.

INTERNET RESEARCH

To find out more about the Sex Discrimination Act, visit the website of the Equal Opportunities Commission at www.eoc.org.uk.

For more information on the Race Relations Act, visit the website of the Commission for Racial Equality at www.cre.gov.uk

Race Relations Act 1976

The Race Relations Act was amended in 2000, after the Stephen Lawrence enquiry, and now it extends to all public authorities, including the police.

The act makes it unlawful to discriminate against an individual, either directly or indirectly, on racial grounds. This not only covers employment but also education, housing and the purchasing of goods, facilities and services. Discrimination can occur when an individual is treated less favourably because of their race, colour, culture or ethnic origin.

Direct discrimination takes place when an individual is treated less favourably because of their racial background, compared to someone else of a different race in similar circumstances. Indirect discrimination can take place when employment conditions would mean that a smaller proportion of people from a particular racial group would be accepted for a job vacancy.

Disability Discrimination Act 1995

The Disability Discrimination (Amendment) Act 1995 Regulations came into force on 1 October 2004. The amendments were introduced as a result of the European Directive on Equal Treatment in Employment and Occupation. The directive prohibits direct and indirect harassment on the grounds of:

- religion or belief
- disability
- age
- sexual orientation

This applies to the fields of employment, self-employment, occupation and vocational training. The main reason for the changes to the existing act is that there is a desire to expand the discrimination protection to:

- employees
- contract workers
- police officers
- job applicants

The law prohibits harassment against disabled people and removes the old threshold. This threshold meant that employers with less than 15 employees were excluded from disability discrimination laws.

Age discrimination

In October 2006 the Employment Equality (Age) Regulations came into force. These new regulations apply to both employment and training. For the first time they outlaw both direct and indirect age discrimination. They also tackle harassment or victimisation on the grounds of age. The regulations make an impact on retirement, but also:

- remove the upper age limit for unfair dismissal and redundancy rights
- allow pay and non-pay benefits to continue when they are related to the length of service an employee has had with an organisation
- remove the age limits for statutory sick pay, maternity pay, adoption pay and paternity pay
- remove the upper and lower age limits for redundancy schemes.

There is no fixed state retirement age in Great Britain. The intention of the government is to raise the age at which state pensions are paid to 65 for both men and women by 2020.

Employers set mandatory retirement ages and this new legislation now allows employees to continue working beyond this date if they wish to.

> **Question**
>
> What are an employee's rights under sex and discrimination law? *(8 marks)*

Impact of legislation: consumer protection

LEARNING OBJECTIVES

- ▶ British law
- ▶ Statutory consumer protection and contracts
- ▶ Sale of Goods Act 1979/1995
- ▶ Supply of Goods and Services Act 1982
- ▶ Consumer Protection Act 1987
- ▶ Consumer Credit Act 1974
- ▶ Trade Descriptions Act 1968
- ▶ Understanding consumer protection legislation

British law

Under British law, consumers have the same rights as in any other forms of trade. The government is also striving to change existing laws to clear up any ambiguity in current law to help e-commerce and ultimately consumer protection across the Internet. The key legislation includes:

- The Data Protection Act 1998
- The Consumer Protection Act 1998
- British Codes of Advertising and Sales Promotion
- The Distance Selling Regulations 2000
- The Unfair Contract Act 1977 and 1999 regulations
- The Sales of Goods Act 1979
- The Consumer Credit Act 1974
- The Trade Descriptions Act 1968

Statutory consumer protection and contracts

Although there have always been laws to determine the validity of contracts, and courts have made hundreds of rulings, it is a relatively recent trend for there to be a comprehensive raft of statutory consumer protection. Successive governments and the European Union have recognised the fact that businesses routinely enter into thousands if not millions of contracts each day. It is also the case that many customers are unaware of the terms of the contract that they are entering into, and the businesses themselves sometimes do not inform them of the contractual terms.

Unsurprisingly, the thousands of consumers who have found themselves at serious disadvantage, having entered into contracts with businesses, have found little recourse in law. Many contracts are simply stacked too far in the favour of business, with no room for manoeuvre or fairness. As a result, it has become a trend to identify key areas where there are contractual problems and to bridge the gaps in existing law in order to deal with them, so that consumers have recourse to law.

Some of the statutes that have become law in Great Britain emanate not necessarily from our own parliament, but from either the translation of a European Union directive, or from a simple application of a directive. This is part of a process within the European Union to harmonise all aspects of business relations, so that businesses can enter into contracts across the continent in the knowledge that similar contractual terms will apply.

Sale of Goods Act 1979/1995

According to the Sale of Goods Act 1979, traders must sell goods that are as described and of satisfactory quality. If consumers discover that products do not meet these requirements they can reject them and ask for their money back. They can also ask for a repair or replacement or claim compensation.

The Sale of Goods Act has been replaced by the Sale and Supply of Goods to Consumers Regulations (2002). Under the new regulations, consumers can now demand repair, replacement or partial or full refund on any goods that were faulty or defective at the time of purchase.

Supply of Goods and Services Act 1982

This law states that certain terms are implied in every transaction for the transfer of goods and that the goods must:

- correspond with the description given
- be of satisfactory quality
- be fit for purpose

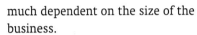

Consumer Protection Act 1987

The Consumer Protection Act 1987 safeguards consumers from products that do not reach a reasonable level of safety. The main areas dealt with are:

- *Product liability* – the Act allows injured persons to sue producers, importers and own-branders for death, personal injury or losses. Defective products are defined as being those where the safety of the product is not such as people are generally entitled to expect.
- *Consumer safety* – the law requires producers and distributors to take steps to ensure that the products they supply are safe, that they provide consumers with relevant information and warnings, and that they keep themselves informed about risks.

Consumer Credit Act 1974

The Consumer Credit Act 1974 regulates consumer credit and consumer hire agreements for amounts up to £25,000. Its protections apply to agreements between traders and individuals, sole traders, partnerships and unincorporated associations, but not agreements made between traders and corporate bodies such as limited companies.

A new Consumer Credit Bill was announced in November 2004. The key benefits of the new law will be that it:

- Protects consumers and creates fairer and more competitive credit.

- Improves consumer rights and redress, gives power to consumers to challenge unfair lending and more effective options for resolving disputes.
- Improves the regulation of consumer credit businesses by ensuring fair practices and, through targeted action, drives out rogues.
- Makes the law more appropriate for different types of consumer credit transaction by extending protection to all consumer credit.

Trade Descriptions Act 1968

The Trade Descriptions Act 1968 aims to prevent misleading descriptions of all goods and services. The Act protects consumers from misleading or false descriptions of goods.

The law applies to suppliers, manufacturers and retailers of goods, as well as services, facilities and accommodation. The law states that it is the business's responsibility to ensure that the goods, services, facilities and accommodation sold or provided are not falsely described. Legislation on misleading prices was made under the Consumer Protection Act 1987.

Understanding consumer protection legislation

Many businesses do not provide any customer information about their policies for refunds, complaints and customer care. In many cases, where information is provided, the nature of it and how it is provided is very much dependent on the size of the business.

Customers need to have confidence in the products and services they buy and also in the business that they are dealing with. Information about the business and its customer care policies should be readily available and easily accessible.

Generally, business awareness of consumer protection legislation is poor. Many companies are unsure if there is a specific body dealing with complaints for their business or industry. There is enormous confusion about the roles and responsibilities of various agencies.

It is important that businesses are familiar with consumer protection arrangements generally and not just the bodies relevant to their business. It also means that employees need to be aware and it is the responsibility of the business to inform them and keep them up to date with the legislation.

> **Question**
>
> British businesses have only themselves to blame for the introduction of consumer protection legislation. No wonder we are known as 'rip-off Britain'. Discuss. *(12 marks)*

Impact of legislation: health and safety

Health and safety

It is the responsibility of employers to ensure that their employees know what hazards and risks they may face and how to deal with them. For this reason employers will arrange health and safety training during working hours. It is important for the organisation to make sure that it is not just existing employees, in post, that receive this training. Some may have particular training needs:

- new employees
- employees changing jobs or taking on extra responsibilities
- younger employees (statistically more likely to have an accident).

Ultimately, the Health and Safety Act states:

- employees must be trained and clearly instructed in their duties
- employers and host companies must ensure that any contractors are properly trained and can work safely and competently.

Supporting health and safety

There are many health and safety requirements in the workplace. Specifically, these require the employer to:

- provide a safe working environment
- provide adequate welfare facilities
- ensure that entrances and exits are safe and clear
- ensure equipment and systems are safe and that they are serviced on a regular basis

- take steps to ensure that the handling of heavy objects and the storage of dangerous items is a priority
- provide instruction, training or supervision as required
- ensure that all accidents are rigorously investigated and the causes of the accidents eliminated.

Health and Safety at Work Act 1974

Prior to 1974, employees did not have legal safety protection in the workplace. The purpose of this act is to provide a legal framework to promote, stimulate and encourage the highest possible standards of health and safety in the workplace. Everyone has a responsibility to comply with the act. This includes:

- employers
- employees
- trainees
- self-employed workers
- manufacturers
- suppliers
- designers
- importers of equipment that will be used in the workplace.

As far as employers are concerned, they have a general duty to 'ensure so far as is reasonably practicable the health, safety and welfare at work of all their employees'. This means that employers are required to:

- provide and maintain safety equipment and safe systems of working
- make sure that materials used are properly stored, handled, used and transported

- provide training, information, instruction and supervision
- ensure that employees are aware of instructions that may have been provided by manufacturers and suppliers
- provide a safe working environment
- provide a safe place of employment
- provide a written safety policy
- provide a written risk assessment
- ensure the safety of others, including the public
- have continued conversations with safety representatives.

In addition to this list, employers cannot ask employees to carry out tasks that could prove to be hazardous to them, particularly if they lack necessary safety equipment to carry out the job.

As far as employees are concerned, they must:

- be aware of their own health and safety and that of others
- be aware that their actions may have legal implications
- cooperate with employers
- not interfere with equipment or anything that has been provided in the interests of health and safety.

In order to ensure that employers comply with the Health and Safety at Work Act, local authorities have environmental health officers. A representative may visit large manufacturing, construction sites and other industrial sites from the Health and Safety Executive. Both representatives can carry out inspections. They have the following powers:

- They can enter the premises without appointments at reasonable times.
- They can investigate and examine the premises and equipment.
- They can take equipment apart and take samples of substances and equipment.
- They can see any documents and take photocopies of them if necessary.
- If they are barred from entry they can ask the police to ensure they gain access.
- They can ask employers and employees questions under caution.
- They can seize any equipment or substances if they feel there is an immediate danger from them.

If employers continue to avoid following the requirements of the act they will face enforcement action. Two things may happen. These are:

1 They will be issued with a legal notice, requiring them to improve the situation within a set period of time or the notice will prohibit them from using equipment or unsafe practices immediately and until solved.

2 They could be prosecuted, as could employees, facing a maximum fine of £5,000 in a magistrates court or an unlimited fine and a prison term in a crown court.

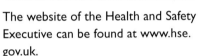

INTERNET RESEARCH

The website of the Health and Safety Executive can be found at www.hse.gov.uk.

Occupational health screening

Some health screening is driven entirely by health and safety at work considerations. For example, employees working in a factory environment may have to have regular hearing tests.

Potential job candidates may have an employment screening to test their fitness for the job before they even start work as an employee.

The main purpose of occupational health screening is to:

- establish and maintain a healthy working environment
- ensure the best physical and mental health in relation to work
- adapt work to the capabilities of employees in relation to their physical and mental health.

At its very basic level occupational health screening is used to confirm an employee's fitness to continue work. Key occupational health issues include:

- smoking, and drug and alcohol abuse
- stress
- repetitive strain injury and back pain
- control of hazardous substances
- disease prevention and control
- violence, bullying and harassment
- work/life balance.

CASE STUDY HEALTH AND SAFETY RISK ASSESSMENT

The office manager of a call centre that occupies a single floor of a ten-storey office block has been asked to carry out a health and safety risk assessment. There are forty staff working at the call centre, 20 of whom are part-timers and two are wheelchair users. The staff turnover is around 30% per year. The centre is staffed from 8am to 8pm every day. The offices contain typical office furniture and equipment; there is a staff kitchen, toilet and washing facilities.

Question

Suggest how a general health and safety risk assessment could be carried out by the manager. *(8 marks)*

Business responses to a change in political and legal environment

Government and business

There are both costs and benefits if businesses continue to be allowed to use monopolies, mergers and restrictive practices. Therefore government competition policy has tended to focus on these aspects. This has also been a major part of EU legislation. Specific rules apply to restrictive practices, dominant businesses and merger controls.

The relevant British legislation is the Competition Act 1998 and the Enterprise Act 2002. The latter, for example, makes cartel agreements a criminal offence and mergers over a certain size have to be investigated before approval.

Most British and EU legislation on anti-competitive practices focus on competition, rather than agreements between businesses or market dominance. Businesses face severe fines if they are found to be carrying out practices that are detrimental to competition.

The British government has also recognised the importance of technology in continued economic success. The government is in the process of formulating an embracing technology policy to ensure that Britain remains competitive.

If British businesses are left to their own devices then technology is developed rapidly enough to a socially desirable level. This is assisted by tax breaks on research and development. Subsidies are available for research and development, as are coordination and advisory assistance.

The British government accepts that businesses are the primary provider of technological change and has therefore kept its role to a minimum. It is slightly different in Europe, where governments have been more interventionist and have developed a range of initiatives to encourage greater levels of research and development.

Training policy in Britain has been largely left to businesses and the result has been that it has been less than impressive compared to other countries, such as Germany. In the last 20 to 25 years training and education policy has focused on vocational courses. This is in recognition of the fact that economic performance can be improved by enhancing productivity, enabling change and supplying scarce skills and policies that aim to reduce wage costs.

For more about technology see the Focus on Business and the Technological Environment on pp. 234–9.

Government and the markets

Pollution is a negative externality and, as such, environmental policy has focused on trying to ensure that the full cost of production or consumption is paid for by those producing and consuming products and services, including the cost of undesirable environmental impact. It is difficult to estimate the cost of environmental pollution, and therefore to actually frame an efficient environmental policy. Broadly, environmental policy can be either market-based or non-market-based and in some cases it is a mixture of the two. Government has used taxes and subsidies to provide a market-based solution, and regulations and controls over non-market-based solutions. British industry has had to accommodate both approaches. The major problem with using taxes and subsidies is in identifying appropriate levels, since they will vary according to the environmental impact of the production processes.

Actually making some production processes illegal or placing limits on discharges is extremely difficult, but the government obviously assumes that these precautionary measures are preferable when the environmental costs are unknown.

If a business can cheaply reduce its pollution below a certain level, it can sell this advantage to another business that finds it more costly to do so. This is a cheap and efficient way of limiting pollution, though it can lead to pollution being concentrated in certain areas.

Another key area with markets has been transportation. For businesses, their use of transportation depends on demand and supply. Demand depends upon the price of using transportation and the costs relate to alternative means of transport, or providing products and services. One major issue with transportation that has adversely affected British businesses is congestion and the increasing pressure on road space. There has been regulation and legislation banning large vehicles from certain areas (such as the emission zone in central London), encouragement to use railways rather than roads and subsidising alternative means of transport, particularly public transport for employees instead of cars. Unfortunately, building additional roads has not been a workable solution because public transport in particular has declined. This has attracted additional traffic to roads and caused additional environmental costs.

British businesses have been affected by government policy to reduce congestion. This is primarily focused on additional fuel taxes, which have pushed up the costs of delivering products and services and so had an adverse impact on prices. Many British businesses do not have an option other than to use road transport to service their customers. Government policy seems to be moving in the direction of electronic road pricing, effectively charging vehicles for every road mile covered.

One of the biggest impacts of government policy over the past 25 years has been the massive privatisation programme. This has impacted on nearly every area of British industry. The argument for privatisation was that it would encourage greater competition, reduce government interference, raise revenue and finance tax cuts. However, the arguments against privatisation were that certain industries needed tight regulation, or these industries provided services where there was a high risk of market failure. In order to deal with the newly privatised businesses, regulation has come in the form of ombudsmen and watchdogs. They usually operate informally, negotiating and bargaining with the industries to behave in the public interest. These newly privatised businesses have had to restrict their price increases to broad changes in the retail price index and undertake to pass cost reductions on to the consumer. If an industry does not abide by these conditions, then the regulators can revise the industry's licence or price formula.

> ## Question
>
> Explain why the government intervenes in the market.
> (18 marks)

Case studies, questions and exam practice

CASE STUDY FLEXIBLE WORKING AND THE EMPLOYMENT ACT

'Flexible working improves recruitment and retention, reduces absenteeism and increases motivation and performance,' said John Blackwell, Managing Director of JBA Ltd. 'Unfortunately, many companies remain unprepared for the changes this new legislation will bring. Britons already work the longest hours in Europe, with an average of 43 hours a week, compared with 40 hours in other countries. Forty per cent of UK managers work in excess of 51 hours per week, and one in six works in excess of 60 hours per week. Research has shown that more than 80% of us have felt under pressure to stay longer at work, even when the working day has finished. In addition to the immediate changes in the short term, we believe the Employment Act signals the beginning of pivotal changes in the workplace, attitudes to work, and the traditional infrastructure supporting it.'

According to the Office of National Statistics, just 7% of the UK workforce (1.8 million people) currently work from home. By 2020, this figure is expected to be 25%. The UK workforce will increase over the next 10 years by 1.5 million. Eighty five per cent of them will be women. With the ongoing pressure to find balance between work and home, flexible working will become a *de facto* part of everyday working, rather than an exception to the norm.

'Twenty-five per cent of managers today are female and 78% of UK women with children work,' added Blackwell. 'Although legislation is behind the enforcement of flexible working, we believe socio-economic insecurities will also force a new set of workplace dynamics that more accurately reflect the lifestyles, demographics and needs of the changing workforce. We also believe it signifies the death of the 'job for life', as it will become more commonplace for people to have 'portfolio careers' with shorter assignments and multiple employers.'

Source: www.onrec.com

Questions

1 What do you think is meant by the term 'traditional infrastructure'? *(4 marks)*
2 Why is it likely that more women will enter the workforce over the next ten years? *(4 marks)*
3 Why might employers be unprepared for the increased demand for flexible working patterns? *(4 marks)*

CASE STUDY BRITISH ARMS INDUSTRY SUBSIDIES

The British government subsidises the arms trade to the tune of hundreds of millions of pounds, which means that far from benefiting financially from the arms trade, the British taxpayer is shelling out to finance it.

The exact amount of government subsidy is difficult to gauge, due in large part to the lack of official information and secrecy, but the Campaign Against Arms Trade's 2004 estimate was that the government subsidy to arms exports was around £900 million. This support includes:

- The Defence Export Services Organisation (DESO). This is a government unit that exists solely to market and sell UK military equipment and services, DESO co-ordinates most of the direct government support for arms exports. It provides marketing assistance and advice on negotiation and financing arrangements, as well as organising arms exhibitions and promotional tours. It has around 500 civilian and military employees in London and overseas. DESO's net operating costs for 2004/05 were £17 million.
- Related Promotional Activity. UK embassies play an explicit export promotion role, particularly via their defence attachés. In countries that are major arms customers, other embassy staff and resources are also employed to promote UK arms exports.
- UK ministers, including the prime minister, civil servants and members of the royal family also make high-level visits to potential or existing arms-purchasing countries. The Government's own records detailed 29 occasions in 2002 and 2003 when ministers from the Foreign and Commonwealth Office and the Ministry of Defence (MoD) promoted specific military sales and a further 13 occasions where details have been kept confidential.
- The Export Credits Guarantee Department (ECGD). The ECGD insures UK exporters against payment default and subsidises the interest rate paid by buyers of UK exports in all sectors. However, on average, between 2000 and 2003, while arms deliveries made up only 1.6% of all visible UK exports, they accounted for 43%

of the ECGD's guarantees.

The MoD's own estimates show that 65,000 jobs are sustained by military exports, just 0.2% of the national labour force. The MoD York report, which was co-written by MoD economists, concluded in 2001 that halving military exports over a two-year period would lead to the loss of almost 49,000 jobs, but that 67,400 jobs would be created in non-military sectors over the following five years. The report concluded that 'the economic costs of reducing defence exports are relatively small and largely one-off.'

The area with most jobs directly related to arms exports is the South East, which has virtually full employment. Where specific towns have a high concentration of jobs dependent on arms export, government and community initiatives could create new training and employment opportunities for those whose jobs are affected. Past military redundancies have had the least negative impact when military companies have worked in partnership with trade unions, local authorities and agencies to assist people to find alternative employment. In fact between 1995 and 2002, jobs dependent on military exports fell from 145,000 to the present level of around 65,000 with no major impact on the economy.

Source: adapted from Campaign Against Arms Trade

Question

The hundreds of millions of pounds saved by reducing or ending the UK arms trade could be invested in other industries, such as renewable energy and transport. This would create new, highly skilled jobs. It would also be a far more ethical use of public funds.

Discuss. (18 marks)

Changes in the social environment: demographic factors

LEARNING
OBJECTIVES

▶ Trends
▶ Challenge for society
▶ Challenge for organisations and managers
▶ Key issues

Trends

The management guru Peter Drucker warned that there would be changes in developed countries as the population changes from a mostly young population to an older population, and that this change was not being addressed by organisations. As the population in developed countries decreases, the proportion of older people is increasing.

- Life expectancy in the developed world is rising year on year.
- Birth rates in Europe are falling. In many countries the birth rate is now below the replacement rate. Italy has the lowest birth rate, with 1.3 children per two adults. In Britain this figures stands at 1.6 children per two adults. Obviously there are some instances where immigration from outside the European Union offsets this population decline, but overall the population of Europe is falling.
- The population of Europe is also becoming older. This means the dependency rate is increasing. The dependency rate refers to the ratio of the population that is over 65 compared to those aged 15 to 64. This is a significant ratio, as the taxes paid by those of employment age effectively support those who have retired.
- In Britain, around 19 million people are over the age of 50. This figure is projected to increase to around 22 million by 2020. At the same time, the number of younger people is expected to fall.
- Around 69% of men in Britain over the age of 50 are still currently working. This represents a significant fall from 1979 when the proportion of men aged over 50 and still in work was 89%.

Challenge for society

Over the coming years the average age of the UK population will continue to increase significantly. This will present a number of challenges. There will be enormous changes in markets, as the population will want to buy different things, added to which there will be fewer people in work to pay the necessary pension contributions to support non-working, older people. This also has an impact on markets, as, without sufficient income, the markets will decrease in size.

Immigration is a much debated topic. Most European countries do not have enough people to maintain their economies. There are enormous skills gaps and large-scale immigration programmes are needed in order to deal with this issue. There is still strong resistance to immigration, but what this means is that there will have to be a more rapid influx of immigrants at some stage in the future, rather than a steady trickle, and this in itself will cause problems.

The numbers of older people needing support is increasing and government and businesses need to find new ways of caring for the elderly.

There have been the beginnings of a trend away from prolonged education for the young. Younger people need to enter the labour market at an earlier stage and this will have enormous implications for the education system. New flexible ways of delivering learning will have to be created by the education system and private training agencies.

Challenge for organisations and managers

Many British businesses are already suffering from labour supply problems. This is especially acute when the business needs trained and skilled workers. The problem is accelerating and unless attention is paid to training for the young or the retaining of older workers, the situation will become critical. However, many organisations currently discriminate on the grounds of age. Britain has outlawed direct and indirect age discrimination and this is beginning to have a marked impact on employment law and on employers' responsibilities.

Business management is only slowly responding to changes in demographics, but managers need to be thinking about these issues now in order to prepare for the gradual impact of the changes, otherwise the businesses will not be able to function correctly and will become less and less competitive.

Key issues

Most businesses have a form of retirement policy, but in the future, due to pension problems, many members of staff will want to or will have to work past the ages of 60 or 65. Pensions are becoming less reliable. This means that people will need to, and fortunately should be more able to work for longer.

Current work patterns tend to focus around the five-day week and the eight-hour day. This is much less popular with those who had planned to have their own leisure time at later stages in their lives. Although enormous strides have been taken in establishing work/life balance and flexible working practices, this will have to be taken even further and businesses will have to consider limited and flexible hours, sabbaticals, teleworking and other flexible working practices.

Flexible working is becoming more common; businesses have to be flexible to ensure that they meet the needs of their employees. This is especially important because of labour market shortages and the fact that staff retention is now more important than it has ever been.

While it is desirable to retain older employees, they are likely to have less formal training and qualifications than younger people and their skills will become obsolete. Businesses need to take more responsibility for their learning as a key part of their job.

Increased immigration from the developing world does fill population shortages, but this means that businesses will have to cope with increased cultural diversity, language barriers and racism. Businesses may also have to consider remote working skills, as business units may be more efficient if they are based in countries in Asia or Africa, where there may be larger pools of potential workers.

The role of businesses and management in handling the complex changes in the demographic structure of the workforce is becoming more and more important. It is important not only to the business, but also to the economy and the country as a whole.

> ### KEY TERM
>
> Sabbatical – an organised and agreed extended period of leave, either for education or travel.

> ### Question
>
> Peter Drucker wrote:
>
> 'One of the challenges will be using these retired people, who are in perfect physical and mental condition, making them useful to the society. It is important to learn how to work with older people; it could be an enormous competitive advantage. I even believe that, in the next 20 or 30 years, the age of retirement in the developed countries will have to be higher. Or at least, retirement will not mean coming out of the working world. Working relationships will probably become very heterogeneous and increasingly flexible.'
>
> How might British businesses respond to this? (12 marks)

Changes in the social environment: environmental issues

LEARNING OBJECTIVES

▶ Business and the environment
▶ Sustainable consumption and production
▶ Environmental reporting
▶ Why should businesses bother with the environment?
▶ Environmental product management
▶ Discharges and emissions

Business and the environment

Businesses have a major role to play in helping to protect and enhance the environment, in line with wider goals of sustainable development.

In particular, business has a pivotal role in meeting the Johannesburg goals (World Summit on Sustainable Development 2002) on sustainable consumption and production, and corporate responsibility.

In March 2005 the Government launched the UK Sustainable Development Strategy – *Securing the Future*. It highlights the need for businesses' approach to corporate responsibility to extend throughout their supply chains, tackling issues from extraction of raw materials through to engagement with consumers about the products and services they buy and eventually discard.

Sound environmental management of processes and products is regarded as a core business issue that can help promote a company's products and services, and improve its corporate standing.

Government has a key role to play and will work closely with business to encourage more sustainable patterns of production and consumption:

- encouraging wider take-up of corporate responsibility practices, including environmental reporting and management systems
- enabling investors to deliver more sustainable consumption and production

- providing information and advice to business on environmental issues
- working directly with business sectors to improve environmental performance.

Sustainable consumption and production

Increasing prosperity in the UK and across the world has allowed many people to enjoy the benefits of goods and services that were once available to only a few. Nevertheless, the environmental impacts from our consumption and production patterns remain severe, and inefficient use of resources is a drag on the UK's economy and business.

Sustainable Consumption and Production (SCP) is about achieving economic growth while respecting environmental limits, finding ways to minimise damage to the natural world and making use of the earth's resources in a sustainable way. It is therefore not a challenge restricted to a few countries or areas of the world, but one that must engage the whole global community.

The current strategy is for:

- better products and services, which reduce the environmental impacts from the use of energy, resources, or hazardous substances
- cleaner, more efficient production processes, which strengthen competitiveness
- shifts in consumption towards goods and services with lower impacts.

Environmental reporting

In 2006, the government produced a set of environmental reporting guidelines to help companies identify and address their most significant environmental impacts. Companies that measure, manage and communicate their environmental performance are inherently well-placed. They understand how to:

- improve their processes
- reduce their costs
- comply with regulatory requirements and stakeholder expectations
- take advantages of new market opportunities.

Failure to plan for a future in which environmental factors are likely to be increasingly significant may risk the long-term future of a business. Good environmental performance makes good business sense. Environmental risks and uncertainties impact to some extent on all companies, and affect investment decisions, consumer behaviour and government policy.

Why should businesses bother with the environment?

In recent years, the volume of environmental legislation has increased. Breaking the law can carry serious criminal and financial penalties, as well as generating bad publicity. Planning ahead to take account of new environmental standards can minimise the costs of modifying or replacing equipment and updating working practices:

- Good environmental management can bring substantial cost savings, such as in raw materials, waste disposal, energy and transport.
- Increasingly, customers prefer to buy from environmentally responsible businesses. Many large companies are 'greening' their supply chain. Some will buy products only from suppliers that satisfy strict environmental criteria, and many consumers will pay a premium for environmentally friendly products.
- Business partners are increasingly looking at companies' environmental profiles. Some banks, insurers and other sources of finance may avoid businesses that do not take environmental matters seriously and expose themselves to unacceptable risk.
- It is easier to recruit employees, and many employees are better motivated when working for an environmentally responsible employer.
- Failure to act in an environmentally responsible way can bring a company into conflict with stakeholders, such as the local community and pressure groups.

Environmental product management

Environmentally responsible products and production processes offer marketing advantages. The careful design of products and processes can reduce the use of resources. Businesses are increasingly designing products that can be reused (notably packaging materials and 'green bags'). Products can be reused, repaired and easily recycled. Businesses increasingly use recycled and recyclable packaging. In fact, businesses with an annual turnover of £2 million, or more handling more than 50 tonnes of packaging per year, are legally required to 'recover' and recycle a percentage of their packaging waste.

Businesses are encouraged to use environmentally responsible materials. This means avoiding:

- scarce natural resources
- supplies with excessive packaging
- hazardous substances (complying with legal restrictions)
- materials that produce toxic by-products when processed.

Businesses face regulations and fines (and subsidies if appropriate) if they use environmentally responsible production methods and machinery. New refrigerators, for example, do not use the ozone-damaging CFC coolant, and they use less electricity. There are also tax incentives available if the business uses energy-saving plant and machinery.

FOR EXAMPLE

If a business plans to replace existing equipment, such as lighting, boilers or insulation, with a more energy-efficient version, they may be able to obtain an interest-free loan of between £5,000 and £100,000 to fund it via the Carbon Trust (www.thecarbontrust. co.uk).

Businesses must also use appropriate labelling. Primarily this is to inform customers about how their products and production processes take account of the environment and how to recycle or dispose of products properly.

Discharges and emissions

Discharges of effluent are strictly controlled. A business can discharge ordinary domestic effluent (water) into ordinary sewerage drainage. Accidental or careless discharges are the business's responsibility and the business may be prosecuted even if they are not its fault.

A business may need authorisations for any emissions into the air. It will have to comply with the terms and conditions of the authorisations. Any unauthorised emissions may lead to prosecution. Businesses need to make sure that emissions do not affect the local population:

- This can include not only discharges and emissions, but also noise, litter, dust and smells.
- Transport to and from businesses can be a concern (e.g. lorry noise and fumes).
- Local authorities have powers to protect people from nuisance caused by businesses.
- Business need to assess the potential environmental impact before carrying out any large projects.

Question

What is an environmental review and what is likely to be involved? *(12 marks)*

The changing nature of the ethical environment

Ethical decision-making

Ethics and social responsibility related to businesses have become increasingly important and much-debated issues in recent years. Essentially, there is an inherent conflict between the desires of the business, the industry, society in general and the consumer. All may have mutually exclusive goals and objectives. Ethical issues arise when one group's values conflict with another. In many cases there are multiple levels of conflict arising out of different sets of values.

The marketing industry has sought to pre-empt governmental intervention by establishing professional associations and accrediting bodies who are concerned with self-regulation. An example of this is the American Marketing Association (AMA), which suggests that marketing behaviour follows certain rules set out in the table below.

There is considerable conflict between the main purposes of marketing, the ethical criteria as stated by organisations such as the AMA, and the goal of making a profit. Given the fact that the major promotional objectives include accentuating the value of the product, the provision of information, the stabilisation of sales, the stimulation of demand, and the differentiation of the product, it is clear from these inherent marketing responsibilities that it is difficult to retain an ethical balance.

Making ethical decisions is always complex because they often have a number of considerations, including:

- several different alternatives
- consequences that may have a knock-on effect
- uncertain circumstances
- outcomes that can have economic, legal and social benefits
- outcomes that can have economic, legal and social costs
- personal implications for the managers and employees of the business, as well as implications for the business itself.

Ethical decisions can also often involve the business's stakeholders, who can have goals and interests that oppose or conflict with those of the business.

Businesses often have innumerable complexities to unravel in order to ensure that they are not behaving in an unethical manner, including:

- ensuring that their goals are compatible with ethical considerations
- ensuring that their route to meeting their goals is ethically acceptable
- ensuring that their motives for meeting their goals are not selfish and non-ethical
- considering the consequences of their activities on others, including the stakeholders.

Guidelines	Description
Responsibility	The AMA urges those involved in marketing to accept a responsibility for the consequences of their actions and activities. They are asked to consider their decisions, recommendations and subsequent actions in the light of satisfying and serving all stakeholders.
Honesty and fairness	The AMA urges marketers to show integrity, honour and dignity as professionals.
Rights and duties	The AMA suggests that there should be an inherent relationship between businesses and their customers, firmly based on the notion of trust. Products and services should be safe and fit for the uses for which they were intended. The Association also stresses that marketing communications should be truthful and that products and services should be sold in good faith. In the case of disputes, a grievance procedure should be established.
Organisational relationships	The AMA also suggests that those involved in marketing should be clearly aware that their actions are intended to influence the behaviour of others: given their persuasive role, they should not encourage unethical behaviour or apply undue pressure to those they target.

As can be seen in the following table, there are various terms associated with ethical standards:

Ethical system	Problem
Eternal law	These are moral standards for which there are innumerable interpretations.
Ethical egoism	This could be seen as a contradiction in terms as it revolves around cooperation and productivity and it is difficult to determine whether one business's (or an individual's) interests are more or less important that those of another.
Utilitarianism	These ethical standards relate to the outcome of a decision or an action and its effect on others. Again, this can be difficult to determine, particularly if the business's actions have a positive impact on a number of other businesses, or groups or individuals, but a negative one on a few.
Universalism	This applies to the intention of an action or a decision by a business or an individual, as opposed to the outcome of that action or decision.
Enlightened self-interest	Similar in many ways to utilitarianism, enlightened self-interest requires the business, or the individual, to ensure that their long-term interests conform to those of society at large.
Interdependence	This ethical system or belief applies to the ability to compromise in order to comply with, or to provide, a dependent business or individual with what they need in order to achieve their goals.

Performance indicators

Performance indicators are the key measurement of performance in a business, and are continually monitored and assessed. They aim to identify particular strengths and weaknesses. Many businesses adopt a series of key performance indicators (KPIs), measuring efficiency (input versus output), adaptability (reconfiguring time), financial performance (return on equity) and effectiveness (non-defects produced). Others divide them into the following key areas:

- *behavioural* – relating to the management of staff, including labour turnover, absenteeism, accidents, etc.
- *confidence* – examining the relationship between the organisation and its broader environment, specifically its stakeholders
- *ethical* – considering the standards of behaviour of the organisation against set criteria
- *operational* – considering profitability, product mixes, portfolios, productivity and output
- *specific issues* – such as profit per employee, returns on investment, delivery speed and quality targets
- *strategic* – considering the overall effectiveness of the organisation.

Businesses will attempt to identify leading indicators that will help them respond quickly to conditions just as the situation is beginning to impact on their operations. They can then make adjustments to their processes before unexpected outcomes affect them.

CASE STUDY TRANSCO BUSINESS ETHICS

'We want to operate to the highest ethical standards. Standards of Conduct have been in place for more than a decade in the US and, in April 2004, we communicated our Code of Business Conduct to all UK employees. We operate 24-hour ethics helplines, where inappropriate conduct can be reported. Reported breaches are thoroughly and promptly investigated and, where appropriate, acted on, with any necessary improvements implemented. The employee opinion survey confirmed that the majority of staff believe that we are an ethical organisation, that we are aware of the codes, and that we feel comfortable that reported issues will be properly and thoroughly investigated.'

Source: adapted from Investis

Question

Ethical statements such as these are meaningless. Discuss. *(12 marks)*

Social environment and corporate responsibility

External stakeholders

External stakeholders are individuals who can either affect or be affected by the organisation. There are clear indications that as long as the organisation pays attention to the stakeholders, considerable synergy can be achieved.

Theoretically at least, the relationship between the organisation and its stakeholders should be mutually beneficial. Stakeholders exercise a series of controls or influences on the organisation, in return for which the organisation should engage with the stakeholders. The primary relationships are explained in the table below.

External stakeholder	Influence on the business	Business response
Government	Regulatory compliance	Compliance
Investors	Capital providers	Risk reduction
Consumers	Demand for products or services	Quality products or services
Industry	Standards of practice	Fair dealing
International bodies	Best practices	Fair dealing
Local communities	Operating licences	Community relations programmes
Business partners	Transparency	Fair dealing

Stakeholder analysis

Stakeholders are people or organisations who either:

- stand to be affected by a project, or
- could make or break a project's success.

They may be winners or losers, included or excluded from decision-making, users of results or participants in the process. Stakeholder analysis is the identification of a project's key stakeholders, an assessment of their interests in the project, and of the ways in which those interests may affect the project. The reason for undertaking stakeholder analysis is to help identify:

- which individuals or organisations to include in any considerations
- what roles they should play and at which stage

IMPORTANCE — HIGH / LOW

BOX A high importance, high influence
- Stakeholders who stand to lose or gain significantly from the project, *and* whose actions can affect the project's ability to meet its objectives.
- The project needs to ensure that their interests are fully represented in the coalition. Overall impact of the project will require good relationships to be developed with these stakeholders.

BOX B high importance, low influence
- Stakeholders who stand to lose or gain significantly from the project, *but* whose actions cannot affect the project's ability to meet its objectives.
- The project needs to ensure that their interests are fully represented in the coalition.

BOX C low importance, high influence
- Stakeholders whose actions can affect the project's ability to meet its objectives, *but* who do not stand to lose or gain much from the project.
- They may be a source of risk; and you will need to explore means of monitoring and managing that risk.

BOX D low importance, low influence
- Stakeholders who do not stand to lose or gain much from the project AND whose actions cannot affect the project's ability to meet its objectives.
- They may require limited monitoring or informing of progress but are of low priority. They are unlikely to be the subject of project activities or involved in project management.

INFLUENCE — HIGH / LOW

Corporate social responsibility

Corporate social responsibility reflects any sense of obligation an organisation may feel is appropriate to include as an integral part of its strategic decision-making.

The options and application can best be summarised as follows:

BOOK RESEARCH

Harvard Business Review, *Harvard Business Review on Corporate Responsibility*, Harvard Business School Press, 2003.

- whom to build and nurture relationships with
- whom to inform and consult about the project.

It will also help the organisation justify its decisions. A business will find that the initial list of stakeholders is very long. For practical reasons, it will have to prioritise the most relevant before carrying out its analysis.

It is difficult to identify key stakeholders in one step. One method that can be used is to brainstorm a list of potential stakeholders and then position them on a matrix (see opposite page) that indicates relative importance to, and influence on, the project. The business can then consider which stakeholders to present in the tables. First, the business will brainstorm a list of stakeholders by asking:

- Who stands to lose or gain significantly from the project?
- Whose actions could potentially affect the project's success?

Then position each one at the appropriate point between the axes. 'Importance' (along the x axis) means the degree to which a stakeholder stands to lose or gain from the project. 'Influence' (along the y axis) refers to the relative ability of a stakeholder to affect a project's success.

Factor	Corporate social responsibility	Corporate social responsiveness
Initiation	Business itself and managers	Stakeholders
Time frame	Long term	Medium term
Motivation	Trusteeships	Stakeholder power
Action	Philanthropic Paternalistic	Practical response to demands of stakeholders

Corporate social responsibility is important in the following senses:

- it can avoid adverse publicity
- it can avoid buy-outs, law suits or legislative procedures
- it can resolve issues before they reach a critical stage.

Social issues clearly include a wide variety of environmental issues: businesses seek to formulate policies to deal with them. These policies can come about either through the business's own actions, or by government legislation.

Typically, the following steps would be taken by a business:

Steps	Detail
Identification of issues/trends/public expectations	Scanning the environment for trends and issues, tracking these trends and issues as they develop, identification of those applicable to the business
Evaluation of impacts and priority setting	Assessment of impacts and probability of occurrence, assessment of organisational resources needed to respond, preparation of priorities for further analysis
Conducting research and analysis	Categorisation of issues, ensuring that priority issues have staff assigned to them, involvement of functional areas, development and analysis of position strategies
Development of strategy	Analysis of position and strategy options, decision of strategic options available, integration with overall business strategy
Implementation strategy	Dissemination of agreed policies and strategies, development of tactics which are consistent with overall strategies, development of alliances, establishment of internal and external communication flows
Evaluation of strategy	Assessment of results, modification of implementation plans, undertaking additional research (if necessary)

For more on stakeholder analysis see Differing stakeholder perspectives on pp. 180–1.

Question

How might a thorough stakeholder analysis help a business respond to the changing social environment? (14 marks)

Case studies, questions and exam practice

CASE STUDY BOTTLED WATER – IS IT IMMORAL?

Drinking bottled water should be made as unfashionable as smoking, according to a government adviser.

'We have to make people think that it's unfashionable just as we have with smoking. We need a similar campaign to convince people that this is wrong,' said Tim Lang, the Government's natural resources commissioner.

Bottled water generates up to 600 times more CO_2 than tap water

Phil Woolas, the environment minister, added that the amount of money spent on mineral water 'borders on being morally unacceptable'.

Their comments come as new research shows that drinking a bottle of water has the same impact on the environment as driving a car for a kilometre. Conservation groups and water providers have started a campaign against the £2 billion industry.

A BBC Panorama documentary, 'Bottled Water: Who Needs It?', said that, in terms of production, a litre bottle of Evian or Volvic generates up to 600 times more CO_2 than a litre of tap water.

Source: adapted from the *Daily Telegraph*

Question

Are products such as bottled water immoral both ethically and environmentally? *(12 marks)*

Effects of technological change

LEARNING OBJECTIVES

▶ General effects of technological change
▶ Marketing
▶ Processes and systems
▶ Technology management

General effects of technological change

The effects on business of continuous technological change and innovation are significant. In almost every area of business, regardless of the sector of industry, there have been changes that have altered the ways in which products and services are created, delivered and serviced. Automation has continued to improve the ways in which products are made, reducing faults and waste as well as ensuring standardisation and high levels of quality. Improved internal and external communications systems have ensured closer contact and cooperation with partners in the supply chain, allowing manufacturing techniques such as 'Just in Time' to work. Improved communications have also meant that there are more efficient and effective ways to interact with customers and consumers, and this has affected marketing, sales, after-sales service and general customer service issues.

Technology has also touched the way in which organisations are structured, and reduced the need for all employees and managers to be working on the same site. Remote working, homeworking, teleworking and telecommuting are all common features of modern-day business.

On this spread we look at only a small selection of key changes, but you should be aware that there is barely a single aspect of a business operation that has not been touched by technological change, and that the pace of change is accelerating year on year.

Marketing

Customer relationship management (CRM) and narrowcasting are two examples of how technology has radically changed marketing and marketing techniques.

CRM is based on the assumption that there is a relationship between the business or the brand and the customer. This is a relationship that needs to be managed both through the individual buying stages and in the longer term. CRM is very much related to fostering customer loyalty and, in the longer term, customer retention.

CRM can be used in call-centre support and direct marketing operations. Software systems assist in the support of customer service representatives and give customers alternative means by which to communicate with the business (such as mail, email, telephone, etc.). Some sophisticated CRM software programs have email response systems which process incoming e-mails and determine whether they warrant a personal response or an automated response. Recent figures indicate that systems such as these can handle around 50% of the requests from customers (typically, requests for additional information, passwords and responses to e-mails sent by marketing).

Other CRM software systems incorporate the facility for customer representatives to take part in live chat rooms or co-browsing, offering the business a less formal environment in which to make contact with customers. CRM software can also queue customers based on their profiles, by requesting that the customer logs in to the website. It is then possible to pass the customer on to individuals in the customer service team who may be better suited to dealing with customers with similar profiles. CRM software also provides the facility to maintain and update a database of information about each customer (in other words a case history).

Narrowcasting is a term most closely associated with the relaying of advertising and promotion messages to small, but clearly defined groups of individuals. For the most part, the term has tended to be used in Internet marketing campaigns where specific groups such as subscribers or users of particular websites can be easily targeted. However, the term is equally valid for marketing or advertising campaigns aimed at any small target group by the use of defined media.

In the field of the broadcast media, narrowcasting refers to situations when the programmer or producer assumes that only a limited number of people or a specific demographic group will be interested in the subject matter of a programme. This is the very nature of most cable television companies' programming strategies as they follow the format or characteristics of specialised magazines. Most US cable television programmes or channels emphasise one subject or a few closely related subjects, and so appeal to only a narrow segment of the potential viewing market.

Processes and systems

Automation refers to manufacturing processes that are largely controlled by machinery driven by software and monitored (and amended) by employees.

There are, generally, three different forms of automation, as can be seen in table on the right.

Technology management

The management of technology involves the linkage of engineering, science and management in order to:

- Plan technological capabilities
- Develop technological capabilities
- Implement technological capabilities

This management system seeks to shape and accomplish the technological goals, both strategic and operational, of the business.

This is achieved in a three-part process:

- Accomplish the goals of the organisation by creating value through technological development
- Focus on the development of the technological capabilities which can be used to improve or create production/service processes
- Establish links to all other parts of the organisation

Technology management has developed considerably since the 1950s as can be seen in the table below.

Type of automation	Features	Considerations
Fixed automation	Uses high-cost and specialised equipment for a fixed sequence of operations offering low cost and high volume. The main limitations are the lack of variety of the units and high costs associated with major changes in products or processes.	The most rigid of the three types as it uses high-cost equipment in a series of fixed processes. Ideal for high-volume, low-cost units where there is little variation.
Programmable automation	Effectively, computer-aided manufacturing (CAM) or Computer Numerical Controlled (CNC). The main limitations of these machines are the employee skills needed to program them and the machines' inability to detect wear and variations in materials. The system could also incorporate Directed Numerical Control (DNC) machines, which are controlled by a computer, or robots that are powered pneumatically, hydraulically or electronically.	Highly flexible, but uses high-cost and general purpose machinery. Process sequence changing is relatively simple and the automation process should be capable of producing a wide variety of low-volume products in small batches. The use of CNC and robots are typical. Computer-aided manufacturing (CAM) ranges from robots to fully automated quality control.
Flexible automation	Essentially includes three options: - Manufacturing Cell (MC), in which a small number of CNCs are used to produce similar products - a Flexible Manufacturing System (FMS), where a group of machines can be reprogrammed to produce a variety of similar products, or - Computer Integrated Manufacturing (CIM), which deploys an integrated computer system to link a range of manufacturing processes.	These systems are derived from programmable automation, except that they use more customised equipment. FMS requires shorter change over periods, allowing the organisation to have almost continuous operation and the ability to produce a wide variety of products. FMS typically uses supervisory computer control and automatic material handling as well as robots.

Factor	1950s	1970s	1980s	1990–2000s
Management approach	Research and development	Innovation strategy	Technology strategy	Value management
Resources	Plentiful	Reduced	Accountability	Accountability
Innovation	Internal development	New venture divisions	Business links	Technology focus
Resource allocation	Funding of research and development	Funding of new technologies	Funding of market opportunities	Funding of business development

> **Question**
>
> What are the benefits to a business of CRM? *(12 marks)*

Response of businesses to technological change

LEARNING OBJECTIVES

▶ Responding to technological change
▶ Problems with introducing new technology
▶ Technology as an opportunity
▶ Technical strategy
▶ Technological myopia

Responding to technological change

The rate of technological change continues to accelerate. Businesses were initially reluctant to introduce computers to replace manual and electric typewriters. Many were also slow to introduce mobile telephony.

Many businesses still retain fax machines, although these are outdated and have been largely replaced by scanned images attached to an email. Every piece of equipment and technology owned by a business raises the question of when to jettison it and replace it with a newer model. It is undoubtedly the case that whenever a decision is made to invest in new technology, there is inevitably another business, probably a competitor, already using an even better version of it.

Product development in technology is extremely fast, meaning that products get to the market far quicker than most other types of products and services. New technologies have an even shorter product lifecycle, which is an issue not only for the business creating the technology, but also for those buying into it.

The greatest danger is that an investment in new technology either does not end up making the business more efficient, or that the technology has to be replaced before it has paid for itself. Unfortunately businesses are not in the best position to hold back from adopting new technology, as their competitors undoubtedly will have made the investment and they will simply be left behind.

Problems with introducing new technology

The introduction of new technology, at whatever level in the business, will mean high costs. Tens or hundreds of thousands of pounds will have to be spent on installing a new networked computer system. Hundreds of thousands or millions of pounds may be needed to install an automated production line. Because of the costs it is not always possible for a business to make this investment when it is needed.

Added to this is the difficulty of not knowing precisely when to buy. As a new technology emerges, many businesses are reluctant to commit to it until it has been tried and tested. But if they wait too long, that technology will have already been overtaken with a new development and the business will find itself in precisely the same position again.

 The *Focus on* Implementing and managing change *can be found on pp. 300–05.*

Another major problem for businesses is that they cannot part-buy into a new technology, as it may not be compatible with other technologies they are currently using. The result is that parts of the organisation are able to adopt new technologies, or sections of the factory become automated, while other functions are still carried out using traditional manual methods.

The impact of the adoption of technology on the workforce is another major concern. Factory automation, for example, inevitably means that less semi-skilled manual labour is needed. Employees who are retained will have to learn new skills to use in conjunction with the technology.

As we will see in the last topic, 'Managing change', technology is just one potentially disruptive factor that can cause conflict and imbalance within an organisation.

FOR EXAMPLE

The technology investment problem is also faced by consumers. In a few short years Betamax video, then VHS video, then DVD and now Blue Ray have all been developed and have rendered the previous technology almost obsolete.

Technology as an opportunity

While technology may offer a series of challenges to businesses, it does also provide enormous opportunities. Technology has often been viewed suspiciously, as it is assumed that it will replace humans in the workplace. What is certainly the case is that routine work can be replaced, but that in most cases work can be speeded up, problem solving made more straightforward and, above all, working life made easier. It also makes individuals more productive.

Technology also creates new markets for businesses. There were few mobile phones just twenty years ago, and it has been only relatively recently that e-mails have begun to replace traditional letters. Technology has allowed us to interact with businesses in different ways and this has brought about new job opportunities.

The precise benefits a business may enjoy will often depend on its ability to predict what type of technology and what changes may occur in the near future. Failing to keep up with the market and its requirements can mean disaster for a business and increasingly this does not just mean the products and services the business offers, but also the ways in which it offers its services.

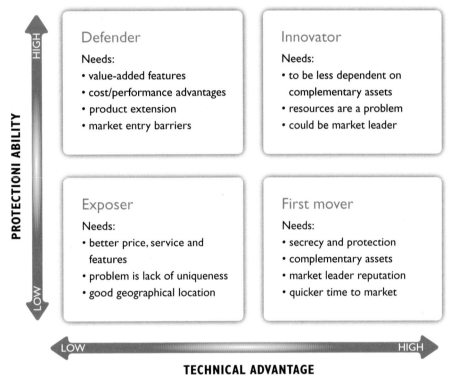

Technical strategy

Technical strategy refers to a model adopted by businesses who seek to protect their technical advantages. The strategies are illustrated in the diagram above.

BOOK RESEARCH

J. Wyman, 'Technological Myopia: The Need to Think Strategically about Technology', *Sloan Management Review*, 26(4) pp. 59–65, 1985.

Technological myopia

Technological myopia can be defined as a business's inability to understand, appreciate or utilise the potential benefits of technology. Technological myopia has been exemplified in recent years by the failure of many business's Intranets. While businesses had secured the technical expertise to install and set up the infrastructure for the Intranet, they had failed to train managers and employees sufficiently, and had also failed to fully utilise the benefits of the new system.

> **Question**
>
> How has technology changed British banking? *(12 marks)*

Case studies, questions and exam practice

CASE STUDY LEARNER SHOPPERS

The next generation of shoppers sees technology as a core part of grocery retailing. Greater use of technology is seen as an obvious solution to make food shopping easier and to improve overall levels of satisfaction, according to research carried out by IGD (the Institute of Grocery Distribution) with 'learner shoppers' – young consumers who have only recently started shopping for themselves. Some suggest a hybrid of the current home-shopping service, where the shopper e-mails the retailer with their order, but still collects it from the store at a time most convenient to them. They simply need to text the store to say they are on their way.

The ideal solution for some is the use of technology to replace personal service. As a generation that has grown up with rapidly evolving technological advances, many learner shoppers are happy to try new technology applied in-store and show none of the hesitancy of older generations. Many identify imaginative solutions to assist the overall shopping experience – for example, using computerised devices attached to trollies to locate products they cannot find, or to check availability of products.

Many learner shoppers embrace new technology and often keep up-to-date with developments in this arena. Some are aware of the development of Radio Frequency Identification (RFID) tagging devices, or at least the principle of these if not the name. They see this technology as a vast improvement in the overall shopping experiences, making shopping more convenient by eliminating time and effort unloading and re-packing the trolley at the checkout.

There is some concern, however, about the implications this technology may have for privacy, and a preference for the devices to be deactivated upon leaving the store. Perhaps surprisingly, learner shoppers are unsure when technological developments are applied to food. For example, most are doubtful about functional foods. They are uncertain of the benefits these products offer and prefer the more traditional approach of a healthy balanced diet.

Question

What is RFID technology and what are its implications?
(12 marks)

Changes in the competitive structure: new competitors and dominant businesses

LEARNING
OBJECTIVES

▶ The competitive environment
▶ Modeling the competitive environment
▶ New entrants
▶ Substitute products and services

The competitive environment

The most important aspect of a business's external environmental factors is its industry or competitive environment. Clearly each different industry has its own characteristics, but in more complex organisations, involved in a number of different markets or different overseas environments, the complexity of dealing with the competitive environment becomes all the more crucial.

It is widely believed that, in order to assess the industry or competitive environment, a business has to consider seven key issues. These are:

- the nature of the industry's dominant features, specifically the economic features
- the nature and strength of the competition
- changing factors that are impacting on the industry's competitive structure and general environment
- an identification of the major competitors and their relative competitive strength
- an anticipation of any strategic initiatives that competitors are likely to make
- an identification of any key factors that will determine competitive success
- the attractiveness of the industry in terms of drawing in new competitors, and the ability of the business to attain a reasonable (sustainable) level of profitability.

Modelling the competitive environment

While the most used model of diagnosing either the industrial or competitive environment is Porter's Five Forces Model, it does require a degree of detailing, particularly in relation to the relative strengths of the importance of specific forces relevant to a particular industry. Typically, any form of competitive analysis will begin with an investigation of the rivalry among existing businesses. In this respect, the rivalry concerns direct competition, and perhaps this is the most important of all of the five forces. Specifics regarding the rivalry include the following:

- *The rate of market or industry growth* – in fast-growing markets businesses may not be overtly competitive, as there is sufficient demand for all. However, should a market be in decline, or be experiencing slow growth, then it is inevitable that the businesses in that market will seek to seize market share from their competitors.
- *The existence of capacity surplus* – in many cases, while businesses are forced to fund their fixed costs, or are reluctant to leave a market due to the high exit barrier costs (*see below*), they are in a position where they have excess capacity. This clearly means that supply exceeds demand. In these cases, the price expected for products and services

is depressed, and consequently a business's profits suffer
- *The size and number of competitors* – when business competitors in a market are broadly equal in terms of their capabilities and size, there is a tendency for competition to increase. Customers will also switch from one supplier to another when there are sufficient numbers of options available to them. In these cases, rivalry is at a high level.
- *New competitors* – this aspect of examining the competitive environment deals with what may be known as either diverse or relatively new competitors. In effect, these new competitors challenge one another and the existing businesses, as they may have different ideas regarding competition. Dangerously, there are unknown factors. New competitors come into the market without a precise knowledge of the competitive boundaries and may well adopt strategies that were hitherto unknown in the industry. While smaller new competitors can, comparatively speaking, be easily dealt with, larger businesses that have acquired a business which will now compete more vigorously in the market are a much more dangerous proposition, as they have the funds and the resources to back their competitive bid.
- *Standardisation of products and services* – it is clearly the case that the more similar products

and services appear, the greater the definition needs to be made in order to retain customers. When products and services are, to all intents and purposes, interchangeable, businesses tend to be more competitive and will resort to drastic pricing or promotional strategies in order to gain a competitive advantage.

- *High exit barriers* – if it is particularly difficult for a business to leave an industry or market due to the high costs of exit, they are left with one simple option. This option is to compete, and perhaps to compete on a more extreme basis than they have done before. This represents the only key to their continued survival.

New entrants

Another significant aspect of investigating the competitive environment is an analysis of any potential new entrants to the market or industry. Some industries are less susceptible to this form of additional competition, as customers may be reluctant to switch from one supplier to another, or there may be especially high barriers to entry. Typical barriers to entry include the following:

- The requirement to acquire specific or specialised resources, such as financial backing, technology or economies of scale.
- Highly differentiated products or services, which means it may be difficult for potential new entrants to find a ready market for their products or services as customers are already matched to the most appropriate products or services offered by existing businesses.
- High capital requirements – significant investment compared to possible returns can be a major dissuading factor for potential entrants.

- Limited access to distribution channels – assuming that many of the distribution channels are already dominated by existing business and that there are no viable alternatives to the traditional channels, it may deter new entrants as they will find no easy way to get their products and services to the end user.
- Regulatory restrictions – in certain cases, public or private monopolies exist that effectively bar new entrants from specific markets. This factor has been particularly the case in many infrastructure-based industries, notably transport. While there has been deregulation in the UK, for example, of the train networks, there are still only single businesses providing services on specific lines. It is therefore impossible for new entrants to offer alternative services.
- Tariffs and trade restrictions – in certain cases, under the terms of the General Agreement on Tariffs and Trade (GATT), countries may erect tariffs, quotas or other forms of trade restriction, to effectively protect their domestic markets from overseas competition. While such protectionist policies are on the decline, they are still a considerable impediment to potential new entrants to a market if either their products or services become too expensive as a result of tariffs, or their volume of exports is reduced due to quotas or other restrictive trade practices.

New entrants tend to be successful and represent a considerable competition risk if they can create a synergy with their existing lines of business. Equally, they are a threatening prospect if they have access to considerable financial resources, alternative technology or government assistance or can penetrate the distribution channels.

BOOK RESEARCH

Arthur A. Thompson and A.J. Strickland, *Strategic Management*, New York: McGraw Hill Education, 2001.

Substitute products and services

Substitute products or services are also a concern in terms of competition. In strict terms these substitute products may either be existing or new products and services. In the first instance an existing product, which could be used as a substitute, is effectively transferred into a new market, although it might not necessarily have been associated with that particular market before. A prime example is e-mail, which has become an effective substitute for postal services. New products or services are strictly those that did not necessarily exist before and represent a major improvement over the products and services that were originally available. Prime examples from the past include the virtual replacement of typewriters by computers or word processors, and electronic watches replacing traditional mechanical watches. In recent years, music and film, for example, have seen a number of major changes. Traditional acetate records were gradually replaced by cassette tapes, which in turn were replaced by CDs, now in the process of being replaced themselves by Internet music files.

> **Question**
>
> How significant is rivalry as part of the competition between businesses? *(12 marks)*

Changes in the competitive structure: customers and suppliers

LEARNING OBJECTIVES

▶ Customers
▶ Suppliers
▶ Integration

Customers

A major factor in assessing the competitive environment is the buyers themselves. Buyers can be either other businesses or consumers, and in cases where buyers have numerous available sources for products, they have a relatively strong position. Customers are also very significant in markets where there are very few of them and demand is therefore always considerably less than supply. In cases when buyers can easily substitute one product or service for another, they have relative strength, assuming that the products and services are not in themselves sufficiently differentiated. The final major consideration regarding buyers is also the fear that they may decide to engage in backward integration.

The relative strength of buyers is affected by:

• Number and concentration of buyers relative to suppliers – bargaining power will be influenced by whether it is the buyers or the suppliers in the industry who are more powerful. The number of buyers and the alliances between them will be important, as will the number of purchases each buyer makes.
• Buyers' price sensitivity – buyers will be considerably stronger if they are able to negotiate prices.
• Product differentiation – if some products seem more attractive than others, then the strength of the buyers will be reduced. If all

the products are equally attractive then the strength of buyers will be greater.
• Switching costs – if it costs money to switch suppliers, then the buyers' strength will be less Information – the more information available to buyers about the products and services and other potential suppliers, the greater the strength they will have.

Suppliers

The other major consideration in terms of the competitive environment is the strength of the suppliers in that market. This refers to suppliers of businesses operating in a given market. Some suppliers are more powerful and can dictate the course or fortunes of the competition within the market, usually under the following circumstances:

• They are strong when there are few suppliers and demand for their products or services is high.
• They are also strong when they have a large number of customers and have options open to them regarding who they sell to and at what price.
• Strength can also be found in cases when suppliers produce unique products or services that are otherwise difficult to obtain.
• Strength can be derived from circumstances where the suppliers have access to greater financial resources than the businesses

operating within the market.
• The final consideration regarding supplier strength is that they could decide to engage in forward integration.

Integration

Markets and sectors are in a state of constant change. This inevitably means that the balance of power between the suppliers, the business and their customers is always shifting. A business will be looking to the ultimate goal of creating and sustaining a competitive advantage. The diagram opposite outlines some of the common strategies and how they might give the business that edge.

You will already be aware of many of the concepts featured in the diagram, such as concentration, diversification and integration as well as the variants of each of these approaches.

Mergers occur when two companies combine to form a single business. A merger is very similar to an acquisition or a takeover, except that in a merger existing shareholders of both businesses retain a shared interest in the new operation.

In an acquisition, one company purchases the bulk of a second company's shares, which creates an unequal balance of ownership in the new, combined business.

Mergers are sought for a number of reasons:

• A profitable business may acquire another organisation that is less

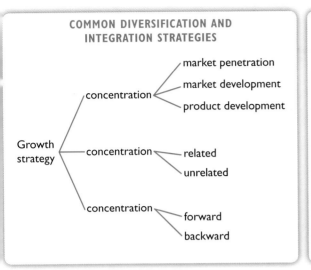

COMMON DIVERSIFICATION AND INTEGRATION STRATEGIES

IMPLEMENTATION STRATEGIES

COMPETITIVE STRATEGIES

COMPETITIVE ADVANTAGE

profitable. It can use the losses of the acquired business to write off tax to offset its profits.

- Increasing market share is another major reason for a merger. Merging with a major competitor, the new business can become a dominant business in the marketplace and give them more power with regard to pricing and buyer incentives. The problem with this kind of merger is when two dominant companies join together, as this may trigger complaints from other businesses and be referred to the Office of Fair Trading, on the grounds that a monopoly has been created.

- Another merger motivator may be that the businesses make different but complementary products. Sometimes this may involve buying a business that controls an asset that the businesses uses somewhere in its supply chain. A manufacturer may buy out a warehousing chain or a travel agent may buy an airline.

FOR EXAMPLE

PayPal merged with eBay, as it allowed eBay to avoid having to pay the fees that they had been paying PayPal, while simultaneously tying two complementary businesses together.

CASE STUDY VIDEO GAME GIANTS

Activision and Blizzard, the games companies behind *Call of Duty* and the *World of Warcraft* announced their merger in December 2007. The deal was worth £9.15 billion. The two businesses were hoping that their different strengths would combine to create a business that was more powerful on every gaming platform across the world. Blizzard is particularly strong in Asia, and Activision has franchises such as Spiderman and produces games for Microsoft, Sony and Nintendo consoles. Around nine million people pay a monthly subscription to play *World of Warcraft*. The merged business will be known as Activision Blizzard. Blizzard itself is owned by the French media group Vivendi. Blizzard will invest $2 million in the new company and Activision will invest $1 billion. Blizzard's last *World of Warcraft* expansion game, *Burning Crusade*, sold nearly 2.4 million copies within 24 hours of its release.

Question

Explain why a merger such as this represents synergy. *(12 marks)*

Evaluating responses to a change in the competitive environment

Responding to changes

The diagram on the right shows Porter's Five Forces and provides some elaborating detail. It also gives useful pointers to the possible responses to change.

In addition to the changing basis on which competition is now taking place, a business also needs to be aware of the changing environment in which it takes place. There are many factors influencing this, including:

- increasing trends towards globalisation
- increasing customer power
- changing regulatory patterns
- increasing trade liberalisation.

These factors are impacting on the business, whether they are aware of them or not. The challenge begins at realising that these factors, and their impact, are real. Impact specifics must be understood and strategies for dealing with these factors need to be developed and implemented to ensure continued survival.

There has been a massive increase in competition with many more providers of goods and services, both in the domestic market and overseas. But 'overseas' no longer means simply a handful of firms in the advanced industrialised nations serving largely dependent and captive markets. Now there are newly industrialising countries competing aggressively for a share not only of their local markets but also in the heartland of the old

These factors tend to increase supplier bargaining power →

These factors tend to raise barriers to market entry by new entrants

ENTRANTS
- Economies of scale
- Differentiation
- Capital requirements
- Switching costs
- Access to distribution
- Cost disadvantages beyond those of scale
- Government policy

BUYERS
- Concentrated
- Buy in volume
- Big ticket items
- Standardised or undifferentiated products
- Low switching costs
- Low profit margins
- Threat of backward integration
- Purchase not important to buyer
- Buyer has all relevant information

INDUSTRY COMPETITORS (RIVALRY)

SUPPLIERS
- Dominated by a few suppliers
- Suppliers are more concentrated than buyers
- No substitutes
- Supplier has more important customers
- Supplier's input is critical
- Differentiated product
- High switching costs
- Threat of forward integration

SUBSTITUTES
- Numerous rivals
- Equally balanced
- Slow growth
- High fixed costs
- Low differentiation
- Low switching costs
- Large capacity increments
- Diverse competitors
- High stakes
- High exit barriers

These factors tend to increase rivalry among existing competitors

These factors tend to increase customer bargaining power

established manufacturing nations. Japan's export model provided an example successfully followed by other nations on the Pacific Rim to the extent that their growth rates are among the fastest in the world.

For the customer, the range of choice of products and services is bewildering. However, it is becoming clear that competition for customers puts a degree of power in their hands. They can now begin to demand better levels of service, better-quality products, better delivery and support, and greater specificity in what they buy. Such power is often increasingly concentrated in the hands of key groups, such as food retailers, who can exert enormous influence on manufacturers in terms of what they are asked to produce. New products and processes – for example, disposable nappies made without the need for bleaching, or the

use of recycled newsprint – emerge as a result of strong pressure groups. Estimates suggest that a significant proportion of consumers, especially women, would be prepared to pay more for products that have a positive environmental image.

Another source of influence is the regulatory environment that operates in and between countries. This can act to shape the rate and direction of change, for example, by imposing legislative controls on certain kinds of products or processes. The case of environmental pollution legislation in recent years has had a marked impact on what firms can do and the costs associated with their different approaches to production.

Another factor that has introduced considerable instability into the environment has been the growing trend towards trade liberalisation. In a variety of countries external forces – especially the major financial institutions such as the International Monetary Fund (IMF) and World Bank – have been acting to lower tariff and other trade barriers and expose markets to open competition. This poses a considerable threat to many firms which have traditionally been insulated from the full extent and level of global competition. The challenge is, often in a short space of time, to recognise the new rules of the game and to develop capabilities to compete under these rules. Typically this will involve considerable technological change.

Buyer-supplier relationships

Given the fact that the average business spends more on supplied resources than on those resources it employs within the organisation, the relationship between suppliers and the business is a vital concern.

The buyer-supplier relationship has distinct strategic importance and studies have increasingly sought to understand the relationships. The creation of partnerships or relationships tends to revolve around the following aspects:

- trust
- length of relationship
- number of suppliers involved
- types of asset acquired from suppliers

The two key considerations in regard to the relationships are:

- *Supplier coordination* – gaining an understanding and a synergy between the buyer and the supplier in order to anticipate and satisfy each others' needs.

- *Supplier development* – bringing the supplier into the decision-making at the earliest stage to ensure quantity and conformity of supplier items.

The overall relationship is typified in the following diagram:

CASE STUDY ARGENTINIAN BEEF

Beef has been a tradition in Argentina for two centuries. It had always exported salted meat and later chilled beef, but with the establishment of trade barriers, and with other environmental factors such as the Second World War, Argentina's international beef market contracted, and so it standardised the domestic market. Argentina's beef consumption per capita is almost four times that of Western Europe (70–80 kgs compared to 15–25 kgs).

Despite its recent domestic orientation, Argentina is still the world's third largest beef producer and fourth in exporting terms behind Australia, Germany and the US. Its traditional export markets for lower-value products (boned and manufactured beef) have been lost to subsidised EU supplies and because of other developed country protection measures.

However, Argentina has maintained or increased its export of high-value products (boneless cuts, canned beef, frozen beef) which now account for over 80% of its export value. Argentina's export value is now near the $800 million mark, although this accounts for only 10% of its total agricultural exports.

The Argentina beef industry faced all the macro forces described by Porter internally and externally, and the threat of new entrants, but survived. This success was not necessarily built on favourable trading conditions but on its ability to maintain international competitiveness through

rampant inflation, currency overvaluation, heavy taxation, potential uncertainty and increased competition from substitute products internationally and from the Argentine cereals subsector which was clamouring for more resources.

Its success was sustained by:

- low-cost production of quality beef (climate and extensive grasslands)
- well-developed, flexible and transparent livestock marketing system
- innovations in beef distribution domestically (butcher chain stores, vacuum packing)
- development of new, international market outlets (Middle East)
- debt rescheduling by banks for livestock and trading enterprise.

With recent measures to make the industry viable again, including capacity rationalisation, Argentina beef is now back in profit and exporting a little more.

Source: adapted from the United Nations

Question

How might Porter's Five Forces explain the competitive responses by this industry? *(12 marks)*

Case studies, questions and exam practice

CASE STUDY NINTENDO Wii IS MARKET LEADER

Two years ago, very few analysts would have predicted that the Nintendo Wii would be the market leader of this generation against the established PlayStation and Xbox brands. But analysts can be in error: Vgchartz.com data, which is based on sample data from retailers all over the world, indicates that in the week ending 18 August 2007, Nintendo's Wii had achieved sales of 10.57 million consoles since its launch in November 2006. The Microsoft Xbox 360 – released a year earlier – had achieved lifetime sales of 10.51 million units by the same time. Nintendo was the new market leader in both the home and handheld videogame console businesses.

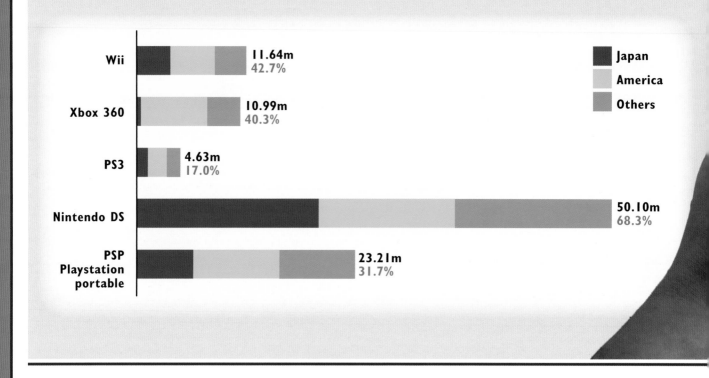

	Sales	Share
Wii	11.64m	42.7%
Xbox 360	10.99m	40.3%
PS3	4.63m	17.0%
Nintendo DS	50.10m	68.3%
PSP Playstation portable	23.21m	31.7%

Japan
America
Others

In just two years, home console sales for the three major manufacturers have effectively reversed. This will have a large impact on third-party publishers and will undoubtedly influence the decisions they make in the future. One factor that has no doubt helped Nintendo's Wii to gain so quickly is the console's broad appeal across all age groups, demographics and countries. Current sales are fairly evenly split between the three major markets – 3.46 million have been sold in Japan, the American market (including Canada and South America) accounts for sales of 4.24 million units, and other markets (including Europe and Australia and a few niche markets) account for sales of 2.87 million units.

Source: adapted from *Agence Française pour le Jeu Vidéo*

Question

How might these figures influence suppliers, customers and publishers of games for the consoles? *(12 marks)*

Introduction

This is the last of the three core themes for the *Business environment and managing change* unit. In this part of the unit we examine how organisations operate in a changing environment. We also look at how change creates both opportunities and threats, how a business can plan for and manage change, and how it is important to appreciate the fact that external and internal change are linked.

There are six parts to this topic. The first focus area examines the internal causes of change. We will be examining changes in organisational size, changes in ownership and leadership, and how poor business performance is often a catalyst for internal change.

The second focus area examines how a business plans for change. We will look at the purpose of corporate plans and how these are influenced by both internal and external factors. We will also look at the value of corporate plans and how it is important for a business to create its own contingency plans as a response to potential changes in the future.

The third focus area examines the first of the key influences on the change process: leadership. We will look at the meaning of leadership and at a range of leadership styles. And we will examine various leadership theories and how they seek to identify the prime characteristics of leadership, as well as identifying the key differences between leadership and management. The topic also looks at how internal and external factors influence leadership style, the role of leadership in managing change, and the overall importance of leadership to an organisation.

The fourth focus area continues the theme of key influences in the change process and switches emphasis to organisational culture. We will examine the different types of organisational culture and the problems organisations often face in attempting to change their culture. We will also look at the importance of organisational culture and how it often determines how a business responds to change, while continuing to perform its usual processes and activities.

The fifth focus area looks at making strategic decisions. We will examine the importance of information management and how there are a number of different approaches to the decision-making process. It also looks at influences on corporate decision-making.

The final focus area examines the implementation and management of change itself. We examine the various techniques that can be used to implement and manage change in a successful way. We also identify the factors that promote and resist change.

FOCUS ON INTERNAL CAUSES OF CHANGE

- Changes in organisational size ▶ page 250
- New ownership, leadership and poor business performance ▶ page 252
- Case studies, questions and exam practice ▶ page 254

FOCUS ON PLANNING FOR CHANGE

- Corporate planning ▶ page 256
- Influences on corporate plans ▶ page 258
- Approaches to planning ▶ page 260
- Assessing the value of corporate plans ▶ page 262
- Contingency planning ▶ page 264
- Case studies, questions and exam practice ▶ page 266

FOCUS ON KEY INFLUENCES ON THE CHANGE PROCESS: LEADERSHIP

- The meaning of leadership ▶ page 268
- The range of leadership styles ▶ page 270
- Transformational leadership ▶ page 272
- Factors influencing leadership style ▶ page 274
- Role of leadership in managing change and achieving success ▶ page 276
- Assessing the importance of leadership ▶ page 278
- Case studies, questions and exam practice ▶ page 280

FOCUS ON KEY INFLUENCES ON THE CHANGE PROCESS: CULTURE

- Types of organisational culture ▶ page 282
- Significance of organisational culture ▶ page 284
- Reasons for and problems of changing organisational culture ▶ page 286
- Assessing the importance of organisational culture ▶ page 288
- Case studies, questions and exam practice ▶ page 290

FOCUS ON MAKING STRATEGIC DECISIONS

- Significance of information management ▶ page 292
- Value of different approaches to decision-making ▶ page 294
- Influences on corporate decision-making ▶ page 296
- Case studies, questions and exam practice ▶ page 298

FOCUS ON IMPLEMENTING AND MANAGING CHANGE

- Techniques to implement change ▶ page 300
- Assessing the factors that promote or resist change ▶ page 302
- Case studies, questions and exam practice ▶ page 304

Changes in organisational size

Mergers and takeovers

You will already be familiar with these two terms – a merger being a voluntary agreement between two businesses, and a takeover when the situation is forced by one of the businesses involved.

Mergers are examples of integration, one of the most common being horizontal integration, where competing businesses in the same industry merge together. Vertical integration is also possible, where businesses at different stages in the production chain merge together. Lateral integration takes place when two businesses with unconnected ranges of products and services in different industries join together.

Businesses are keen to merge because they can make savings by being bigger (known as economies of scale). They are better placed to compete with larger competitors, or the merger can simply be to eliminate a competitor.

Organic growth

Organic growth occurs when a business achieves better revenue results with what they already have. This is notably their current product, market and customer portfolios. Organic growth can come from changes to market segmentation and target market definition, strategies for pricing, positioning, advertising and promotion, line extensions, packaging, merchandising, sales effectiveness, distribution channels or e-marketing.

Market penetration	
Market segmentation	Size and growth rates of specific market segments
Competitive position	Market share, competitors' market shares, intent-to-buy research
Market portfolio management	Mix of sales (revenues and margins) by market segmentation (described by demographics, psychographics, lifestyles, attitudes, Standardised Industrial Classification codes (SIC codes) or other measures)
Media position	Share of traditional and e-media expenditure; awareness, recognition, usage and attitude
Account or customer penetration	
Cross-selling	Share of customer's expenditures secured by company
Customer penetration	Expenditures by age of account (time the account has been a customer)
Customer retention	Expenditures by age of account (time the account has been a customer)
Customer portfolio management	Mix of sales (revenues and margins) by customer cluster (usually described by customer behaviours, size of customer, customer profitability or strategic value)

Businesses look for ways to grow organically primarily because there are so few attractive alternatives. Mergers and acquisitions do not offer a simple way to ensure growth, as they often destroy shareholder value rather than create it. Four ways of achieving organic growth are:

- *As an imitator* – growing by process or asset replication. Competitors have a successful asset – for example, a store model (as in Tesco and McDonald's) – and they become expert at reproducing that asset in ways that keep costs down.
- *As an inventor* – growing by exploiting technological superiority. Making the business's products and services consistently superior to those of the competitors. Invention lies not just in capabilities, but in inventing the right products and services for customers.
- *As an insider* – growth is driven by customer relationships. Marketing superiority is a powerful organic growth engine.
- *As an illuminator* – growing by seeing the gaps in the marketplace more clearly and sooner than competitors, and filling them first. A business's organic growth is driven by anticipating unspoken customer needs. Procter & Gamble call these gaps 'white spaces' – places where they can deliver new products or services that expand their core business.

The strategies of businesses striving for organic growth tend to be long-term, with an emphasis on sustainability and focus, but execution is ultimately more important than strategy. Products and services need to be closely tuned to the needs of customers within serviceable market segments. These businesses have a view that centres on what the market needs and what their business model can deliver quickly and efficiently. Their organisation and governance structures are networked rather than hierarchical, accountability is well established, and decision-making is delegated and distributed. They are decentralised, which is another way of saying that they are close to the customer, with few intervening layers in the organisation. Their leaders are patient, persistent, focused, and eager to learn and guide – typically not the swashbuckling type. And their business processes and information systems are highly adaptable, and focused on organisational interaction and integration.

Retrenchment strategies

Retrenchment strategy is exemplified by moves that a business may seek to make in difficult times, or when the markets or the external environment are unpredictable. They may opt for a scaling down of operations, perhaps identifying current areas of business activity which are most under threat. They will partially or completely remove themselves from weaker parts of the market, or divest themselves of business operations in order to refocus on stronger areas of the business. Retrenchment often involves a considerable regrouping through both cost and asset reduction in response to declining sales and profits. Retrenchment is often referred to as a turnaround or a reorganisation strategy. In essence, it seeks to strengthen the business and force it to return to its distinctive core competences. Retrenchment can involve the sale of land, buildings, the reduction of production lines, the closure of marginally profitable businesses, the closure of an obsolete manufacturing unit or automated processes, a reduction in employees or the institution of stringent expense-control systems.

Organisation development

Organisational development (OD) is a planned process of change. It requires performance improvement in which a business will seek to align more closely with the environment and markets in which it operates in order to achieve its strategies efficiently and effectively. OD can involve developing organisations in terms of culture, values, people, structures, processes and resources.

OD is a complex issue and often specific in terms of process, timing and those involved. There are, however, some overarching processes and elements that can be identified as common to many OD situations. These tend to begin with research into the current situation to assess all the issues. This research will inevitably involve the following aspects:

BOOK RESEARCH

Fred Davis, *Strategic Management Concepts*, New York: Prentice Hall, 2001.

- clarifying the impact obligations, which have to be honoured
- the availability of appropriate resources, such as skills, facilities and finances
- the desires and career aspirations of those who will be affected
- the proposed plan's overall fit with future business strategy.

Once the research process is completed, the organisation should have a better view of how the OD will work in practice. This begins with planning the change programme, which may involve the design of the new organisational structure, job descriptions and evaluation, salary and benefits provision, physical resources, phasing of the overall project and the management of impacts on existing employees.

Throughout the process, the organisation needs to ensure that it conducts communication, development and counselling events to assist the establishment of the new organisational structure. It may also be necessary to reshape or re-profile certain areas of the organisation with the intention of improving retention and the best use of skills and expertise in order to make the intended developments in efficiency.

> ### Question
> Explain why organic growth may be the most desirable form of business growth. *(12 marks)*

New ownership, leadership and poor business performance

LEARNING OBJECTIVES

▶ Reasons for change
▶ New ownership or management
▶ Poor business performance

Reasons for change and responses to change

There are many reasons for organisational change:

- strategic change
- structural change
- cultural change
- new technology change
- merger and acquisition change
- break-up and spin-off change
- downsizing change
- expansion change.

Senior managers facing such changes are asking their employees to join them in a collective leap into the unknown. The initial responses to change are typically: instability, stress and uncertainty. These reactions can pose enormous problems for management as they are closely linked to power, anxiety and control.

As part of their strategic planning, many companies review the merits of reorganising their existing operations. The option to relocate the business may not be available due to time, cost or other factors and the need to consolidate the business may require drastic changes to an existing infrastructure. The need to reorganise a factory or site becomes a higher-profile issue whenever there is a major change in a company's business operations or when production output reduces.

As businesses rarely make drastic changes in their site operations, it is unlikely that an organisation will have the necessary experience or skills to research, plan and generally undertake the reorganisation project in-house. The pressures already put on a business usually mean that existing resources are heavily loaded and the failure costs of poorly planned or poorly executed reorganisations brought about by time pressures are real and very public. Reorganisations are more often undertaken by an experienced project management company working alongside key client staff. Such a company will understand that the client project manager already has a 'day job'. Successful factory and site reorganisations will always recognise the need to maintain continuity of service to customers, and to cause as little disruption as possible to the business in terms of customers, employees and other stakeholders.

The reasons for a business needing to change its operations (factory reorganisation, site reorganisation, building changes etc.) are varied. The business might be reacting to an increase or decrease in product demand, or to changes in manufacturing methods. Or it might be responding to practical issues, such as the unsuitability of existing premises that need to be upgraded to meet new legislation.

An increasingly common reason for a business to decide to commit to a site reorganisation is that it decides to outsource its products to a third party. This is especially true for commodity items that can be sourced from overseas at much lower cost. Businesses can decide to source all their requirements from global or local suppliers or retain some of the high added value and complex products. Either way, there is a major reduction in the facilities required by the new operation and the associated ongoing costs.

New ownership or management

A management buy-out involves the acquisition of a business by its existing management. In many cases the management group will establish a new holding company which then effectively purchases the shares of the target company. There are variations of management buy-out, notably management buy-in, where external management buys the business and buy-in management buy-out, which is a combination of the two.

Management buy-outs may arise as a result of any of the following:

- A group may decide to sell a business because it has become a non-core activity
- A business may find itself in difficulties and need to sell part of its business
- The owner of a business may choose to retire
- A receiver or administrator may sell the business as a going concern

For more on the management of change see the Focus on Implementing and managing change on pp. 300–05

Poor business performance

Poor business performance can be a major catalyst for internal change. The poor performance may be judged in a number of different ways and may be only comparative (e.g. the sales figures are lower than the previous year, or profits have fallen compared to the same time last year). The overriding issue is that the internal change seeks to address the problem before it permanently and adversely affects the ability of the business to continue to operate.

The diagram on the right illustrates why it is important for a business to intervene and put corrective steps into action before the situation gets out of control.

We can see from the diagram that the business owners or leaders only have a limited period of time before which the situation slips out of their control. Note also that the 'informal' process refers to steps that the business can take before external agencies, such as debt collection and courts, become involved.

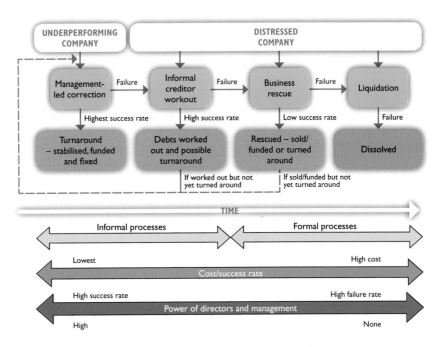

CASE STUDY POOR PERFORMANCE

In 2006, Intel began a cost-cutting reorganisation. The electronic chip-maker's chief executive, Paul Otellini, stated that restructuring would cover all parts of the company in a bid to 'adjust to the business realities of today [and] tomorrow'. Otellini did not reveal whether the reorganisation would lead to redundancies, but did promise to 'deal with non-performing business units' and to evaluate key metrics, such as productivity and cost per unit.

Intel had seen its market share slide in recent years, and had warned that 2006 revenues would drop by three per cent relative to the previous year. Profitability was believed to have decreased by 6.5 percentage points to 24.7%.

The chip giant cited lacklustre growth in PC shipments as well as a build-up of inventory over the past six months. Intel had already committed to cutting spending by $1 billion and reducing capital expenditure, but Otellini admitted that this would be 'insufficient'.

Source: adapted from VNU

Questions

1 Define the term 'restructuring'. *(2 marks)*
2 What is meant by the term 'key metrics'? *(4 marks)*
3 What might be the consequences of restructuring for the workforce? *(6 marks)*

Case studies, questions and exam practice

CASE STUDY A LITTLE BIT OF HISTORY

In the winter of 1981 Bud Lynn, Executive Vice President, responsible for overseas operations at the American parent company Woolworth, started negotiations with a British consortium to sell their British subsidiary. This was not because of any problems in Britain, but because of the need to raise funds back in America.

American colleagues (and many executives) believed that the British management was buying the company out. Many felt guilty at the way the American parent had taken billions of dollars of dividends out of the British company over 73 years trading for a once-off investment of £50,000, and thought the sale was only fair.

Little did they know that actually the company was being sold from under the feet

of the board to a completely new owner.

The media generally liked the idea. They had been strongly critical of the Woolworth management (because they were diversifying too much and moving up-market), but seemed happy with the new owners and their declared plans for the business. The sale was completed in autumn 1982.

The BBC News reported that 'for the first time Woolworth is in British Ownership', against a backdrop of the flagship Oxford Street store. It was everyone's last chance to see that store as a Woolworths, as it closed only weeks later.

Oxford Street had never been a profitable store, and it was a very valuable piece of real estate, so people could understand the closure – but many of the other early closures were opportunistic ways of releasing asset value from the business, that took no account of the profitability of the store, or the value of the building.

The new owners had recognised the potential of the Woolworth business, and the advantages of spreading their portfolio between in-town and out-of-town stores. Spurred on by a hostile takeover bid from Dixons in the 1980s, they later did a lot to bring Woolworths up-to-date, establishing a new trading formula for the company. But investment was rationed and given only when there were no more interesting projects around for the Kingfisher business development team.

No-one will ever know whether the original Woolworth management would have had the focus to develop B&Q into such a fantastic business. They did not have a good track record of seeing ideas through to fruition, which is how, 18 years after it was launched, Woolco was still only small, while Tesco and other retailers had expanded massively out of town.

In late 2008, disaster struck for Woolworths. All 815 of their stores were facing the threat of closure, and the 26,000 staff were facing redundancy. There were rumours that Sainsbury's, Tesco, Poundland, Asda and Iceland were all interested in some of the high-street locations, and discussions were underway with potential buyers for the whole chain.

But nothing came of the negotiations. Woolworths went into administration on 26 November 2008, owing £386 million. And there was worse to come. Woolworth's music, DVD and games distribution subsidiary, Entertainment UK, also went into administration. Zavvi (formerly Virgin Records) was a major customer and this caused supply problems. Then Zavvi went into administration on 24 December. Steadily, the administrators began closing the stores, some were sold off to rivals HMV.

Questions

1 What is a hostile takeover? *(4 marks)*
2 How might a hostile takeover be dealt with by the target business and why are they invariably successful? *(10 marks)*

Corporate planning

Corporate planning

A corporate plan is a document that provides guidance for people who work in an organisation, and information for stakeholders through a high-level statement of how the organisation proposes to go about its work over the next few years.

Strategic or corporate planning is an integrated and systematic approach to the management and coordination of the total range of activities of an organisation, to move it from where it is now to a desired future position. At its heart, it is a recipe for survival. It involves the entire organisation and all its assets: physical, financial, human and intellectual. The strategic plan for an organisation is a 'blueprint' or framework for the development of specific operational plans within business units to move in the future corporate direction.

The strategic plan looks to the future by requiring a business to:

- review its purpose
- assess where it is now
- determine where it ought to be at a future time (e.g. 3–5 years) in response to requirements (incorporating all of its stakeholders)
- establish how and when it should get there
- monitor and evaluate its progress
- initiate corrective actions as necessary.

The strategic planning process seeks to answer three classic questions:

- *Where are we now?* This means an analysis of the current and forecast external environment in which the organisation will be operating, and its existing strengths and weaknesses.
- *Where do we want to be?* This incorporates a statement of purpose (mission and broad objectives); a set of hierarchical objectives; the strategic objectives, and the tactical objectives with time-based targets.
- *How do we get there?* This includes a formulation of strategies, programmes and activities directed towards achieving the agreed objectives.

There are a number of advantages associated with strategic (corporate) planning:

- It gives greater purpose and direction for the whole organisation.
- It designs the future, and invents ways of bringing about that future.
- It allows the sharing of common goals by the various components or business units.
- It develops a 'team' approach to management.
- It creates an organisation that is sensitive to the external environment (both macro and micro).
- It helps in the identification of strategies to react to that environment and an assessment of the risks involved.

- It also provides a step-by-step process towards the future.

The strategic or corporate planning process provides a framework for continuous performance improvement. Performance can then be evaluated by results achieved against explicit objectives and targets. Diagnostic analysis identifies constraints or reasons for under-achievement (negative feedback). Identification of measures minimises constraints (positive application of negative feedback).

Because this is a dynamic process, it is necessary for the fundamental mission statement and corporate objectives of an organisation to be reviewed on a regular basis. This is the role of the senior management (a top-down process), but communication and feedback from key stakeholders (such as government) and staff (a lateral and bottom-up process) should be an integral part of the review.

The use of confusing language is counter-productive and should be avoided at all costs. Concise and meaningful mission statements are hard to write. Similar comments apply to the review of corporate objectives. It is vital that for corporate objectives to be of value they should be:

- meaningful
- achievable
- measurable

The role of management

The strategic planning process needs to be driven by executive management. The role of management is to provide the necessary leadership and support to produce the plan. The process is driven from the top down. Lower levels of management within the organisation develop the details within the strategic framework established by the executive. The Board of Directors overviews the plan, particularly the strategic implications, and sanctions the plan and management processes to be set in place.

In driving the process, the role of management is to:

- Determine corporate and lower-level objectives;
- Harness and guide the people and other resources required to successfully achieve the objectives, including capital, intellectual capital, human resources, plant and equipment and materials
- Monitor and control
- Communicate with stakeholders

CASE STUDY TASMANIA'S CORPORATE PLAN

The corporate plan is our primary planning tool. It articulates our vision, mission and values, as well as the outcomes we hope to achieve for the community and the factors that we have identified as critical to our success.

The development of the corporate plan is intrinsically linked to the delivery of government outcomes and ensures that the allocation of resources is directed to the Government's priorities.

As a result, the corporate plan outlines what we will be doing and why, how we are going to do it, and the resources needed. The corporate plan is not a static document; it evolves to meet the new priorities and challenges we face.

All staff work together in the corporate planning cycle to frame our strategic direction, to identify our priorities and our strategic challenges and to identify and develop the initiatives we need to achieve our vision and mission. The corporate planning cycle is also used to ensure that our work is directly related to achieving the Government's outcomes, and that the results of our work are monitored and measured.

Source: adapted from the Tasmanian Government

ONGOING 12-MONTH CORPORATE PLANNING CYCLE

TREASURER'S ENDORSEMENT (June/July)
The Corporate Plan is finalised and subsequently endorsed by the Treasurer

SENIOR MANAGEMENT CONFERENCE (Oct)
Strategic direction setting for the coming year

BRANCH PLANNING (Oct–Nov)
Branch Operating Plans are developed. These underpin the Corporate Plan

REVIEW OF BRANCH OPERATING PLANS (May)
This ensures that activities remain focussed on the achievement of the Government's current objectives and priorities, and can be funded

CORPORATE PLANNING CYCLE

ENDORSEMENT OF BRANCH OPERATING PLANS (Nov)
The draft Branch Operating Plans are considered in detail. The Department's budget for the coming year is allocated across branches

BUDGET PRESENTATION (April–May)
Budget allocations are included in the State Budget

INDIVIDUAL WORKS PLANS (Feb, July)
Twice yearly, branches establish individual work plans for each staff member, based on the Branch Operating Plan

REVIEW OF THE CORPORATE PLAN (Feb, April, July, Oct)
The Corporate Plan sets out a number of milestones to be achieved. Progress towards these is monitored and reported on.

Questions

1 What is meant by the phrase 'not a static document'? *(4 marks)*

2 Explain how the corporate plan is monitored and amended. *(8 marks)*

Influences on corporate plans

Influences and stages

There are a great many descriptions of corporate planning methodology, regardless of the model selected. The corporate planning process can be employed successfully if it is applied with regard to the situations in which the organisation exists. No real standardised planning method is applicable to all organisations, as each plan needs to take into account the particular environment and the management systems, authority, leadership and culture of the organisation.

The essence of the corporate planning process consists of the elements shown below – most are developed as a sequence, but some of the earlier steps can be carried out at the same time. It is important to appreciate that many organisations skip backwards and forwards in the planning process in their attempt to create a workable plan.

Communication

The entire process is based on communication as the process could not work at all without open communication up, down, and across the organisation. The key to getting the information flowing is the participation of the people who will be responsible for executing the plan. Normally, the extent of participation in deciding on the organisation's overall directions and corporate goals will not be that broad. Ultimate responsibility lies with the senior management. However, once operational objectives are established and action plans developed, participation should be as wide as possible. Without participation in implementing the long-range aims set by senior management, the most vital ingredient of corporate planning – commitment – is missing.

Two other vital ingredients of a successful corporate planning system are flexibility and control. The management team must be flexible in both organisation structure and the plans that pull the structure along. If flexibility is not built into the system, and if the organisation cannot adapt to changing situations, then it will ultimately fail.

Managers must make a careful assessment of the amount of oversight to exercise with each subordinate. If too little control is exercised, there is a possibility that problems could arise and grow unsolvable before any management action can be taken. There is a fine balance between what might be too little control and what could be described as excessive control. In translating plans to actions, that balance must be found.

STEP BY STEP, THE PLANNING PROCESS INCLUDES:

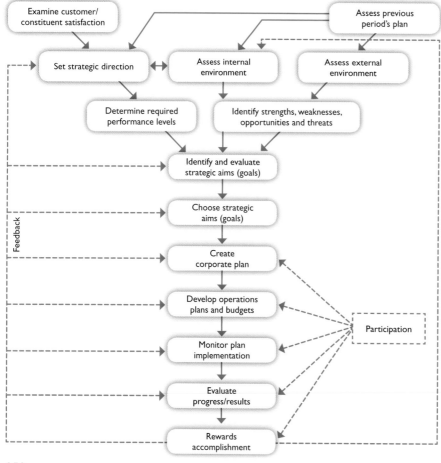

Step	Influences
Assessing the previous period's plan to determine (a) the progress of the organisation against the plan, (b) areas where problems were encountered and where special attention needs to be paid in the future, and (c) planning material that is still current and appropriate. This is an important step, as it ensures that there is continuity from one year's plan to the next.	Internal influences from different departments and functional areas of the organisation as they feed back on their experiences and observations from last year's plan.
Analysing customer satisfaction with the products and services received – problems and opportunities will be included in the plan.	Customer feedback and the views of those in the organisation who have close contact with customers (such as sales and marketing).
Setting the strategic direction of the organisation – this is a critical step, undertaken by the senior managers. It sets the tone for the planning process and gives everyone in the organisation a good idea of where the senior management sees the organisation heading.	Senior management (with reference to the wishes and priorities of the major stakeholders).
Assessing the organisation's internal environment – this means looking at human, physical, and financial resources and then drawing conclusions based on the analysis. Included is an assessment of the organisational culture, climate, and working conditions.	Various internal inputs from different parts of the organisation.
Assessing the organisation's external environment, including economic and social factors, financial or budgetary constraints, political and environmental considerations, and community or government regulations. The focus should be on identifying challenges from outside the organisation.	All external stakeholders that can exert an influence (or potential influence) on the organisation.
Determining the kinds of products and services that will be offered during the planning period and the levels at which those products must be provided. This forecasting activity involves projecting future market needs as well as internal performance targets, such as return on investment, productivity increases, or improved responsiveness to customers.	Input from various parts of the organisation including sales, marketing, production, distribution and accounts.
Determining the organisation's strengths, weaknesses, opportunities, and threats (SWOT).	Input from various parts of the organisation including sales, marketing, production, distribution and accounts.
Identifying and evaluating strategic aims. These goals should relate directly to the SWOT factors and concern a range of outcomes which the unit could move towards in order to fulfil its mission.	Management and senior management.
Developing operational plans to guide the implementation of the goals. These short- to intermediate-term objectives define the major results that must be accomplished for the organisation to move towards attaining the goal.	Operational plans from each major department or division of the organisation.
Evaluating progress and results against the objectives to determine the extent to which movement toward the goal has been realised. If problems are noted, adjustments can be made to action either the steps or the schedule.	Feedback and input from all parts of the organisation.

CASE STUDY BARNET'S CORPORATE PLAN

Building on its successes of the last five years, Barnet Council has risen to the challenges set by central Government, improving its 3* score in its assessment of the Council to a 4* score, despite much tougher inspection regimes. This means it is 'improving well' overall and that all its services have been recognised as 'good' by the Audit Commission. Most importantly, its residents agree – 72% surveyed think the Council is 'doing a good job' which is well above the London average.

This is a notable achievement in challenging times, but Barnet recognises that there is still more to be done. Central government has set out its expectations of local authorities for stronger communities and local and national prosperity. Through action at a local level, Barnet Council needs to continue to work with residents and businesses to sustain its success, and it has bold ambitions to develop the area further as an attractive and safe place to live and a vibrant and prosperous place to work and do business. This will involve working with central government and the private sector to develop innovative ways to raise the money to deliver the infrastructure required for growth, and keep the cost to communities as low as possible.

Question

Identify Barnet Council's likely stakeholders and their influences. *(12 marks)*

Approaches to planning

LEARNING
OBJECTIVES
▶ Corporate planning process
▶ Balanced scorecard
▶ Cost benefit analysis

Corporate planning process

As with any level of management, a planning process must be undertaken in order to outline, monitor, implement, continue to monitor and assess the outcomes of any plan. In order to do this, the senior management must first identify and agree both operational and financial performance levels. Typically, they will also identify when these particular performance levels should be reached. At corporate level, the planning process can be fairly complex; not only does it have to incorporate a series of both qualitative and quantitative objectives and measurements, but it also has to achieve the overall support of those within the organisation. While there is no definitive model of the corporate planning process, the conceptual model on the right indicates the series of steps that need to be taken in order to achieve a viable corporate level plan.

The business needs to formulate a plan that is in broad accord with its posture and position, otherwise it will be impossible for it to have any hope of achieving its performance objectives. The planning process should also indicate the journey the business is about to embark on, in order to achieve the objectives and its new posture and position in the future. None of this planning can take place without attention to the external environment. The business needs to analyse the environment and use this information as the basis for its forecasting. It is only

CONCEPTUAL MODEL OF THE PLANNING PROCESS

then that the business can begin to develop performance objectives and decide how those objectives will be achieved. In other words, the business must apply a series of rational criteria, linked to its current position and posture, in order to move forward.

The model for a planning process that incorporates issue management can be seen in the diagram below.

This model shows how the

business can at first recognise that a decision related to the overall plan has to be identified and then a decision taken on it. The issue cannot be advanced until there is a commitment by the organisation and a policy formulated in order to deal with it. Only at this point can that element of the plan be implemented.

If the policy implementation is satisfactory, then regular feedback and control may reveal new issues for which commitment and policy formulation need to be developed. The implementation policy is rarely a smooth process, and there may be a policy learning phase, where the business and its employees and management gradually incorporate the new policy into their day-to-day thinking. At this stage the detail of the plan can come into operation, with detailed procedures regarding the new policy. Eventually the policy will become integrated into the overall business operations. Again, regular feedback and control systems will identify new issues for which policy formulation and implementation will have to follow.

CONCEPTUAL PLANNING MODEL INCORPORATING ISSUE MANAGEMENT

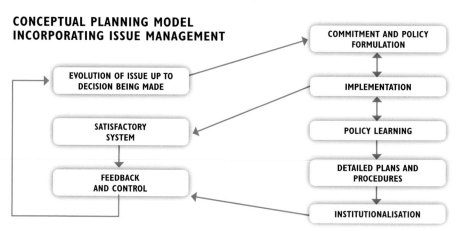

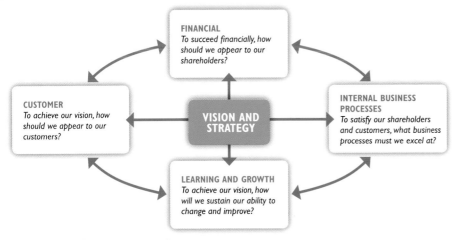

Balanced scorecard

The concept of the balanced scorecard was developed in the early 1990s by Robert Caplan and David Norton. Essentially, the balanced scorecard is a management system which enables organisations to clarify their vision and strategy and then translate them into actions. It provides feedback on both the internal business processes and external outcomes in order to facilitate continually improving strategic performance and results.

The balanced scorecard suggests that an organisation should develop metrics, collect data and then analyse it in relation to each of the four perspectives, which are:

- *Learning and growth perspective* – including employee training and corporate cultural attitudes related to both the individual and corporate self-improvement. Metrics are used here to help managers ascertain where training funds can be best deployed.
- *Business process perspective* – dealing with internal business processes. Metrics can be used to show how well the business is performing and whether the products and services match customer expectations.
- *Customer perspective* – focusing on customer satisfaction and analysing the different types of customer and the processes by which products and services are delivered.
- *Financial perspective* – recognising that timely and accurate data is of vital importance. Metrics include cost benefit analysis and financial risk assessment.

Cost benefit analysis

Cost benefit analysis is the technique that seeks to assess the value of the benefits of a particular course of action and then subtract any costs associated with it. The majority of benefits can be typified as those received over a period of time, while costs may either be one-off episodes or ongoing. In effect cost benefit analysis allows a business to work out a payback period for a particular course of action.

In its simplest form, cost benefit analysis could simply use financial costs and financial benefits. This would make it relatively easy for a business to assess and analyse the costs and benefits associated with any particular scheme. Restricting the analysis to purely financial terms does not mean that all costs and benefits have been assessed, as there may be human resource, environmental, production, or a host of other costs and benefits that have not been taken into the equation. Therefore, a more sophisticated approach to this form of analysis can attempt to put a financial value on what would be intangible costs and benefits – although this is notoriously subjective.

Cost benefit analysis can be a powerful tool, particularly if the intangible items are incorporated within the analysis.

CASE STUDY THE BALANCED SCORECARD – WHO'S DOING IT?

Increasingly, as balanced scorecard (BSC) concepts become more refined, the Balances Scorecard Institute has had more inquiries asking for examples of organisations that have implemented the BSC, and how the BSC applies to a particular business sector.

By 2004 about 57% of global companies were working with the balanced scorecard. Much of the information in the commercial sector is proprietary, because it relates to the strategies of specific companies. Public sector (government) organisations are usually not concerned with proprietary information, but also they may not have a mandate (or much funding) to post their management information on websites.

Source: adapted from the Balanced Scorecard Institute

Question

Using the case study, and Internet research, describe the nine stages or steps of the balanced scorecard process. *(18 marks)*

Assessing the value of corporate plans

LEARNING OBJECTIVES
▶ Value of corporate planning
▶ Risk management
▶ Environmental scanning

Value of corporate planning

The planning models used by many businesses are unable to stand up to current requirements as the basic conditions in the environment have changed. In particular, the annual budgeting process is time-consuming, costly in terms of resources, and ties management capacity, but is too rigid to allow rapid adjustments to be made. The planning data is often out-of-date even by the time budgeting has been completed.

In many cases there is a lack of orientation towards the organisation's corporate strategy and key targets. Sub-plans (such as sales, turnover, overheads, etc.) are not focused enough and are often not integrated to any real extent.

Planning instruments and tools barely meet the challenges of a complex and dynamic planning environment.

The figure above shows a more integrated approach to corporate planning. Note the sales and operational planning (S&OP) on the left-hand side. This is a key component of the planning process, and fundamental in driving the targets in the strategic growth plan.

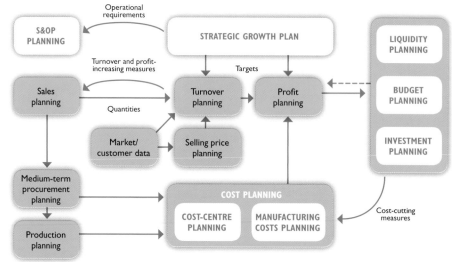

The key benefits of integrated corporate planning are:

- Increases in efficiency due to a reduction in duration and costs of planning processes.
- Increased flexibility by assessing the number of planning levels (no detailed budgets in all areas) and planning horizons (if necessary transition to rolling planning).
- Synergy effects due to uniform planning models that cross over functional and divisional boundaries.
- Decrease in manual planning and coordination effort by using

modern planning instruments (such as software applications).
- Illustrating the planning processes using standard software helps to exploit benefits e.g. high level of data integration and data consistency (for master data and transaction data) and maintainability of systems.

Risk management

One of the many advantages of carrying out corporate planning is that it enables the business to look at the possible risks that it might

1. STANDARD RISK MANAGEMENT MODEL

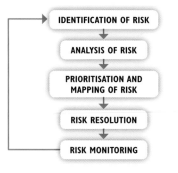

2. COMPLEX RISK MANAGEMENT MODEL

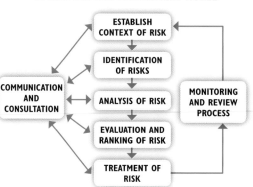

3. PROACTIVE RISK MANAGEMENT MODEL

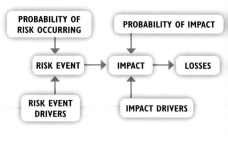

face, and assess their likely impacts. Risk management is an integral part of managerial responsibility. Risk management does not just apply to managers in senior positions, as it takes place on a daily basis at various levels of risk. There are no tried and trusted methodologies of risk management, but there have been several attempts to create a standard model (see diagram 1, opposite).

This is, however, a rather simplistic means of assessing risks and dealing with the risk management procedure, since it suggests that risks can be addressed one by one, when in fact risk management often involves dealing with several risks simultaneously. Therefore a more complex risk management model (diagram 2) may be employed.

Other businesses prefer to take a more proactive approach to risk management (diagram 3) and may evaluate the probability of risk and its

impacts prior to the risk even taking place or threatening to take place.

Environmental scanning

Environmental scanning is the process of monitoring and detecting external changes in the environment. In essence, environmental scanning can be seen as a way of identifying new, unexpected, major and minor possible impacts on the business. Environmental scanning, however, needs to be systematic for two main reasons. Firstly, indiscriminate collection of information is somewhat random and it may not be possible to identify the relevant from the irrelevant. Secondly, it provides early warnings for managers of changing external conditions in a measured and paced manner.

The key objectives of environmental scanning are:

- to detect scientific, technical, economic, social and political trends and events of importance.
- to define the potential threats, opportunities and changes implied by those trends and events.
- to promote future thinking in both management and staff.
- to alert the management of trends which are converging, diverging, speeding up, slowing down or interacting in some way.

At the heart of environmental scanning is the notion that decision-makers need to be aware of the environment in which they operate. In this respect environmental scanning provides the business with strategic intelligence, which can help to frame their organisational strategies. Environmental scanning should help a business to forecast in the light of the expectation of change.

CASE STUDY ST ALBANS

St Albans Council, like all local authorities, has a corporate plan. It is, however, externally and independently judged on its ability to meet its performance plan (which effectively details the targets it has set to achieve its overall plan). The independent review is of great value to the council and the local community in assessing the progress of projects and initiatives put forward by the council.

The assessors looked at the way the council is run as well as its performance in specific service areas. They were particularly interested in how well the council manages housing and public space functions. They looked at the standard of council-owned homes and the housing market generally, as

well as the environment, community safety, and work with young people. The assessors also used information such as performance indicators, and relied on the auditors' judgement and result of the benefits inspection to feed into the process.

The council was assessed under ten themes:

- ambition
- prioritisation
- focus
- capacity
- performance management
- achievement in quality of service
- achievement of improvement
- investment
- learning
- future plans.

Question

Suggest some of the criteria that could be used under each of the ten themes. (20 marks)

Contingency planning

LEARNING
OBJECTIVES
▶ What is contingency planning?
▶ Contingency planning process

What is contingency planning?

Contingency planning is a systematic approach to identifying what can possibly go wrong in a situation. Rather than hoping that everything will run smoothly at all times, an organisation should try to identify contingency events and be prepared with plans, strategies and approaches for avoiding, coping, or even exploiting them (as they may not be a disaster, they may be an opportunity).

Contingencies are relevant events anticipated by an organisation. These will include low-probability events that would have major impacts on the organisation. Contingency planning is essentially a skill to anticipate 'what ifs'. This is an important skill for organisations that operate in contested and competitive markets. The primary objective of contingency planning is not just to identify and develop a plan for every possible contingency, as that would be impossible and would represent a waste of time. Instead, the objective is to encourage the business to think about major contingencies and possible responses.

In practice, very few situations actually unfold according to the assumptions of a contingency plan. However, businesses that have given thought to contingencies and possible responses are more likely to meet their major goals and targets. The following questions can help a business develop contingency plans:

- What events might occur that require a response?

- What disasters might happen during execution of the plan?
- What is the worst-case scenario of events for the situation?
- What scenarios are possible for the situation?
- What event would cause the greatest disruption of current activities and plans?
- What happens if costs of the plan are excessive?
- What happens if delays occur?
- What happens if key people leave the organisation?
- What are the expected moves of antagonists and competitors?
- Who or what might impede implementation of the plan?

Contingency planning process

Contingency plans should be developed for every critical process or function. The business begins by reviewing all alternatives and identifying the best plan or alternative process for the situation. These plans will vary with each system, process and intended purpose. This generic outline will help the business visualise what a contingency plan should include and can serve as an outline for almost any process. Contingency plans can range from very simple to very complex. A business will design each plan based on its organisational needs:

- *Contingency plan title* – a descriptive title for the system or process that the contingency plan aims to address.
- *System mission description* – the basic functions and outputs of the system or process.

- *System specifics* – the detail of the system or process specifics.
- *Critical processes and outputs* – what the system does in terms of specific processes and outputs.
- *Key contact information* – lists personnel that have responsibility for the system or process.

The business will then address the main objectives of the contingency plan:

- *Risks of failure* – what is the risk of failure, and how would it impact the business?
- *Risk of contingency plan* – what are the risks involved with using the chosen contingency plan alternative, and how might it impact the business?
- *Desired outcomes* – what are the desired outcomes in terms of output and level of service, and how long does the business intend to operate under the contingency mode?
- *Potential impact* – what is the anticipated impact on the business or organisational unit in lower service or functional levels?

The next stage would be to identify the resource requirements of the plan:

- *Time estimates* – time required to implement the plan.
- *Cost estimates* – the plan's budget for the cost of equipment, supplies services, staff overtime, etc.
- *Source of funding* – where will the money come from?

Next, attention turns to implementing the plan:

- *Implementation criteria* – what will be the situation that prompts the decision to implement?

- *Trigger events* – what are the various scenarios that could lead to a trigger event?
- *Responsibilities* – who is responsible for making implementation decisions?
- *Duration* – what is the estimated length of time that contingency operations will cover?

The plan will then detail the operation and management of the contingency plan:

- Describe the management structure that will be used to ensure smooth operations.
- Who will be making the decisions to implement, change and discontinue the contingent operations?
- What support personnel will be used to implement and operate processes under the plan?
- Provide details on who will do what under the plan.

- Determine the teams that will be used to respond to emergencies or breakdowns.
- Detailed information on the team that will run the process or system.

The next stage is to outline the personnel and notification procedures:

- Describe how the business plans to notify staff that the plan is being implemented.
- Describe how the business plans to manage records issues.
- Describe the processes to be employed to ensure data security, recovery, integrity and confidentiality.

Assuming that the crisis is over, the plan then seeks to explain how things will be returned to normal:

- How the business will determine that it is time to discontinue the contingency mode and return to the normal operation mode.

- Describe the conditions or events that would lead to returning to normal operating mode.
- Describe the detailed procedures required to return to normal operating mode.
- List key personnel who have responsibility for returning the system or process to its normal operating mode.
- Who will be making the decisions to discontinue the contingent operations and begin the recovery process?
- List the key operational resource personnel needed to return to normal operations.
- Detailed information on the team that will run the process of resuming normal operations after the contingency period.
- List any business partner relationships (internal and external) that will be involved in resuming normal operations.

CASE STUDY FOOTBALL LICENSING CONTINGENCY PLANS

The 1985 European Cup Final was held at the Heysel stadium in Brussels. The ageing ground had been chosen as the venue for the final, despite misgivings from both Liverpool and Juventus. The Heysel disaster on 29 May 1985 led to the deaths of 39 supporters and a blanket ban of English clubs from European competition for five years.

At around 7pm local time, an hour before kick-off, trouble erupted between rival fans. A section of Liverpool fans stormed an area of Juventus fans, and as the Juventus fans tried to escape, a wall collapsed. Many fans were crushed, 39 Italian and Belgian fans died and hundreds were injured. The game went ahead to prevent further trouble, Juventus winning 1–0. The Heysel stadium continued to stage athletics events but no more football matches after the disaster. In 1995 the stadium was demolished and replaced with the King Baudouin Stadium built on the same site.

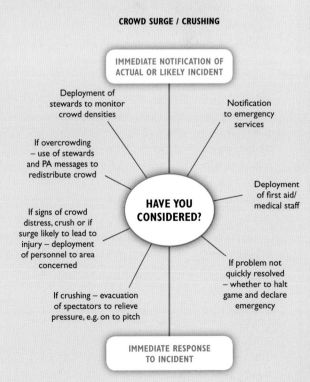

CROWD SURGE / CRUSHING

IMMEDIATE NOTIFICATION OF ACTUAL OR LIKELY INCIDENT

Deployment of stewards to monitor crowd densities

Notification to emergency services

If overcrowding – use of stewards and PA messages to redistribute crowd

HAVE YOU CONSIDERED?

Deployment of first aid/ medical staff

If signs of crowd distress, crush or if surge likely to lead to injury – deployment of personnel to area concerned

If problem not quickly resolved – whether to halt game and declare emergency

If crushing – evacuation of spectators to relieve pressure, e.g. on to pitch

IMMEDIATE RESPONSE TO INCIDENT

Questions

1 What other contingency plans, such as the crowd-surge contingency plan, could be prepared by a football club? *(8 marks)*

2 Suggest the contents of a contingency plan for crowd trouble. *(8 marks)*

Source: adapted from the Football Licensing Authority and the BBC

Case studies, questions and exam practice

CASE STUDY UNIVERSITY OF SOUTH AUSTRALIA

The provision of high-quality Higher Education by Australian universities is being undertaken in a climate of challenge and change. New opportunities and threats are constantly emerging to which the University of South Australia (UniSA) must react quickly, carefully and decisively. The corporate plan provides the specific organisational strategies and objectives for the pursuit of the university's aspirations – detailed in UniSA's statement of strategic intent.

The process is designed to:

- involve and engage staff, stakeholders and the community in the shared vision
- reflect on performances and position
- enhance understanding of current and future operational environment
- identify strengths and weaknesses
- facilitate innovation and improvement, and
- commit the university to action.

At an individual level, feedback and commitment is encouraged through performance management. Performance management plans are aligned to the goals and objectives – the medium-term strategic plans (MTSPs) – of the individual's work area (e.g. a division, school, institute or unit). Note: Sometimes, for large work areas, these are facilitated by team plans/operational plans. Work areas review their performance on at least an annual basis and summarise their findings in their annual review report.

Source: adapted from the University of South Australia

Undertaken by corporate planning group
- Scans competitive environment to benchmark current performance and consider implications of change in the environment
- Consider priorities in relation to university-wide plan: *equity strategic plan; teaching and learning strategy; international strategic plan; indigenous education strategy; research and research education management plan*
- Consider and synthesise information from local *medium-term strategic plans and medium-term financial plans*
- Formulate plans for the medium term to achieve:
  - university-wide priorities for teaching and learning; research, research education and commercialisation; and people and services
  - priority projects

CORPORATE PLAN AND BUDGET

CORPORATE PLANNING AND BUDGETING PROCESS

LOCAL A

LOCAL MEDIUM-TER STRATEGIC PLANS AND MEDIUM-TERM FINANCIAL PLANS

IMPLEMENTATION

LOCAL LEVEL REVIEW PROCESS

LOCAL REVIEW REPORTS

Undertaken by schools, divisions, institutes, units
- Review financial performance and achievements against plans
- Review quality of coursework programs and research degrees, and outcomes of other quality reviews
- Assess risk profile and opportunities
- Identify major achievements and areas for improvement
- Develop *Review* reports

CORPORATE REVIEW PROCESS

CORPORATE REVIEW REPORT

Undertaken by corporate planning group
- Scans competitive environment to benchmark current performance and consider implications of change in the environment
- Consider division, institute, unit review reports, discuss issues with division and unit executives, teaching and learning committee, research policy committee, research degrees committee
- Evaluate performance against key performance indicators, achievements against priorities and review financial performance
- Review implications of performance, identify areas for improvement in the medium term, including:
  - university-wide priorities for teaching and learning; research, research education and commercialisation; and people and services
  - priority projects

REVIEW AND PLANNING INFORMED BY:

- Statement of strategic intent
- UniSA 2010
- Environmental scan
- Risk register
- Academic profile 2010–2015, *Towards a teaching and learning framework 2010–2015*

LOCAL PLANNING PROCESS

Undertaken by schools, divisions, institutes, units
- Revise local statement of strategic intent
- Plan contribution to achievement of corporate priority projects and to supporting teaching and learning; research, research education and commercialisation; people and services
- Access contribution to corporate key performance indicators
- Develop *medium-term strategic plans*
- Develop *medium-term financial plans*

Questions

Why might the university carry out environmental scanning?
(12 marks)

The meaning of leadership

LEARNING
OBJECTIVES

▶ What is a leader?
▶ What is a manager?
▶ What is the difference?
▶ Turning a manager into a leader

What is a leader?

There are leaders and there are managers. Some leaders are managers and some managers are leaders. Leadership requires the creation of new systems and vision to see something new and means being prepared to take calculated risks. It also means looking beyond the status quo, something a manager tends not to do.

Managers need to 'think outside the box', which means looking for better and more efficient ways of doing things. It might mean the creation of dynamic teams and the ability to accomplish goals. Leaders aim to inspire, to strip out layers of management that can stifle an organisation, shifting responsibility, forcing out non-producers and rewarding those who do produce.

Leaders tend to understand the value of self-management and self-motivation; above all they understand the importance of empowerment.

What is a manager?

Being a manager means being an individual whose principal employment responsibilities consist of supervising or directing (or both supervising *and* directing) human or other resources, and a person employed in an executive capacity. This does not really tell us that much, but it aims to give a comprehensive view of the range of work that a manager might do.

What does it tell us about being a manager? When we consider the term, we might think about football managers and what they do. A football manager supervises and directs, and looks after human and other resources. However, in this example, the term is blurred. What is a coach and what is a director of football? Are they managers? A coach would have responsibilities solely related to the training of the players while a director of football would manage and control expenditure and resources, not just the squad.

A manager is someone who oversees one or more employees or departments to ensure they carry out assigned duties as required. Depending on the size of the business there might be a single, dual or triple management layer involved. In bigger organisations, there could be even more. In large organisations, management is usually divided into three tiers: upper or senior management, middle management and lower management. Lower management includes managers who operate at basic functional level. Mid-level management oversees lower management and generates reports for senior management. Senior or upper management commonly consists of a board of directors or owners of the business responsible for making key decisions that affect the company.

Manager	Leader
Managers have employees	Leaders have followers
Managers only maintain command and control, many times to excess, thereby demotivating employees.	Leaders empower and inspire their followers.
Managers want stability	Leaders want flexibility
Managers follow a course and expect their employees to follow rules and procedures to deal with situations	Leaders set the course, inspiring their followers to solve their own problems and make their own decisions
Managers make decisions, solve problems as they arise, and give orders.	Leaders teach their followers to be leaders in their own right and to better themselves, their organisations, and those around them
A manager accepts the organisation's make-up and culture and does what she can to cement the company's status quo	Leaders are always looking for better and more efficient ways of doing things

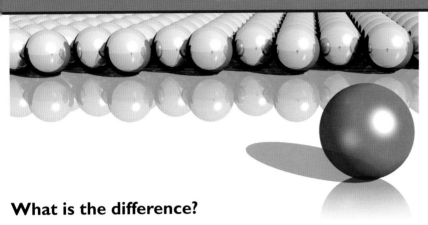

What is the difference?

It may appear that the words manager and leader are at opposite ends of a continuum. We can accept the fact that the term manager often refers to the more controlled, analytical, structured and rule-bound end of the continuum. The term leader brings with it the concepts of being visionary, unstructured, flexible, passionate and experimental.

The truth is that managers and leaders are different both internally and externally. Both see work and the success of the organisation as being important; however they treat people in different ways and respond to things in different ways. Both allow employees to have their own focus, but they also limit employees in different ways. Some of the differences can be put down to the organisational culture and the reactions from the employees that are actually being managed or led.

Leaders generally display the ability to inspire, engage and satisfy their followers in situations where there is conflict, competition or change. Their followers take on a shared vision. Leaders have to have values that they understand as well as their followers. For leaders,

value-based activity is the basis for commitment. While a manger may rely on the mind and muscles of their employees, a leader not only engages their followers but also instils purpose.

Leadership style is the pattern of influence used by leaders. The first element of this is the creation of directive behaviours such as:

- goal setting
- planning in advance
- defining timelines and deadlines
- specifying priorities
- establishing ways of evaluating progress and contribution
- defining roles and establishing who has authority to make decisions
- illustrating how outcomes can be accomplished.

A leader also has to create a series of supportive behaviours, on both a group and individual basis, including:

- listening skills
- praise and encouragement
- seeking ideas and input
- sharing information
- assisting others to problem solve
- providing a rationale for actions.

Turning a manager into a leader

In order to be transformed from a manager into a leader, an individual needs to have a great deal of character and many qualities beyond simple management skills. Good leaders share many of the same characteristics and qualities. The following attributes are essential:

- vision and the ability to communicate this to others
- effective communication (as important as the vision)
- integrity and being more concerned with doing the right thing than what is expedient.

This may suggest that leaders are born and not made, but a manager can become a leader if they can acquire and believe in the essential skills required. They need to let those around them realise that they feel a commitment to the employees as well as the organisation itself. Equally essential is for employees to trust the manager; this will need to be earned by actions and not demanded. A leader will show loyalty to their employees and in return the employees will be loyal to them.

> ### Question
>
> Distinguish between a manager and a leader. *(18 marks)*

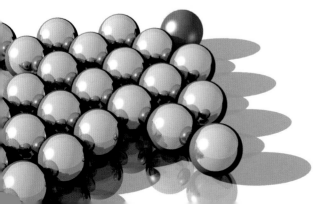

The range of leadership styles

LEARNING
OBJECTIVES

▶ Douglas McGregor
▶ Rensis Likert
▶ Tom Peters
▶ Blake and Mouton

Douglas McGregor (1906–64)

McGregor was a management consultant theorist and a social psychologist. He formulated two models that he called Theory X and Theory Y.

Theory X assumes that the average human has an inherent dislike of work and will do all that is necessary to avoid it. This assumes the following:

- Because people dislike work they have to be controlled by management and often threatened in order to work hard.
- Most people avoid responsibility, need to be directed by management but seek security within work as a primary concern.
- Managers who adhere to the Theory X approach rarely give their subordinates any opportunity to show traits other than those associated with Theory X.

Theory X has given rise to what is often known as tough or hard management, typified by tight control and punishment. Soft management adopts the alternative view, which aims to create a degree of harmony in the workplace.

Theory Y assumes the following:

- Most people expend the same amount of energy or effort at work as in other spheres of their lives.

- If the individual is committed, or encouraged to be committed, to the aims of the organisation in which they work, they will be self-directing.
- Job satisfaction is the key to involving and engaging the individual and ensuring their commitment.
- An average individual, provided they are given the opportunity and encouragement, will naturally seek responsibility.
- In ensuring commitment and responsibility, employees will be able to use their imagination, ingenuity and creativity to solve work problems with less direct supervision.

Managers following Theory Y are often seen to be using soft management, and the intellectual potential of employees is vital to the success of the business. In many cases it is argued that businesses ignore the Theory Y benefits and under-utilise their employees.

McGregor saw his two theories as being very different attitudes. He believed that it was difficult to use Theory Y for large-scale operations, particularly those involved in mass production. It was an ideal choice for the management of professionals. For McGregor, Theory Y was essential in helping to encourage participative problem-solving and the development of effective management.

Rensis Likert (1903–81)

Likert was a management theorist concerned with human behaviour within organisations. He examined different types of organisation and styles of leadership. At the heart of his theories was the belief that an organisation needed to make optimum use of its human assets in order to achieve maximum profitability via good labour relations and high productivity. Likert believed that the workforce should be organised into work groups supported by other similarly effective groups. He identified four different types of management style:

- *Exploitative/authoritative* – where decisions are made by the management alone and motivation is ensured by threats. Higher-level management has the bulk of the responsibilities while lower-level management has little responsibility other than day-to-day operations. The system is characterised by having poor upward communication and downward communication, as well as the absence of teamwork.
- *Benevolent/authoritative* – this is essentially a master-and-servant relationship between the management and employees. It is on this basis that trust is maintained and motivation is assured through rewards. Management is made to feel responsible for its employees, but there is little communication up and down the organisation, and little developed teamwork.

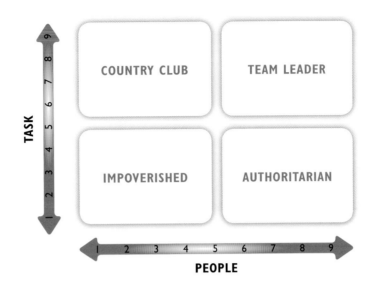

- *Consultative* – this system shows that management has a degree of trust in its employees, but not a total belief in their abilities or ideas. Motivation is achieved through reward and the opportunity to be involved, at least partially, in the decision-making. Higher management is primarily responsible for achieving organisational goals. Horizontal communication and vertical communication, as well as teamwork are used moderately.

- *Participative group system* – this illustrates circumstances where managers have confidence in their subordinates. Motivation is based on economic rewards, firmly based on goals that have been set in participation. All personnel have a responsibility to achieve the organisational goals. As a consequence, all forms of communication are high and cooperative teamwork is encouraged. This is the system that Likert believed ideal in order to ensure profit and concern for employees.

Tom Peters

Although Tom Peters has written extensively on broader issues regarding the success of businesses, his central message is the use of leadership, or rather the habits of leaders. He prefers to use term leadership rather than management, as he suggests that a manager should focus on leadership qualities, specifically motivating and facilitating their employees. He therefore places leadership at the centre of all aspects of the business, including creating new ideas through innovation, satisfying customers and, above all, deploying people (employees) in the most effective manner.

Blake and Mouton

Robert Blake and Jane Mouton developed a grid that provides an opportunity to identify styles adopted by managers in specific situations. By completing a questionnaire, the individual tallies its people or task-related scores and then cross-references them to discover to what degree they accord with the four broad types of manager identified on the grid.

The Country Club manager is typified by an individual who tries to avoid problems and considers productivity to be subservient to staff contentment. Anything that disturbs the balance is avoided.

A team leader or manager manages to maintain a high simultaneous concern for both productivity and employees. The focus is upon providing the employees with the means by which they can achieve organisational objectives. Employees are encouraged to participate, state their opinions, not avoid conflict and approach all working relationships with honesty.

An impoverished manager is not interested in either productivity or employee relations. The manager does not encourage creativity or initiative, seeks to avoid conflict and does not seem to wish to contribute. This is an individual who is just concerned with survival.

An authoritarian is, essentially, a task-orientated autocrat who shows little concern for employees. All issues are subservient to productivity, conflict is suppressed and social aspects of work discouraged.

At the very centre of the grid is a mid-point which illustrates that managers could, at various times, adopt the characteristics of any of the four categories. Typically, this point describes the manager as being 'middle of the road' where there is equal concern for productivity and for employees. Conflicts usually end in compromise and creativity is encouraged, provided it is not too revolutionary.

> ### Question
>
> How might management theory help us understand the skills needed as a manager? *(18 marks)*

Transformational leadership

LEARNING OBJECTIVES

▶ Transformational leadership
▶ Action-centred leadership
▶ Fielder's contingency model

Transformational leadership

James MacGregor Burns' concept of 'transforming leadership' stated:

'Leadership is the relationship of mutual stimulation and elevation that converts followers into leaders and may convert leaders into moral agents. It occurs when one or more persons engage with others in such a way that leaders and followers raise one another to higher levels of motivation or morality.'

Transformational leadership is about the ability of the leader to motivate and empower their followers as Bass and Avolio noted in 1994:

'The goal of transformational leadership is to 'transform' people and organisations in a literal sense – to change them in mind and heart; enlarge vision, insight, and understanding; clarify purposes; make behaviour congruent with beliefs, principles, or values; and bring about changes that are permanent, self-perpetuating, and momentum building.'

You will discover that transformational leadership is often contrasted with transactional leadership. Transactional leadership focuses on gaining the commitment of others on the basis of the exchange of pay, benefits and security in return for a reliable and consistent level of work.

In order to understand what transformational leadership is we must appreciate that it is a process which aims to change and transform

1. TRANSFORMATIONAL V TRANSACTIONAL LEADERSHIP

TRANSACTIONAL
• Reward for effort
• Recognises basic subordinate needs
• Clarifies expected outcome
• Clarifies roles
• Gives sufficient confidence
• Goals may not be questioned
• Role authority
• Tasks and process focus

CHARISMA (INTERCONCEPT)
• Self-understanding
• Awareness of others
• Excitement, optimism
• Vision building
• Personal esteem
• Sense of mission

INSPIRATION (OUTER CONCEPT)
• Giving purpose
• Communicating high expectations
• Focus on key activities
• Uses simple, open communication

INDIVIDUAL CONSIDERATION AND CONFIDENCE
• Identifying individual requirements
• Giving personal attention
• Giving responsibility
• Instilling pride, respect, independence and trust

INTELLECTUAL STIMULATIONS
• Generating challenge in others
• Stimulating new ways

individuals. Transformational leadership means having the ability to get people to want to change, to improve themselves and to be led. It involves assessing their motives and needs, and valuing them.

There are four key factors in transformational leadership (often referred to as the Four Is). These are: idealised influence, inspirational motivation, intellectual stimulation and individual consideration. The importance of each of these factors is outlined in the table below.

Effective transformational leadership should result in performance that exceeds organisational expectations. There is what is called an additive effect of transformational leadership because managers need to bring together various components to reach this performance beyond expectations, as seen in diagram 2 opposite.

Each of the four components describes the characteristics that are essential to the transformation process. If a manager is a strong

Factor	Explanation
Idealised influence	This describes managers who are exemplary role models. Managers with idealised influence can be trusted and respected by others to make good decisions for the organisation
Inspirational motivation	This describes managers who motivate others to commit to the vision of the organisation. Managers with inspirational motivation encourage team spirit to reach goals of increased revenue and market growth for the organisation
Intellectual Stimulation	This describes managers who encourage innovation and creativity through challenging the normal beliefs or views of a group. Managers with intellectual stimulation promote critical thinking and problem-solving to make the organisation better
Individual consideration	This describes managers who act as coaches and advisors to others. Managers with individual consideration encourage others to reach goals that help both the associates and the organisation

2. ADDITIVE EFFECT OF TRANSFORMATIONAL LEADERSHIP

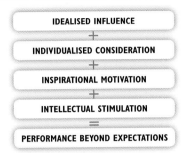

IDEALISED INFLUENCE
+
INDIVIDUALISED CONSIDERATION
+
INSPIRATIONAL MOTIVATION
+
INTELLECTUAL STIMULATION
=
PERFORMANCE BEYOND EXPECTATIONS

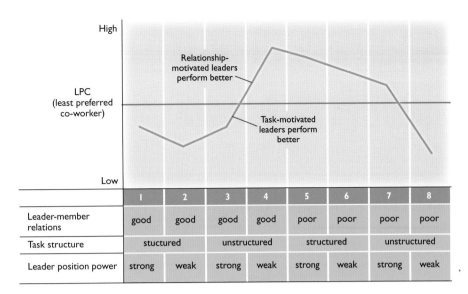

	1	2	3	4	5	6	7	8
Leader-member relations	good	good	good	good	poor	poor	poor	poor
Task structure	stuctured		unstructured		structured		unstructured	
Leader position power	strong	weak	strong	weak	strong	weak	strong	weak

role model, an encourager, an innovator and a coach, they are making use of the Four Is to help transform their employees into better, more productive and more successful individuals. However, with any theory, there are strengths and weaknesses:

- Strengths are widely researched (using well-known leaders). They effectively influence others on all levels (from one-on-one to the whole organisation), and strongly emphasise others' needs and values.
- Weaknesses have many components that seem too broad, they treat leadership more as a personality trait than as a learned behaviour, and have the potential for abusing power.

Because the theory of transformational leadership is broad, there are no specific steps that a manager has to follow, but it should be noted that transformational leadership is a process. It needs to be applied with conscious effort by the manager who needs to adopt the transformational style. In understanding the basics of transformational leadership and the Four Is, the manager can begin to apply this approach. The manager either has to already have, or be prepared to show, the following qualities:

- The ability to empower followers to do what is best for the organisation.
- The strength to act as a role model with high values.
- The ability to listen to all viewpoints to develop a spirit of cooperation.
- The ability to create a vision, using people in the organisation.

- The ability to act as a change agent within the organisation by setting an example of how to initiate and implement change
- The ability to assist the organisation by helping others contribute to the organisation.

Action-centred leadership

John Adair proposed a model that argued that it is not who you are but what you do that marks you out as a leader. In his view, a leader needs to balance the needs of the task, the team and the individual. This is shown in a version of his diagram (*below*) that uses three circles. As far as Adair was concerned, an effective leader carries out the functions and demonstrates the behaviours appropriate to the circles. They also have the capacity to vary the level according to the needs of the situation. A leader has to balance the three circles, sitting in a helicopter above the process, ensuring the best possible overview of what is taking place.

TASK

TEAM   INDIVIDUAL

Fielder's contingency model

In Fielder's model, leadership is effective when the leader's style is appropriate to the situation, as determined by three key factors:

1 *Leader-member relations* – the nature of the interpersonal relationship between leader and follower, expressed in terms of good through to poor, with qualifying modifiers attached as necessary. A leader's personality and the personalities of subordinates play important roles in this variable.
2 *Task structure* – the nature of the subordinate's task, described as structured or unstructured, associated with the amount of creative freedom allowed for the subordinate to accomplish the task, and how the task is defined.
3 *Position power* – the degree to which the position itself enables the leader to get the group members to comply with and accept their direction and leadership.

Question

Compare and contrast the theories of transformational leadership and action-centred leadership. (*12 marks*)

273

Factors influencing leadership style

LEARNING OBJECTIVES

▶ Determinants of leadership style approach
▶ Cognitive choice
▶ Personality
▶ Self-concept and sources of motivation
▶ Role expectations
▶ Reinforcement: social learning
▶ Performance pressures

Determinants of leadership style approach

Leadership style is most often viewed as a dependent variable, where the focus is on how leadership style influences individual behaviour and attitudes, and group or organisational performance. However, the determinants of the leadership-style approach examine the factors influencing a given leader's dominant style or how it is developed. On this spread we will look at the various ways in which a manager can arrive at a particular leadership style.

Cognitive choice

This is based on the assumption that managers will deliberately choose a style of leadership that will aim to maximise an individual or group performance. It is seen to be the most rational of approaches as it suggests that a manager looks at the task, subordinates and environment and then decides which leadership style is most appropriate to get the job done.

Typically, the following theoretical approaches apply to this explanation:

- Expectancy theory – make the effort and it will lead to good performance
- Theories by Vroom, Yetton and Jago support the choice process
- Klein's control theory can also be applied.

INTERNET RESEARCH

Find out more about Vroom, Yetton and Jago by carrying out a simple Internet search on their theories.

Personality

This approach suggests that the leadership style adopted by an individual leader is more an extension of their personality, than a result of the situation in which they operate. The Myers-Briggs Type Inventory (MBTI) is one approach that links a leader's cognitive style to their leadership style.

The MBTI is an instrument that attempts to measure cognitive style. It has strong validity and reliability measures, but its accuracy is very dependent on the honesty of the individual completing the test that provides the basis of the analysis. Cognitive style, as a variable, measures the strength of an individual's preference for the manner in which they process information.

INTERNET RESEARCH

Try the personality test out yourself and find out what kind of leader you are at www.personalitytype.com/quiz.html.

Self-concept and sources of motivation

This approach suggests that an individual's dominant source of motivation plays an important role in determining their leadership style. Central to this is the concept of social identity. This means that the role of leader is viewed as a role-specific social identity that has associated traits, competences and values (known as TCVs).

It could be applied in the following way:

- Instrumental leaders see the organisation as an exchange system (similar to an employee in the transactional theory). The leader bases their actions on seeking extrinsic rewards (pay and promotion). Their interest in group performance increases when pay, promotion and performance appraisal are directly linked to group performance.
- A leader dominated by self-concept external motivation is interpersonally based. The leader uses interpersonal techniques to influence others. They are dominated by receiving praise and acknowledgement on the basis that group success is as a result of their efforts and skills. These leaders tend to keep much of the praise and credit to themselves.
- A leader that is self-concept internally motivated will focus on achievement and self affirmation of their internal set of standards and goals. They will attribute success to their activities, and are happy for others in the group to take the credit for success; they do not seek public recognition themselves.
- Leaders who internalise the goals of the group are better placed to accept ideas and to give credit to group members. They are interested in accomplishing goals, regardless of pay, promotion, status and recognition.

| Sources of motivation | Motivational driver | Motivational inducement systems | | | |
| | | Reward system | Leadership style | Task system | Social system |
Conditions for motivation		Pay and promotion	style	Job design	Culture
Intrinsic	Enjoyment		Laissez-faire leadership	Job rotation	Social activities
Process					Quality of work/ life programmes
Enjoyment					
Instrumental Increase in pay and/or promotion is linked to high performance	Increases in pay and promotion	Merit pay commissions			
		Incentive pay-gain sharing			
		Profit sharing bonuses			
		Promotion			
Self-concept: external Increased status, recognition and external validation are associated with high performance	Group acceptance	Promotion	Recognition	Job enlargement	Peer recognition
	Individual worth		Empowerment		Customer recognition
	Group status		Positive reinforcement		Team building
	Group influence				
Self-concept: internal Skills, abilities and values are validated through high performance	Achievement		Empowerment	Job enrichment	
	Validation of competencies		Participation in problem-solving	Knowledge of results	
			Linking skills to mission		
Goal identification High performance is essential in the accomplishment of key goals or benefits to others	Accomplishment		Vision creation	Alignment activities	
			Goal-setting	Knowledge of results	
			Empowerment in mission development		

Role expectations

Theorists who suggest this approach argue that social systems set and communicate particular role expectations of leaders. Individuals in a leadership role will enact these expectations, with the expectations being learned either directly or indirectly:

- Direct learning takes place through a process of application, feedback and reinforcement. When a leader achieves success with a particular leadership style, they will 'save' that style and use it again and again without really questioning whether it is still working.
- Indirect learning takes place through social learning, where the leader copies the style that has been adopted (and seen to work), by other leaders.

Returning to the MBTI approach, 'judging' leaders are more likely to adopt role expectation approaches. The attribution model of leadership suggests that leaders look at what they consider to be successful organisations and they attribute that success to the leaders of that organisation. They then look for traits and behaviours used by those leaders and use them as a role model.

Reinforcement: social learning

Using this approach, it is argued that the style used by a leader is a function of the feedback and reinforcement received from three important elements of the leader's role set:

- their subordinates
- their peers
- their own managers

Performance pressures

The performance pressure approach argues that leaders respond to two fundamental pressures facing a work group:

- The pressure for task accomplishment – when this is strongest, leaders tend to use task styles.
- The pressure for group maintenance, membership and relationship building – when this is strongest, leaders tend to use socio-emotional styles.

> ### Question
> To what extent can theory explain the factors that might influence leadership style?
> *(18 marks)*

Role of leadership in managing change and achieving success

Change management

There are many theories regarding change management. Many of these focus upon the way in which a business thinks about change and the way it drives change. As there are a number of different theories, it is, perhaps, prudent to focus on just some of the ways in which change management can be achieved. Although change may not necessarily be driven by a human resources department, it is often the role of the department to manage the intricacies and complications arising out of change. There are innumerable theories on not only how change impacts on individuals and groups within a business, but also the ideal ways of managing that change.

Stace and Dunphy took the view that change management could be packaged in terms of its size and complexity and then organised accordingly (*see diagram 1 below*).

Costello's approach sought to set the parameters purely by the size and scope of the change being envisioned and then to suggest strategies by which the change could be facilitated (*diagram 2*).

Bate, on the other hand, considered the whole process of change to be a cycle which had clearly identifiable phases (*diagram 3*).

Julie Hay's theory

Julie Hay's approach used Transactional Analysis (TA) to understand how change could be managed by considering three sets of seven inter-related aspects. Her three areas of concern were:

- individuals' responses to change
- needs of an individual going through change
- the seven acts of management to meet the seven stages of change and the needs of employees.

Julie Hay's theory, often referred to as the 'seven, seven and seven approach' is summarised in the table on the right.

1. STACE AND DUNPHY

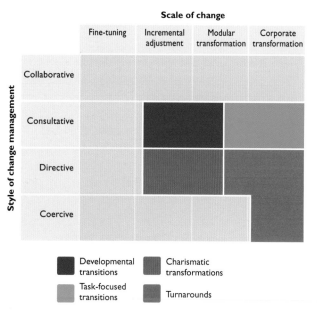

2. COSTELLO

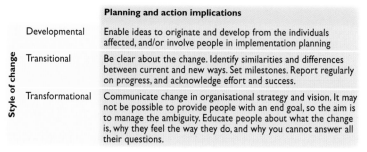

3. BATE

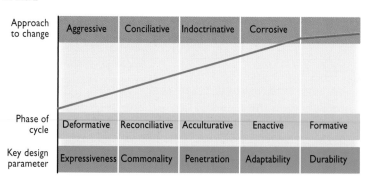

Kurt Lewin's theory

Kurt Lewin, in the 1950s, identified three stages that individuals, groups or organisations pass through when dealing with change:

- *Unfreezing* – management and Human Resources make it clear to employees that a change is required in the business. Employees are consulted, changes are planned and organised, and schedules and appropriate training arranged.
- *Changing* – the implementation of the change that rests on the flexibility of the planning process and steps taken during the unfreezing stage.
- *Refreezing* – once the change has been implemented, an assessment needs to be made of how effective and satisfactory the change has been. Whatever the new systems or procedures that have been put in place, these are effectively the new ways of doing things and should now be accepted by the employees and the organisation as a whole.

Understanding the leadership of change

Throughout periods of changes, leaders need to move people from change avoidance to change acceptance. There are five steps accompanying change (Conner, 1993):

- *Denial* – cannot foresee any major changes
- *Anger* – at others for what they're putting me through
- *Bargaining* – work out solutions, keep everyone happy
- *Depression* – is it worth it? doubt, need for support
- *Acceptance* – the reality

Diagram 1 (*below right*) illustrates the process that takes place when change is negatively perceived. This is potentially damaging and disruptive for an organisation.

As an alternative, positively perceived change is both a shorter and a much less disruptive process for the organisation, as can be seen in diagram 2.

By changing their employees'

attitude from avoidance into acceptance, leaders can help the change process. To bring about this change of attitude it is necessary to move:

- from *'Why?'* to *'What new opportunities will this provide?'* – focus on the benefits that the change will provide them and the organisation
- from *'How will this affect me?'* to *'What problems will this solve?'* – anything that prevents something from being better is a problem
- from *'We do not do it this way'* to *'What would it look like?'* – provide plenty of explanations
- from *'When will this change be over so we can get back to work?'* to *'What can I do to help?'* – employees to become involved in implementing the change
- from *'Who is doing this to us?'* to *'Who can help us?'* – focus on the challenges that must be overcome.

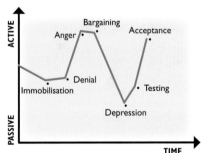

I. NEGATIVELY PERCEIVED CHANGE

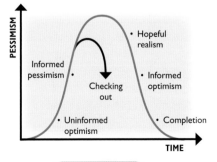

2. POSITIVELY PERCEIVED CHANGE

Criteria	Responses	Needs	Management
Immobilisation	Shock. Individual does nothing.	Seeks reassurance.	Make information available and give employees time and space.
Denial	Acting as if nothing is happening.	Needs the organisation to show patience.	Listen and recognise that this is the most difficult stage.
Frustration	Blame others for changes. Internal fighting between colleagues.	Needs the organisation to recognise that this is normal and needs space and time.	Tolerate and accept that anger is directed towards management.
Acceptance	Realisation that the past is gone and positively considering the future.	Needs help to redefine their new position.	Offer advice and be employee-focused.
Development	Gradual acquisition of new knowledge and skills.	Requires training and coaching and possibly a role model.	Offer more advice and provide training and coaching when needed.
Application	Realisation of where the individual fits in.	Needs positive encouragement and a means of monitoring their progress.	Encourage.
Completion	Now settled and competent without considering the past.	Contentment and a strong advocate of the change.	Continue to encourage and help develop.

> **Question**
>
> How might theories of change help us understand a leader's role in managing change and ensuring the success of an organisation? *(18 marks)*

Assessing the importance of leadership

LEARNING OBJECTIVES

▶ Why leadership is important
▶ The meaning of leadership
▶ The work of the leader
▶ Visionary leadership
▶ Leaders versus administrators and managers
▶ The nature of leadership

Why leadership is important

Without leadership, organisations move slowly and can stagnate and lose their way. Most theories of leadership tend to focus on the decision-making abilities of leadership, but this is too narrow an approach. The assumption is that decision-making is always timely, correct and complete. Yet a decision itself actually changes nothing – the challenge is to implement that decision, and that is the role of the leader. Leaders have to be able to influence behaviour, change the course of the organisation, and overcome resistance to change. Investors recognise the importance of good leadership and the fact that a good leader can make a success from a poor business plan, while a poor leader can make a mess of the best business plan.

The meaning of leadership

Leadership is the process by which one individual influences the thoughts, attitudes and behaviours of others. Leaders set a direction, help the organisation see what lies ahead, help it visualise what might be achieved, and encourage and inspire. Without leadership an organisation will quickly degenerate into argument and conflict, because people see things in different ways and lean toward different solutions. Leadership helps to ensure that everyone pulls in the same direction and harnesses their efforts. Leadership is the ability to get other people to do something significant that they might not otherwise have done.

The work of the leader

Taking a leadership position means several things: A leader must have a vision of the future of the organisation and its members. As we have seen, being a leader means:

- having a vision about what could be achieved
- making a commitment to the mission and to those being led
- taking responsibility for the accomplishment of the mission and the welfare of those being led
- assuming the risk of loss and failure
- accepting the recognition for successes.

A leader must be able to express their vision clearly and in a compelling manner so that others are engaged by it. People will judge a leader by their commitment and will not commit themselves beyond the commitment of the leader. The leader will have to assume a considerable amount of responsibility, not just for the goals at hand, but to urge others to accept responsibility themselves.

A leader also has to assume risk, as without risk there is little need for leadership. The risk is that some people will try to avoid making decisions that could lead to failure. Leaders need to accept that risk and gain the commitment of others to help ensure that the risk is offset by positive and meaningful actions.

Leadership is often associated with high levels of authority – in other words, the senior management (or those in higher positions in the hierarchy) have considerable influence over others in the organisation. The assumption is that authority requires a degree of leadership – the higher the position and the more authority, the greater the leadership skills expected. The challenge for individuals in this situation is to get others to take decisions that could involve a degree of risk.

Visionary leadership

A visionary leader needs to create a vision, a mission and a strategy. They then have to communicate these aspects to others and convince them to 'buy into' the vision. In organisations, this is essential to ensure that the business continues to grow, evolve and adapt to changing circumstances and environments. A leader has to provide a mission statement – a clear indication of what needs to be done. They need to provide a strategy or a path, which maps out how to accomplish the mission and achieve the vision. This needs to show clearly how the group or organisation will get there. A leader has to clearly communicate these aspects as they are crucial to motivating action. A vision cannot be rigid; it needs to have the capacity to adapt. If it does not have this capacity, it will quickly become obsolete and lose the power to excite and motivate others.

Leaders versus administrators and managers

Leadership is not the same as having a position of authority. It is possible to have a position of authority and not be a leader. Usually this means being more of an administrator than a leader. Administrators can be very effective, but essentially they are bureaucrats dealing with rules, regulations and their enforcement. An effective organisation has to be led and administered, but being an administrator is not the same as being a manager. Management, as we have seen, has a distinct set of skills. We can therefore suggest that a truly effective organisation has to have leaders, managers and administrators.

BOOK RESEARCH

Rich Teerlink and Lee Ozley, *More Than a Motorcycle: The Leadership Journey at Harley-Davidson*, Boston: Harvard Business School Press, 2000.

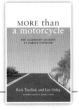

The nature of leadership

Leadership is complex; many leaders confuse personal style and positions of authority with leadership. The following can be said of leadership:

- Leadership is not primarily a particular personality trait. A trait that is closely linked to leadership is charisma, but many people who have charisma are not leaders.
- Leadership is not primarily a set of important objectives. It involves getting things done.
- Leadership is not primarily a formal position. There have been great leaders who did not hold high positions (for example, Martin Luther King, Jr.), and there are those who hold high positions who are not leaders at all, but perhaps administrators.
- Leadership is not primarily a set of behaviours. Many leadership theories suggest that what actually makes a leader are qualities such as delegating and providing inspiration and vision. However, people who are not leaders can often do these things, and some effective leaders do not do them all.

Leadership is often confused with personality, formal position and specific behaviours. It certainly includes all of these things, but it is not limited to them. An effective leader is often a complex individual. A description of Oliver Cromwell, the Lord Protector of England in the 17th century, explains this complexity:

'There was no single Cromwell – that is, a clear-cut individual ... Instead, there was a multiplicity of Cromwells, each linked to the other by his enormous vitality ... Firstly, there was the very human, simple and compassionate man, a visionary and a romantic. Secondly, there was a violent, boisterous and irascible bully. Thirdly, there was the resolute and iron-willed general ... Fourthly, the calculating politician, the man of expedients who had no guiding principles. And lastly, there was ... the Cromwell ... who, as the interpreter of God's will, was capable of committing any atrocity.'

Source: J. F. C. Fuller, *A Military History of the Western World*, Vol. 2, New York: Funk & Wagnalls, 1955

Question

Why is leadership important to an organisation? *(12 marks)*

Case studies, questions and exam practice

CASE STUDY NHS LEADERSHIP QUALITIES FRAMEWORK

The leadership qualities framework aims to provide a blueprint for effective leadership in the National Health Service (NHS).

It provides a foundation for:

- setting the standard for leadership in the NHS
- assessing and developing high performance in leadership
- individual and organisational assessment
- integrating leadership across the service and related agencies
- adapting leadership to suit changing contexts
- benchmarking – by enabling the development of a database about leadership capacity and capability.

The framework describes the key characteristics, attitudes and behaviours to which leaders in the NHS should aspire. It has been tested within the NHS and validated. It sets the standard for outstanding leadership in the NHS.

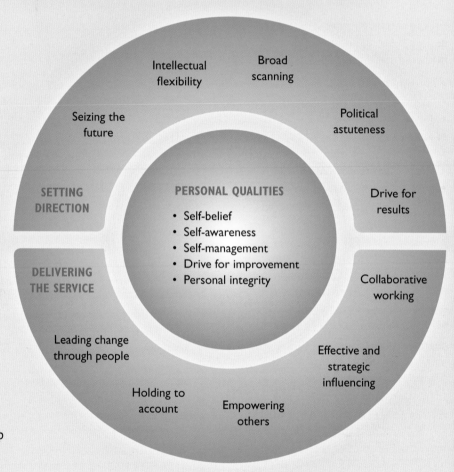

The framework has a number of applications and it describes the qualities expected of NHS leaders, now and in the future:

- personal development
- board development
- leadership profiling for recruitment and selection
- career mapping
- succession planning
- connecting leadership capability
- performance management.

Source: adapted from the NHS

Question

Explain what is meant by 'the applications of the framework'? *(14 marks)*

Types of organisational culture

LEARNING OBJECTIVES

▶ Organisational culture
▶ Harrison and Handy
▶ Deal and Kennedy
▶ Quinn and McGrath

Organisational culture

There are a number of ways in which an organisation's culture can be classified. The main ideas have been suggested by a number of researchers, including Harrison and Handy, Deal and Kennedy, and Quinn and McGrath. As years have passed, so these classifications have become more developed, making it possible to approach them only in broad terms.

Harrison and Handy

In 1972, Harrison suggested four main categories of organisational culture: power, role, task and person. Charles Handy reworked Harrison's theory and developed descriptions of the four categories – outlined in the table below.

Deal and Kennedy

During the 1980s, Deal and Kennedy developed their own set of theories about organisational culture and the way in which it affected how management made decisions and formed strategies. Their conclusions are shown in the table opposite.

Culture	Description
Power	This type of culture is based on trust and good personal communication. There is little need for rigid bureaucratic procedures since power and authority is based on only a few individuals. The power culture is dynamic in that change can take place quickly but is dependent on a small number of key, powerful individuals. This culture tends to be tough on employees because the key focus is the success of the organisation, often resulting in higher labour turnover.
Role	This type of culture tends to be bureaucratic in nature, thus requiring logical, coordinated and rational processes with heavy emphasis on rules and procedures. Control lies with a small number of employees who have high degrees of authority. They tend to be stable organisations, operating in a predictable environment with products and services that have a long lifespan. Not considered to be innovative organisations, they can adapt to gradual, minor change, but not to radical ones.
Task	This type of organisational culture relies on employee expertise. The matrix structure tends to prevail in these organisations, with teams of individuals specialising. They need and tend to be flexible organisations with individual employees working with autonomy allowing fast reaction to changes in the external environment and having set procedures in place to address this aspect.
Person	This type of culture relies on collective decision-making, often associated with partnerships. Compromise is important and individuals will tend to work within their own specialist areas, coordinating all aspects and working with autonomy without the need to report to other employees.

Culture	Description
Macho	This type of organisation has to make decisions quickly and adopt a tough attitude towards its employees and fellow managers. There is a high degree of internal competition and the operations tend to be high-risk. The majority of these organisations do not form strategies or plan for the long term but are short-termist, with a low level of cooperation within the organisation itself. There is a high labour turnover resulting in a weak organisational culture.
Work hard/ play hard	This type of culture tends to be associated with sales. The majority of individual employees are sales-oriented but the level of risk is low. It is the employees' ability to accumulate sales that is important and the culture tends to encourage team building and social activities for employees. It also promotes competition and offers rewards for success, but does not necessarily rate quality as highly as volume.
Company	This type of organisation is often in a high-risk area and operates on the basis that decisions take a long time to come to fruition. Decision-making takes place at the top of a hierarchical organisation and the overall approach can often be old-fashioned. Each new invention or technical breakthrough will pose a threat to the business.
Process	This type of culture operates in a low-risk, slow feedback environment where employees are encouraged to focus on how they do things rather than what they do. They tend to be based on systems and procedures, requiring employees to work in an orderly and detailed fashion, attending meetings and work groups. There will be rigid levels of management in the hierarchical structure, but because the organisation operates in a predictable environment. Reactions from management are often slow.

Quinn and McGrath

Quinn and McGrath also identified four different organisational cultures, as shown in the table on the right.

It should be remembered that no one organisation fits neatly into any one of the categories mentioned and the majority are too complex to be categorised generally. The classifications should be regarded only as a reference point for comparison of extremes.

Culture	Description
Rational	The rational culture is firmly based on the needs of a market. The organisation places emphasis on productivity and efficiency and encourages management to be goal-oriented and decisive. All activities are focused on tangible performance and employees are rewarded on achievement.
Adhocracy	This type of culture is an adaptive, creative and autonomous one where authority is largely based on the abilities and charismatic nature of leaders. These organisations tend to be risk-oriented and emphasis is placed on employees' adherence to the values of the organisation itself.
Consensual	These types of organisation are often concerned with equality, integrity and fairness and much of the authority is based on informal acceptance of power. Decisions are made by collective agreements or consensus, and dominant leaders are not often present. Morale is important, as is cooperation and support between employees in order to reach organisational objectives. Employee loyalty is high.
Hierarchical	This type of culture relies on stability and control through the setting of rigid regulations and procedures. Decisions are made logically on facts alone with the management tending to be cautious and conservative. The employees are strictly controlled, with management expecting obedience.

> **Question**
>
> What is corporate culture and why is it difficult for corporate culture to adapt to changes in the wider community? *(14 marks)*

Significance of organisational culture

LEARNING
OBJECTIVES
▶ Organisation types
▶ Organisational behaviour
▶ Organisational design
▶ Organisational evolution
▶ Organisational norms
▶ Organisational politics
▶ Defining organisational politics

Organisation types

There are many different forms of organisational type, which can be typified as being primarily related to the way in which the organisations coordinate themselves; the degree of their centralisation or decentralisation; and the aspect of the organisation which it considers to be of primary importance. The table on the right illustrates the different configurations, although any such treatment or coverage of organisation types cannot hope to incorporate all the variants.

Configuration	Prime coordinating mechanism	Key part of organisation	Type of decentralisation
Entrepreneurial organisation	Direct supervision	Strategic apex	Vertical and horizontal centralisation
Machine organisation	Standardisation of work processes	Techno-structure	Limited horizontal decentralisation
Professional organisation	Standardisation of skills	Operating core	Horizontal decentralisation
Diversified organisation	Standardisation of outputs	Middle line	Limited vertical decentralisation
Innovative organisation	Mutual adjustment	Support staff	Selected decentralisation
Missionary organisation	Standardisation of norms	Ideology	Decentralisation
Political organisation	None	None	Varies

Organisational behaviour

The study of organisational behaviour incorporates both an academic and a practical approach. Any such investigation begins with the primary definition of the word organisation, or organisational. Clearly it refers to a form of social collectivity, or in the organisational sense, a series of collectivities. The study of organisational behaviour can be a highly specialised area of investigation. Typically, researchers and theorists will tackle many of the different aspects of organisational life, including performance, goal, product or service-related issues and general performance.

The dominant approaches to the study of organisational behaviour tend to revolve around culturalist, institutionalist or utilitarian explanations. Undoubtedly the study of organisational behaviour began with a simple study of organisational structure and functions. This moved further into the field of the behaviour of groups and individuals. The study draws heavily on psychology and sociology, but later studies have begun to incorporate industrial relations, political science, economics and engineering.

The study of organisational behaviour does derive elements from both the theoretical and the empirical. It attempts to understand how and why organisations develop particular ways of regulating their operations, their employees and their management. The studies of F. W. Taylor could be considered to be a scientific management approach to organisational behaviour. Much of the structural theory is derived from Max Weber, and the group theory from Elton May (Hawthorn Experiments).

Organisational design

The way in which an organisation decides to configure its activities can be depicted in terms of organisational design. The primary objective of any organisational design is to ensure that the structure conforms to the following:

- the business objectives
- the business resources
- the environment in which the business operates.

It is the structure, or the design, of the organisation that describes the relationship between the different parts of the organisation and those who work within it. The design also specifies the following:

- the divisions of work
- the hierarchical structure
- the authority structure
- formal links within the organisation.

Organisational design is therefore the process of actually configuring the organisation in relation to its strategies to attain optimum performance. Organisational design has to be reactive and flexible in the sense that changes may have to be made if discontinuity occurs. The net effect of not changing the design is to create a gap between the way in which the organisation works and the strategy objectives. It is therefore imperative that the organisational design does not impact on the performance of the business. The following problems may be encountered, and strategies adopted:

- As the organisation grows, the design is amended to decentralise decision-making, making it easier for experts in certain areas to take control.
- Changes in strategy must be matched with changes in design.
- Changes in priority must be matched with changes in design.
- Technology changes may mean changes in information, communication and decision-making; all need to be reflected in organisational design.

Organisational evolution

It was inevitable that the general theory of evolution would be eventually applied to organisations. The theory of organisational evolution revolves around the following concepts:

- Human practices and norms are a direct result of human action.
- Therefore, management theory and organisational theory are a direct result of human actions.

Organisational norms

Organisational norms reinforce the socialisation process of individuals within a business. The norms and socialisation work together in order to instil in the management and employees the organisational goals. Organisational norms seek to identify the ways in which individuals spend their time, manage information, communicate, take responsibility and make decisions. In other words, organisational norms involve the moulding of attitudes and behaviours in order to achieve collaboration and performance.

Organisational politics

Organisations are essentially political systems and power is used on a day-to-day basis to determine organisational relationships. Politics within the organisational context are a means of recognising and ultimately reconciling various competing interests. While in the past the politics within organisations was controlled rigidly by management, politics have increasingly developed into various forms of democratic

working environments, based on a non-coercive set of circumstances. Organisations, in term of their politics, can range from the autocratic to the democratic. Within these two extremes there are bureaucratic organisations, which run their politics on a very formalised basis, and technocratic systems, in which the politics are based on skills and abilities. Politics, therefore involve what can often be non-rational influences on decision-making. It is widely believed, however, that successful organisational politics lead to higher levels of power and ultimately to more reasoned organisations that can adapt and change, as well as become more effective in their decision-making. In order to understand organisational political behaviour, the table below may prove to be a useful starting point, as it identifies three key dimensions. These are:

- Where the political activity takes place – internal (inside) or external (outside the organisation).
- The direction of the influence – either vertical or lateral
- The legitimacy of the political action.

DEFINING ORGANISATIONAL POLITICS

Dimensions		
Internal/external	Internal examples: Exchange of favours, reprisals, obstruction, symbolic protests	External examples: Whistle-blowing, legal action, information leaks
Vertical/lateral	Vertical examples: By-passing chains of command, complaining to managers, interaction between peers	Lateral examples: Exchanges of favours, formation of coalitions or groups
Legitimate/illegitimate	Legitimate examples: Any actions taken with the overall organisational procedures and policies	Illegitimate threats

Question

We mentioned the Hawthorne Experiments by Elton Mayo on this spread. Find out about these experiments and explain their significance. *(18 marks)*

Reasons for and problems of changing organisational culture

LEARNING
OBJECTIVES

▶ Reasons for changing
organisational culture
▶ Problems with changing
organisational culture
▶ Force Field Analysis

Reasons for changing organisational culture

There can be a variety of reasons behind attempts or desires to change the organisational culture of a business; some are derived from internal forces, while others are driven by external factors:

Change driver	Explanation
Merger or takeover	Both an internal and external driver, the new organisation will either have to adapt to a new culture that has been acquired or imposed upon it by the new ownership or if it is the parent or acquiring company then it will have to impose the existing culture on the newly acquired business
Performance	Poor performance (such as low productivity or profits) could be a key driver to change the culture of the organisation. The leadership of the organisation will have to create and transmit the newly desired culture throughout the organisation
Downsizing	This could force a major culture change, with reduced workforce and the fact that many of the previously internally controlled processes are either outsourced or passed on to suppliers and partners
Leadership or management	Changes in leadership and management or a change of viewpoint could be a key driver in the desire to create a new culture
New corporate goals	A change in the goals and objectives of the organisation could be a major influence on the entire culture of the organisation. New procedures and processes will be introduced and new ways of working required
Public to private	Typical of organisations that were carrying out a range of activities in the public sector (such as waste management, transport etc.) and have now been privatised. The ethos of the organisation will have radically changed from one of service and value for money to one of productivity and profit
Market	A business may well have to consider changing its culture in order to remain competitive and stay up-to-date in terms of changes in the market. Older working practices may no longer be cost-effective or workable in the new conditions

Problems with changing organisational culture

Henry Mintzberg wrote:

'In the past, some large organisations treated people paternalistically, but reasonably decently, but many have destroyed that contract. It's significant that the two most popular management techniques of all time – Taylor's work study methods (to control your hands) and strategic planning (to control your brain) were adopted most enthusiastically by two groups: communist governments and American corporations.'

In the majority of cases, potential changes planned for an organisation will be resisted by the culture. Given the fact that change aims to move an organisation from its current situation to another, we should appreciate the fact that change will cause uncertainty or unwillingness to give up existing practices. To begin with, many individuals will deny that the change is actually necessary and will resist it utterly, or avoid the changes once they have been introduced. The management structure needs to be able to determine why there is resistance to change and attempt to overcome it. If individuals feel threatened by change, they will not be able to recognise the potential advantages of embracing the change. If management can explain why the changes are necessary and the opportunities that are presented by this action, then there is more possibility of commitment being received from those who are hesitant. There are a number of different reasons why individuals will feel a need to resist change. These include situations where:

- their security has been undermined
- their competence is being questioned
- familiar relationships are under threat
- their territory or responsibilities are being impinged upon
- they do not understand the direction in which they are supposed to be moving.

For all individuals there needs to be a period of transition from resistance or denial to exploration and commitment. This would include the need for the organisation to fully appraise all employees and give them time to understand and internalise information. Those who are resisting will not acknowledge, accept or respond to this approach, but should be encouraged through support to explore the potential advantages of the change. Once this has been achieved, commitment will be gained through team-building activities, rewards, and the gradual move towards the new objectives.

Force Field Analysis

Kurt Lewin put forward the theory of Force Field Analysis, which considers that situations of change can be best visualised by two mutually opposing forces operating against one another.

One set of forces supports the change and the other resists the change. The main purpose of force field analysis is to enable the management to identify the nature of these forces in advance of any implementation of change. The next step is to attempt to remove or minimise each of the forces that restrain the organisation from making the change, while, at the same time, bolstering the forces that support or encourage the change.

We can best see the current state in which the organisation finds itself as a solid line with, some distance away, a dotted line showing the desired state (*see the diagram above*). The driving forces can then be

seen as arrows pushing the current state line towards the desired state line. There are matching arrows attempting to restrain the current state line from moving towards the desired state line. Some of the forces will be stronger than others. It is the manager's responsibility to try to match and exceed the restraining forces in order to push the organisation towards its desired state. If the two opposing forces are equal then the organisation will remain where it is. If the driving forces are stronger, or the restraining forces become weaker, then the line will move towards the desired state.

> **Question**
>
> Why might there be resistance to changes in organisational culture? *(14 marks)*

Assessing the importance of organisational culture

LEARNING OBJECTIVES

▶ Culture as an asset
▶ Reducing conflict
▶ Coordinating and control
▶ Reducing uncertainty
▶ Improving motivation and effectiveness
▶ Influence of organisational culture

Culture as an asset

One of an organisation's key assets should be its culture. If we examine what constitutes an organisation's culture we see that it is made up of the following elements that combine to define organisational purpose and deliver organisational goals:

- organisational values and beliefs
- human attitudes and behaviour patterns
- organisational structure.

The primary asset to the organisation is the influence that can be exerted on human attitudes and thus behaviour patterns through the development of a sound organisational culture. A secondary asset is the influence on trading partners and customers from a set of sound and fair organisational values and beliefs.

Reducing conflict

As we have seen, organisational culture includes the sharing of assumptions, beliefs and values. Individuals within the organisation will learn how to act in certain sets of circumstances. One of the principal reasons for the development of organisational culture is that it helps to reduce the amount of conflict within the organisation. In other words, there is a degree of social cohesion within the business. Providing individuals can accept a particular type of organisational culture, it will assist them in being able to cope with external pressures in the business environment. Not only this, it will also allow them to survive and adapt to changes by developing a

series of integrated internal processes.

There needs to be a generally accepted way in which the mission statement and objectives of the organisation are interpreted. As the principal goal is to achieve the various objectives of the organisation, the business needs to develop a generally accepted strategy in order to achieve this. This form of consensus allows the organisation to develop its personnel in such a way that they will act together, understanding how and why things need to be done. It will also reduce the degree of ambiguity in certain situations.

Coordinating and control

Organisational culture is not only important to reduce the level of conflict within the organisation, it will also help the management to coordinate and control the organisation itself. Certain courses of action will become an integral part of the organisation's operations. This will enable the management to make a series of decisions without any reference to the employees themselves, as they will be expecting this particular type of response. There will be a series of preconceived ideas and expectations in certain situations. Individuals will readily accept the fact that they need to respond in a particular way. This will facilitate the coordination of various activities. The adoption of various rules and procedures will also reinforce management controls and there will be a generally accepted recognition of power and authority within the organisation.

Reducing uncertainty

As we mentioned earlier, there is a degree of uncertainty at the beginning of an organisation's existence, and indeed a level of uncertainty from new recruits entering a business. However, the adoption of a standardised form of organisational structure will generally reduce the level of uncertainty. If there is a coherent culture within the organisation the individuals can attempt to predict various courses of action which may be put forward by the management. This means that when there are conflicts of interest, for example, there will be generally accepted ways of coping with these conflicts. This is not to say that the resolution of these problems will necessarily be rational, even though they may be predictable.

Improving motivation and effectiveness

If the organisation has developed a culture then the individuals within the organisation are generally considerably more motivated, making 4them more efficient and effective. This is, of course, assuming that the organisational culture is one which is fully embraced by most members of the organisation. The individuals working within the organisation will understand the ways in which demotions, punishments, bonuses and wage differentials are calculated. If the employees can readily identify with an organisation and its culture then they have a tendency to be far more loyal. This means they have fully embraced the beliefs and values of the organisation itself. It is then assumed that the performance of these employees will be greatly enhanced.

Influence of organisational culture

Organisational culture will naturally exert a considerable influence over the strategies of a business. There are a number of reasons for this:

- The organisation needs to continually scan the environment to identify situations that they are uncertain about, but which they feel capable of controlling. There will be certain cultural assumptions within the organisation that will affect the scanning process
- The organisation needs to be aware that it will have various filters in place that will determine the attitude towards certain information and activities in the external environment. This selective perception of the different situations will have been built up as an integral part of the organisation's culture.
- The organisation needs not only to collect and interpret information, but also to appreciate the fact that its own culture will have a different set of demands arising out of the information and this will determine their response.
- The organisation's culture will have an ethical component to it which will determine the way in which the strategies are formulated and implemented. Whatever the dominant set of values and norms within the organisation, there will be a variety of different ways in which the organisation will either restrict its response or direct its actions.

BOOK RESEARCH

Jon Sutherland and Diane Canwell, *Organisation Structures and Processes,* Pitman Publishing, 1997 and 2007.

Any new strategy will put forward at least two questions that can be directly related to culture:

1 What behavioural changes are required of the culture in order to incorporate the new objectives?
2 Does the behavioural change or degree of change determine whether the objectives can be achieved?

The organisation could take a number of approaches to culture when considering its strategic possibilities:

- It could ignore the culture itself, but this might be dangerous.
- It could try to manage the strategy around the culture by making modifications to the plan.
- It could try to modify the culture to the plans.
- It could try to adapt the plans to the culture.

Question

What are the major advantages of organisational culture?
(12 marks)

Case studies, questions and exam practice

CASE STUDY MILLER BREWING

Miller Brewing Company, a subsidiary of the tobacco giant Philip Morris, is the second largest brewery in the United States. Its parent, Philip Morris, is considered to be the largest packaged goods organisation in the world. The other main Philip Morris subsidiary, the recently acquired Kraft Foods, is responsible for this distinction. Miller holds roughly 21% of the US domestic beer market with its approximately 50 brands of beer. It runs breweries in seven different US states from coast to coast and has made steps to break into international markets. Miller is currently the leading import beer in Ireland, South Korea, Norway and Mexico, and the sixth largest brewer in the world, selling beer in about 100 countries worldwide.

The company prides itself on its strong commitment to high-quality brewing techniques and end products. Its 7,000 employees are encouraged to pay attention to detail and make all the beer produced, 'perfectly Miller.' Employees are highly valued at Miller. Evidence of this fact can be seen on the company's website, which boasts, 'Miller Brewing employees make Miller Time!'

Many of today's organisations are changing towards worker-friendly cultures within their firms. It is a strong belief that making the wellbeing of people a top management priority will lead to a more successful business in the long run. Miller Brewing Company is no exception to this belief. In 1996, Mark Spear became the new Director of Management and Organisational Development of the Milwaukee-based brewer. Spear states that his mission is to help Miller Brewing reinvent itself through a process of changing its internal culture.

He intends to change the core culture of the company by altering the main factors, or observable culture, that affect or mould the core beliefs of the employees and the organisation. This is no small task. He must change the most basic elements of the company's culture – the stories, rites and rituals, hero figures and the symbolism that the workers and the organisation as a whole hold dear to their hearts. His first and foremost method of attacking the core culture problems he saw involved revamping the employees' perception of their place within the company and the beer industry. Spear said, 'I think one of the foundations of changing an organisation is having people really understand the business, where they add value to it and how they impact the bottom line.' Spear chose to focus on the rites and rituals section of observable culture with the hope that his changes would bring about a new and improved corporate culture for Miller Brewing. Spear, along with a team of experts, compiled information on each individual employee role and how each role in turn affected the end product and level of success for the brewery. The team emerged with a finished product called *Brewery Business Understanding*. Every step to having a successful brewery is covered in this program. One of the biggest innovations that the team has given Miller is a slide rule that will tell a worker exactly how his or her actions will impact on the economic situation of the entire brewery. Miller is currently using this as a type of training rite and has implemented it for all hourly wage earners and their supervisors within the business.

Spear has also implemented a similar program for salaried workers called *Business Understanding*. This program, rather than using a slide rule, uses tools called business literacy maps to explain to middle management exactly where they fit in the overall scheme of things. There are four business maps, each covering a different area of the organisation. The first gives an overview of the customer/consumer/competitor landscape. The second sheds light on the distributor relationship of the company. The third explains the flow of revenue in both domestic and foreign arenas. The fourth explains the chain of command at Miller Brewing.

Spear once said, 'Until our people better understand the broad business and how they add value upstream and downstream in relationships with the distributors, consumers and suppliers, it's hard to move the organisation forward.' With these two new rites – the *Brewery Business Understanding* and *Business Understanding* programs – worker confusion over roles within the organisation will cease to exist, and awareness of how one person can make a difference will increase by leaps and bounds. These programs will promote progress among both the hourly wage workers and middle management, which will in turn create higher overall levels of wellbeing, productivity and quality within the organisation.

Spear also employs observable culture aspects that were already in place before his takeover of command at Miller Brewing. Miller has always used their stories, or more appropriately their history, to create and enhance a positive core culture. The organisation holds the core belief that with innovation comes success. Because of this, Miller holds many firsts within the beer industry.

When the historical stories are told of Miller having the first nationally distributed light beer, the core belief of innovation is reinforced.

Symbolism is another area on which Miller has focused in order to manipulate its core culture values. When browsing the Miller Brewing website one will find a link directly to a page discussing the Miller Brewing organisation. Underneath the main heading in bold is a sentence that says it all, 'Miller Brewing employees make Miller Time!' The subsequent paragraphs describe the commitment and dedication of the employees of Miller Brewing. They also emphasise the importance of the Miller Brewing employees in the quality of the beer itself. Miller utilises web space like this in order to make symbolic gestures to its employees to let them know that they are appreciated. This will increase employee well-being, loyalty and overall performance.

Mark Spear has made a large impact on the culture at Miller Brewing. Because of his innovative techniques the employees at Miller have a much better understanding of where they stand within the company. They understand the connection that they have to the beer they produce and the customers they serve, no matter how far removed from the process their jobs may seem. In the end, Miller is given a happier and more productive workforce and, in the long run, a more prosperous organisation.

Source: adapted from Ohio University and Miller

Question

Mark Spear introduced a form of employee engagement. What does this mean? Give examples of this process from the case study. *(18 marks)*

Significance of information management

LEARNING
OBJECTIVES

▶ What is information management?
▶ Scope of information management
▶ Management information systems
▶ Competitive information systems
▶ Competitive intelligence

What is information management?

Information management is concerned with identifying, organising, evaluating, storing and disseminating information in the most effective and efficient manner. This involves understanding how information systems can be developed to meet requirements. It also involves understanding how organisations work, and how information strategies must take into account people's needs and behaviour. Information is recognised as one of the most important assets of any organisation.

FOR EXAMPLE

In public sector organisations, a large proportion of the administrative budget is typically spent on information handling activities of one kind or another. Information is needed at all levels of government to support business functions and assist in the achievement of business aims and objectives, and it serves as evidence of the way government operates and the transactions it carries out.

In order for an organisation to efficiently use the information it has, a number of things are important:

- Employees must have ready access to all the information they need to do their jobs, at all levels in the organisation.
- Information assets need to be fully exploited, through information-sharing within the organisation and with other organisations, and through commercial arrangements with the private sector where appropriate.
- The quality of the organisation's information has to be maintained, and the information used in the business must be accurate, reliable, up-to-date, complete and consistent.
- Legal and other requirements for maintaining the privacy, security, confidentiality, authenticity and integrity of information must be observed.
- Information has to be made available conveniently to stakeholders through a variety of channels.
- The organisation needs to achieve a high level of efficiency and economy in its information-handling activities.

Information is a key resource of the organisation, together with people, finances and material assets. Through effective management of the organisation's information resources and information systems, corporate managers can:

- add value to the services delivered to customers
- reduce risks in the business
- reduce the costs of business processes and service delivery
- stimulate innovation in internal business processes and external service delivery.

Generally, an organisation will maintain the following information types:

- *Structured data* – Data held in databases is typically used to support operational activities and business transactions. Databases hold structured records containing details about the subjects of interest to the business, such as individual customers, financial holdings, companies, buildings and other resources inside and outside the organisation.
- *Unstructured data* – These may include images, photographs, maps, videos and sound recordings.

Scope of information management

Four areas of management are usually included within the scope of information management:

Area	Explanation
The management of information resources	All the information resources need to be managed. The governance of information in the organisation must ensure that all these resources are known and that responsibilities have been assigned for their management
The management of information technology	The management of the IT that underpins the organisation's information systems is typically the responsibility of the 'supply-side' function, managed within the organisation or delivered through an external service provider. The management of the organisation must be able to operate and access the IT-based products and services it needs and acquires
The management of information processes	All business processes will give rise to operations involving one or other of the information resources of the organisation. The processes of creating, collecting, accessing, modifying, storing, deleting and archiving information must be properly controlled if the organisation is to exercise satisfactory governance over its information resources
The management of information standards and policies	The organisation will need to define standards and policies for its information management. These will typically be developed as an element of its IT strategy. Management policies will govern the procedures and responsibilities for information management in the organisation; technical policies and standards will apply to the IT infrastructure which supports the organisation's information systems

BOOK RESEARCH

Kenneth C. Laudon and Jane P. Laudon, *Management Information Systems*, New York: Prentice Hall, 2003.

Competitive Information Systems (CIS)

A CIS is a marketing data capture system which aims to collect, collate and assess intelligence regarding the operations of competitors. Ideally, it needs to encompass the following:

- a clear decision regarding the information that needs to be collected
- the design of appropriate data capture methods
- a system by which the data can be analysed and evaluated in a timely manner (old data may be of little value or, at worst, may suggest strategies that are no longer appropriate)
- a communications system that allows the dissemination of the information
- the incorporation of the data into the decision-making process, and an ability to assess the quality of the data collected so that systems can be refined.

Competitive Intelligence

Competitive Intelligence (CI) is increasingly seen as a distinct business management discipline, which provides an input into a whole range of decision-making processes.

There are four stages in monitoring competitors, known as the four Cs:

1 Collecting the information
2 Converting information into intelligence (CIA: Collate and catalogue it, Interpret it and Analyse it)
3 Communicating the intelligence
4 Countering any adverse competitor actions.

Management information systems

A management information system (MIS) is a computer application that is used to record, store and process information which can be used to assist management decision-making. Generally a business will have a single integrated MIS into which data from various functional areas of the business is fed and to which senior management has access.

There are two additional sub-types of MIS, which are decision support systems and executive information systems. Decision support systems also collect, store and process information accessible by management. They contain data on the business's operational activities and allow managers to manipulate and retrieve data using modelling techniques to examine the results of various courses of action. An executive information system (EIS) provides similar facilities for senior management, combining internal information with external data. It is used to support strategic decision-making and presents the information in a variety of formats, primarily aimed at enabling the users to identify trends.

> ### Question
>
> An organisation will need to consider the information requirements across all of its business units and functions. It is often recommended that a life-cycle approach is used to look at the use of information in business processes. What should the organisation review regarding its use of information? *(12 marks)*

Value of different approaches to decision-making

LEARNING OBJECTIVES

▶ Investment appraisal and break-even analysis
▶ Cost benefit analysis
▶ Expected values
▶ Ishikawa diagrams

Investment appraisal and break-even analysis

Investment appraisal can refer to an internal appraisal of the potential benefits of a project, which is primarily carried out by the management or employees of a business. It can also refer to an investment appraisal made by an external individual, business or investor, with a desire to become involved in some way with a business.

Typical ways in which investment appraisal can be undertaken include payback, which can be considered as a fairly simplistic way of calculating the viability of a project. It is one of the most common ways in which investment appraisals are made. The business would normally identify a period within which the investment would be expected to pay for itself. After this period of time the project would be expected to move into profit. It is possible to calculate the relative payback periods for a number of competing projects or investments. A business will bear in mind that all investments will be at the expense of other projects. This means that businesses need to know which, potentially, will be the best investment to proceed with.

Essentially this is a question of opportunity cost, which is addressed purely in cash terms. Not all investments are made purely to provide a quick cash return; there may be other motivations behind

the investment. Whatever the case, payback does allow a business to look at a number of competing projects and, at least in monetary terms, it can assist them in making a decision.

Average rate of return is a means by which a business's annual profits on a particular investment can be calculated as a percentage of the original amount paid. In using the average rate of return for a particular project the business would be able to see whether it would be more profitable to leave the money in the bank, rather than risk the investment on a project that may not repay at the same level. The average rate of return, when coupled with a close examination of interest rates, enables a business to identify the opportunity costs of an investment and allows it to compare one project against another.

An alternative is the internal rate of return (IRR), which is the discount, when used in cash flow, that makes the net present value equal to zero. The business needs to discover the rate of return when the net present value is zero. This is used to compare the market rate of interest with the internal rate of return, so that the business can make a decision about the potential investment. As the rate of interest represents the actual

cost of the capital, if the internal rate of return is higher, the project is worth considering. However, the organisation may set its own discount rate, which may be higher than the interest rate. In these cases, even if the project looks as if it will match the interest rate, it will still not be accepted because it still does not reach the minimum discount rate set by the business.

Another alternative to investment appraisal is consideration of discounted cash flow. The interest rate and time will determine the return on a particular project. Using this concept it is obvious that money earned (or paid) in the future is worth less than it is today.

Finally, businesses may consider either a form of break-even analysis or a cost benefit analysis. In the latter case, the business will take a broader view of the potential costs and benefits associated with a decision. This means that the normal considerations with regard to costs and benefits are extended and may include any relevant external costs and benefits which may be either unavoidable, or, in some cases, desirable. Social costs, for example, may be brought into the equation, as may the longer term impact of a particular project upon the rest of the operations routinely being carried out or provided by the business itself.

Cost benefit analysis

Cost benefit analysis is the technique that seeks to assess the value of the benefits of a particular course of action and then subtract any costs associated with it. The majority of benefits can be typified as being those that are received over a period of time, while costs may be either one-off or ongoing. In effect, cost benefit analysis allows a business to work out a payback period for a particular course of action.

In its simplest form, cost benefit analysis can use simply financial costs and financial benefits. This would make it easy for a business to assess and analyse the costs and benefits associated with any particular scheme. Restricting the analysis to purely financial terms does not mean that all costs and benefits have been assessed, as there may be human resource, environmental, production, and a host of other costs and benefits which have not been taken into the equation. Therefore a more sophisticated approach to this form of analysis can attempt to put a financial value on what would be intangible costs and benefits, although this is notoriously subjective.

Cost benefit analysis can be a powerful tool, particularly if the intangible items are incorporated within the analysis.

BOOK RESEARCH

James T. Fey, Elizabeth D. Phillips and Catherine Anderson, *What Do You Expect: Probability and Expected Value*, New York: Pearson Prentice Hall, 1997.

Expected values

Expected value can be calculated as the sum of the products of each possible outcome of a situation and the relative likelihood that it will occur. Typically expected value can be applied when making the necessary calculations for a decision tree.

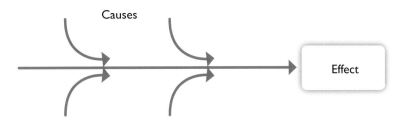

Causes

Effect

Ishikawa diagrams

The Ishikawa, or fishbone, diagram was created by Kaoru Ishikawa and is, to all intents and purposes, a cause and effect graphic representation. The diagram is designed to identify all the possible causes leading to a specific effect. In this respect the Ishikawa diagram is also referred to as being either a cause and effect diagram, or root cause analysis.

An Ishikawa diagram is a graphic tool often used as means to note the progress and content of a brainstorming session where the aim has been an attempt to identify the causes of a problem.

The diagram is named after the inventor of the tool, Kaoru Ishikawa (1969). It is called a fishbone diagram because the name of the basic problem is entered at the right of the diagram at the end of the main bone. The causes of the problem are then drawn as bones off the main backbone.

BOOK RESEARCH

Kaoru Ishikawa, *Guide to Quality Control*. Asian Productivity Organisation, 1986.

Typically, four Ms are used as a starting point: materials, machines, manpower and methods, although different categories can be used if needed. The main point of the exercise is to have between three and six main categories, which cover all possible influences.

Brainstorming allows the addition of causes to the main bones of the diagram, with more specific causes then adding more bones to these. The subdivision of the problems continues for as long as there are identified problems that can be subdivided. Usually, the diagram has between four and five levels, and when the fishbone has been completed, the individuals involved will be able to view a full picture of all of the possibilities related to the root cause of the problem.

> ### Question
> 'Investment appraisal is the only foolproof way of underpinning decision-making'. Discuss. *(18 marks)*

Influences on corporate decision-making

LEARNING
OBJECTIVES

▶ Ethical position
▶ Availability of resources
▶ Relative power of stakeholders

Ethical position

Ethics and social responsibility in relation to business has become an increasingly important and much-debated issue in recent years. Essentially, there is an inherent conflict between the desires of the business, the industry, society in general and the consumer. All may have mutually exclusive goals and objectives. Ethical issues arise when one group's values conflict with those of another. In many cases there are multiple levels of conflict arising out of different sets of values.

Making ethical decisions is always a complex procedure for a number of reasons, including:

- different alternatives
- consequences that may have a knock-on affect
- uncertain circumstances
- outcomes that can have economic, legal and social benefits
- outcomes that can have economic, legal and social costs
- personal implications for the managers and employees of the business, as well as implications for the business itself.

Ethical decisions can also often involve the business's stakeholders who can have goals and interests that conflict with those of the business.

Businesses often have innumerable complexities to unravel in order to ensure that they are not behaving in an unethical manner, including:

- ensuring that their goals are compatible with ethical considerations

What are the consequences of your decision?

How can the option be implemented?

Which option is the most ethical?

Consider your options.

Think through the ethical dilemma and identify all components as objectively as possible.

STEPS TO ETHICAL DECISION-MAKING

- ensuring that their route to meeting these goals is ethically acceptable
- ensuring that motives for meeting their goals are not selfish and non-ethical
- considering the consequences of their activities on others, including the stakeholders.

Availability of resources

The concept of resource dependency takes the view that organisations are rather like living creatures and that they are dependent upon their external environment. In other words, they require certain resources to prosper and survive. The relationship between the organisation and its resources is illustrated in the diagram below:

Resource dependencies have a direct impact on the organisation's strategies and structures, and, as such, they often determine the structures and the opportunities to implement the strategies.

Typically, organisations will seek to create links with their key resources and possibly to gain control over them. It is often the case that businesses include what is known as boundary spanning units in order to control their most important resources. This will achieve the following:

- insights into the external environment to understand, monitor and perceive impacts on resources
- an understanding of how external factors can affect the business's policies and procedures.

Relative power of stakeholders

The relative power of stakeholders for influencing can be summarised on a three-point scale: high (3), medium (2), and low (1). Stakeholders with no resources would effectively have no stake (0) and would therefore not figure in an analysis of the current situation. However, they could become important future actors if empowered in some way. Clearly some stakeholders are more powerful than others, but none of them can be ignored because one of the challenges is that the relative power of stakeholders varies over time.

FOR EXAMPLE

In food retailing, for example, the suppliers used to hold the power, but now with the growth of the supermarket chains, the power has in effect shifted to the retailers, such as Tesco and Sainsbury's. Moreover, improvements in global communication technology (Internet and SMS) allow even small stakeholders to have a significant impact. As Anders Dahvig, CEO of Ikea, said: 'The world has changed enormously in the past decade… All of us now act in ways we did not 10 years ago. Globalisation means stakeholders and responsibilities everywhere, which have to be managed. It's quite a different level of complexity.'

CASE STUDY ROYAL BANK OF SCOTLAND'S STAKEHOLDER ISSUES

Top issues

- Lending practices including rates and charges: how we sell and market all financial products.
- Customer service: providing service suited to customer needs.
- Financial crime and corruption: protecting financial security.
- Financial inclusion and capability: access to our products and understanding of them.
- Project finance and the equator principles: management of the social and environmental impact of the projects we finance.
- The environment: managing and minimising our direct environmental impact.
- Employee practices: managing, developing and rewarding our people.
- Supporting SMEs / encouraging entrepreneurialism: providing support and encouragement to start-ups and small businesses.
- Community investment: our support to the communities in which we operate.

CUSTOMERS
EMPLOYEES
INVESTORS
NGOs
GOV/REGS
MEDIA

TOP TEN ISSUES
Lending practices including rates and charges
Customer service
Financial crime and corruption
Financial inclusion and capability
Employee practices
The environment
Project finance/Equator principles
Supporting SMEs/entrepreneurs
Community investment

Stakeholders

A number of different groups of people are impacted by, and can have an impact on the business. These groups are all the business's stakeholders. It is important that what they think is understood. There are direct and indirect stakeholders:

- **Direct stakeholders** – customers, employees and investors – those with whom the business has a close relationship.

- **Indirect stakeholders** – the Government and regulators, the media and NGOs (Non-Governmental Organisations) – are those who have a broader interest in, and impact on, the financial services sector.

Question

How might the RBS have discovered this information and set of priorities for its stakeholders? *(8 marks)*

Case studies, questions and exam practice

CASE STUDY DECISION TREE

Decision trees are tools that assist managers in deciding between several different courses of action. As graphical representations of the options, it is possible to use them to investigate the outcomes that would be associated with the choosing of the different options. Decision trees can therefore be used to form a balanced picture. An example of a decision tree is shown on the opposite page.

In order to create a decision tree, a small box is drawn to the left-hand-side of the page. Lines are then extended to the right which relate to each possible solution or option. The name or description of the solution is written along the line. At the end of each line a circle is drawn if the result of taking that decision is unclear. Alternatively, if the initial option leads to another decision needing to be made, another square is drawn and the procedure repeated and continued. Squares on a decision tree represent decisions, while circles represent uncertain outcomes.

It is now possible to note on each of the lines what each of the options means. All the possible options can now be compared. Normally a business or a manager would assign a cash value or a score to each possible outcome. At each of the points represented by a circle, an estimate of the probability of each outcome needs to be calculated. These can be either fractions, which add up to 1, or percentages.

Once the value of each of the outcomes has been calculated, the actual values of each of the decisions or options can now be calculated in monetary terms.

Source: adapted from *Key Concepts in Strategic Management*, Sutherland and Canwell (Palgrave 2004)

Question

Using the data from the decision tree on the right, should the business open a new outlet in London or refurbish its existing one? Show your calculations.
(18 marks)

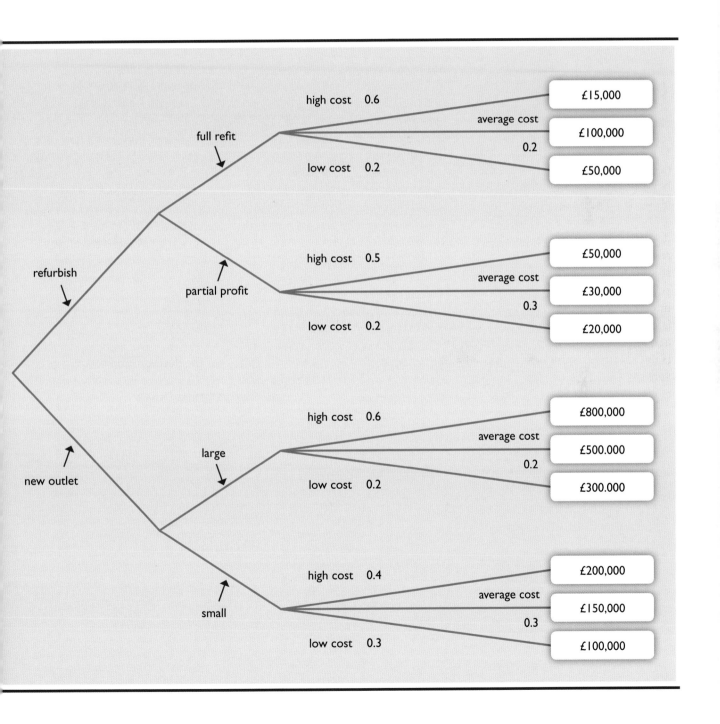

Techniques to implement change

Models for the management of change

There are a number of theoretical approaches that can be used to manage change. Effectively there are three main approaches. These are:

- the action research model
- the three-step model
- the planned phase change model.

Action research proposes that the most effective way of solving an organisational problem is to make a systematic and rational analysis of all the criteria and circumstances involved. This means collecting information from every group or stakeholder and then taking their views into account before proposing a solution to the problem. In effect, any attempt to make a change in the organisation is a learning process. By involving itself in change and investigating how the changes are made, the organisation is effectively carrying out action research. It usually has three main aspects:

- The organisation itself carries out the research, usually via a senior manager.
- The subjects of the change carry out the research, as they are the individuals who will be most affected.
- A change agent may be involved, who is not usually a member of the organisation but may have been brought in as a consultant.

The main point of the exercise is for all three groups to agree common terms of reference before the process can begin. Once this

has been achieved, data is gathered and analysed on a participative basis. Each group will have its own viewpoint, which needs to be taken into account. Once the data has been analysed, a proposal can be created. The process depends on correctly analysing the situation and identifying all possible alternatives. A major problem is that over-analysis can mean a lack of response and a considerable amount of time spent judging and evaluating each alternative. There needs to be considerable cooperation, despite the fact that this is essentially a top-down process. Action research is seen as a primary means by which effective change can be imposed on an organisation.

The second model for change management is based on Kurt Lewin's three-stage model. The first step is to unfreeze the way in which things are currently done. The second step is to move the organisation along to its new position with new sets of policies and procedures. The final stage is to refreeze the organisation once all the changes have been incorporated. Any change from one set of behaviours to another will involve the development of new values, behaviours and attitudes. If these have not been properly developed there will be a tendency for the organisation to slip back into its previous form.

The theorists, Bullock and Batten, suggested that there are four main planned change phases – detailed in the table below – and this is, perhaps, one of the most useful ways of looking at the management change.

Change phase	Explanation
Exploration	This is an opportunity for the organisation to decide what changes need to be made and what level of resources they will need. The organisation needs to be aware that change needs to happen, that it might need assistance and establish criteria to judge the progress of the change.
Planning	This involves the organisation carefully considering the nature of the problem. The organisation begins the process of collecting data and diagnosing the problem. They will assign goals and actions to decision-makers, who will be expected to support and approve the proposed changes.
Action	This involves the organisation implementing the change. They will move away from their current status quo to a new position that incorporates support mechanisms. The organisation will also begin to evaluate the impact of the changes and make necessary adjustments.
Integration	This takes place directly after the changes have been implemented. The aim is to stabilise changes so that they become part of the organisation's accepted set of norms and values. This may involve retraining and redeployment.

Change options matrix

The change options matrix links the main areas of human resource activity. The three main areas of strategic change are work, cultural change and political change. The change options matrix was developed by Beer, Eisenstat and Spector (1990) when they provided a six-point plan on how best to proceed with change:

1. Mobilise commitment through joint diagnosis.
2. Develop a shared vision of how to organise and manage for competitiveness.
3. Create a consensus for the new vision along with the competence and cohesion to act on it.
4. Revitalise departments by pressure from senior management.
5. Ensure change through the adoption of policies, systems and structures.
6. Monitor and adjust strategies as required.

For more on the ways in which leaders and managers manage change and achieve success, see Key influences on the change process: Leadership *on pp. 268–81.*

CASE STUDY CHANGE AND GROWTH

As an enterprise grows and develops a foothold in its market, the need to adapt dynamically to changing market conditions and to diversify into new fields becomes ever greater. Yet a culture of fear and resistance to change will usually become the 'norm': individuals' empire-building, teams with long-standing friendships and a general lack of visibility of others in the business, often cause an enterprise to become static and virtually impossible to adapt.

Understanding the requirement to adapt and then empower employees, will make change far less of a burden on the business and keep a competitive edge.

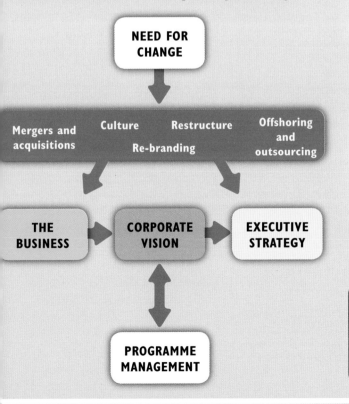

Requirement	Corporate vision function
Visibility of milestones for both change and work within a programme	Milestone tracking that can be rolled up and drilled down through the business
The ability to plan and incorporate change into a programme at an early stage	Business Planning (as opposed to task-based planning) takes the bigger picture of a programme for a more realistic model of the problem
An understanding of the requirements of a change programme and its potential impacts on the business	Portfolio management, scenario planning and capacity planning together give you complete visibility of the business and its ability to complete a project
Management of people outside their parent teams and departments	Resource management allows you to manage and track resources across all areas of the business
Reduction of the cultural resistance to change	Visibility of all the issues in a programme and the visibility of resource and demand across the business reduce managers' and employees' anxiety and empower them to do their jobs
Align change programmes and strategy	Strategic planning and portfolio management tools allow better alignment

Source: adapted from Atlantic Global

Question

Read the case study. Find out about the theories of Rosabeth Moss Kanter and her views of empowerment and change. What are the main points of her theory? *(12 marks)*

Assessing the factors that promote or resist change

Changeability

Business changeability is a measure of an organisation's agility or flexibility. The flexibility of a business is measured by the degree to which the organisation can adapt its operations to changes in the market.

A generic changeability or agility diagram is shown below:

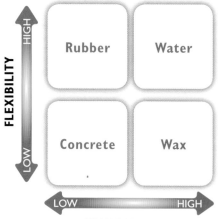

Reason for resisting change	Description
Parochial self-interest	This category suggests that the individual is more concerned with the impact of change on themselves and how it might affect their future, rather than the continued success of the business. Change for these individuals means losing something which they value and, as such, they will resist it. There is a danger that if enough individuals feel this way, then they will collaborate to block the change.
Misunderstanding	Essentially this is a communication problem. Inadequate information has been passed to the employees by the management and, as a result, much of what the employees know and understand has been derived from grapevine communication. At the root of this, the employees do not trust the management and will seek to find alternative justifications for why the management is instituting the changes.
Different assessment of the situation	Not all employees will see that there are good reasons to be instituting the changes. Each will seek to find reasons why the changes are being proposed and each will come to their own conclusions, which may inevitably lead to resistance. It should not be assumed that even with the most complete and open consultation process individuals will reach the same conclusions.
Low tolerance to change	These individuals value their security and stability in work. The introduction of new systems or processes will tend to undermine their self-belief. Management will need to recognise that there is fear and reassure the employees, otherwise they may resist the change.

As the diagram implies, organisations with low flexibility and changeability characteristics resemble concrete, in that they do not have the capacity for movement and are inflexible. Those with high scores on both counts resemble water, being able to flow and adapt as required.

Kotter and Schlesinger

Kotter and Schlesinger recognised that many employees are inherently resistant to change. There are enormous implications arising out of change that could affect an individual's opportunities of promotion, pay, or the fact that they may need to travel to an alternative location. The theorists attempted to classify why employees may be resistant to change and suggested four broad categories, as shown in the table above.

Kotter and Schlesinger suggested a number of ways in which management could seek to minimise resistance to change:

- through education and communication
- through participation and involvement
- through facilitation and support
- through negotiation and agreement
- through manipulation and co-opting
- through explicit and implicit coercion.

Conflict management

Conflict management involves situations when there may be opposition, incompatible behaviour and antagonistic interaction, or the blocking of individuals from reaching their goals. Conflict behaviour can range from questioning or doubting to a desire to annihilate the opponent.

Typically conflicts will arise out of disagreements, disputes or debates. Conflict is not always a negative aspect for a business and there is no specific need to reduce all conflicts as they ebb and flow and become an inevitable part of organisational life. Indeed many consider conflict to be essential for growth and survival.

BOOK RESEARCH

J.P Kotter and L.A. Schlesinger, 'Choosing Strategies for Change'. *Harvard Business Review* 57 (106–14). 1979

BOOK RESEARCH

Bernard S. Mayer, *The Dynamics of Conflict Resolution: A Practitioner's Guide.* New York: Jossey Bass Wiley. 2000.

Therefore, conflict management includes aiming to both lessen conflict and increase it.

There are various forms of conflict but they can be broadly distinguished as being either functional or dysfunctional.

Functional conflict, or constructive conflict, was first suggested in 1925 by Mary Parker Follett. It increases information and ideas, encourages innovative thinking, allows different points of view to be raised and reduces organisational stagnation.

Dysfunctional conflict, on the other hand, usually arises from tensions, anxieties and stresses. It reduces trust and can lead to poor decisions because of distorted or withheld information. Management tends to be obsessed with dysfunctional, high-conflict situations.

There is also a sub-division – dysfunctional low conflict – which again is negative in the sense that few new ideas are presented, there is a lack of innovation and a lack of information-sharing, all of which leads to stagnation.

Conflict management also involves three levels of conflict. Clearly there could be conflict between or within the organisation itself. There is also group conflict within the organisation and individual conflict between individual members of the groups.

Generally it is considered that there are three conflict episodes. These are:

- *Latent conflict* – behaviour that starts a conflict episode
- *Manifest conflict* – the observable conflict behaviour

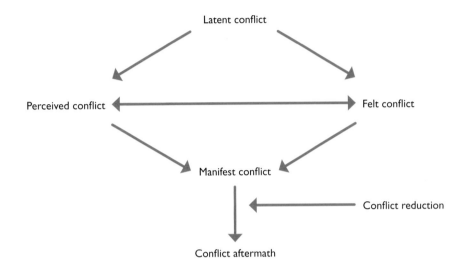

- *Conflict aftermath* – the end of a conflict episode, which can become the latent conflict for another episode in the future

Conflict management appears between the manifest conflict and the conflict aftermath, which seeks to lower the level of the conflict itself.

A more complete view of the conflict episodes and the place of conflict management within this system can be seen in the diagram above. Perceived conflict occurs when an individual becomes aware that they are in conflict. Conflict can be perceived when no latent conditions exist. A prime example is misunderstanding another individual's position on an issue. Felt conflict is the emotional or personalising part of the conflict and is exemplified by oral or physical hostility. These are the hardest episodes for managers to control.

The various episodes link the conflict aftermath to future

latent conflict. Effective conflict management breaks this connection by discovering the latent conflicts and removing them. An ideal conflict management model that would seek to maintain conflict at functional levels would include the following:

- no complete elimination of conflict
- an increase in dysfunctional low conflict
- choosing a desired conflict level based on perceived conflict requirements
- a tolerance to conflict.

> **Question**
>
> Suggest reasons why conflict may be desirable and why undesirable, and suggest types of conflict that could occur in the workplace due to managerial actions. *(12 marks)*

Case studies, questions and exam practice

CASE STUDY THE CASE FOR MANAGING CHANGE

Most organisations and their project teams are familiar with the business resistance/acceptance cycle associated with major change projects and are aware of the need to consider change management during implementation. However, all too often this awareness translates into broad change management exercises typified by training and communications plans. A true awareness of change management allows for a 'shallowing' of the change curve, resulting in the following benefits:

- lower risks to current day-to-day operations.
- lower project effort and costs
- faster path to benefit realisation.

Organisations don't always easily adapt to new technological, organisational or process changes. While these issues are recognised by most project teams, all too often a general, common approach is used. In reality, issues often differ by stakeholder groups, business units and/or geographies. Understanding these differences is vital as, prior to implementation, any disruption or disaffection with proposed changes can present risks to the current 'business as usual'.

The extent to which change management is planned and addressed prior to, and in the early stages of the project, dictates the total change effort that will be required not only to achieve implementation, but to

SUCCESSFUL CHANGE MANAGEMENT ADDRESSES THREE KEY FACTORS

ensure the full changes are embedded in the organisation. The earlier and more targeted the change management effort, the lower the total effort, and the better the use of the project's limited budget and resources.

The better prepared the organisation and its people, the faster the benefits will be delivered and felt. The time to achieve the new state of 'business as usual' and the associated business case represents a significant opportunity cost for the project. The more insight the business has into where and with whom issues are most likely to arise, and the earlier the warning, the more quickly it can identify strategies and accelerate the adoption of the new changes.

Source: adapted from Leadent

Question

It is not just the business that can be affected by organisational change. What technique can be used to identify those staff who will be affected, and how should they be handled? *(14 marks)*

CHECKLIST AND REVISION

CHECKLIST

- [ ] Understanding mission, aims and objectives

- [ ] The relationship between businesses and the economic environment

- [ ] The relationship between businesses and the political and legal environment

- [ ] The relationship between businesses and the social environment

- [ ] The relationship between businesses and the technological environment

- [ ] The relationship between businesses and the competitive environment

- [ ] Internal causes of change

- [ ] Planning for change

- [ ] Key influences on the change process: leadership

- [ ] Key influences on the change process: culture

- [ ] Making strategic decisions

- [ ] Implementing and managing change

MOCK EXAM

SECTION A

ANSWER <u>ONE</u> QUESTION FROM THIS SECTION

1 Read **Article A** and answer the question that follows.

ARTICLE A

TESCO CORPORATE GOVERNANCE

We aim for the highest standards of corporate behaviour. This requires strong leadership, clear governance and effective communication to staff of the behaviour we expect of them.

The Board considers strategic reputational risks every time it meets and discusses Corporate Responsibility strategy bi-annually. The Executive Committee receives regular updates on Corporate Responsibility performance, assesses future risks and opportunities, and develops our strategy in this area. Accountability for managing operational risks is clearly assigned to line management.

Formal risk assessments are carried out routinely throughout the UK and our international businesses. Significant risks and any control failures are escalated to senior management and the Board, as necessary.

Corporate Responsibility leadership is provided by a cross-functional committee of senior executives, chaired by one of our Executive Directors, Lucy Neville-Rolfe. Members of the Corporate Responsibility Committee are drawn from across the business, which ensures that corporate responsibility is at the heart of our daily operations.

As our business grows internationally, we recognise the importance of International Tesco participation in our Corporate Responsibility Committee and the work we do on the environment and in communities.

The Committee has a remit to:

- assess risks
- develop corporate responsibility strategy
- review our social, ethical and environmental policies and practices
- encourage best practice throughout the business
- identify opportunities to improve the effectiveness and sustainability of the business using the Community Plan and other initiatives
- review, agree, monitor and report on our Corporate Responsibility Key Performance Indicators (KPIs)
- increase internal awareness of Corporate Responsibility
- improve stakeholder communication and engagement.

The retail sector is undergoing rapid change, with increasing expectations of business on sustainability and community. *Forum for the Future*, supported by Tesco and Unilever, is conducting a wide-ranging exercise looking at possible futures for the UK retail industry in 2022, and the implications for corporate sustainability strategies. The project will first seek to understand the major trends and factors that will influence the retail sector's development over the next 15 years. The second stage will use this information to develop possible futures for the retail sector in the UK in 2022. The third stage will use the scenarios to inform strategic conversations about sustainable development in Tesco and Unilever.

> (Question)
>
> I With reference to the article above and your own research, discuss the view that corporate governance is a marketing function in that it is public relations driven. (*40 marks*)

2 *Read* **Articles B and C** *and answer the question that follows.*

ARTICLE B

INFLUENCES ON BUSINESS ETHICS

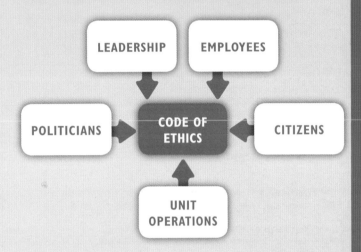

ARTICLE C

ASDA v. ACTION AID

The supermarket chain Asda wants overseas suppliers excluded from a new code of conduct that is designed to ensure that the big grocers do not use their buying power to impose unfair trading terms. The UK arm of US-based Wal-Mart has included the demand in its response to the Competition Commission's 'remedies' statement, published after a near-two-year inquiry into the £125 billion grocery market. In that statement the commission suggested setting up an ombudsman service to help protect small suppliers and farmers, and supermarkets may be forced to appoint compliance officers to ensure they treat suppliers in accordance with a new and wide-ranging code of practice.

In its response Asda says overseas suppliers should be excluded from the proposed code because they have customers in other countries. It is understood that Asda is the only one of the main supermarkets to have made the demand. The current code of practice, which is widely thought to have failed to make any impact on trading terms, does apply to overseas contractors, but only if they are direct suppliers and no middleman is used.

continued.../

ARTICLE C

ASDA v. ACTION AID continued

ActionAid, which lobbies on behalf of overseas suppliers to UK food retailers, said Asda should not oppose measures that could help workers in other countries on low incomes. Jenny Ricks, corporate campaigner at ActionAid, said: 'Faced with a true test of their ethical credentials, Asda has failed miserably. Their response clearly shows why we urgently need sensible regulation that will ensure supermarkets clean up their supply chains overseas. Ethical trading cannot continue to be a sideline for big UK supermarkets. This unmasks the fact that despite their ethical protestations, business as usual is continuing. We urge Asda and other supermarkets to prove they are serious about cleaning up their act by accepting the commission's remedies and stop fighting proposals that would help poor workers overseas.'

ActionAid had written to Asda's chief executive, Andy Bond, pointing out that 'responsible retailers have nothing to fear' and that British firms should help raise standards worldwide. It argues that if the code does not apply to all, retailers are likely to shift sourcing to those that are not protected.

In 2007 ActionAid published a report highlighting the conditions in which some overseas workers produce goods for UK supermarkets. It found women in Bangladesh who were paid as little as 5p an hour for up to 14 hours a day to make clothes for Asda and Tesco. It also reported on cashew-nut-processing workers in India who were paid 30p a day, 1% of the retail price of the cashews.

Asda has made clear recently that it is turning the screw on suppliers in order to keep prices down in the face of rising global food costs. Bond said recently: 'We will be as aggressive as we possibly can ... I am not going to squeeze suppliers, but I am going to be very assertive.'

In its submission to the Competition Commission, Asda also claimed that the new code of practice would harm competition. It rejected the idea of a full-time supermarkets ombudsman, suggesting instead that the Office of Fair Trading should monitor compliance with the suppliers' code. Yesterday a spokesman for Asda said the commission had not provided any evidence that a tougher code of practice was necessary, but the supermarket chain was committed to treating overseas suppliers fairly. 'We have always complied with the spirit and the letter of the existing code of practice and believe in treating all our suppliers fairly, particularly those who are small or from developing countries.'

The supermarkets emerged almost unscathed when the Competition Commission published its preliminary conclusions about whether the grocers abuse their market position, drive small rivals out of business or abuse their suppliers. The commission has also suggested changes to the way planning decisions are made, to prevent supermarkets imposing conditions on land they sell that stops rivals buying the sites.

Source: Julia Finch, *The Guardian* © Copyright Guardian News & Media Ltd 2008

Question

2   With reference to Articles B and C and your own research, to what extent do you believe that most businesses apply business ethics only as far as they are compelled to do so, and that ethics only really extend to their immediate stakeholders? *(40 marks)*

SECTION B

ANSWER ONE QUESTION FROM THIS SECTION

Questions

3   Leadership is essential to businesses in a rapidly moving market. Discuss. *(40 marks)*
4   The use of ICT is essential to all business success. Discuss. *(40 marks)*
5   The environment in which a business operates is in constant flux, and if a business cannot adapt to the changing circumstances then it is doomed to failure. Discuss. *(40 marks)*

PICTURE CREDITS

The publishers would like to thank the following for permission to reproduce images in this book.

p.1: (t to b) © Sergey Galushko–FOTOLIA, © jeff Metzger–FOTOLIA, © Yegor Korzh–FOTOLIA, © Anton Zhukov–FOTOLIA, © frenta–FOTOLIA, © Emilia Stasiak–FOTOLIA; p.3: © Sergey Galushko–FOTOLIA; p.4: Kingfisher plc (x2); p.5: Kingfisher plc; p.6: © Sergey Galushko–FOTOLIA; p.7: © Lai Leng Yiap–FOTOLIA; p.9: Kingfisher plc (x2); p.10: © jeff Metzger–FOTOLIA; p.13: © monti–FOTOLIA; p.14: © Marlee–FOTOLIA; p.15: Flybe.com; p.16: PA Photos; p.17: PA Photos; p.18: © absolut–FOTOLIA; p.21: © K. Geijer–FOTOLIA; p.22: © endostock–FOTOLIA; p.23: www.cartoonstock.com; p.25: © Akhilesh Sharma–FOTOLIA; p.27: © Alex Hinds–FOTOLIA; p.28: © iofoto–FOTOLIA; p.29: (l) © Leah-Anne Thompson–FOTOLIA, (r) © DebbieO–FOTOLIA; p.33: © jeff Metzger–FOTOLIA; p.35: © Kay Ransom–FOTOLIA; p.36: © kentoh–FOTOLIA; p.38: © Andres Rodriguez–FOTOLIA; p.39: © Ljupco Smokovski–FOTOLIA; p.41: (t) © Miqul–FOTOLIA, (b) © Les Cunliffe–FOTOLIA; p.45: © rgbdigital.co.uk–FOTOLIA; p.48: © Andrei Filonov–FOTOLIA; p.49: © Scott Maxwell–FOTOLIA; p.52: © Stenmark–FOTOLIA; p.53: © maromarez–FOTOLIA; p.55: © Yegor Korzh–FOTOLIA; p.59: PA Photos; p.61: PA Photos; p.65: © Radu Razvan–FOTOLIA; p.67: © senor nunez–FOTOLIA; p.69: (r) Alamy/eye35.com, (b) Alamy/Peter Schneiter, (l) Alamy/Viewpictures Ltd; p.75: courtesy of MCS; p.76: Montblanc UK Ltd; p.77: courtesy of FireAngel Ltd; p.78: Reprinted with permission from DSG international; p.80: PA Photos; p.81: The Coca-Cola Company (x2); p.83: Apple Inc.; p.87: Benetton Group; p.89: (t) © Chad McDermott–FOTOLIA, (b) Facebook Inc. (x2); p.90: (l) Tesco plc; p.90, (r) courtesy of Gillette; p.91: Science Photo Library/Pasieka; p.93: © Anton Zhukov–FOTOLIA; p.94: © Tom Mc Nemar–FOTOLIA; p.97: (t) © Aviator70–FOTOLIA, (b) © laura–FOTOLIA; p.98: PA Photos; p.99: PA Photos; p.100: © Prod. Numérik–FOTOLIA; p.102: © Scott Maxwell–FOTOLIA; p.104: (front) © Douglas Stevens–FOTOLIA, (back) © Ella Batalon–FOTOLIA; p.107: © Springfield Gallery–FOTOLIA; p.109: Apple Inc.; p.111: © Peter Penner–FOTOLIA; p.113: © Anton Zhukov–FOTOLIA; p.115: © terex–FOTOLIA; p.116: © frenta–FOTOLIA; p.118: (l to r) Microsoft logo reprinted with permission from Microsoft Corporation, McDonalds Inc., Shell Group, The Coca-Cola Company; p.120: © crazed–FOTOLIA; p.121: © diego cervo–FOTOLIA; p.127: PA Photos; p.129: © Dreef–FOTOLIA; p.131: © frenta–FOTOLIA; p.132: © TebNad–FOTOLIA; p.134: © kentoh–FOTOLIA; p.135: © Christopher Dodge–FOTOLIA; p.136: © Mario Ragma Jr.–FOTOLIA; p.139: © frenta–FOTOLIA; p.149: © David Humphrey–FOTOLIA; p.157: © kolesn–FOTOLIA; p.159: © Yuri Arcurs–FOTOLIA; p.165: © iofoto–FOTOLIA; p.166: Nationwide Building Society; p.167: Nationwide Building Society; p.168: © Emilia Stasiak–FOTOLIA; p.171: (t to b) © ville ahonen–FOTOLIA, © Scott Maxwell–FOTOLIA, © Frog 974–FOTOLIA, © Emilia Stasiak–FOTOLIA; p.173: © ville ahonen–FOTOLIA; p.175: © NataV–FOTOLIA; p.182: Gudellaphoto–FOTOLIA; p.183: jenny–FOTOLIA; p.184: Scott Maxwell–FOTOLIA; p.187: © Joe Gough–FOTOLIA; p.188: © Scott Maxwell–FOTOLIA; p.192: © Stephen Finn–FOTOLIA; p.193: © c–FOTOLIA; p.196: © Studiotouch–FOTOLIA; p.197: © Robert Mizerek–FOTOLIA; p.198: © Saniphoto–FOTOLIA; p.200: © pmtavares–FOTOLIA; p.202: www.nikebiz.com; p.206: © Freeze Frame Photography–FOTOLIA; p.207: (t) Nestlé Group, (b) © sharply_done–FOTOLIA; p.209: © Fineas–FOTOLIA; p.211: © Alena Yakusheva–FOTOLIA; p.213: © Sascha Tiebel–FOTOLIA; p.214: © Varina Patel–FOTOLIA; p.215: © Varina Patel–FOTOLIA; p.216: © Graça Victoria–FOTOLIA; p.217: © Rob Byron–FOTOLIA; p.221: © LVDESIGN–FOTOLIA; p.222: © Douglas Freer–FOTOLIA; p.225: (l) © iofoto–FOTOLIA, (r) © Rob–FOTOLIA; p.226: © Pavle–FOTOLIA; p.227: © matteo NATALE–FOTOLIA; p.232: (l) © Edyta Pawlowska–FOTOLIA, (r) © rlat–FOTOLIA; p.233: © mr.REPORTER–FOTOLIA; p.236: (l) © Sergey Galushko–FOTOLIA, (r) © Johanna Goodyear–FOTOLIA; p.238: (l) © Orlando Florin Rosu–FOTOLIA, (r) © TheThirdMan–FOTOLIA; p.239: © Letty–FOTOLIA; p.243: (l) PayPal Inc., (r) eBay Inc.; p.247: © dinostock–FOTOLIA; p.248: © Frog 974–FOTOLIA; p.251: © jovica antoski–FOTOLIA; p.253: © cornelius–FOTOLIA; p.254: Woolworths Group Plc; p.263: © Simon Lane–FOTOLIA; p.269: © petrol–FOTOLIA (x2); p.273: © caraman–FOTOLIA; p.279: © Csaba Peterdi–FOTOLIA; p.281: (l) © moodboard–FOTOLIA, (r) © Alan Heartfield–FOTOLIA; p.282: © Levente Janos–FOTOLIA; p.283: © Levente Janos–FOTOLIA; p.289: © CHEN–FOTOLIA; p.290: © Carl Durocher–FOTOLIA; p.292: © Srecko Djarmati–FOTOLIA; p.305: © Peter Galbraith–FOTOLIA; p.306: (t) © Emilia Stasiak–FOTOLIA, (b) Tesco Plc; p.308: © Emilia Stasiak–FOTOLIA.

Every effort has been made to contact copyright holders, but if any have been inadvertently overlooked, the publishers will be happy to make the necessary amendments at the first opportunity.

In the case studies in this book, some businesses, people and products are given their real names and have genuine photographs as well, but in some cases the photographs are for illustrative or educational purposes only and are not intended to identify the business, individual or product. The publishers cannot accept any responsibility for any consequences resulting from this use of photographs and case studies, except as expressly provided by law.

INDEX

Bold page numbers indicate key terms.

A

ACAS (Advisory Conciliation and Arbitration Service) 165
accelerator effect **190**
accountability 142
accounts 10–53, 136
acid test ratio 30
acquisitions 242
    see also mergers
action-centred leadership 273
action research model 300
Adair, John 273
additive effect 272–3
adhocracies 283
administrators 279
advertising 58, 87
    see also marketing
age discrimination regulations 215
ageing workforces 145, 224–5
aims 4, 172–83
air travel 51, 97, 102, 207
American Marketing Association (AMA) 228
Ansoff's matrix 74–5, 82–3
Apple organisation 78, 82–3, 109
ARR (average rate of return) 50, 294
asset-led businesses 68
asset turnover ratio 32
assets 18–19, 22–3, 26–7, 44, 48, 288
attribution model of leadership 275
Australia 192, 266–7
authority 270–1, 278–9
automation 234–5
autonomy **116**, 153
average rate of return (ARR) 50, 294
averages 36–7, 64, 68

B

B&Q case study 4–5, 8–9
B2B (business-to-business) markets 68–9
B2C (business-to-consumer) markets 69
balance of trade 204–5
balance sheets 18–19, 22–3, 26, 28, 34
balanced scorecard 261

banks 51, 74, 204, 208, 297
Barnet Council case study 259
barriers to entry 102, 186, 212, 241
behavioural factors 279, 284, 289
benefits 48, 108, 114–15, 146
    see also cost benefit analysis
Benetton clothes 66, 87, 91
Blake, Robert 271
booms (economic) 191, 200
Boots chain 80
borrowing 18–19, 40, 201
    see also loans
bottled water case study 232–3
bottlenecks **100**, 101
BP Group mission statement 175
brain research 175
break-even analysis 85, 112, 294
breweries 110–11, 290–1
British exchange rates 192–3, 201
broadcasters 60–1, 234
brown sugar case study 104–5
budget analysts 142
budgeting 12, 88–9, 262
    see also numerical forecasts
buildings 27, 48
bulk buying 100
business angels 39, 47
business cycle 186, 190–1, 200
business-level strategy formulation 177
business-to-business (B2B) markets 68–9
business-to-consumer (B2C) markets 69
buyer-supplier relationships 187, 245
    see also customers

C

CAM (computer-aided manufacturing) 235
capacity 100–3, 240
capital 18–19, 22, 31, 40–1, 48, 196–7
capital expenditure 40–1
capital-intensive strategies 102, 105, 133, 195
Car Free Weekend case study 182–3
cartels 189

cash, terminology problem 27
cash-flow 44, 50–2, 294
    forecasting 40
    targets 12, 14
Centaur case study 42–3
centralised structures 152–3, 284
chains of command 154
challengers **62**
change
    assessing 184–247
    management 248–305
    planning for 256–67
change options matrix 301
changeability 302
Chelsea FC case study 16–17
children's advertising 58
China 9, 119
CI (Competitive Intelligence) 293
CIS (Competitive Information System) 293
clothing market 59, 66, 87, 91, 96
Coca-Cola 76, 81
cognitive choice 274
collateral **26**
collective bargaining **133**
communication 101, 116, 160–1, 166–7, 234, 258
comparisons 24, 34, 81
Competition Act 1998 220
competitive advantage 6, 7, 96, 107
competitive environment 96, 186–9, 206, 210, 220, 240–7
Competitive Information System (CIS) 293
Competitive Intelligence (CI) 293
competitive strategies 87, 177
competitive structures 150–9
compressed working week 157
computer-aided manufacturing (CAM) 235
concentric diversification 78–9
conceptual model of planning 260
conflict management 288, 302–3
congruent goals 177
consensual culture 283, 288
Consumer Credit Act 1974 217
consumer markets 69, 226
    see also customers
Consumer Prices Index (CPI) 194

consumer protection 216–17
contingency plans 7, 85, 191, 264–5
contracts 216
controls 84–5, 154–5, 179, 199, 258, 288
convergence in economic growth 197
coordination of business 101, 288
corporate aims 172–83
corporate culture see culture
corporate objectives 2, 4–7, 172–83, 200, 256
corporate planning 177, 179, 256–63
    see also strategic planning
corporate responsibility 226, 230–1, 306–7
corporate strategies 84, 177, 178–9
correlation 64–5, 68
cost benefit analysis 40, 261, 294–5
cost centres 14, 26, 39–41
cost focus/leadership strategies 72–3
cost-volume analysis 95, 112–13
costs
    innovation 108–9
    investment decisions 48–9
    location decisions 114–15, 119
    marketing strategy evaluation 81
    minimisation 12, 14, 40–1, 133
    operational objectives 95
    profit-and-loss accounts 20
CPI (Consumer Prices Index) 194
CPM (critical path method) 124
credit industry 40, 217
creditor turnover ratio 32
critical path analysis 124–5
CRM (Customer Relationship Management) 234
Crocs Shoes case study 75
culture 86, 150–1, 282–91
current ratio 30
customers 6, 157, 234, 242–5, 250
cycle time 126–7
cyclical changes 190–1

D
Deal and Kennedy 282–3
debentures **31**
debtor days 32
decentralised structures 152, 284
decision-making 292–9
    employee representation 162
    ethical 228–9
    financial data 24–5, 28
    issue management 179
    leadership 278
    organisational structures 152
    political decisions 212–13
    see also investment decisions; location decisions
decision trees 295, 298–9
deficit on trade 204, 205
degrees of competition 188
delegation 152–3
demand
    inflation 194
    operational objectives 97
    price elasticity of 65
    resource mix 102–3
    transportation 221
    workforce plans 141, 143, 148–9
demographic factors 224–5
dependability objective 95
dependency rate 224
depreciation 22–3, 27
deregulation of markets 210
design issues 106
    see also organisational design
development of workforce 146–7
    see also training needs
differentiation strategies 72–3
direct costs 20
direct marketing 67
direct stakeholders 297
directors 2, 47, 154–5, 163
    see also leadership
Disability Discrimination Act 1995 215
discharges 227
discounted cash flows 51–2, 294
diseconomies of scale 101
dispute resolution 164–5
diversification 57, 74, 78–9, 82–3, 100, 191
dividends 15, 20, 23, 33
downsizing businesses 286
downturns 186, 190–1, 200

E
economic factors 35, 58, 186–205
economic growth 196–7, 201, 204–5
economies of scale 100
education policies 211, 220, 224
effectiveness 289
efficiency ratios 32, 34
    see also return on capital employed
elasticity 65, **201**
emissions 227

employee representation **134**, 135, 162–3
employees 101, 108, 133–5, 160–7, 218–19, 290–1
employers 133–5, 160–7, 218–19
Employment Act 2002 214, 222
employment policies 119, 134, 165, 204, 214–15, 222
empowerment **116**, 152, 153
engagement 161, 290–1
enlightened self-interest 229
Enterprise Act 2002 220
entrants see new market entrants
environmental issues 5, 51, 59, 220–1, 226–7
environmental scanning 263
Equal Pay Act 1970 214
ethics 5, 46, 228–9, 289, 296, 307–8
European Union 193, 204
    human resource management 134–5
    industrial tribunals 165
    organic juice market 73
    packaging market 70–1
    subsidies 206–7
    trade issues 212–13
evaluation methods 6, 80–1, 88–9, 141, 200–1, 244–5
evolutionary theory 285
exchange rates 112–13, 119, 192–3, 200–1, 208
exit barriers 241
expansionary fiscal policy 209
expected values 295
exports 193, 212, 223
external stakeholders 181, 230
extrapolation 64–5, 68

F
Facebook case study 89
farming subsidies 207
fashion market see clothing market
Fayol, Henri 154–5
feedback systems 179
Fielder's leadership model 273
financial data 18–29
    see also benefits; costs
financial efficiency ratios 32, 34
financial objectives 10, 12–17
financial strategies 10–53, 58, 86, 100
fiscal policies 186–7, 209
fishbone diagrams 295
fixed assets 19, 23
fixed automation 235

fixed costs 113
flat organisational structures 154
flexibility 95, 102, 235, 258
flexible working 156–60, 222, 225
Flybe airline 15
focus strategies 72–3
followers **62**
food retailing 120–1, 297
football clubs 16–17, 265, 268
Force Field Analysis 287
Ford company 98, 118, 123, 127
forecasts 24, 40, 44–5, 84, 85
free trade 210, 212–13
Freeminer Brewery case study 110–11
functional objectives 2–9
functional organisational structures 151
functional strategies 2–9, 177
funds, terminology problem 27
Fyffes Plc case study 19, 21

G

gap analysis **84**, 85, 141, 143, 148–9
GDP (gross domestic product) 197, 205
gearing ratios 31, 34
general fund accounts 15
General Motors case study 127
Glisten Plc case study 21
global manufacturing 198, 202–3
globalisation 198–9, 201–3
goals 6, 176–8, 228, 286
    see also objectives
government
    economic intervention 204–5
    environmental role 226
    fiscal policies 186–7, 209
    growth level/rate 196
    market intervention 220–1
    monetary policies 186, 208–9
    trade policy 213
gross domestic product (GDP) 197, 205
gross profit margin 30
growth 43, 196–7, 201, 204–5
    change and 301
    competitive environment 240
    functional objectives 5, 8–9
    global 198–9
    market analysis 62
    organic 250–1
    ratio analysis 37
growth level/growth rate 196

H

Handy, Charles 150, 282
harmonisation **134**
Harrison and Handy 282
Hay, Julie 276–7
head-hunters 135
Health and Safety Act 1974 218–19
health screening 219
hierarchical structures 151, 154, 283
horizontal diversification 78
HRIS (human resource information systems) 136–7
human resource management (HRM) 132, 134–5, 137, 139
human resources 86, 130–67, 174
    accounting/audits 136
    objectives 132–9
    plans 134, 137
    strategies 130–67

I

immigration 224, 225
implementation issues
    change management 300–5
    contingency plans 264–5
    corporate plans 260
    marketing plans 88–9
    policy learning phase 179, 260
    workforce plans 144–5
income-based investment decisions 48–9
income elasticity **201**
income levels 186
income statements 20–1, 26
    see also profit-and-loss accounts
indirect costs 20
indirect stakeholders 297
industrial disputes/action 164–5
industrial markets see business-to-business markets
industrial relations 133, 164–5
industry averages 36–7
industry structures 188–9
inflation 34, 194–5, 200–1, 204–5, 208
information systems/management 66–7, 122, 136–7, 292–3
infrastructure 112–13, 207, 209
innovation 106–11, 210
instrumental leadership 274–5
insurance company case study 52–3
intangible assets 27
integration 242–3
    see also mergers

Intel case study 253
interdependence 229
interest rates 192–3, 200–1, 208
internal rate of return (IRR) 294
internal stakeholders 181
international businesses 8–9, 118–19
    see also overseas businesses
inventories 126–7
investment appraisals 44–5, 50–1, 113, 294
investment criteria 46–7
investment decisions 24–5, 44–53, 113, 168–9, 294
    financial objectives 14
    interest rates 201
    technology 236
investment ratios 33
IRR (internal rate of return) 294
Ishikawa diagrams 295
issue management 179, 260
IT professionals 142

J

Jaguar Cars case study 98–9
Japan 119, 126–7
JIT (just-in-time production) 126–7
job descriptions 132
juice companies case study 73
just-in-time production (JIT) 126–7

K

KaBloom franchise 117
kaizen strategy 127
Kingfisher case study 4–5, 7–9
Kotter and Schlesinger 302

L

labour cost minimisation 133
labour-intensive strategies 97, 102, 105, 133, 195
labour market 142, 200, 210–11, 224–5
labour productivity growth 196, 197
labour relations 165
    see also industrial relations
land and buildings 27, 48
lead times **100**, 101, 126–7
leaders **62**, 268, 269, 273, 278
leadership 252–3, 268–81, 286
    see also management
lean production 122–9
Learner Shoppers case study 238–9
learning organisations 144
legal factors 204–23

legislation 134, 165, 214–19, 222
legitimacy 285
Lewin, Kurt 277, 287, 300
liabilities 18–19
liberalisation of trade 210, 212, 244–5
Likert, Rensis 270–1
liquidity 12, **13**, 18
liquidity ratios 30, 34
living standards 197
loans 38–9
  see also borrowing
location decisions 112–21, 132, 143, 195, 198
logistics **72**
low-cost strategy 72–3, 114–15
lower management 268

M

McDonaldisation 199
McGrath 283
McGregor, Douglas 270
management
  accounts use 26
  buy-outs 252
  capacity management 103
  change management 248–305
  conflict management 288, 302–3
  contingency plans 265
  corporate plans 257
  cost minimisation 12
  culture changes 286–7
  demographic changes 224
  economies of scale 100
  employee representation 162–3
  environmental product management 227
  Fayol's theory 155
  goal management 176
  human resources 132, 134–5, 137, 139
  information management 292–3
  issue management 179, 260
  multi-site locations 116–17
  operations management 94
  organisational structures 154–5
  risk management 7, 262
  strategic management 178
  technology 234–5
  workforce plans 142, 145
  see also leadership
managers 268, 269, 279
manifest conflict 303

manufacturing sector 94, 195, 198, 202–3, 205, 235
market access 212–13
market analysis 62–71
market-based policies 210–11, 220–1
market changes 200, 286
market development 57, 74, 77, 82–3
market failures 189
market-led businesses 68
market penetration 57, 74–5, 250
market position 62
market segments **57**, 62
market share 5, 37
market structure 62, 188–9
marketing
  economies of scale 100
  ethics 228
  mix 84–5
  objectives 56–9, 62, 84–5
  plans 84–91
  research 85
  strategies 54–91
  technology 234
matrix structures 151
maximisation of profits 5, 46
mergers 138–9, 242–3, 250, 286
mid-level management 268
Miller Brewing Company 290–1
minimisation of costs 12, 14, 40–1, 133
minimum wage legislation 134
MIS (management information systems) 293
mission statements 4, 174–5, 256, 278
missions 4, 6, 174–83
Mitchell Charlesworth case study 79
monetary policies 186, 208–9
monitoring marketing plans 88–9
monopolies 188, 189
motivation 101, 108, 274, 289
Mouton, Jane 271
moving averages 64, 68
Muda (waste) 126–7
multi-site locations 116–17
multinationals 118–19
multiplier effect **190**
music industry 57
Myers-Briggs Type Inventory 274, 275

N

narrowcasting 234
National Trust case study 153
Nationwide Building Society 166–7
net present value 50–2
net profit 20
net profit margin ratio 30
new businesses 37
new market entrants 187, 240, 241
  see also barriers to entry
new ownership/leadership 252–3
NHS case study 147, 280–1
niche markets 62
Nike case study 202–3
Nintendo Wii 63, 246–7
non-financial benefits 48
norms 285
numerical forecasts 84, 85

O

objectives 2–9, 172–83, 256
  change strategies 200
  definition 176
  financial 10, 12–17
  human resources 132–9
  investment decisions 46, 51
  marketing 56–9, 62, 84–5
  operational 58, 94–9
  workforce plans 140, 143
  see also strategies
occupational health screening 219
OD (organisational development) 251
OECD (Organisation for Economic Cooperation and Development) 212
oligopolies 188, 189
Olympic Movement case study 59–61
ombudsmen 221, 307, 308
operational objectives 58, 94–9
operational strategies 5, 92–129
operations management 94
opportunity cost 49
opportunity, technology as 237
optimisation
  locations 114–15
  resource mix 102–3
ordinary shares **13**
organic growth 250–1
organic juice case study 73
organisational culture 86, 150–1, 282–9
organisational design 284–5
  see also organisational structures

organisational development (OD) 251
organisational mapping 151
organisational size 132, 250–1
organisational structures 150–9, 283–5
out-of-town locations 115
over-trading 12
overdrafts 38
overseas businesses 8–9, 80, 112–13, 115–19, 132, 198
ownership changes 252–3

P

packaging 70–1, 227
participation schemes 162–3, 271
partnerships 144
patents 106, 108–9
payback method 50, 294
PayPal 215, 243
PDSA (People's Dispensary for Sick Animals) 67
pensions 215, 224, 225
perfect competition 188
performance assessment 178–9, 229
    change management 253, 256, 260, 266, 286
    competitors 96
    financial data 18–29
    marketing plans 85
    ratio analysis 34–5
performance indicators 229
performance pressures 275
person-based organisational culture 282
personality factors 274, 279
PESTEL model **84**
Peters, Tom 271
Phillips Curve 195
planned phase change model 300
planning 4
    change planning 256–67
    contingency plans 7, 85, 191, 264–5
    corporate plans 177, 179
    horizons 6, 24
    human resources 134, 137
    marketing plans 84–91
    time management 122
    workforce plans 140–9
plants within plants (PWPs) 103
policy learning phase 179, 260
political factors 58, 204–23, 285
pollution 189, 220–1
poor business performance 253

population changes 224
Porter's Five Forces 187, 240, 244
Porter's generic strategies 72
power-based culture 282
predictability 199
preference shares **13**
price elasticity of demand 65
prices 65, 189, 201, 204
primary efficiency ratio
    see return on capital employed
privatisation 210, 221, 286
proactive businesses 6, **7**, 262
procrastination 122
production issues 94, 226
productivity growth 196–7, 205
products 68, 97
    development 57, 74, 76–7, 82, 86, 106
    lifecycles 56, 86
    management 227
    markets 210
    positioning 85
profit
    centres 14, 26, 38–41, 43
    evaluation 81
    maximisation 5, 46
    quality 23, 27
    utilisation 23
profit-and-loss accounts 18, 20–3, 26, 39
profitability ratios 30–1, 34
programmable automation 235
protectionism 119, 241
public sector 180, 286, 292
purchasing 86
push/pull factors 114
PWPs (plants within plants) 103

Q

qualitative approach **25**, 44, 51, 81, 112, 114
quality circles (QCs) 162
quality objectives 95, 98
    see also profit, quality
quantitative approach **25**, 44–5, 50–1, 112–14
Quinn 283

R

Race Relations Act 1976 215
Radio Frequency Identification (RFID) 90–1, 238
raising finance 38–9
ratio analysis 30–7

rational culture 283
reactive businesses 6, 7
recessions 186, 190–1, 200
recoveries (economic) 191, 200
recruitment issues 135, 145, 147, 195
regulatory restrictions 241, 244
reinforcement, leadership 275
related diversification 78–9
relative power of stakeholders 297
relocating businesses 114–15, 195
reporting processes 116–17, 226
repositioning strategy 77
representation, employees **134**, 135, 162–3
research and development (R&D) 106–7, 109
reserves 19
residual value of assets 48
resistance to change 286–7, 301–3
resources
    dependency on 296
    optimal mix 102–3
    time management 126–7
    utilisation 96
    see also human resources
responses to change 200–1, 220–1, 236, 244–5, 252
responsibilities 142, 204–5
    see also corporate responsibility
restructuring businesses 253
Retail Prices Index (RPI) 194
retail sector 117, 120–1, 297, 307
    see also supermarket chains
retained profits 20, 23, 38
retention of workforce 147, 157
retirement ages 215
retrenchment strategies 251
return on capital 13–14, 30–1, 81
revenue costs 49
RFID (Radio Frequency Identification) 90–1, 238
risk assessments 219
risks
    aversion 51
    contingency planning 264
    innovation 108–9
    investment decisions 47–9
    leadership role 278
    management 7, 262
    marketing strategies 74, 78
    reduction strategies 100
rivalry analysis 187, 240–1
ROCE (return on capital employed) 13–14, 30–1

Rojee Tasha Stampings Ltd 128–9
role-based culture 282
role expectations 275
roles in workforce planning 142
Rotherham Metropolitan Borough
    Council 161
Royal Bank of Scotland 74, 297
RPI (Retail Prices Index) 194

S
sabbaticals **225**
safety legislation 218–19
St Albans Council case study 263
Sale of Goods and Services Acts
    216
sales and operational planning
    (S&OP) 262
sales forecasts 7
sales patterns 63
sales revenue 27
savings rates 197
scale of production 100–1
school uniform business 28–9
scoring and weighting method 48
SCP (Sustainable Consumption and
    Production) 226
segmentation of markets **57**, 62
self-concept, leadership 274–5
senior managers 142, 268
sensitivity analysis 49
services 86, 94
    see also products
Sex Discrimination Act 1975
    214–15
shareholder ratios 33
shareholders 13, 15, 20–1, 23, 38
shrinking markets 62
situational analysis 84
size of businesses 132, 250–1
skills of workforce 132, 145, 236
Slough Borough Council case study
    158
SMART criteria 56, 80
social environment 224–33
social identity 274
social learning 275
social objectives 5
social responsibility 226, 230–1,
    306–7
socialisation 285
software for market analysis 66–7
solvency ratios 30, 34
Sony products 63, 77
spans of control 154–5

speed objective 95
spending rates 197, 201
stagflation 195
stagnant markets 62
stakeholder analysis 181, 230–1
stakeholders 26, 180–1, 183, 259,
    304
    corporate responsibility 230–1
    operations management 94
    relative power 297
standardisation 199, 240–1
standards
    communication 161
    of living 197
statutory consumer protection
    216
stock turnover ratio 32
stock valuation 27
strategic decision-making 292–9
strategic management 178
strategic planning 134, 140–2, 144–
    5, 177, 256–7
    see also corporate planning
strategic thinking 177
strategies 2–9, 177–9, 256–7,
    292–9
    change 200–1
    financial 10–53, 58, 86
    formulation 177
    human resources 130–67
    marketing 54–91
    operational 92–129
    organisational design 285
    retrenchment 251
    technical 237
    workforce plans 148–9
    see also objectives
strikes 164
structured data 292
subsidies 206–7, 223
substitute products/services 187,
    241
successful leadership 276–7
sugar industry 104–5
supermarket chains 189, 297, 307–8
    see also Tesco supermarkets
suppliers 187, 242–3, 245
supply, workforce plans 141, 143,
    148–9
supply side policies 210–11
surplus on trade 204, 205
Sustainable Consumption and
    Production (SCP) 226
SWOT analysis 6, 58, 259

synergy effects 78, 262

T
takeovers 250, 255, 286
    see also mergers
talent acquisition 145
target markets 85
targets 4, 12–14
tariffs **212**, 213, 241
task structures 273, 282
Tasmania case study 257
taxation 20, 206–7, 211
Taylor, F.W. 123, 284
technical strategies 237
technocratic systems 285
technological myopia 237
technology 234–9
    change effects 234–5
    economies of scale 100
    globalisation 198–9
    government intervention 220
    management 234–5
    market analysis 66–7
    marketing objectives 58–61
    organisational design 285
Tesco supermarkets 74, 90, 152,
    189, 297, 306–8
test markets 64
Thanet District Council case study
    15
Theory X/Theory Y 270
three-step change management
    model 300
time management 122–3
total cost 95, 113
total quality management (TQM)
    162
Toyota 126–7
trade 204–5, 210, 212–13, 241,
    244–5
Trade Descriptions Act 1968 217
trade-offs 204–5
trade unions 133, 163–5
training needs 134, 144, 146–7,
    211, 220
transactional leadership 272
Transco case study 229
transfer payments 186–7, 209
transformational leadership
    272–3
transportation 221
trend analysis 24, 63–5, 224
tribunals 165
turnover ratios 32

U

uncertainties 48–9, 192–3, 288
undistributed profit 20, 23, 38
unemployment 195, 200–1, 204
unfair competition 189
unique selling point (USP) 73
United States 186, 190, 199
universalism 229
University of South Australia 266–7
unrelated diversification 79
unstructured data 292
USP (unique selling point) 73
utilitarianism 229

V

valuation of assets 27
values 174–5, 269
VAT (Value Added Tax) 206, 207
venture capitalists 39, 47
vertical diversification 78–9
video games 63, 243, 246–7
visions 6, 174, 278
    see also mission statements

W

waste reduction strategies 126–7
water providers 232

WCM (world-class manufacturing) 128–9
weighting and scoring method 48
Woolworths case study 254–5
worker directors 163
workforce analysis 142–3, 148–9
workforce plans 140–9
workforce potential 132–3
workforce skills 132, 145, 236
working capital 22, 40
works councils 162
world-class manufacturing (WCM) 128–9
World Trade Organisation (WTO)